D1571853

# The
# American
# War Film

Henry Wilcoxon as the Vicar in *Mrs. Miniver*, giving the sermon "This is the people's war . . ." in a bombed-out church. Winston Churchill had the speech copied and distributed to the Allied forces. Filmed on the back lot at MGM, 1942. Photofest.

# THE
# AMERICAN
# WAR FILM

## History and Hollywood

Frank McAdams

Westport, Connecticut
London

**Library of Congress Cataloging-in-Publication Data**

McAdams, Frank, 1940–
    The American war film : history and Hollywood / Frank McAdams.
        p.   cm.
    Includes bibliographical references and index.
    ISBN 0–275–96871–5 (alk. paper)
        1. War films—United States—History and criticism.   I. Title.
    PN1995.9.W3M395   2002
    791.43'658—dc21            2001053086

British Library Cataloguing in Publication Data is available.

Library of Congress Catalog Card Number: 2001053086
ISBN: 0–275–96871–5

First published in 2002

Praeger Publishers, 88 Post Road West, Westport, CT 06881
An imprint of Greenwood Publishing Group, Inc.
www.praeger.com

Printed in the United States of America

The paper used in this book complies with the
Permanent Paper Standard issued by the National
Information Standards Organization (Z39.48–1984).

10 9 8 7 6 5 4 3 2 1

**Copyright Acknowledgments**

The author and publisher are grateful to the following for granting permission to reprint from their materials:

SAN FRANCISCO BE SURE TO WEAR FLOWERS IN YOUR HAIR, Words and Music by John Phillips. © Copyright 1967 UNIVERSAL-MCA MUSIC PUBLISHING, A DIVISION OF UNIVERSAL STUDIOS, INC. (ASCAP). International Copyright Secured. All Rights Reserved.

Interview with Gregory Peck, conducted by the author on June 8, 1998, courtesy of Gregory Peck.

Interview with Edward Dmytryk, conducted by the author on February 3, 1998, courtesy of Jean Dmytryk, trustee.

To those absent classmates and comrades
who crossed my path as we journeyed into the fray.

Thomas Dineen
Allan Herman
Edward Jory
Edward Keeble
Joseph Laslie
Barry Levin
Allan Loane
Donald Perkins
Vincent Venuti
Fred Williams

# Contents

*Photo essay follows page 158*

# Preface

For generations American films have reflected the politics, attitudes, and tempo of the times in which they were produced. The emergence of sound sadly ended the production of silent films. But it also created the musical genre, just as the Great Depression gave rise to the gangster film. World history enhanced the background for another genre, the American war film.

Just as wars have changed throughout the twentieth century, so has the war film genre, which reflects their statements, through drama, of what those experiences entailed.

The American war film has been written about in countless books. These works are mostly confined to certain periods, common elements, or one particular war and its effects.

What I have concentrated on here is a look at American history in this century—with its base in the previous—through the lens of the American war film. These films are a cinematic reflection of what this nation did in the twentieth century, good and evil, not just to each successive enemy at the time but to ourselves.

The staple of the American war film has characteristically been a group of men, and women, from diverse backgrounds, fighting for survival amid the threat of chaos. The ending of that threat is found not just in conquering the enemy but also in overcoming our own fears, allowing us to move on.

Through cultural snapshots captured in American war films, this nation can see itself not only in handsome profile but marked occasionally with warts. Generations can point to these films, their influences, and the statements they made to audiences worldwide.

And like any artistic endeavor, there will be mixed interpretations. A Vietnam veteran once observed that war films were responsible for many young men and women joining the military—just as they were likewise the cause for others to avoid it.

There is probably no other film genre than the war film that reflects so completely the struggles this country has endured during the twentieth century.

This is a film genre that not only shows us where we have been—it can guide us to where we are going.

# Acknowledgments

Any work of nonfiction admittedly has a foundation in research and tedious legwork. This book is no different.

What came about after a University of Southern California (USC) Cinema faculty meeting launched me on an eight-year odyssey where I often realized the price of grabbing the proverbial tiger by the tail. One resource led to another. And the files began to grow.

Several journeys were far-reaching, moving, and informative, beyond my wildest thoughts. Two of these were the Rendezvous with War Conference, in April 2000, at the College of William & Mary, and a nostalgic 1998 trip to the Pearl Harbor naval base. These trips, along with a wide spectrum of resources, made me realize how research is ongoing and never ending. Yet there comes a point where it has to stop. But does it?

My debts in this book are like my travels, far and wide.

At the UCLA (University of California at Los Angeles) Special Collections Library Julie Graham gave me access to the first-draft scripts of *Apocalypse Now* and *Buffalo Ghost*, which became *Coming Home*.

Ned Comstock, at the USC Cinema Library, pointed me toward more resources.

Barbara Hall, at the Academy of Motion Picture Arts and Sciences, Oral History Project, offered appreciated guidance and all-important corrections.

Faye Thompson and Libby Wharton, Academy of Motion Picture Arts and Sciences, answered questions, leading to more questions, and always with answers.

Scott Miller, Academy of Motion Picture Arts and Sciences, helped me in legal directions.

Author Herman Wouk was responsive and considerate in giving insights, particularly on *The Caine Mutiny*.

Friend and latter-day tennis partner, acclaimed author E.M. "Mick" Nathanson gave me much needed background on his own *The Dirty Dozen, A Dirty Distant War*, and *Knight's Cross*. The phone calls on the *Dozen* were never ending, along with lunches and dinner conversations.

The late Edward Dymytrk, whom I first met on the USC Cinema faculty, was supportive and gave me valuable information including insight on directing war films with noted actors. In his own way he fought the good fight, as evidenced by a packed memorial service in June 1999.

I am doubly indebted to the Peck family. Stephen Peck served in the U.S. Marine Corps as a combat officer in the same period the author served and today supervises the Westside Los Angeles program to help homeless veterans. We were in Vietnam at the same time and remained in touch. His father, Gregory Peck, gave the war film genre more than just superb acting; Gregory Peck granted me an interview that went on wonderfully long, topped off with honey tea and cucumber sandwiches, served by Carmen.

J. Michael Lennon, past president of the James Jones Society and vice president of Wilkes University, helped tremendously regarding the early stages of *From Here to Eternity*, along with the life of James Jones.

The same can be said for screenwriter Daniel Taradash, who turned a corner in film adaptation in his script of *From Here to Eternity*. In a later generation Eric Roth did the same thing for *Forrest Gump*.

On several occasions I was offered the hospitality of Gloria Jones, the widow of James Jones, and daughter Kaylie at their Long Island home.

The late Barry Levin, a thrice-wounded Vietnam veteran and former Los Angeles police officer who built a successful law practice geared toward helping veterans and police officers in trouble, gave me added insight on Vietnam and its aftermath. Like many of us, Barry neither forgot the war nor the men who fought it. Sadly, he left us too soon.

Two other Vietnam veterans also helped with political opinions, reflections, and insights: screenwriter Patrick S. Duncan and retired Marine Captain Russ Thurman. They never fought together, but they work well together.

Retired Lieutenant Colonel Gary Andresen, USMC, helped with suggestions and observations on the Vietnam experience. As lieutenants, we commanded "Rough Rider" truck convoys through the Hai Vanh pass more times than we like to remember. To this day we are grateful for simply surviving.

Author William Conrad Gibbons, this author's brother-in-law, showed me how the history of the Vietnam War paralleled the films of the war. "W.C." wrote the five-volume history *The U.S. Government and the Vietnam War*. Much of his work has been reflected in subsequent articles and books. More, no doubt, will be forthcoming.

ABC's Don North and Associated Press's Rick Pyle gave me support and more resources regarding the Hue City massacre. Peter Arnett of CNN contributed as well.

Colonel Herb Fix, U.S. Marine Corps, Retired, gave me a superb account of the fall of Saigon, this from a man who was there.

Screenwriter Nancy Ellen Dowd gave me an unusual look into her UCLA master's thesis script *Buffalo Ghost*, which became the basis for *Coming Home*.

Susan Golant, a fellow instructor in the UCLA Extension Writers Program, outlined to me what a nonfiction book proposal should contain. Suddenly locked doors opened. That is why you are reading this.

The late Carl Foreman, one of my judges in the Samuel Goldwyn Competition, not only offered opinions on his many war films but also gave me a new perspective as a World War II veteran whose service to his country was forgotten while he was blacklisted. I had no idea how beneficial the meetings with him in his office at Universal Pictures would eventually be. Likewise, his memorial service at Mount Sinai, in Los Angeles, was a packed house.

Finally, there are two people who know the years-long effort contained in these pages: My wife Patty, who endured the combat separation of Vietnam, offered numerous suggestions over countless dinner conversations. As the project lengthened, so did the rejections, forty-six in all. She never wavered through all of it. Even when I thought events were at their darkest, she saw some light.

Screenwriter Heather Hale, my first-line editor, constantly took the devil's advocate position. Often she made me rethink many observations, both in films and in history. I will always remember the luncheon conversations, endless phone calls, and the exchanges of pages.

At Praeger Publishers I would like to thank Jim Sabin, Dave Palmer, and Susan Badger for their support, communication and professionalism. So many items had to be checked, double-checked, and triple-checked.

All of these people share individual credit for what they did to make this work possible. I like to think that they contributed not only to film but to the history of it.

# Introduction:
# A Theatrical Education

It is well that war is so terrible,
that we should grow too fond of it.
— General Robert E. Lee, 1862

The only thing I have in common with Pearl Harbor is that I learned about war on Sundays.

Sunday afternoons in my family were special times, marked by going to a film. On the "right side of fifty" today, I can still vividly recall those boyhood weekends by film title.

Many of those films were in the war genre.

Coming from a large Irish Catholic family on the south side of Chicago, Sunday mornings were spent attending Mass with my class from St. Philip Neri Grammar School. However, as I sat there in the pew, under the watchful eye of a Dominican nun, my mind was elsewhere, knowing that later in the afternoon I would be in a darkened downtown theater watching American movie actors performing scripted heroics against the background of a war.

From the 1930s to the 1960s the first-run films came into Chicago to the "Loop" movie theaters, the downtown shopping and business area encircled by the elevated tracks. Some of these theaters are gone now. But I can still remember them from those Sunday afternoons: the Oriental, the United Artists, the Garrick, the Woods, and the RKO Grand. Over on State Street were three more, the State-Lake, the Chicago, and the Roosevelt. The Clark showed older re-release films. Today it would be called an "art house."

Sunday afternoons were my mother's time alone. We were a family of seven children, four boys and three girls. Usually there would be relatives, or a legal associate from my father's law office, scheduled as dinner guests. But the afternoon hours were my mother's time to rest from the preceding week and the never-ending duties of caring for seven children.

My father would herd all of us, the older boys and girls plus any school friends who wanted to tag along, into the station wagon for a first-run downtown film. This was a treat.

I would see the film again when it came to the neighborhood. If the story was exceptional, in my uncritical schoolboy judgment, I would see it a third time, which afforded me the trivial luxury of learning the dialogue and the base of a three-act structure. Naturally I didn't know it at the time, but these experiences would have a payoff in later life.

The next day, in the schoolyard, I would impress my classmates with the new war movie downtown, reeling off the story line until I got to the denouement. They would wait breathlessly. I would never tell them the end. And then I would smile and add, "Go see the movie."

One of my uncles, known for his rigid lack of humor, brought up the fact to my mother that I was spending too much time in movie theaters. He often told me that it was "time wasted, sitting in the dark watching foolish movies."

As I began the outline for this book, I found myself thinking of that now-departed uncle and how his opinions affected me in a way he hadn't intended.

My father, Frank McAdams Jr., was a World War II naval officer. So naturally war films from his era held a personal appeal. He was commissioned as a "90-Day Wonder" from the Naval Indoctrination Program set up on college campuses. He went through the Princeton program in the months following Pearl Harbor. My mother, Irene, was extremely unhappy about this. They were already parents of three. But it was a world war, and every qualified man under the age of thirty-five was draft bait.

Years later, my father took me back to the Princeton campus. We visited his room in Cuyler Hall, which he shared with four other midshipmen. After the war he learned that he was the only survivor of that group of roommates.

I later found out, from some of the members of my father's naval amphibious squadron, that when General Douglas MacArthur landed in the Philippines on October 20, 1944, at Leyte Beach in that classic photograph taken by Major Gaetano Faillace of him and his staff wading ashore, my dad's landing ship was already unloading materiel less than 100 yards up the beach.

At 2:30 the next afternoon, dad was seriously wounded, in an artillery bombardment, while supervising unloading operations from the bridge of his landing ship, the LSM-201. He wasn't even supposed to be up there. He took the watch of one of his officers who had been up all night. Three of the men standing on the bridge with him were killed.

Six years later, after extensive therapy and operations at four naval hospitals, his wounded right arm was amputated below the elbow because of dead nerves. Bluish shrapnel scars dotted the calves of both his legs. After the war, he got on with his life and seemed to carry his war wounds with unusual grace. It wouldn't be until years later when the war's true toll came to bear on him. It came in the Irish tradition of alcohol, the "creature." Tragically, for my father, it caused a bittersweet law career to end without gaining its full potential.

Despite the missing arm, he could tie a tie faster than most men. I used to marvel at how fast he could tie his shoelaces with one hand. He would put his shoe up on a chair and move the fingers of his left hand so fast that I couldn't keep track of the laces. All of a sudden the shoe was tied, as if by magic.

Driving a car presented no problem. He could even drive a stick shift by moving his left arm through the wheel fast enough to do the shifting. Often he would accelerate the car rapidly from an intersection, then shift from first to third. The first time I tried to imitate that move I killed the engine.

Once I remember proudly wearing my father's navy campaign ribbons to school. On the top row was the Purple Heart for his wounds at Leyte. I recall taking a message into one of the higher-grade classrooms at St. Philip's. The nun, Sister Jean Philip, stopped in the middle of her morning presentation and asked me if I was wearing my father's ribbons. I nodded yes and pointed to the Purple Heart, right in front of the entire class.

"I remember the Sunday when they announced at Mass that he had been wounded in the Philippines," she said. "We all prayed for him." She then proceeded to tell her class about how my father was wounded in the Western Pacific in 1944.

That afternoon in the schoolyard one of the older boys from Sister Jean Philip's class called me over, under a tree.

"You should take those off," he said, pointing at the ribbons.

I remember staring at him for a moment. I didn't like his tone. "Why? They're my dad's ribbons," I countered.

"Right. And you didn't earn them," he argued.

"Why are you saying this?" I asked.

"My dad's got the same Purple Heart. And a couple of others like your dad." Then he paused and looked around the schoolyard. "Only my dad didn't come back. He's buried in Belgium." I can still remember how he pointed to the Purple Heart. "I have them at home. They're his ribbons. Always will be." He looked at me, directly in the eye. "You're wearing something you didn't earn."

I went home that afternoon and took the ribbons off. I never wore them again. Years later, as a commissioned Marine Corps officer, each time I pinned on my own ribbons I would recall standing under that tree, learning a lesson from a fatherless youth about the hard price of war.

My school friends always remembered the first introduction to my father because he would extend his left hand for a handshake. The unsuspecting person would suddenly realize that there was no right hand. It was always an awkward moment with a look of embarrassed surprise. My father came to enjoy it in a strange way. Only if someone asked did he or she learn it was because of the Leyte invasion in World War II.

Years later when my sister's children were young, my nephew, Michael Berardi, asked my father what happened to his right arm.

My dad smiled. "A bear bit it off."

Before World War II my father was always drawn to the western genre in films. After his generation returned as heroes from their war, he added the war film to his favorite categories. His favorite movie actors were James Cagney, Spencer Tracy, Gary Cooper, Clark Gable, Jimmy Stewart, and Randolph Scott.

And, of course, the "Duke" himself, John Wayne.

He thought Robert Taylor was boring.

After seeing John Wayne in *Sands of Iwo Jima*, my father was quick to point out that Marion Michael Morrison, once an aspiring tackle at USC, never wore a uniform or served in combat. Heavily influenced by the combat roles Wayne had played, I refused to believe it. It was later when reality hit me. Yes, it was true. John Wayne never experienced combat or wore an active duty uniform. It was here, at the age of eight, where I had to realize that sometimes there was a difference between life and art.

It was on one of those Chicago Sunday afternoons in a downtown theater when I watched Gregory Peck, in an Oscar-nominated performance, in *Twelve O'Clock High*. Right from the beginning I was drawn to his character because of the contrast of strength and vulnerability. I sat there, gradually drawn in, throughout the film. I recall feeling the pain as I watched Peck, portraying the young General Frank Savage, head toward an emotional breakdown brought on by the stress of a wartime Eighth Air Force bomber command.

In Peck's climactic scene, he has driven himself into a state of exhaustion where he is unable to climb up into the nose hatch of his B-17. His body had finally reacted to what Peck's mind shut out, seeing so many of his men die. He freezes and cannot lift himself into the plane. He is taken away yelling, arms extended as one of his field-grade officers takes his place to lead the dangerous daytime mission into Germany.

I can still recall riding home in the station wagon that late afternoon, staring out of the window across the Illinois Central railroad tracks as we passed Soldier Field, into the approaching darkness. Like most boys my age, I wondered if the time would ever come when I would be tested like General Frank Savage. The film surprised me because I initially thought that Peck and his men would end the drama as victors, walking off as music swelled in the background. I was unprepared for the emotional price that the writers, who were Army Air Force veterans, put into the script.

My father often told me of his feelings of holding a wartime command, being the skipper of a navy landing ship. He knew if anything adverse happened while at sea, he would be held responsible. In rough seas he never slept, preferring to be on the bridge. And he often told me that a good officer leads by example. To this day the surviving members of his amphibious squadron speak of him with admiration and respect.

The first time I ever heard the expression "draft dodger" was from my father.

Often, during election time in Chicago, when a candidate's resume was being scrutinized in the press, dad would check out the candidate and quickly point out if there was time spent in uniform. He often explained how some candidates would take glamorous license with their military records.

Several times, while reading a profile, I would see him pause. He would then mutter, "What a fake."

Once, at a political breakfast, after Senator John Kennedy had announced his presidential candidacy, the subject came around to the senator's controversial wartime experience in the Solomon Islands when his navy torpedo boat was rammed in a nighttime operation. Kennedy and his crew were missing, presumed dead, for days. After they were eventually found, Kennedy was awarded the Navy-Marine Corps Medal for heroism. It was later recounted in *The New Yorker* magazine, a book, and then a movie, *PT 109*.

One of the men at the table, a successful businessman, questioned Kennedy's Ivy League and silver spoon background and leadership potential. "What kind of an officer would allow his boat to get that close to a Japanese destroyer and get cut in half?" The man snickered.

Dad stared at him for a beat. I knew the look. The gentleman was so unprepared. Oh, my God, I thought. Now it's coming.

And it did.

Dad softly put his fork down. He then swung his right stub up on the table so everyone could see that there was no arm in his sleeve. "We're about the same age, wouldn't you say?" The man nodded. "Matter of fact, Senator Kennedy is younger than you and me." The man nodded again. "I'd say the difference is that Kennedy went. As a matter of fact, Kennedy pulled some strings to get a combat command." Dad took a stage pause to insure that the entire table was listening.

The table was listening.

And then Dad continued. "Let me ask you, what did *you* do in the great World War II?"

I don't think I've ever seen anyone caught so off guard in a social situation. The man paused, noticing everyone at the table looking at him, suddenly realizing what he had walked into. Beads of perspiration were forming on his forehead. "Well, I, uh, had a business to run. But I did contribute to the war effort."

"You mean back here in the States?" asked dad.

"Uh, yes. Back here. You see, I had a family."

"So did a lot of *us*," said dad, emphasizing the word *us*. "Yet you can criticize someone who wore a uniform and put his life on the line." Dad paused again and looked around the table. "I think we should realize how fortunate some of us are, to be able to survive a world war." He then took another pause, going in for the kill. "Where some of us went. And others, who are now critics, didn't."

A strange silence came over the table. Dad's steely eyes were boring a hole through the man, as the silence continued. And then dad picked up his fork and continued eating as if nothing had happened.

The successful businessman finished his meal quickly. At the first opportunity, he got up and left the table.

Dad walked out of the breakfast with a smile, and Kennedy narrowly won the controversial election, with the help of certain Cook County, Illinois, votes.

I knew that my father would never change that man's vote, in the close 1960 election, since Vice President Richard Nixon was also a naval officer in the war. But I do know that that man would never forget meeting my father, if only to get a sampling of the lasting effect of a war.

I recall asking my father why he liked war films so much. His answer was straightforward. "Because most men never have to face the ultimate test of combat. You come face to face, in an instant, between living and dying. And that, young man, is the basis of classic drama."

Then he added, "That's why war films will always be with us. It's a film genre that will never go away because man is combative by his very nature."

My mother often told me how she and my father learned of the Pearl Harbor attack. They pulled into the garage of their apartment building after Sunday morning Mass.

The parking attendant, a black man by the name of Don, approached them. "Did you hear the news?"

"What news?" asked my father.

"The Japs bombed Pearl Harbor this morning." He paused and looked at both of them. "Looks like we're going to war."

My mother recalled exchanging dreaded looks with my father. Minutes later they were listening to the latest reports coming from Washington and Hawaii. They didn't know it at the time, but their lives, along with the lives of millions of other men and women and their sons and daughters, were about to change.

Forever.

And so would the American war film genre.

The
American
War Film

# 1

# Something New

As long as war is regarded as wicked it will always have a
certain fascination. When it is looked upon as vulgar it will
cease to be popular.

—Oscar Wilde

In one of his famous fireside radio chats President Franklin Roosevelt proclaimed, "Ah hate wah!" He even added that his Scottie dog Fallah hated war.

Most Americans hate war. To suffer the casualties of four major wars in less
than a century says something about a nation. To establish our independence
we had to fight. To keep from splitting into two nations we had to fight. And
as the world became smaller, and more complex, we chose to fight.

That said, we can now look at the contradiction: Movie audiences, particularly
American movie audiences, hate war, *but* they *keep coming* to see war films
because they are fascinated by the conflict and drama.

Before making a decision on the secret bombing of Cambodia, in 1970, President Nixon went through a decision-making process. Part of that process, reportedly, included the viewing of *Patton* in the White House screening room.
Nixon even advised his staff to see the film to understand wartime decisions.

On March 24, 1997, the Academy of Motion Picture Arts and Sciences gave
*The English Patient* the award for Best Picture of 1996. Written and directed
by Anthony Minghella, from the novel by Michael Ondaatje, this film told an
old love story set against a war background. Two people, one of them married,
fall in love, and that relationship becomes complicated because of the war.

One could be talking about *Casablanca, Gone with the Wind, Mrs. Miniver,*

*The African Queen*, or *From Here to Eternity*. These became Academy Award–winning films about love relationships with war backgrounds.

Hollywood did not discover anything new with *The English Patient*. Through the years films with war backgrounds have won the Oscar in the Best Picture category an astounding seventeen times. Naturally that number would be higher if all Academy categories were considered.

In her obituary after dying of brain cancer at age fifty-one, former Columbia Pictures president Dawn Steel was quoted as to what initially attracted her to the film industry: "It wasn't until I saw 'Rocky' that I realized movies could affect people beyond mere entertainment."[1]

## THE BLOSSOM ROOM

The first Academy Awards ceremony had all the hoopla of a sit-down dinner, which is exactly what it was. Approximately 250 people gathered in the Blossom Room, the main ballroom of the Hollywood Roosevelt Hotel, at 8:00 P.M. on Thursday, May 16, 1929.

For the first time the newly formed Academy of Motion Picture Arts and Sciences came together to honor the best films of the 1927–1928 season.

"It was more like a private party than a big public ceremony," Janet Gaynor later recalled.

The awards were handed out by Douglas Fairbanks in less than five minutes total. Naturally, at the time, no one knew that this would become a glitzy world-wide annual televised event.

At the Hollywood Roosevelt dinner Emil Jannings (who was in Germany at the time) was given the award for Best Actor in *The Way of All Flesh*. Janet Gaynor was named Best Actress for *Seventh Heaven*. The Best Picture award was given to Paramount Pictures for *Wings*.

It was a war film.

Even Janet Gaynor's Best Actress award, in *Seventh Heaven*, was a role with a war background. In the 20th Century Fox film, Gaynor played a Paris street waif who is befriended by a sewer worker portrayed by Charles Farrell. When the war comes, Farrell goes off but returns blinded. Benjamin Glazer won the Oscar for Best Screenplay, and Frank Borzage won for Best Director.

The Academy wasn't the first organization to give film awards. Reportedly, *Photoplay Magazine* had begun the practice seven years prior. Film awards were becoming more accepted.

A golden statuette, a stalwart man holding a sword and standing on a reel of film, designed by MGM art director Cedric Gibbons, was officially designated as the award. The sculptor was George Stanley. One story has it that Margaret Herrick, the noted film librarian, saw the prototype and studied it for several moments on her first day of work in 1931. She thought the statuette looked like a Texas relative.

"He looks like my Uncle Oscar," she said.

Like the origin of the name of Hollywood, there are other versions as to how the Oscar got its name. At one time, Bette Davis claimed to have named Oscar. When she won the award for Best Actress in 1935, Davis examined the statuette and said that its backside reminded her of her then-husband Harmon O. Nelson. "Since the *O* in Harmon O. Nelson stood for Oscar, Oscar it has been ever since," said Davis.

The press was not to be left out. Hollywood columnist Sidney Skolsky claimed that he was the first to use the word "Oscar" in 1933. Skolsky was irritated at what he thought was snobbery around the award and wanted to make it human.

Of the three versions, Hollywood insiders prefer the Herrick quote.

"The little gold-washed statuette was thought, by skeptics and art lovers, a bit on the amatuerish side," wrote MGM screenwriter Frances Marion. "Still I saw it as a perfect symbol of the [movie] picture business: a powerful athletic body clutching a gleaming sword with half of his head, that which held his brains, completely sliced off."[2]

*Wings*, directed by William Wellman, was a World War I drama with a love story triangle, filmed mostly around San Antonio, Texas. The simulated aerial sequences involved no (fake) process shots. It wasn't the first war film produced, nor would it be the last in the Silent Era. The previous war films had their action taking place on the ground. Wellman lifted the action off the ground and took it airborne.

The credit for the impressive and daring aerial sequences goes to Wellman and John Monk Saunders, both of whom served in the Army Air Service during the war.

The critics and audiences loved *Wings*, just as critics and audiences loved and appreciated *The English Patient*. The war genre had once again survived the test of time.

The Academy gave Steven Spielberg's 1998 efforts in directing Robert Rodat's screenplay *Saving Private Ryan* the Oscar for Best Director. Spielberg was in competition with Terrence Malick, who directed and wrote the adaptation of James Jones's sequel to *From Here to Eternity, The Thin Red Line*.

## IN THE BEGINNING

The first recorded American war film was a dramatic short, centered around the Spanish-American War, *Tearing Down the Spanish Flag*, filmed in New York City in 1898 by J. Stuart Blackton. It emphasized the elements of patriotism and propaganda, something that would be repeated with future American war films.

What Blackton did was revolutionary for the embryonic industry: to use an American historical event to tell a drama. This was not lost on the studios and production companies when audiences began to wait in line to see these "flickers."

In a *Newsweek* Special issue on the effect of movies in the twentieth century Jack Kroll and Tessa Namuth wrote, "It's doubtful if the human race will ever be as astounded by a new form of entertainment as it was by the advent of the movies."[3]

Gloria Swanson, as Norma Desmond in *Sunset Boulevard*, has a scene where she tells William Holden, portraying Joe Gillis, a struggling screenwriter, "There was a time in this business where we had the eyes of the whole world!"[4]

In 1903 Edwin S. Porter's *The Great Train Robbery*, a twelve-minute single reel film shot in upstate New York, was shown at a theater in Pittsburgh. The film had fourteen scenes. It was the first American film to tell a realistic story in a time frame.

The early film companies, the majority of which were located on the East Coast, kept the story lines simple. An art form was still being discovered.

The theaters were small and unventilated, with uncomfortable seats. The price of admission was one good old American nickel. Hence the moniker "nickelodeon." By 1907 there were approximately 5,000 nickelodeon screens in the United States. As these profits swelled, the independent film companies felt that they were being victimized by the distribution firms that were consistently raising their fees in this fledging market.

To survive, the new film companies realized that they had to produce the "flickers" year-round. The very best that the East Coast could offer, for exterior shooting, was approximately six months. And that was if the clouds and Divine Providence were kind. It was now time to follow the sun, and a Mediterranean-type climate, not only to produce more flickers but to get away from the unfair distribution trusts.

Several locales were considered, Florida, the Gulf Coast, and south Texas. There were also several cities in southern California between Santa Barbara and San Diego—and right in the middle was Ciudad de Los Angeles.

Next to Los Angeles was an undeveloped area known as "Hollywood." Like Oscar's background, several stories conflict as to the exact origin of Hollywood. One version, told mostly by tour guides, is that the region's name came from the wild holly bushes that grew along the roadsides. However, the tour guides fail to mention that holly is difficult to grow in a Mediterranean climate. Like many things in Hollywood, some publicist obviously used poetic license.

Another version is that Hollywood got its name from Daeida Wilcox Beveridge, the widow of Harvey Henderson Wilcox, a prohibitionist and a devout Methodist who developed much of the land around Los Angeles. By the time of her death, in 1914, the section around her home on the boulevard was known as "Hollywood." The more accepted version has Mrs. Beveridge taking the name from a friend's eastern estate.

As the rattle of war became louder in Europe the eastern film companies began setting up shop in Hollywood to work year-round.

In 1915 the Mutual Film Production Company released *The Birth of a Nation*. The screenplay was written by an actor, David Wark Griffith, and Frank Woods, based on the novel *The Clansman* by Thomas Dixon. It told the story of two families who found themselves on opposite sides of the Civil War.

If there is any one historical chapter that most influenced and fascinated this country, it has to be the Civil War, where the American experiment with democracy was severely tested, interspersed with romance and tragedy and colorful personalities who spanned the dramatic spectrum.

One of the more noted Civil War personalities was photographer Mathew Brady. By 1860, at age thirty-seven, he had a reputable portrait gallery in New York City, with a branch in Washington, D.C. Nine years before, he had won first prize in the international daguerreotype competition at London's Crystal Palace Exhibition. He was constantly experimenting with new techniques. By the time Fort Sumter was fired on, Brady was already using the "wet plate" process, which used collodion, a light-sensitive solution that made it mandatory for the image to be developed within an hour. From the wet plate negative, multiple prints could be produced on paper.

By the first Battle of Bull Run, Brady's "photo team" consisted of three people. Besides himself, he had recruited Alexander Gardner, a Scotsman who had a reputation in his own right. The third person was Timothy O'Sullivan, a noted photographer of the day. Brady knew he needed help if he was to embark on recording this monumental American struggle.

Ironically, the most famous American photographer of the nineteenth century was plagued by increasingly poor eyesight. As a result, many of the noted camp and field photographs, in the first year of the war, were taken by Gardner and O'Sullivan, with Brady closely supervising. As the war widened, Brady recruited more photographic teams. At one point, he had as many as twenty such teams documenting the battles and living conditions.

Brady invested approximately $100,000 of his own money, an enormous sum at the time, into his "Civil War Project." Tragically, many of his plates were lost after the war ended. By then Gardner and O'Sullivan had struck out on their own.

By 1875, when the federal government bought the remaining collection, Brady was close to poverty. The famous New York gallery had long been closed. In 1895 he was forced to sell the Washington gallery. He died the next year.

And two years later J. Stuart Blackton filmed *Tearing Down the Spanish Flag*.

Despite the tragic financial price that Mathew Brady paid, what he left behind was to influence not only future photographers but filmmakers who saw what he had captured: American history through a war that tore the nation apart, that would be engraved into this country's persona well into the succeeding century. His legacy included more than 3,500 photos of almost every major Civil War engagement. In addition, he photographed eighteen U.S. presidents.

A *New York Times* reporter visiting Brady's studio a month after Antietam, wrote,

Mr. Brady has done something to bring home to us the terrible reality and earnestness of war. . . . There is a *terrible fascination* about it that draws one near these pictures. . . .

You will see hushed, reverend groups standing about their weird copies of carnage . . . to look in the pale faces of the dead, chained by the strange spell that dwells in dead men's eyes.[5]

D.W. Griffith gave motion to the Brady photographs. In many of the battlefield photos, Brady showed the aftermath, the broken, twisted bodies, stiff in death, on their sides, their backs, their stomachs, sightless eyes opened to the clouds. One can only wonder what sort of look *The Birth of a Nation* would have had if the Civil War had not been so documented with photographs, particularly Mathew Brady photographs.

Soon after its release *The Birth of a Nation* found itself in the midst of a heated political debate. Blacks in several cities rioted because of the depiction of the Ku Klux Klansmen who sought revenge for what they considered injustice. This also clouded the film's use of innovative camera angles, plus the reenactment of historical incidents such as President Abraham Lincoln's call for volunteers and John Wilkes Booth's assassination of the president at Ford's Theatre.

President Woodrow Wilson described the film as "history written in lightning." Wilson later backed away from this statement, under pressure because of the racial element. The controversy continues to this day.

The audiences were being fed the usual genres, westerns (known as "oaters"), screwball comedies, romantic melodramas, family stories, and biblical epics. The comedies made instant stars of Charlie Chaplin, Ben Turpin, Harold Lloyd, and Buster Keaton. These comedians were basically trained as clowns and mimes and fit perfectly into the new medium with their timed perfection of sight gags, facial reactions, and pratfalls.

As the European war intensified, many observers knew it was just a question of time before the United States became involved, a historical element that would be repeated in the next generation.

From the war's outset former President Theodore Roosevelt repeatedly criticized the Wilson administration for not taking a harder line, to get into the war on the Allied side.

On May 17, 1915, the British ocean liner *Lusitania* was torpedoed by a German submarine and went down with 1,198 men, women, and children, among whom were 124 Americans. While the country was still reeling from this shock, British Viscount James Bryce, former ambassador to the United States, released an official report of some 1,200 alleged atrocities by German soldiers, mostly against Belgians. Although much of the report was later proved false, it still caused controversy in the American press and fed sensationalism. Then, on August 19, 1915, 2 Americans were lost when another British liner, the *Arabic*, was sunk by a German submarine.

Roosevelt became enraged at both incidents and assailed Wilson for being "too proud to fight," implying that the occupant of the White House was a coward. He held President Wilson personally accountable for the recent loss of American life.

Running for a second term, President Wilson used the campaign slogan "He Kept Us Out of War." The war in Europe was now a hot campaign issue. Some thought that Wilson would be turned out of office because of his neutral stance.

The election was in doubt for two days after the polls closed. Many thought that Republican candidate Charles Evans Hughes was the new president. Hughes won over Wilson in the Northeast and in the upper Midwest with the exceptions of New Hampshire and Ohio. On election night, the *New York Times* conceded the race to the challenger, and Wilson went to bed thinking about his release from "carrying the burden." He was even planning his moving schedule out of the White House.

The morning after the election a reporter called Hughes. An aide answered, explaining that "President Hughes does not wish to be disturbed."

The final tally showed that Wilson had won not only the Democratic bastion of the South but all of the western states with the exceptions of South Dakota and Oregon. Women were a decisive factor. As a bloc American women, in the states where they had the vote, voted for Wilson because of his desire for peace and avoidance of war.

The stage was now set for one of the most important turns in American history, one that the war film genre would continue to reflect: the entry into a modern, twentieth-century world war.

Early the following year, with its seaports blockaded, Germany announced unrestricted submarine warfare. Wilson, going against his peace platform, asked Congress for a Declaration of War. While reading his request for a Declaration of War, in a joint session of Congress, Wilson's hands trembled. He knew, with the passage of the declaration, that thousands of Americans would ultimately end up in cemeteries. Later, while alone, he wept.

## ROYALTY REPLACED

Wilson appointed General John J. Pershing to command the American Expeditionary Force (AEF) heading for France. At this same time the White House was developing a unique and revolutionary idea, with Wilson's approval, to use motion picture stars to market the war effort in the coming Liberty Loan drives. These drives would raise money and sell the war to the American public. Like so many other things in the twentieth century, this was something new. The Liberty Loan drives would supply about two-thirds of the $33.5 billion that the war would cost the United States.

In the late nineteenth century, and for approximately the first ten years of the twentieth century, America's "Royalty" were the rich. The California Gold Rush, the Civil War, the railroad, and the opening of the western states created fortunes. Many of these fortunes grew indecently, founded by the colorful and scandalous robber barons.

Initially the nouveaux riche were looked down upon. And it stayed that way until more of the new rich came along. Many of these were from immigrant families sharing the so-called American Dream.

The Spanish-American War established the United States as a world power. The superrich families were ensconced in and around the major American cities. Even though the parents had modest—or vague—educations, many of their children attended the best universities, frequently in the Ivy League. And their comings and goings, parties, weddings, divorces, and scandals gave birth to a separate section in the metropolitan newspapers. How these people partied, who they married, and where they went on vacation were always news. These families grew to be America's "Royalty." And they enjoyed it, reading about themselves and wondering how the less fortunate managed.

And then came Hollywood. Emerging from Hollywood came celebrated persons that the media dubbed "celebrities."

In a 1997 *Daily Variety* column, Timothy Gray wrote:

Celebrities are like the gods of Mount Olympus: They are flawed, but their lives are greater than those of mere mortals, and their experiences encompass every human trait and emotion. . . . Celebrities are our religion, and their lives provide us with lessons, myths and fantasies. Since the August 31, 1997 death of [Princess] Diana, many in the media have lamented that she got more attention than Mother Teresa who died days later. Are they kidding? Why bemoan celebrity worship? . . . But everybody in the world knows the stories of Muhammed [sic] Ali and Elizabeth Taylor. Celebs are the closest thing we've come to a global religion.[6]

In a 1997 newspaper interview, just before the Academy Awards ceremony, Hollywood producer David Brown said,

[A] great proliferation of media has created a level of celebrity that was unknown in early times. Which may mean that the celebrities of today pale a bit in comparison with someone like Harry Houdini, who was able to became world famous without the benefit of satellite television. . . . [O]f course, the star is the one who sells the tickets at the box office, so it's appropriate they [sic] be treated like royalty.[7]

The American stage community looked upon motion pictures as an aberration that would soon fade. An actor, with classical training, would never lower himself or herself to act in "flickers." This was the beginning of a professional rivalry that would last for generations.

But now, as flickers graduated to dramatic film stories, the new medium gained wider acceptance. It was apparent that audiences were not only captivated; they identified with and loved the people in these films. A stage actor would be exposed to a limited audience, whereas a film actor received instant recognition with just one film released nationwide. With succeeding films, the actor's name soon became a household word from coast to coast.

The old money generation came to find it particularly disgusting that they had to share the "Style" and "Society" pages with movie actors, many of whom came from the "hoi polloi" and had less-than-mediocre educations.

But now the country was in a world war. And that took precedence over the Style and Society pages. The government needed to finance its part in the European war.

Wilson created the Committee on Public Information (CPI), chaired by George Creel. Creel had his committee start a propaganda campaign never before seen in this country. An estimated 75 million pieces of pamphlet literature provided the official line on the war. War posters appeared everywhere to encourage enlistments and the purchase of Liberty Bonds.

At Paramount, Adolph Zukor reacted by distributing 100,000 propaganda posters to theaters nationwide. Liberty Bond trailers were tacked onto studio serials.

What the rich were forced to realize, in this changing world, was that they were being replaced as America's Royalty. It became a classical dump, American style.

In a 1980 essay in the *New York Review of Books*, Gore Vidal wryly observed, "All Americans born between 1890 and 1945 wanted to be movie stars."[8]

This was one of the first social changes of the new century. To the chagrin of America's rich, they would never, as a class, regain their former status. The steady appeal of films, and film magazines centered around celebrities, would keep movie stars safely perched at the top of America's twentieth-century social hierarchy.

It took a world war to bring about this social change. And after the war, propaganda began to be studied in a very different light. In 1922 F.M. Cornfield penned a new definition of propaganda that is often quoted today. Propaganda, Cornfield wrote, is "that branch of the art of lying which consists in very nearly deceiving your friends without quite deceiving your enemies."[9]

The movie stars lent their celebrity to the Liberty Bond tours, singing the virtues of democracy and sniping at all things German. Pretzels were removed from saloon counters in Cincinnati. German measles were renamed "liberty measles." Sauerkraut was now called "liberty cabbage"; German shepherds were dubbed "police dogs." Local ordinances banned Brahms and Beethoven from major concert halls. Works of German literature were removed from schools and libraries. Theodore Roosevelt suggested prohibiting the teaching of the German language in the nation's schools.

Like many American boys, Roosevelt was raised on the image of bravery tested by war. He would read about the Civil War as a boy, participate in the Spanish-American War as a man, and be devastated by World War I as a father.

"Teddy" (a nicknamed he despised) was born in 1858 to a privileged New York family. On April 25, 1865, he watched from a second-story window as church bells tolled while President Abraham Lincoln's funeral cortege passed below. The event so stayed with him that it led to a lifetime of reading about the Civil War and what he thought was a man's ultimate test, bravery in combat, dramatic stakes at their highest. He would bestow this feeling to his sons, each of whom accepted it and carried it out in their generation with different results.

At Harvard, Roosevelt didn't even live on campus as an undergraduate. His parents provided an apartment nearby. Because of constant health problems, he prided himself—lifelong—on being physically fit. Even when he wasn't.

He finally got his war in 1898. And in July of that year, in Cuba, he led a charge of his regiment, nicknamed the "Rough Riders," up a hill complex known as San Juan Heights. He returned as a war hero and ran for Republican governor of New York and later as vice president. The 1901 assassination of President William McKinley made him the youngest president at forty-two. And like George Washington, Andrew Jackson, William Henry Harrison, Zachary Taylor, Ulysses S. Grant, James A. Garfield, and McKinley, Theodore Roosevelt went to the White House a combat veteran.

But now, in 1917, his time in the White House gone, the young man in Roosevelt desperately wanted a piece of *this* war. Like most middle-aged men, Theodore Roosevelt was forced to accept the fact that combat, in this new century, was a young man's game.

One of Roosevelt's sons, Quentin, volunteered like his father in the previous war. Reflecting new strategies, Quentin joined the Air Service instead of his father's branch, the cavalry.

On July 17, 1918, Lieutenant Quentin Roosevelt's plane was shot down over France. Many people, close to the family, felt that Roosevelt never recovered from this wartime tragedy. On the night of January 6, 1919, he retired to bed, sick and depressed.

The last thing he said was, "Please put out the light."

The "T.R." attitude didn't end with World War I. Two of Roosevelt's other sons would also die serving their country. Kermit, who held the rank of major in both the British and American armies, would die in 1943. Theodore Jr. rose to become the assistant division commander of the 4th Infantry Division in World War II, landing on Utah Beach at Normandy on the first day of the invasion. Before dying of a heart attack in 1944, he was awarded the Congressional Medal of Honor. On January 16, 2001 Colonel Theodore Roosevelt, of the 1st U.S. Volunteers, was awarded the Medal of Honor by President Bill Clinton for his actions at San Juan Heights.

## THE PLAN

The planners of the Liberty Bond tours knew something about the American public: They would turn out to see a movie star. And they would buy whatever the movie star was selling. And so Mary Pickford, Lillian Gish, Harold Lloyd, Wallace Reid, Douglas Fairbanks, and Charlie Chaplin appeared at bond rallies to help America finance its part in the world war.

The Treasury Department contracted western star William S. Hart for a West Coast speaking tour. His emphatic, emotional appeal covered ten days and nineteen cities. In Spokane, Washington, thousands were turned away because of overcrowding. Hart's appearance in one evening raised $52,800 for Liberty Bonds. He made fifty-one speeches that collected $2 million in bond subscriptions.

Mary Pickford went on a New England tour that resulted in $14 million in Liberty Bond subscriptions. Douglas Fairbanks's Midwest tour alone garnered more than $8 million. Other appearances included Charlie Chaplin, William Farnum, Marie Dressler, and Tyrone Power Sr.

Propaganda films and shorts began to appear in theaters. One of the first World War I features was D.W. Griffith's *Hearts of the World* (1918) with Lillian Gish, Robert Harron, Ben Alexander, Noel Coward, and Dorothy Gish. Erich von Stroheim, at his Prussian best, played the evil German officer.

*Hearts of the World* was made by Paramount, at the request of the British government, early in 1917. It told the story of two expatriate families living in France when war erupts. The young man (Harron) decides to join the French army. The love story subplot has Harron in a triangle between the Gish sisters, Lillian and Dorothy. The scenes that shocked American audiences were those that dealt with the Germans plundering the French and Belgian villages.

Griffith went over to France to shoot actual combat footage to be used in postproduction. This was a technique that was consistently copied by directors in World War II films. Griffith also employed Allied advisers. Always breaking new ground, he never received full credit for these types of innovations. In later years other filmmakers copied him repeatedly.

Griffith directed another propaganda film, *The Girl Who Stayed Home* (1919), from a script by S.E.V. Taylor, starring Carol Dempster, Richard Barthelmess, Robert Harron, and David Butler. It was the account of a young man drafted into the army despite his father's influential protests. The youth then becomes a man on the battlefields of France.

Douglas Fairbanks gave a rousing patriotic speech in front of a huge New York City throng in April 1918. His training as an actor, speaking with enthusiasm and intensity, impressed not only the enormous crowd but the Wilson administration.

One month before the Armistice was signed, Frank R. Wilson, director of publicity, Treasury Department, for the War Loan Organization, wrote a letter to actor Wallace Reid in care of Lasky Studios, Hollywood, California. In the letter Wilson thanked Reid for his effort in the fourth Liberty Loan drive. Wilson then requested an autographed photo from Reid.[10]

Comedian Buster Keaton enlisted in July 1918. Despite his many Liberty Bond drive appearances, Charlie Chaplin was criticized for not enlisting. Chaplin, who was born in the slums of London, was one of the Hollywood actors to support not only the Allied effort early on but American's involvement.

What started out as a method to finance World War I with celebrities laid the groundwork for wartime and charity fund-raising for the rest of the century.

As Michael Satchell noted in *U.S. News & World Report* in September 1997,

"Today most major nonprofits depend on famous names to help carry their messages. Elizabeth Taylor and Elton John have become eponymous with AIDS assistance, Alec Baldwin and Kim Basinger with animal rights, Robert Redford with wilderness protection and Sting with rain forests."[11]

More than 30,000 women served in World War I in the roles of nurses either in the army or in the navy Nurse Corps or simply as women members of the military. They were yeomen in the navy, marines, and Coast Guard. Also, women were employed as clerical workers, draftsmen, translators, recruiters, and electricians. By Armistice Day, more than 10,000 nurses were serving overseas. At least 3 army nurses were awarded the Distinguished Service Cross, the nation's second-highest combat medal.[12]

A total of 4,743,826 Americans wore uniforms in World War I. Total battle deaths numbered 53,513. Of that figure, 50,510 of them were army deaths.[13]

## A SILENT COMEBACK

After the Armistice the moviegoing public gravitated to more lighthearted fare. For a while they seemed to want to forget the war that took its toll on the flower of American youth.

A party atmosphere came about as Prohibition, what Warren Harding called "a noble experiment," was selectively enforced, laying the groundwork for another Hollywood genre—the gangster film.

Early marketing techniques noted that the war film was subjected to the fickle taste of American movie audiences. But not for long. The audience pendulum began to swing back. Hollywood reacted to it. The propaganda films were now a thing of the past. War films would be far more reality based.

This syndrome would repeat itself in the next generation.

When Metro decided to film Vincente Blasco-Ibáñez's novel *The Four Horsemen of the Apocalypse* in 1921, it was agreed that they would need a "draw," an actor to attract audiences, particularly women. The studio gambled with Rex Ingram on Rudolph Valentino. It paid off handsomely. Others in the cast were Alan Hale and Wallace Beery. This was the first major post–World War I film to tell a realistic story without jingoism and propaganda.

Valentino played Julio Desnoyers, born into a wealthy Argentine family that is part French. Julio journeys to Paris where he is caught up in a hedonistic lifestyle. There, he begins an affair with Marguerite Lurier (played by Alice Terry). However, the war forces a decision on Julio who also has German cousins. He enlists in the French army and finds himself confronting one of his cousins on the battlefield. Julio dies, leaving his family to contemplate the mythical symbol of the four horsemen: conquest, war, famine, and death.

In 1925 *The Big Parade* was released by MGM, destined to become the largest-grossing silent film to date. If one film led the parade of American war films into the twentieth century, it was this one, complete with a love story subplot that would become a staple of the genre. Studios and producers were discovering that a war film was made richer and deeper with a love story subplot. And, of course, the converse worked, a love story set against a war.

The main story line of *The Big Parade* followed a male trio, played by John Gilbert, Karl Dane, and Tom O'Brien. They meet as recruits and stay together through combat. Gilbert falls in love with a French farmgirl, played by Renée Adorée. During the following harrowing battle sequence, Gilbert loses a leg but survives, while his buddies do not. Gilbert returns home and suffers emotional trauma when those around him fail to understand what he has suffered, a harbinger of things to come in subsequent wars. He returns to France and to the arms of Adorée, who not only understands him but identifies with what he has gone through.

Connecting with veterans, this was the first American film to date that came closest to showing the brutal horrors of a recent war.

Coming in on the heels of *The Big Parade* was 20th Century Fox's adaptation of the successful 1924 stage play by Maxwell Anderson and Lawrence Stallings, *What Price Glory?* with Victor McLaglen, Edmund Lowe, and Delores del Rio in the proverbial triangle, respectively, as Captain Flagg, Sergeant Quirt, and Charmaine. The stage play was bawdy and raucous, irreverent marines in a combat zone with French village girls. On screen, director Raoul Walsh used a script written by Barney McGill, Jack Marta, and John Smith.

The censors were caught completely off guard. Audiences could read the lips and had a better time "seeing" the words. It was a unique trait of the silents. This film cut a new cloth in film censorship.

*What Price Glory?* got its main story message across—that, yes, war is hell. And it's the older men who send the young ones off to die.

As Captain Flagg observes, "It's a lousy war . . . but it's the only one we got!"

The trench warfare scenes were brutal to take, compared with the wild comedy in the first half of the film. Fox remade this, from a script by Phoebe and Henry Ephron, directed by John Ford in 1952, with James Cagney, Dan Dailey, and Corinne Calvet. *The Big Parade*, to which it was always compared, was never remade.

## THE PIVOTAL YEAR

As the Jazz Age grew wilder and crazier, fueled by the hypocrisy of Prohibition, American audiences yearned for more adventure films. It is not lost on film historians that if one pivotal year had to be selected that turned the country and the film industry in a new direction, it was 1927.

In addition to the first Academy Awards and the triumph of *Wings*, 1927 produced several other historical events. Charles Lindbergh, carrying five ham sandwiches, flew the Atlantic Ocean by himself in a single engine plane. He came to personify the all-American hero. In baseball, the New York Yankees, with a batting order dubbed "Murderers' Row," crumbled their opponents with what many sports historians call the greatest team ever.

Science, society's pacesetter, then developed sound for film, making it possible for audiences not only to see what was happening but to hear it. To survive this innovation the studios, and production companies, had to adapt or suffer the fatal economic consequences. Silent films would not be able to compete in the marketplace against sound pictures.

Like most scientific revolutions, the trend began subtly. And slowly a new art form rushed in as its admired and creative predecessor was given "the bum's rush."

In early January 1926, Warner Bros. was in dire financial straits. One of the three Warner brothers, Sam, had been impressed when he saw several short films that were experimenting with the Vitaphone system of synchronized music recorded on a disc. He then approached Western Electric, which owned Vitaphone.

Within months Warner Bros. released *Don Juan*, starring John Barrymore. It was the first feature-length film with a synchronized music score composed. The film did extraordinary business. However, the majority of studio executives, in their everlasting wisdom, dismissed it as a onetime pheonomeon. They felt that this was the proverbial "flash in the pan."

Tilt.

Almost a year to the day when he approached Western Electric, Sam Warner signed Al Jolson to appear in *The Jazz Singer*. This would be the first movie with a few synchronized dialogue scenes in addition to a musical score. Still, nobody seemed to realize that they were witnessing a technical revolution.

William Fox felt the development could go even further. Soon it was accepted that sound on a film track, instead of on a disc, was the more efficient way to go. This realization captured the attention of some insightful studio executives.

In the middle of the summer of 1928, Warner Bros. released the gangster melodrama *Lights of New York*. The story line was simple: A chorus girl played by Helene Costello gets involved with gangsters. What was unique in marketing was that *Lights of New York* was being promoted as the first all-talking feature-length film. Audiences turned out to see the film in droves. All bets on the silents were off; sound was definitely in.

D.W. Griffith was one of sound's early supporters. "Just give them ten years to develop [sound] and you're going to see the greatest artistic medium the world has ever known."[14]

Legendary director Frank Capra was one of those who made the transition to sound films. In an interview, Capra described the differences between shooting a silent film and shooting a sound film:

Shooting your first sound film was a study in chaos. First of all, no one was used to being quiet. Shooting of silent scenes had gone on with hammering and sawing on an adjacent set; the director yelled at the actors through a megaphone, cameramen shouted

"Dim the overhead. . . . Lower the boom!" while everyone howled as if the scene was funny. Suddenly with sound we had to work in the silence of a tomb. When the red lights were on everyone froze in his position, a cough or a belch would wreck a scene. It was like a quick switch from a bleacher seat at Ebbets Field to a box seat at a Wimbledon tennis match.[15]

The development of sound made it possible for the emergence of a new genre: the musical. Audiences would be able to see people dancing, hear the music, and see the characters singing at the same time. What was once confined to the stage was now going to the screen in extravaganza proportions.

However, as with most revolutionary technological achievements, the innovation left casualties in its wake. They came in several groups. The first was musicians. Theaters no longer needed organ players or orchestras to accompany the silents. The studios would provide this. The writers of the dialogue cards and directors who were settled in the silents saw their careers flashing before their eyes.

The tragic casualty list likewise spread to the actor ranks. Ramon Novarro and Vilma Bánky had foreign accents that they had never bothered to correct.

Mary Pickford's voice was weak and high-pitched. There was little that "America's Sweetheart" could do about it. It didn't take long before she realized the end of her career.

Another well-known actress of the day, Polish-born Pola Negri, was never able to lose her thick accent. She accepted the inevitable and departed for Germany.

Mae Murray had a squeak, and Norma Talmadge had Brooklyn coming out of her mouth every time she opened it.

Another group was the comedians, particularly the ones who relied solely on pantomine and sight gags. Buster Keaton fell to secondary roles. Harold Lloyd decided to retire. Charlie Chaplin, who never really felt accustomed to the new wave of sound, didn't venture into the medium until 1940 with *The Great Dictator*.

Two actors whose careers were tragically ended by sound were John Gilbert and Karl Dane from *The Big Parade*. Gilbert, who had a high-pitched voice, died of a heart attack at age forty-one, in 1936, brought on by excessive drinking due to his faded career and personal frustrations. Dane, who was best known as a comedian, kept hoping for a comeback but always carried bitterness for what sound did to his career. He worked as a carpenter and mechanic and suffered a final indignity, being forced to sell hotdogs from a vendor wagon a short distance from the gates of the studio where he was once an "A List" star. Finally, in 1934, he ended everything by sitting in a comfortable chair in his apartment, putting a gun to his head. His body went unclaimed in the county morgue for days before his old studio stepped in and paid the burial expenses.

The development of sound intensified dramas, particularly the war film. Audiences would not only see fear on the faces of soldiers; they would hear the rifle and artillery sounds. They would also hear the screaming agony.

Howard Hughes's long-awaited war film *Hell's Angels* (1930) was greatly affected by the development of sound in film. The film was originally developed as a silent in 1927. Greta Nissen, who was cast as a society girl in a love triangle subplot, had a thick accent. Sound forced Hughes to recast the part to a young actress named Jean Harlow. The film was the most expensive ever produced at the time—$4 million. In 1990s dollars it would have been a $100 million–plus production.

The main story line follows two British brothers, educated at Oxford, who are commissioned in the Royal Flying Corps. James Hall, as Roy Rutledge, is a strong, idealistic young man. His brother, Monte, played by Ben Lyon, is a playboy. They become involved with Harlow, who plays one against the other. When the brothers are captured, in a mission to destroy a munitions factory, they are subject to interrogation by the Germans. Roy is forced to kill Monte to prevent him from giving over information. Roy is then sent to face a firing squad, grief stricken but certain that his actions were justifiable, protecting information that would have cost many Allied lives.

The aerial sequences were meant to supersede *Wings*. Hughes also used two-color technicolor that seemed to conflict with the black-and-white tone of the rest of the film. Since Hughes did not have the assistance of the military or any of its bases, he had to rely on the availability of stunt pilots.

The love story/combat triangle was also employed at Columbia for *Flight*, a 1929 Frank Capra–directed film that had Lila Lee as the nurse who is torn between two rival Marine Corps flyers in Nicaragua. The two flyers, Jack Holt and Ralph Graves (who did a rewrite on the script), begin as friends and then turn against each other when Lee professes her true love to each. The story is not only derivative of *Wings*, but Lee appears as a twin sister to Clara Bow. The aerial sequences gave a good action alternative to the much-used plot. Columbia was obviously trying to add a new twist from the World War I story lines, this time to capitalize on the latest U.S. intervention into Central America.

The same year that United Artists released *Hell's Angels*, Universal Pictures came out with the film adaptation of Erich Maria Remarque's novel *All Quiet on the Western Front*. Remarque had served in the German infantry.

Lewis Milestone directed from a script by George Abbott. Remarque's novel was about an idealistic German youth, Paul Baumer (played by Lew Ayres), and his classmates. They enthusiastically join the German army after hearing a propagandistic speech by a high school teacher. They undergo rigorous training and are sent to the front, where they fall victim, one by one, to the artillery and deadly machine gun.

After Baumer is wounded, he goes home and makes an appearance at his old school, where he warns the youths of the horrors of war in the trenches, the way he saw his friends die. He is shouted down with jeers and realizes, like

John Gilbert in *The Big Parade*, that he has no identification with these people and thus returns to the front.

In the novel, Paul Baumer is killed on an otherwise uneventful day along the Western Front. His death is merely reported and the book ends. Milestone took that ending and made it more visual and dramatic, having Baumer killed in the muddy trenches by an enemy sniper as he reaches out to touch a symbol of nature's beauty: a butterfly. The roll-call epilogue of the film has the ghosts of the young men walking, in uniform, toward the front. The audience then sees Paul Baumer look at them, as if to say, "This is what you've done to the younger generation." He then turns and joins the ghosts of his comrades.

The film was critically acclaimed as a powerful and realistic work, a landmark in American war films yet still pacifistic. The criticism went to the other end, also. Other quarters, in America, looked upon the film as a vehicle designed to cripple the U.S. military.

When the film had its premiere in Berlin, members of the Hitler Youth ran through the theater hurling stink bombs and yelling, "Germany Awake!" They also scattered white mice across the floor, all tactics engineered up by Nazi propaganda minister Joseph Goebbels. When the Third Reich took control of the government, in 1933, the film was banned, and the United States was condemned for producing it.

The powerful statement could not be denied to audiences on either side of the Atlantic. It was ironic that one of the most important American war films was about a German soldier. And the actor who played Paul Baumer, Lew Ayres, became a lifelong pacifist, a decision that brought much controversy to him after the outbreak of World War II.

*All Quiet on the Western Front* impacted entire generations; it also affected Milestone and Ayres in different ways. After appearing as a speaker at a film conference in 1964 in Aspen Meadows, Colorado, Milestone wrote:

In all my years of picture making I'm constantly confronted by two questions. What? And how? In my case the writer answers the first question. I answer the second. How is the director's job. That's me. If the director does his job well the audience will not detect propaganda, although propaganda is there as it must be of one kind or another. In every picture you make, every story you tell.

Remarque wrote a book—an autobiographical book. It was called by some anti-war, pacifist. I hate to tell you what Mr. Schicklegruber (Adolf Hitler's real name) called it. I felt my job was to erase all handles, technical terms and slogans. My wish was to give the audience a ringside seat to war. I believed it was also Remarque's wish, thirty-four years later. I take no chance of appearing immodest when I boldly say we succeeded.[16]

In a 1975 letter to a biographer, Lew Ayres mentioned a 1939 Atlantic Ocean crossing on a German liner:

It was off season. The ship was far from crowded, and hearing that I was a motion picture actor, some of the [German] crew members cordially ringed around me by chance one day on deck asking the names of some of my films. When I mentioned *All Quiet on the Western Front* there was a mutual interchange of startled looks. Some turned and walked away without a word, but two remained long enough to inform me (although they'd never seen the film) they knew by official criticism it was an evil book with a corrupt and degraded philosophy. Widely avoided and almost totally unattended for the rest of the crossing I was greatly relieved to debark in France.[17]

Ayres went on to explain that the film and various events in his life, about 1933, led him toward a pacifistic philosophy.

In 1937 Universal produced Remarque's sequel to *All Quiet on the Western Front*, *The Road Back*. Again, German protests emerged. The story was about war veterans adjusting to postwar civilian life. Even though it was a sequel, *The Road Back*, directed by James Whale from a script by R.C. Sheriff and Charles Kenyon, never achieved the status of the earlier film.

The American war film genre had reached another level, visually arguing that war brings out the best and worst in human nature simultaneously, setting the stage for the ultimate evil that man has to face in drama and contradiction.

## MADNESS LOOMING

In 1933 MGM released *Today We Live*, from a story by William Faulkner titled *Turnabout*. Assisting Faulkner on the script were Edith Fitzgerald and Dwight Taylor. The story had a male triangle with Robert Young, Gary Cooper, and Franchot Tone. The "eternal triangle" had Cooper and Young vying for the affections of an English society girl played by Joan Crawford. The action scenes were well crafted. Some of the stock footage was borrowed from *Hell's Angels*.

While *Today We Live* was playing in theaters, forty-four-year-old Adolf Hitler, a World War I veteran, was named chancellor of Germany, standing in stark contrast to the aging president, Paul von Hindenburg, who was considered a Prussian with a nineteenth-century mentality.

The new leaders in Europe and Great Britain, although born in the nineteenth century, came of age in the twentieth. Regardless of whether they were a Churchill, a de Gaulle, a Mussolini, or even a Hitler, they all had one thing in common: nationalistic attitudes.

Three months after Hitler was named chancellor, newly elected American President Franklin D. Roosevelt told the public, "The only thing we have to fear is fear itself," borrowing the phrase from Henry David Thoreau.

In the mid-1930s the Academy of Motion Picture Arts and Sciences was being torn apart. In an interview with Michael Thomas, reprinted in the *Los Angeles Times*, legendary director Frank Capra contended that the studio heads were using the Motion Picture Academy to destroy the guilds.

Capra added,

They were going to destroy the academy to do it. Well, I didn't want to see that happen. I knew the Academy Awards are the best advertising for the film industry. So in 1935 we decided to try and unite the industry by honoring the man who started it all, D.W. Griffith. Except nobody knew where he was. I found him in a bar in Kentucky dead drunk.

Well, we got him sobered up and brought him back to Hollywood and presented him with a special Oscar [in March 1936] and it worked; it helped to reunite the industry and save the academy.[18]


Back in Germany, when Hindenburg died in 1934, Chancellor Adolf Hitler became führer of the Third Reich and assumed supreme command of the German military. He then put forward a calculated time line to rearm Germany, disregarding the 1919 Versailles Treaty. The European community, although aware of this violation, did nothing.

Hitler also wanted to document his regime. Books and periodicals were fine. But he was also aware of the enormous power and impact of film. He put forth a plan to chronicle the Third Reich, creating a propaganda document for history.

Out of this propaganda film program emerged Leni Riefenstahl's *Triumph of the Will* in 1935. Some observers felt that this was the consummate propaganda film, what sold Adolf Hitler (and the Third Reich) to the German people.

Hitler ordered Propaganda Minister Joseph Goebbels to line up the best of the Austrian and German filmmakers. One of them was Fritz Lang, a staunch German but an ardent anti-Nazi who had written and directed such noted German films as *The Woman in the Moon*, *M* (which gained Peter Lorre international fame), and *Metropolis*. Goebbels summoned Lang for a meeting and informed the director that the führer admired his films, that Lang had been chosen to topline the emerging Third Reich film office. Lang got out of Germany that night on an express train bound for Paris. He turned up in London shortly thereafter. Eventually he found a new home and a welcome artistic reception in the United States. He later fell prey to the "Blacklist Era," for attending meetings that were deemed "suspicious." Fritz Lang happened to be on the crest of an exit wave of artistic and creative people in Europe who knew that madness loomed.

History was starting to repeat itself in America. Should the United States get involved in European entanglements—again?

The nation had passed from Prohibition to a Great Depression and preferred, once again, not to get involved in Europe's troubles. However, many influential Americans, including Charles Lindbergh and Ambassador Joseph P. Kennedy, felt that Hitler was simply restoring German confidence.

Many historians felt that Hitler's charisma came from a natural speaking ability. His military experience was modest, a lance corporal with some battlefield time as a messenger. The son of a customs official, he dropped out of school at sixteen. After the Armistice he was obsessed with avenging the humiliating 1918 defeat. Many of the protests he took part in deteriorated into street riots.

In 1923, Hitler was sentenced to a term in Landesberg Prison near Munich. It was here where he wrote the infamous Nazi credo *Mein Kampf.*

He used time wisely, writing a book while serving a prison sentence. The future chancellor was telling the world what he was going to do. He felt that Germany should strive toward a lasting uniting of the Aryan race. After he was released, he began to employ his strategy.

Soon civil war broke out in Spain. Then Germany declared a two-year military conscription, which provided the opportunity to test the new weapons of the Third Reich.

In 1935 Warner Bros., still mining world history for war film scripts, came up with a story based on the doomed British cavalry charge at Balaclava during the Crimean War in 1854, what came to be known as "the magnificent blunder." An adaptation of Alfred Lord Tennyson's poem of the same name, *The Charge of the Light Brigade* (1936) reinforced Errol Flynn's image as a swashbuckler. Facts did not get in the way of this war film—the film had little to do with the actual event.

As the noble 600 advanced on the enemy's cannons, Tennyson's words crawled up on the screen, letting the audience know that the cavalrymen were riding into certain death. With the timed shots and angles, plus Max Steiner's virtuoso score, it was "pure Hollywood." Steiner even garnered an Academy Award nomination.

When Paramount released *The Last Train from Madrid* in 1937, it received mixed reviews. The story was about a group of people caught in Spain as the civil war begins. The rest of the story is about their plight to get out of Spain. Even though it showed the coming problems with fascism in Europe, the script was laced with a tired story line and clichéd characters. This film did reinforce to American audiences that storm clouds were once again forming over Europe.

The war film genre continued to center around the more popular wars, World War I and the American Civil War. In 1938, Warner Bros. remade the 1930 World War I film *The Dawn Patrol*, using two of the actors from *The Charge of the Light Brigade*, Errol Flynn and David Niven.

This chapter in the Hollywood war film rewrite business showed insiders that sometimes the sequel can be even better than the original. Such was the case, according to a few film critics, with *The Dawn Patrol.*

The 1930 film had a script by John Monk Saunders of *Wings* fame; it was directed by Howard Hawks, also a war film veteran. Saunders won an Academy Award for his screenplay. The original title was *Flight Commander* with an all-male cast, a squadron of British aviators trying to survive the war. The cast included Richard Barthelmess, Douglas Fairbanks Jr., and Neil Hamilton.

Besides Flynn and Niven, the 1938 remake featured Basil Rathbone, Melville Cooper, Donald Crisp, and Barry Fitzgerald. The same aerial footage was used, but the tension and character action were improved upon.

When Macmillan published Margaret Mitchell's novel of the Old South, *Gone with the Wind*, in 1936, word had already filtered out that an American Civil War epic was in the offing. Kay Brown, at the Selznick International office in New York, read the book and immediately wired her boss to grab the film rights. Brown then had the book reduced to a fifty-seven-page outline.

Many Hollywood insiders advised Selznick against buying the film rights to *Gone with the Wind*. A 1935 Civil War film released by Paramount, *So Red the Rose* from the novel by Stark Young, starring Margaret Sullavan and Randolph Scott, fizzled at the box office. Paramount had gone through three screenwriters to adapt the novel.

Selznick was repeatedly told that American audiences were simply tired of war films, particularly about the Civil War. Beyond that, many people in Hollywood took issue with the literary worth of this so-called Civil War epic. Val Lewton, Selznick's respected and erudite story editor, confided to several associates that the book was ponderous trash.

Selznick's father-in-law Louis B. Mayer, who headed MGM, was concerned about the decision not only to produce *Gone with the Wind* but to develop it into a Civil War epic because of the twelve-year time frame and numerous supporting characters. Mitchell's agent was asking for a whopping $100,000 for the screenplay rights.

As Irving Thalberg, the noted MGM executive, reportedly said to Mayer, "Forget it Louis, no Civil War picture ever made a nickel."

Katharine Hepburn was chomping at the bit for her studio, RKO, to get the book. Over at Warner Bros., Jack Warner wanted the book for Bette Davis. Eventually, both Warner and Darryl Zanuck, at 20th Century Fox, dropped out because of the initial asking price. Zanuck stopped bidding at $35,000.

Selznick thought it was "a fine story," but the gamble was too much. In New York, Kay Brown pleaded with him to at least read part of the book. In the meantime, the price of the film rights dropped to $65,000.

Selznick then reread the outline and began to change his mind. People at his studio and at MGM were suggesting actors for Rhett Butler. One of the first suggestions was Clark Gable. Others were Gary Cooper, Ronald Colman, and Melvyn Douglas. Another, Basil Rathbone, actually fit the physical description of the Butler character.

The part of Scarlett was reduced to such casting suggestions as Paulette Goddard, Tallulah Bankhead, Jean Arthur, Joan Bennett, and an unknown British actress—Vivien Leigh—who initially was indifferent to the thought of playing Scarlett.

However, Selznick followed his instincts and negotiated a deal with Mitchell's agent. The film rights to the book were purchased for $50,000. Selznick then took a much-needed vacation to Honolulu, where he finally read the book.

Selznick's enthusiasm went to passion upon his return. He then brought in Sidney Howard, a respected New York playwright, to develop a screenplay.

Howard was the first of many writers to work on the script. He would get the final screenplay credit and ultimately an Oscar posthumously. The director's

assignment was given to George Cukor, who was known as "a woman's director."

Margaret Mitchell's life then began to turn upside down. The Atlanta author,
and former journalist, became deluged with mail that she not cast Clark Gable
as Rhett Butler. Strangers approached her on shopping trips, insisting that Katharine Hepburn would never do as Scarlett O'Hara.

Even though director Cukor favored Hepburn, Selznick was not convinced.
Hepburn felt that Selznick Studios was being forced to take her because they
had to start the film by a certain date.

Hepburn had read the manuscript after Margaret Mitchell sent her a copy.
She then recommended the book to Pandro Berman, head of RKO. Berman gave
it to Joe Sistrom, his assistant, for an evaluation. Sistrom reported back to Hepburn that Scarlett's role was a very unsympathetic part and would be bad for
her career. Powerless to go against her studio and disagreeing with Sistrom,
Hepburn felt that any passionate leading American actress would kill to play a
feisty young Southern woman against a war background.

In her autobiography, Hepburn stated,

I also felt that I would really be a disappointing choice. And I knew that if I did a test
they would sign me, but they would go on looking for an unknown and might find one
and then just dump me.

The final arrangement was that the day before they had to start—*the day before*—I
would agree to start work in the actual picture. I'd been dressed by Walter Plunkett [the
film's costume designer] many times, so I could become a part of everything very speed-
ily. This was clever of me because then they found Vivien Leigh and certainly would
have dumped me.[19]

Margaret Mitchell Marsh was even more frustrated. She wrote, "I suppose
you know that casting this picture is the favorite drawing room game these days
and every newspaper has been after me to say who I want to play the parts. It
has been difficult but so far I have kept my mouth shut. I wish to goodness you
all would announce the case and relieve me of this burden."[20]

After principal casting was completed, with Clark Gable, Vivien Leigh, Leslie
Howard, and Olivia de Havilland, Selznick was ripe for more criticism. Holly-
wood columnists were upset with the Leigh and Howard choices. Scarlett
O'Hara and Ashley Wilkes were definitely American characters of the Old
South. Yet Selznick chose two British actors for the roles.

The search for Scarlett O'Hara has been documented. And it stretched to the
start of production, the burning of Atlanta with Scarlett and Rhett escaping.
Almost from the beginning, there were problems, from the production office to
the set.

On February 13, 1939, Cukor and Selznick released a statement to the trade
papers saying that a directing change was necessary. Many of Cukor's scenes
made the final cut, but feathers were inevitably ruffled. Selznick shut the pro-

duction down for several days while he lobbied and cajoled Victor Fleming, a close friend of Clark Gable's. Fleming was finishing his director's assignment on another 1939 classic, *The Wizard of Oz*.

Rudy Behlmer, editing the much-praised *Memo from David O. Selznick*, noted that Selznick was quoted, in 1947, by Lloyd Shearer in the *New York Times Magazine* as explaining that he and Cukor "couldn't see eye to eye on anything."

Selznick added, "I felt that while Cukor was unbeatable in directing intimate scenes of the Scarlett O'Hara story, he lacked the big feel, the scope, the breadth of the production."[21]

The controversy went on long after the film won its awards. Cukor was quoted in Gwen Robyns's book *Light of a Star* as to the difficulty and tension caused by never-ending script changes, from various screenwriters (including F. Scott Fitzgerald and Selznick himself) and that Selznick was constantly on the set second-guessing Cukor's decisions. Clark Gable was also unhappy with Cukor's supposed preoccupation with Vivien Leigh and Olivia de Havilland.

According to Robyns, Cukor stated,

It is nonsense to say that I was giving too much attention to Vivien and Olivia. It is the text that dictates where the emphasis should go, and the director does not do it. Clark Gable did not have a great deal of confidence in himself as an actor, although he was a great screen personality; and maybe he thought that I did not understand that. . . . For the first time he [Selznick] wanted to come down on the set and watch me direct something that we had worked out together. It was very nerve-wracking.[22]

After he was cast as the romantic Ashley Wilkes in *Gone with the Wind*, Leslie Howard (who would later die in a controversial World War II air battle on a flight from Algiers to London) confided to several people that he felt the novel, at best, was mediocre. He later changed his opinion after the film was released.

Selznick planned the premiere of *Gone with the Wind* in Atlanta on December 15, 1939. Gable was accompanied by his wife, actress Carole Lombard.

According to Jane Ellen Wayne, in her book *Gable's Women*, instead of watching the film, Gable ducked into the ladies' room with Margaret Mitchell for a long-awaited conversation. Many people thought that Mitchell always had Gable in mind when creating the character of Rhett Butler. However, Mitchell told Gable during that conversation that Rhett Butler was patterned after her first husband with whom she had a stormy relationship, which is why she chose to keep the two apart at the end.[23]

*Gone with the Wind*, simply put, was about "a bitch and a bastard" set against an American war.

In the "Twelve Oaks" barbeque sequence of the film, Ashley Wilkes and Rhett Butler acted as the Greek Chorus, foreshadowing the coming bloodbath. Wilkes observes that "most of the miseries of the world were caused by wars. And when the wars were over, no one ever knew what they were about."

Butler then goes further with his "dreams of victory" dialogue. "I think it's hard winning a war with words gentlemen. . . . There's not a cannon factory in the whole south. . . . The Yankees are better equipped than we. They've got factories, shipyards and coal mines. And a fleet to bottle up our harbors and starve us to death. All we've got are cotton, slaves and arrogance."

The film garnered ten Academy Award nominations. It came off with eight Oscars including Best Director for Victor Fleming and Best Actress for Vivien Leigh. Hattie McDaniel became the first black to win an Oscar for the supporting role of Mammy, beating out Olivia de Havilland. McDaniel graciously accepted with a speech written by the studio.

Gable lost out to Robert Donat for *Goodbye, Mr. Chips*. As one of life's strange ironies, Gable was frustrated throughout his years that despite all the noted film work he did his best-known role would be remembered for Rhett Butler in a year where the Academy chose someone else as Best Actor.

## A PLOT POINT IN ENGLAND

During this time, England got a new prime minister. Arthur Neville Chamberlain succeeded Stanley Baldwin. Chamberlain, an elderly and peace-loving man, began to follow a policy of appeasement, beginning in 1937. This attitude allowed the Third Reich to annex Austria easily in 1938. Hitler then planned an armed invasion of Czechoslovakia. Chamberlain was prepared to give Hitler anything within reason to keep peace. Thousands of Czech square miles were turned over to the Third Reich. At that point a violent confrontation seemed to have been averted.

This would soon pass. Hitler felt defrauded of his planned war. His troops were massed on the Czech border, and now he was being asked to forego the military occupation of the Sudetenland. He refused and insisted that his soldiers march into the German-speaking districts of Czechoslovakia at once. Chamberlain refused to submit to this bullying tactic. The French began to mobilize, and the British began to prepare for air raids.

As tension increased, Italian dictator Benito Mussolini came up with an idea of a four-power proposal between Britain, France, Germany, and Italy. Once and for all the Sudeten issue would be settled. On September 30, 1938, in Munich, the birthplace of the Nazi Party, the four leaders signed the agreement, a face-saving document providing for the occupation of the Sudetenland in stages and for the final delimitation supervised by an international commission. Hitler agreed, knowing that he would ultimately follow his own agenda. And peace was preserved—for another year.

In March 1939 Hitler violated the four-power proposal he had signed at Munich when he declared the Czech lands a Reich Protectorate. This showed that the Nazi annexationist drive wouuld spill over to non-German-speaking people. In less than six months, the führer broke the Munich Agreement. He was doing exactly what he had outlined in *Mein Kampf*.

British Prime Minister Chamberlain was both shocked and shaken with the violation of the Munich Agreement. Czechoslovakia would became a "Protectorate" of the Third Reich.

Chamberlain was a man sadly out of his time, dealing with a vindictive, brutal mentality leading to a world war that would change the world and the century.

Chamberlain resigned, embarrassed by the debacle of the Munich Agreement where he proclaimed to have Hitler's word that there would be "peace in our time." First Lord of the Admiralty Winston Churchill was then named the new prime minister. Chamberlain never recovered from that embarrassing tailspin and died shortly thereafter.

## THE CLASSIC YEAR

If any one year stands out as a classic in twentieth-century American film history, it has to be 1939. In that year, Hollywood miraculously accomplished something that would never be repeated: the release of twelve classics in one year: *Mr. Smith Goes to Washington, Ninotchka, Wuthering Heights, The Wizard of Oz, Goodbye, Mr. Chips, Stagecoach, Of Mice and Men, Young Mr. Lincoln, Gone with the Wind, Beau Geste, Drums along the Mohawk,* and *Gunga Din.* It is not surprising that the last four had war backgrounds.

George Stevens got the director's assignment for *Gunga Din,* an adaptation of Rudyard Kipling's poem about the famous Hindu water boy who sacrifices himself in battle to save a regiment. The cast included Cary Grant, Victor McLaglen, Douglas Fairbanks Jr., Eduardo Ciannelli, and Sam Jaffe as Gunga Din.

There was a great deal of correspondence from the Hays Office regarding the censorship of what was to be shown in the battle sequences. And RKO wanted to stay truthful to the spirit of the Kipling poem. The film was shot entirely on location in California, in the Lone Pine, Bishop, Mammoth Lakes area. Research notes were compiled by Hilda Grenier on the methods and table of personnel for the British Army and Bengal Lancers during that period.[24]

This one year, 1939, could be called a classic coincidence, personifying Hollywood's "Golden Era." And it would also be the year where the ultimate twentieth-century experience began.

*Goodbye, Mr. Chips* was adapted at MGM from the James Hilton novel. Sam Wood directed Robert Donat and Greer Garson to Academy Award nominations, including one for himself, along with the screenwriters, R.C. Sheriff, Claudine West, and Eric Maschwitz. However, the only one who prevailed was Donat, portraying the shy schoolmaster from his first teaching assignment at Brookfield Academy to his death. In the middle of the film, the audience sees the toll that World War I took on the flower of British youth. It is also implied, at the fade-out, that the recent graduates of Brookfield will soon be putting on uniforms, as their fathers did before them.

As Hollywood prepared for the release of Margaret Mitchell's *Gone with the*

*Wind*, Nazi air and land forces began their assault on Poland on the first day of September, setting into motion the devastating upheaval for the world, one that would be reflected in film—particularly war films—for the rest of the century.

During the two years after Germany invaded Poland, many contradictory elements occurred both in Hollywood and in Washington. A statement would be issued and then a contradiction would take its place.

While the antiquated, outmanned, and outgunned Polish army attempted a valiant stand against the Nazi onslaught, Jack Warner released a policy statement from his studio that America is neutral. "There will be no propaganda pictures from Warner Brothers."

Shortly thereafter, Warner Bros. released *Confessions of a Nazi Spy* (1939), starring Edward G. Robinson, Paul Lukas, and George Sanders. The script was based on source material taken from former FBI agents. Directed by Anatole Litvak, the film was produced in "docu-drama style," showing how the agents determined who was and who wasn't a Nazi spy in the United States. The film caused an uproar in Europe. The United States was charged, by the Third Reich, with violating international laws of neutrality.

## A QUESTION OF TIME

Even President Roosevelt displayed an inconsistent position. On September 4, 1939, in a special radio broadcast, he reaffirmed America's neutrality. Forty-eight hours later he then announced that the American navy would patrol the Atlantic and Caribbean. Thereafter, more than 100 American destroyers were reconditioned to carry out the president's order.

Over at Republic Pictures, Herbert J. Yates was quoted as saying that his studio would "veer away from pictures of war."

By the spring of 1940, Nazi Wehrmacht forces rolled into France and soon were marching into Paris, issuing occupation orders as to how the French citizens should act. After the surrender signing, in a railway car (where the World War I Armistice was signed), Hitler walked outside and danced a jig. He then toured Paris, including Napoleon's tomb, and returned to Berlin.

In France, the Third Reich's anti-Semitic laws began to be enforced. Jews were prohibited from using public phone booths. Their businesses, like those of German, Austrian, and Polish Jews, were marked with signs. Jews were being picked up in the middle of the night, jammed into personnel carriers, and driven away, never to be seen again. Anyone suspected of taking part or aiding French partisans was immediately arrested. And it was not uncommon to see French partisans executed in public.

From May 27 to June 4, 1940, French and British forces had to retreat to the beach at Dunkirk, where an all-out effort to rescue them—in some cases, plucking them from the water in British powerboats—left most of continental Europe completely occupied by the Third Reich. The Nazis then set their sights across the Channel. The closest landfall to England was Calais. Hitler told his staff that Calais would be the staging point for the coming invasion of the British Isles. It was only a question of time.

In the summer of 1940 the island nation of Great Britain entered into what was to become the great air battle where "never so many owed so much to so few," as Churchill would later proclaim in his praise of the Royal Air Force's stand against Reichsmarshal Hermann Goering's inflated Luftwaffe. The world watched and read accounts every day, while Spitfires and Hurricanes engaged Messerschmitts and Stukas over the Channel and England itself. When the Battle of Britain finally ended, the Luftwaffe withdrew. And the United Kingdom was still standing. Hitler blamed Reichsmarshal Goering for the Luftwaffe's failure to prevail. Goering, in true character, turned around and blamed his staff.

Hitler had only to cross the English Channel. Instead, he pulled back and concentrated on the Russian front. Many historians felt this was a major turning point and led to Germany ultimately losing the war.

## CLOSER TO THE EDGE

Even with a war in Europe taking place, Hollywood continued to use World War I as a film backdrop. In 1940, Warner Bros. released *The Fighting 69th*. The 69th was "the Irish Regiment," attached to New York's 165th Infantry Brigade in France in 1918. The film was stocked with the Warner Bros. contract actors who either were or could act tough and Irish: James Cagney, Pat O'Brien, George Brent, Alan Hale, Frank McHugh, Dennis Morgan, and Dick Foran portraying the doomed poet Joyce Kilmer. Directed by William Keighley, the script had O'Brien as the real-life Father Duffy. The cast, from all sides of New York society, brought out the heroic virtues of honor, loyalty, and teamwork.

That same year, 1940, MGM released *The Mortal Storm*, based on a novel by Phyllis Bottome. It told the story of a typical German family being torn apart by Nazism. The film starred Margaret Sullavan, Robert Young, James Stewart, Frank Morgan, and Robert Stack. Frank Borzage directed from a script by Claudine West, George Froeschel, and Andersen Ellis.

According to Robert Stack, in a letter to the *Los Angeles Times*, Germany seemed ready, while production was taking place, to invade Great Britain. One day a man in a suit appeared on the set, a representative from the Swiss consulate. He was relaying news from Germany that "everyone appearing in two [American] motion pictures, *Confessions of a Nazi Spy* and *The Mortal Storm*, will be remembered when Germany wins the war."[25]

The release of *The Mortal Storm* prompted Nazi Propaganda Minister Joseph Goebbels to ban all MGM films in occupied countries.

In early 1941, President Roosevelt initiated the Lend-Lease program to help the European Allies in "resisting aggression." It was a $50 billion aid package not only to bolster Allied defense but to support U.S. war-related industries. Roosevelt's critics contended that the president was already engaged in behind-the-scenes machinations that would bring America into the war. And the Lend-Lease program was just another example.

In September 1941, Hitler appointed Lieutenant General Reinhard Heydrich as Reich protector of Bohemia-Moravia. Heydrich was a known favorite of the führer's, famous for his ruthless brutality toward Jews in Germany. He was now commissioned to take that same approach with the Czechs, whom he considered "worthless scum."

As the war in Europe escalated, Japan continued its war in China. The imperial Japanese government felt that the United States had its eyes directly pointed toward Europe, whereas Secretary of State Cordell Hull voiced a protest to Japan's prime minister, Prince Konoye, about the fighting in China. Japan's military leaders, led by General Hideki Tojo, were secretly negotiating an alliance with the Third Reich.

Japan had already taken the logistical initiative to stockpile war materials. There was enough for a two-year period. Many of these materials had come from the United States. Because of the American "freezing policy," the Japanese realized that the United States would have to be replaced as a source. By November 1941, the imperial Japanese government came to officially recognize what had long been discussed, that the American policy could not be changed by negotiation. They also realized that if this led to a war, it would have to be won in less than two years.

The ultimate twentieth-century drama was unfolding. The overture was playing in Europe. At this particular juncture, all that was needed to precipitate American involvement was a flash point to raise the curtain.

The major news came from the East Coast and the fighting across the Atlantic. Everyone was watching the day-to-day happenings in England and Europe.

But who was looking out of the back door—California and beyond?

# 2

# A Sleepy Sunday

War is mainly a catalogue of blunders.

—Winston Churchill

It was shortly before seven o'clock on that sleepy Sunday morning when Japanese planes approached the main Hawaiian island of Oahu. Within the next two hours they were going to change the course of their country, America, and the world.

They were also going to have a lasting effect on how American audiences viewed war films for the remainder of the century and beyond.

It is an accepted afterthought that had Japan not attacked Pearl Harbor the United States would have never gotten involved in World War II. And the American war film would have a very different look today. So would the American armed forces.

The pleasant American summer of 1941 eased into the fall. Students went back to school, as they normally did. By October their parents were preparing for the Thanksgiving holidays.

The Selective Service Act had already been passed. Franklin D. Roosevelt was one year into his unprecedented third term with Henry Wallace as his vice president. The *St. Louis Post-Dispatch* won the Pulitzer Prize for meritorious public service.

A three-room apartment in New York City rented for $82 a month. A washing machine cost $38, and a new Studebaker came off the assembly line with a price tag just under $700. A loaf of bread cost $.10, a tube of toothpaste $.33.

Earlier in the year *Rebecca* won the Oscar for Best Picture of 1940. Director John Ford also received a statuette for *The Grapes of Wrath*. James Stewart was named Best Actor for *The Philadelphia Story*. Ginger Rogers was named Best Actress for her performance in *Kitty Foyle*.

Whirlaway, a thoroughbred ridden by Eddie Arcaro, won racing's Triple Crown.

In major league baseball Joe Dimaggio, of the New York Yankees, was named Most Valuable Player in the American League. On October 1 Dimaggio set a major league record, getting a hit in fifty-six straight games. Dolph Camilli, of the Brooklyn Dodgers, was named Most Valuable Player in the National League. In the World Series that year the New York Yankees defeated the Brooklyn Dodgers four games to one. Dimaggio would later enlist in the Army Air Force, serve in Hawaii, and be discharged at war's end as a staff sergeant.

Bruce Smith, a halfback from the University of Minnesota, was about to be named 1941's recipient of the Heisman Trophy as the nation's best college football player. Smith's team, coached by Bernie Bierman, was named college football's national champions for the second straight year. Frank Leahy of Notre Dame was named college football's coach of the year. Within the year, Leahy would set aside his coaching career and apply for a naval officer's commission.

The Chicago Bears were on their way to a second championship year in the National Football League.

Unknown to most of the world that last week in November, a highly trained group of Japanese pilots sailed with a fleet of aircraft carriers and escorts from the Kurile Islands with a mission to launch a crippling air strike against the American Pacific Fleet, most of which was moored at Pearl Harbor, Territory of Hawaii.

Very few Americans even knew where Pearl Harbor was.

Just before dawn the first wave of approximately 180 Japanese attack planes and torpedo bombers, led by Commander Mitsuo Fuchida, were launched from the carriers, less than 250 miles away, north of Oahu.

The attack was years in planning and preparation.

The Empire of Japan, whose thinking was clearly in concert with neither the twentieth century nor the Western world, felt itself being pressured in the Western Pacific. By the fall of 1940, the growing feeling in Japan was that war with the United States was inevitable. The Japanese army and navy were split. Many Japanese admirals opposed the Axis pact, which Japan had signed with Germany and Italy, thereby pitting them against Great Britain and France. After the pact was signed, Admiral Isoroku Yamamoto, naval commander in chief, warned Prime Minister Fumimaro Konoye that he could run wild across the Pacific from anywhere upwards of six months. After that American mass production would begin to have an effect, and Japan would most certainly lose a long and protracted war.

Japanese military leaders led by General Hideki Tojo, an archconservative and a man of narrow thinking, began looking at strategies to mount a military attack after a six-month war resolved with a peace, thereby getting the American fleet out of the Western Pacific.

Prime Minister Konoye's government was already shaky. By the middle of October 1941, it failed, and General Tojo was asked to become prime minister. This move put the military in complete control.

Admiral Yamamoto, thirty-six years a naval officer, was a veteran of the Russo-Japanese War. From 1925 to 1928, he was a naval attaché in Washington, D.C. His thinking convinced others to participate in an operation code-named "Z": A surprise attack on Pearl Harbor was the correct solution and would lay the foundation for a quickly negotiated peace.

An accomplished poker player who knew the American routine, he recommended that the attack occur early on a weekend morning. The detailed planning went to an experienced officer, Commander Minoru Genda. What came out of this planning was how the assault force would be formed. The final plan had the assault force in two waves with an option for a third.

Yamamoto had emphasized that the war had to end in the shortest time frame. He knew what would happen if the United States were given time to arm itself. Yamamoto carried a fatalistic approach. Before leaving to supervise Operation Z, he confided to his geisha Masako Tsurushima, the great love of his life, that he did not see himself surviving the war.

The first wave of Japanese aircraft had been detected by an Army Signal Corps radar team. Just as the morning watch was about to shut down, an operator noticed the approach of the largest set of aircraft he had ever seen on a radar screen. The Signal Corps team then contacted the information center duty officer at Pearl Harbor and reported the huge sighting. The duty officer, an Army Air Force lieutenant, explained to the team leader, "Don't worry about it."

The duty officer had assumed that the radar team had sighted a flight of American B-17 bombers approaching from California that morning.

Approaching the island of Oahu the Japanese formation then split to the various airfields where more than 400 American aircraft lay on the ground. The main part of Fuchida's wave veered toward Ford Island and the American fleet. The second section headed for the Army Air Force planes on the ground at Hickam, Bellows, and Wheeler Fields.

Docked at Ford Island's "Battleship Row" on that sunny morning were the *Arizona, West Virginia, Maryland, Oklahoma, Tennessee,* and *Nevada.* The *Pennsylvania* and the *California* were berthed nearby.

Less than ten minutes after the Ford Island attack began a 1,760-pound armor-piercing bomb hit the forward magazine of the *Arizona* and ignited an explosion that sent approximately 945 men to a watery grave. Secondary internal explosions quickly erupted.[1]

Behind the *Arizona,* the *West Virginia* took a half dozen torpedo hits and quickly joined the *Arizona* on the bottom. The *Tennessee,* which was on the inshore berth, was protected. The *California* took two torpedoes and began flooding. At the head of the row was the *Nevada,* which, though hit, managed to get under way but went aground. The quick thinking of a junior officer saved the ship from sinking and cleared the channel.

At this point the second wave, consisting of 167 Japanese planes, was approaching. However, the major damage had already been done. The main body of Army Air Force planes on the ground was now in flames. They were easy targets, for the Japanese pilots, parked wing to wing because of suspected sabotage.

The attack was so overwhelming that full reports were not released for days in order to prevent what could amount to a panic. The American death toll alone sent heads reeling: approximately 2,400 killed, 1,178 wounded, 916 missing. The total Japanese force of approximately 340 planes lost only 29. In addition, five midget submarines were lost. Total Japanese killed came to less than a hundred.

The American navy reported twenty-one ships either sunk or damaged.

## A GREAT RESOLVE

The attack could have been worse. Part of the American carrier fleet—the *Lexington, Saratoga*, and the *Enterprise*—was out at sea under the command of Admiral William F. Halsey Jr.

The submarine fleet survived the attack virtually intact. Beyond these fortunate turns, Japanese Admiral Chuichi Nagumo refused Commander Fuchida's request for a third strike.

It was a widely held belief that the vastness of the eastern Pacific Ocean saved the American West Coast from a follow-up attack and invasion. However, in the coming weeks California and the West Coast endured a period of panic, with all eyes pointed toward the Pacific horizon and the fear of an immediate Japanese invasion.

The United States was in an easy, carefree mode, right up to the commencement of the Pearl Harbor attack. The previous afternoon UCLA and USC met in the Los Angeles Coliseum for their traditional football showdown. During the first quarter, six members of the USC Sigma Phi Epsilon fraternity snuck into the UCLA cheering section and stole the victory bell. The game ended in a 7–7 tie.

The morning of the attack the *Los Angeles Times* carried the headline "Final Peace Move Seen." But now Los Angeles and California were riddled with war rumors: Thirty Japanese planes were spotted over the northern California coast; the Golden Gate Bridge had been hit; the real objective was an invasion of California; Japanese Americans had already planned an uprising.

The Pasadena Rose Bowl, scheduled for New Year's Day 1942, between Oregon State and Duke, was moved across country to Durham, North Carolina. Oregon State won, 20–16. The gloom of war headlines gave speculation as to the futures of high school graduates and college students.

Within hours after the Pearl Harbor attack, Japanese planes flying from Formosa launched air raids on Clark, Nichols, and Iba Fields in the Philippine Islands. Although American and Filipino ground forces, under General Douglas

MacArthur, had been on full alert for the previous eleven days, they were caught completely off guard.[2]

The American general staff in Manila received confirmation of the Oahu attack. But there was a delayed response, giving the Japanese planes enough time to reach the airfields and destroy half of the American combat aircraft on the ground.

American and Filipino forces then withdrew to the Bataan Peninsula. In March, MacArthur and his staff were ordered to Sydney, Australia, to assume command of the disorganized Pacific forces, leaving the Philippine command to General Jonathan Wainwright. The garrison on the peninsula would hold out until April 9, 1942, when they were forced to surrender.

Wainwright's second in command was Major General Edward P. "Ned" King, a Georgian and a respected artillery officer. All but forgotten today, King shouldered the responsibility and humiliation of surrendering the largest ground force in American history.[3]

During the subsequently brutal and tragic Bataan death march 650 Americans and between 5,000 and 10,000 Filipinos would die, many as the result of bayoneting or beheading. Barely a third of the American soldiers who were forced to surrender would survive the next three years of imprisonment. King and Wainwright, along with other officers, would ultimately live through the war in a Manchurian prison camp.

The Bataan and Corregidor tragedies were black spots on MacArthur's long military record. Wainwright was eventually awarded the Congressional Medal of Honor and stood near MacArthur on the USS *Missouri* at the Japanese surrender signing. King was never acknowledged, and MacArthur never spoke publicly of him again, barely mentioning him in his memoirs.

In Hollywood, the morning after Pearl Harbor Nisei (second-generation) Japanese workers at the film studios were instructed not to report for work. They were to remain at home until they received further word. In the meantime, California Attorney General Earl Warren began sending recommendations to Washington regarding where Americans of Japanese descent on the West Coast should be "relocated to confinement" (for what were called reasons of national security). The recommendations would later include the phrase "for the duration."[4]

This plan quickly resulted in Executive Order 9066, which forcibly confined 110,000 Americans of Japanese descent in "relocation camps." It was to become one of the biggest American scars of World War II. Later, in 1943, Warren (by then governor of California) refused to recommend rescinding the order.

Back in the Pacific, shortly after the Japanese planes returned to their carriers, many of the pilots began celebrating. In a staff meeting, Admiral Yamamoto realistically explained that the hard work and sacrifice were just beginning, that there would be other battles with varied outcomes.

Yamamoto then added, "What we have done [at Pearl Harbor] is awaken a sleeping giant . . . and filled him with a great resolve."[5]

Fulfilling his own mortal prediction, Admiral Yamamoto did not survive the war. While on a staff inspection tour his plane was shot down by Army Air Force fighters near Bougainville on April 18, 1943.

Commander Fuchida, however, did survive the war. He later became a rice farmer, converted to Christianity, and was ordained as a nondenominational minister. In 1966 he became a U.S. citizen. He died in 1976.

## THE OUTFALL

President Roosevelt appointed the Roberts Commission to investigate the American lack of preparation preceding the Pearl Harbor attack. This would result in several investigations.

Two of the command casualties were General Walter Campbell Short, a graduate of the University of Illinois and veteran of the Mexican Expedition of 1916–1917 and World War I. He was known as a staff officer. Although he felt he was misled by intelligence information from Washington, General Short was more impressed with style than substance. He never regained his former military stature. The other was the commander in chief, Pacific Fleet, Admiral Husband Kimmel, a Naval Academy graduate, World War I veteran, and former aide to Assistant Secretary of the Navy Franklin D. Roosevelt in 1915.

Both General Short and Admiral Kimmel were criticized for lack of preparation and leadership and were called to testify in the congressional hearings. Retirement was forced on both. Kimmel spent the rest of his life defending himself against attacks as the man responsible for the American fleet being so unprepared. Ironically, his first priority upon assuming command of the Pacific Fleet, in February 1941, had been to prepare for war. It wasn't until May 1999 when the U.S. Senate voted to exonerate and restore the reputations of Admiral Kimmel and General Short.

The lack of preparedness at Pearl Harbor resulted in a total of eight investigations. However, the Manila debacle (General MacArthur's command being unprepared) resulted in nothing.

## THE STUDIO SYSTEM IN UNIFORM

President Roosevelt, who had seen the remarkable effect that the World War I Liberty Bond drives and subsequent films had had on the American public, realized the potential of Hollywood. If an Allied victory over Germany and Japan was to occur, it would have to be based on the united effort of the entire country. American films would definitely contribute to that effort.

FDR was not going to simply repeat what was done with movie stars in World War I. The situation demanded that he build on it, to sway the American public. The country was going to learn from what America's "Royalty" did in World War I.

A new generation of America's Royalty had come of age, along with the sound experience in Hollywood. And they were going to help put out the message—many in uniform—in the quest for an Allied victory.

President Roosevelt made it clear to every movie studio and production company that he wanted war-oriented films to boost morale and generate propaganda aimed at the Axis's defeat.

Overnight it came. America was in it. And while men and women began exchanging civilian clothes for uniforms, Hollywood turned to directors, writers, and actors to develop war-themed films.[6]

In June 1942, the Office of War Information (OWI) was chartered in Washington with two branches, domestic and overseas. The Bureau of Motion Pictures (BMP), with Lowell Mellett as chief administrator, was part of the domestic branch. The BMP was responsible for the production of informational and training films and consulting with the major studios.

A West Coast office was quickly set up in Hollywood in the Taft Building on Hollywood Boulevard. The OWI would spend much of 1942 and 1943 fighting within itself, on both coasts, and with other government agencies over policy about war information being released to the American media.

Later that year, OWI released a memo on American public opinion including suggested training shorts, such as *The World at War*, *Men of the Merchant Marine*, *Why Are We Fighting?*, *Americans All*, and *Unsung Heroes*.

Directors like Frank Capra, John Ford, John Huston, and William Wyler were called to active duty to produce documentaries, training, and propaganda films. Lieutenant Commander Ford was already in the Naval Reserve and was being assigned as commander of a Field Photographic Unit.

Major Capra was noted for his series *Why We Fight*. Wyler produced and directed *The Memphis Belle*, a documentary about the crew of a B-17 in the Eighth Air Force.

World War II provided the challenge that produced Wyler's greatest contribution to filmmaking. When Wyler went to war, he was forced to get his film assignments completed under the most stressful, life-and-death circumstances.

Many established and struggling Hollywood figures, by choice or by chance of the Selective Service Board, were soon wearing uniforms. This was where Hollywood differed from the previous war. Many established actors not only took part in the bond drives but decided to place their careers on hold to enlist. Some of those who went were:

*Army*: Lew Ayres, Burt Lancaster, Melvyn Douglas, Ronald Reagan, Kevin McCarthy, Stanley Kramer, Josh Logan, Robert Mitchum, Karl Malden, Tony Martin, Charles Durning, Sterling Hayden, Glenn Miller, Sammy Davis Jr., Tony Randall, Carl Reiner, Howard Morris, Charles Bronson, Neville Brand, Pat Brady, Red Skelton, Allen Funt, Richard Egan, Desi Arnaz, Jack Warden, William Holden, Eli Wallach, James Arness, Tim McCoy, Bert Parks, Buddy Rogers, Mickey Rooney, Steve Forrest, Art Carney, Mel Brooks, George Montgomery, Van Heflin, Bob Eberly, Brian Keith, Daniel Taradash, Carl Foreman, Arthur Kennedy, and Craig Stevens.

*Army Air Force*: Jimmy Stewart, Tim Holt, Burgess Meredith, Walter Matthau, Skitch Henderson, Henry Mancini, Gene Autry, Jackie Coogan, Tom Poston, James Daly, Robert Cummings, Cameron Mitchell, Henry Morgan, Merian C. Cooper, Alan Ladd, Jack Palance, John Carroll, Jack Valenti, Clark Gable, and Charlton Heston.

*Navy*: Robert Montgomery, Gene Kelly, Kirk Douglas, Wayne Morris, Sidney Poitier, Douglas Fairbanks Jr., Henry Fonda, Raymond Burr, George O'Brien, Jason Robards Jr., Richard Denning, Billy De Wolfe, John Ford, Logan Ramsey, Aldo Ray, Robert Taylor, Tom Ewell, Pat Hingle, Rock Hudson, Dennis Day, Eddy Duchin, Gene Markey, Lloyd Bridges, Eddie Albert, Jackie Cooper, Ernest Borgnine, Glenn Ford, Johnny Carson, Jack Lemmon, Paul Newman, and Tony Curtis.

*Marines*: Tyrone Power, Louis Hayward, Jonathan Winters, Ed McMahon, George C. Scott, and Lee Marvin.

*Coast Guard*: Sid Caesar, Victor Mature, Buddy Ebsen, Rudy Vallee, and Caesar Romero.

This type of commitment, from Hollywood figures in wartime, would never be seen again.

Jack Warner went on active duty, as a lieutenant colonel, to establish the First Motion Picture Unit through the Army Air Force, working with both the BMP and the OWI. Space was allocated to the unit at Hal Roach Studios in Culver City. The site was quickly dubbed "Fort Roach." And those who reported for duty there were called "Culver City Commandos." Their mission was producing films for training and recruiting. And they would use everything Hollywood could offer, mainly one of its most necessary commodities: movie stars.[7]

The powerful film weapons that came out of Fort Roach, from 1942 to 1945, resulted in more than 300 training films and documentaries.

"It was the studio system in uniform," reflected producer Gregory Orr, whose father, Bill Orr, appeared in several of the First Motion Picture Unit's films.

One of the officers who kept Fort Roach on its schedule during this time was Army Captain Ronald Reagan, the husband of actress Jane Wyman.

This period of inspiring, flag-waving propaganda films reinforced the war effort not only to Americans but to our Allies overseas. Any family that had a member in uniform proudly hung a blue star banner in the living room window.

During this time the Nazis were portrayed as psychotic, whereas the Japanese, consistently referred to as "Japs," emerged as the personification of evil to the point of being subhuman.

Naturally, censorship played an important role. It was forbidden to portray the military in a negative light. And brutal battlefield realities such as open, bloody head wounds, dismemberment, and decapitation were not to be released. This seemed contradictory in light of many of Mathew Brady's Civil War photographs, which showed soldiers lying in groups in an open field or trench riddled with shrapnel and bullets.

The closest a film could come to battlefield reality was to have the audience realize, in its own mind, that such a scene was occurring (off screen), then to see the reaction on the actors' faces.

Fox's *A Yank in the RAF* (1941) had Tyrone Power getting involved with Betty Grable in war-torn London. Grable played a stranded chorus girl, while Power was portrayed as a cocky, gum-chewing, American itching to get into the fight ahead of time. Darryl Zanuck used his pseudonym, Melville Crossman, to work on the script, which was rewritten by Karl Tunberg and Darrell Ware. The Fox team of director Henry King, cinematographer Leon Shamroy, and music arranger Alfred Newman rounded out what was called a flagwaver for recruiting.

Paramount's *I Wanted Wings* (1941), with Ray Milland, William Holden, and Wayne Morris, was nothing more than a recruiting poster, about three candidates for the Army Air Corps. Although the film was released in 1941, it was set in 1938 and stressed being prepared for war. It also had a rousing patriotic score by Victor Young.

The one memorable element that Warner Bros. *Dive Bomber* was noted for in 1941 was that it was the first film to use a color portable camera for the aerial scenes on location in San Diego. The story documents navy dive bomber pilots' medical problems with pilot blackout.

At 20th Century Fox, Fritz Lang, expatriated from the clutches of Nazi Propaganda Minister Joseph Goebbels, directed *Man Hunt* with Walter Pidgeon, Joan Bennett, George Sanders, and John Carradine. The script was adapted from Geoffrey Household's novel *Rogue Male* and was later made into a 1976 TV movie. Pidgeon played a British game hunter who deliberately fumbles a chance to assassinate Hitler. He is captured and tortured and escapes to England, where the plan is turned upside down, and he becomes the prey.

The *New York Times* said that *Desperate Journey*, from Warner Bros., in 1942, was *The Three Musketeers* set in a Nazi prison camp. Errol Flynn, Ronald Reagan, Arthur Kennedy, and Alan Hale were under the direction of Raoul Walsh as the Americans fighting their way back to freedom. Arthur Horman's script contained the memorable fade-out propaganda line, "Now for Australia and a crack at those Japs!"

James Cagney was set for *Yankee Doodle Dandy* (1942) but first had to complete *Captains of the Clouds*, in 1942, with Dennis Morgan, Brenda Marshall, and George Tobias. Cagney played a rogue Canadian Air Force pilot who emerges as a hero under fire.

After spending years in B westerns, John Wayne was finally accepted as a star for his 1939 performance as the Ringo Kid in *Stagecoach*. Then under contract with Herbert Yates and Republic Pictures, Wayne began 1942 with *Flying Tigers*, supported by John Carroll, Anna Lee, and Paul Kelly. The story was molded from the American volunteers who served with the Chinese Air Force unit commanded by Colonel Claire Chennault. In the story Carroll saves Wayne's life while sacrificing his own on a suicide mission.

Americans had to appear brave and challenging. In one scene, after Wayne returns from a dangerous mission, his ground mechanic notices several machine gun holes in the plane's fuselage. With customary American bravado, Wayne shrugs this off and says, "Termites!"

However, in spite of Wayne's rave reviews for *Flying Tigers*, patriotism took a different turn at Republic Pictures.

Studio head Herbert Yates went into a rage when Gene Autry, the celebrated singing cowboy, volunteered for the Army Air Force. Autry, whose films were Republic's bread and butter, simply walked away and put on a uniform. But Yates didn't want to look like a moneygrubbing, unpatriotic tyrant in the press by holding the singing cowboy to his contract. When Wayne began making noises about enlisting, Yates called him into the front office and threatened him. Yates explained to Wayne that if he enlisted like Autry, the studio would sue him for breach of contract. Despite this threat, which went against government policy at the time, Yates added that he would make certain that Wayne would never work for Republic or any studio again. Wayne never pressed the issue again with Yates and continued making films at Republic and other studios as an RKO loan-out.

But Wayne did make another attempt to enlist, this time in John Ford's Field Photographic Unit in 1943. A navy official told Wayne that the navy and marine personnel slots were all filled in Ford's unit, but there were openings on the army side. Wayne then obtained the enlistment forms from the Department of the Army. But before Wayne could complete the forms, Republic cast him in *In Old Oklahoma*, a western being shot on location in Parreah, Utah. He finished the forms but then discovered that Republic had cast him in another film. By then, Wayne learned that the Selective Service Board had extended his draft deferment. And so the one movie star who came to personify the combat serviceman, through sixteen American war films, passed into history never having worn a real uniform and never having served in combat. It was a contradiction that would follow his image for the rest of his life.

Warner Bros. then decided to take three of the stars of *The Maltese Falcon*, with the same director, John Huston, and put them in *Across the Pacific* (1942), a spy thriller set against the war. Huston was on a deadline to finish the film quickly, having accepted a commission in the Army Signal Corps.

The script, written from a serial *Aloha Means Goodbye*, had Humphrey Bogart playing a cashiered army officer who leaves the service just before Pearl Harbor. Bogart is actually working undercover against a Japanese plot, concocted by Sydney Greenstreet, to blow up the Panama Canal. Mary Astor was cast as his love interest. Chinese-Hawaiian passenger Richard Loo came aboard as the Asian enemy that American audiences were supposed to hate. The violent ending was imposed by the studio, according to Huston. Vincent Sherman finished the ending when Huston was called to active duty.

An American aircraft factory set the background for *Joe Smith, American* (1942) at MGM. Robert Young portrayed an American assembly-line worker with a special engineering talent who is kidnapped and tortured by Nazis who want information on a new bombsight design. Young not only escapes but leads the FBI back to his captors. This was one of many in a spate of the domestic propaganda war films that Hollywood was churning out.

One of the first notable films in this time frame was *Mrs. Miniver* (1942), based on a novel by Jan Struther. Viewed today, this opus of a British family caught up in the throes of early wartime, when England stood alone, seems overly sentimental and surrealistic. But the film took off after MGM released it, in 1942, winning six Oscars including Best Picture. It was shot entirely on the Metro back lot in Culver City.

The vicar's speech, in a bombed church, delivered by Henry Wilcoxon, at the end of *Mrs. Miniver*, is to the Allies. We are hearing the word of God, to stand up against tyranny and oppression—"This is the people's war."

This set a precedent for a stirring, patriotic speech at film's end. The vicar's speech so impressed British Prime Minister Winston Churchill that he requested the studio to reprint it for Allied troops. Churchill also confided to an aide that, for propaganda purposes, the film was worth a hundred battleships.

In winning the Oscar for Best Actress as *Mrs. Miniver* Greer Garson's "lengthy" acceptance speech went over the acceptable time frame. And then a Hollywood legend was created.

Joan Fontaine, who won the award the previous year for *Suspicion*, presented the Oscar for Best Actress. As the names of the nominees were read, photographers began jockeying for position around Garson who was considered the heavy favorite. And then she was announced.

What began as an unprepared acceptance speech went on for five and a half minutes. "This is the most wonderful thing," said the Irish-born actress. "I feel just like Alice in Wonderland." She then prophesied, accurately, "[that] I may never win another statuette."

The Academy members began glancing at their watches as Garson went on to discuss the controversy of acting as a competition.

Producer George Jessel later quipped that it took the king of England less time to abdicate his throne.

Legend quickly overshadowed fact. In *Inside Oscar*, by Mason Wiley and Damien Bona, Garson became increasingly irritated at the humorous reaction to her speech. In a later interview, she said, "Please clear up this myth. It was funny for two weeks, but now I'm quite tired of it."

The film *Citizen Kane*, a controversial biography loosely based on the life of media magnate William Randolph Hearst, was nominated for eight Oscars. It received only one, for Best Original Screenplay. That honor was shared by Herman J. Mankiewicz and twenty-five-year-old Orson Welles, who also directed and played the title role.

## A NEEDED LIFT

The dark days of the war grew darker. Singapore fell and the British withdrew from Malaya. Lonely American garrisons, in the Philippines, were holding out on Bataan and Corregidor. General Douglas MacArthur, with family and staff, was now directing defenses from Sydney, Australia. The American and Filipino soldiers captured on the Bataan Peninsula were forced into the now-infamous death march.

The White House, in top secret meetings with the War Department, gave the go-ahead to a plan that called for Army Air Force B-25 bombers to be launched from the carrier *Hornet* with the objective of bombing Tokyo, Kobe, and Yokohama. It was felt that the country, and the Allies, needed a psychological lift. The B-25 was chosen because of being a light bomber; it could be launched from a carrier within striking distance of Japan.

The April 18 raid, led by Lieutenant Colonel Jimmy Doolittle, caused little damage but did give the United States and Allied side a much-needed shot in the arm. It also shocked the Japanese Imperial Command that American bombers so easily reached their shores.

## THE CARAVAN TOUR

The OWI, with Army-Navy Relief, began to coordinate the Hollywood Victory Caravan, a whistle-stop train tour. The kickoff, hosted by Eleanor Roosevelt, was a tea reception on the White House lawn on April 30, 1942, boasting movie stars from every studio. The first train stop, Boston, came the following day. There, movie stars paraded through five miles of streets jammed with thousands of people. *Life* magazine reported that Joan Blondell and Cary Grant were so moved by the overwhelming affection of the people that tears welled in their eyes.[8]

In Philadelphia people besieged a restaurant where stars like Bob Hope, James Cagney, and Judy Garland were dining.

In Chicago the Hollywood Victory Caravan drew a house of almost 20,000 people and netted $90,000. Movie fans followed them all the way down to the train station to wave good-bye.

By the time the caravan from Boston to Houston ended, $600,000 was raised for army and navy relief. The actors played to 125,000 people, not counting thousands who lined the streets and the train stations.

One of the Hollywood tough guy actors, John Garfield, who grew up as Julius Garfinkel on New York City's Lower East Side, had the idea of developing what was to become the Hollywood Canteen. This was right in the middle of Hollywood at 1415 Cahuenga Boulevard, a block off Sunset Boulevard in a building that was an abandoned nightclub.

Garfield was making *Tortilla Flat* with Spencer Tracy and Hedy Lamarr at MGM the week Pearl Harbor was attacked. During his subsequent army physical, he was found to have a heart murmur and was classified "4-F: physically unfit to serve." He attempted several times to get the classification changed. When he was finally notified that he would get his greetings within ninety days, he suffered his first heart attack.

Perhaps through guilt, or frustration, Garfield sought to do something for the thousands of servicemen who were passing through southern California without the opportunity to take advantage of the area or see movie stars. Garfield was reportedly inspired by the idea of New York City's Stage Door Canteen. His idea was supported by Bette Davis, who got the ball rolling and established "a home away from home" in the Hollywood Canteen for thousands of American servicemen passing through Hollywood from 1942 to 1945.

The canteen had bleachers on either side of the entrance, wrote Roy Hoopes in *When the Stars Went to War*. "People paid $100 each to sit there on opening night and watch three thousand soldiers, sailors and marines enter."[9]

Garfield's heart problems would be exacerbated by the politics of a coming era. Six years after getting the patriotic idea of creating the Hollywood Canteen, Garfield was subpoenaed to appear in front of the House Un-American Activities Committee (HUAC). Garfield suffered a fatal heart attack days before. Friends later claimed that it was caused by the stress of being an unfriendly witness.

## THE RANKS GROW

Japanese forces were now in complete control of the Western Pacific. Within days the Battle of the Coral Sea had begun. The Battle of the Coral Sea was the first naval engagement between carriers of two fleets that never actually saw each other, owing to the use of new radar and aircraft reconnaissance. However, the American carrier *Lexington* was sunk. The *Yorktown* limped away with the Japanese assuming it had been sunk. A major breakthrough from the battle was that American intelligence had broken the Japanese radio code.

By the end of 1942 the total ranks of the American army, navy, and marines numbered 3.85 million, as compared to the 1.8 million of the previous year. By 1945 that number would quadruple to approximately 16 million.[10]

The blatant propaganda speeches in the films of this time frame seemed to be in competition with each other. In American films they represented a unique element never to be repeated in such an exaggerated, sledgehammer manner. Suspended realism was normal. Glorified combat conditions, filmed on back lots, motivated many a young man to enlist ahead of the draft.

In these early propaganda films, it wasn't unusual to see an actor jumping up in the middle of an intense firefight, without being hit, to pull a hand grenade pin with his teeth. And with an accurate "All-American" throw, the grenade would result in several enemy soldiers being blown to bits.

Events both in Europe and in the Western Pacific were being monitored daily by every studio's story department. Anything that remotely constituted dramatic screenplay elements was outlined for a possible movie. This defined the publicity cliché "From the headlines to the screen."

A new trend was developing in American war films, where an actual wartime incident would, within a year, be transformed into a dramatic film. These movies were not simply documentary films or totally fictional scenarios, as in World

War I; they used the incident as a start point of a new era of poetic license to develop gripping, emotional stories. Facts never got in the way of a good movie.

## BRUTALITY IN CZECH

On May 27, 1942, in a suburb of Prague, a team of Czech commandos ambushed thirty-eight-year-old Nazi Lieutenant General Reinhard Heydrich, the Reich Protector. The special operation, administered by British Intelligence, carried the code name "Anthropoid." Heydrich, rumored to be the führer's successor, was on his way to sign the morning mail before boarding a plane for a conference with Hitler at Nazi field headquarters. Heydrich was rushed to a local hospital. The grenade blast caused wounds that were thought to be only superficial. On the morning of June 4, he died.

Heydrich was selected as the target because of his notorious record. He often presided over mass executions of Czech partisans and imprisoned Jews. Immediately thereafter Heydrich would return to his office to eat lunch and sign more execution orders.

Reinhard Heydrich was the chairman of the infamous Wannsee Conference at police headquarters in Berlin on January 20, 1942. It was here where the "final solution" was presented. In order to complete the plan for the ultimate extermination of European Jews, and others deemed undesirable, additional "camps" would have to be constructed.

The führer was so impressed with Heydrich's handling of the Czech Jews and partisans that Hitler set his sights even higher. It had long been rumored that Hitler was considering transferring Heydrich to Paris so a similar reign of terror could be employed against the French Jews and partisans. This led to the decision to "hit" Heydrich.

When informed of Heydrich's death, Hitler went into a screaming tirade over the telephone. In retaliation, Hitler ordered the annihilation of a Czech village. Heydrich's second in command, General Karl Frank, attempted to dissuade the führer. But Hitler was adamant. Even though the commandos were still at large, the führer wanted a swift and brutal example set that would prevent any repeat. The village of Lidice, a Prague suburb, was chosen. Nazi intelligence felt that inhabitants of Lidice had conspired in the assassination.

Heydrich was the highest-ranking Nazi to date to be the target of an assassination. At a memorial service in Prague, at Hradcany Castle, Heinrich Himmler praised Heydrich as a fearless Nazi leader.

That evening Hitler phoned Karl Böhme, the Nazi security police commander in Prague, demanding that the Lidice operation begin at daybreak.

Hours later, the village was cordoned off. Males over the age of fifteen, numbering 199, were taken to an area near the town square. Mattresses were tied to a nearby wall. The men were then lined up, in groups of ten, in front of the mattresses and shot.

One hundred ninety-five women were arrested and transported to several concentration camps. Of ninety-five children, eight were considered worthy of being "Germanized" because of their Aryan looks. The rest were sent to concentration camps along with the women.

The houses of Lidice were then set on fire. The ruins were bulldozed by the German Labor Service. Every trace suggesting that a village had even existed was erased. General Frank then remarked, "Corn would grow where Lidice once stood as a permanent reminder to those who defy the rule of the Third Reich."[11]

The Czech commandos were later tracked down and surrounded in a Greek Orthodox church in downtown Prague. They committed suicide rather than surrender. The Gestapo ordered the heads of the commandos be severed and placed on spikes to be publicly displayed.

Before the war's end, the Heydrich assassination and Lidice would provide the background for two Hollywood war films: *Hitler's Madman* (1943) and *Hangmen Also Die!* (1943).

## THE WARTIME STUDIOS

It was timely that when the Pearl Harbor attack occurred, Warner Bros. *Sergeant York* (1941) was already in theaters. The producer was Jesse Lasky, who courted York, always wanting to make the film of one of the most noted American experiences of World War I. Lasky, the brother-in-law of Samuel Goldwyn, had long associations with the other Hollywood moguls. According to Robert Brent Toplin in *History by Hollywood*, Lasky was one of the first Hollywood producers to approach York for the rights to his life story. Many other executives and producers followed through the 1920s and 1930s. But York turned them all down. Lasky tried again in 1938, and this time York changed his mind when offered a chance to work with Warner Bros.[12]

His change of mind came about as York had become increasingly skeptical that America's involvement in World War I actually did any good. He was never boastful about killing the number of German soldiers that were credited to him, but now he saw Nazism as a real threat.

In the World War I film, based on York's wartime experiences, Gary Cooper comes to terms with his rural pacifistic upbringing as he is forced to put on a uniform and stoically head into combat where his deadly marksmanship plays into the final days of the war. In his Oscar-winning performance, Cooper kills 25 German soldiers and captures 132 others one month before the Armistice is signed.

Writing "The Mythical Morning of Sergeant York" in the *Quarterly Journal of Military History*, John Bowers detailed York's extraordinary combat heroism on October 8, 1918, at the northeastern edge of the Argonne Forest. The astonishing figures of enemies killed and captured were later verified. In addition, York silenced thirty-five machine gun emplacements while armed with only an Enfield rifle and a .45 automatic pistol.[13]

When Corporal York marched the German prisoners back to his headquarters, at the battalion level, they couldn't handle the numbers. At regimental headquarters, the answer was the same. Finally, at division headquarters the prisoners were incarcerated. And Alvin York, Kentucky born and Tennessee bred, who never went beyond the third grade, left his German prisoners and marched into history. In addition to his American campaign and combat medals, the Congressional Medal of Honor, and Distinguished Service Cross, he was also awarded the French Croix de Guerre by Field Marshal Ferdinand Foch.

In the end, York signed off on many of the film's fictionalized accounts of his Tennessee life before being drafted into the army. The poetic license taken called for York to ride off to kill a man who supposedly cheated him. York is later knocked off his mount by a lightning bolt that destroys his rifle. The so-called St. Paul Incident was to visually portray York's conversion to pacifism, which would be later confronted for patriotic reasons.

Other literary licenses were taken with the "turkey shoot" scene and being double-crossed during the sale of a farm by a man named Nate Watson. York also did not "shock" range officers with his constant bull's-eyes.

In the film, Cooper returns to a hero's welcome and to his fiancée's open arms. Joan Leslie played the real-life fifteen-year-old Gracie Williams York. By the time of York's death, in 1964, he was a tired, blind, and broken man living on the generosity of friends and a small pension.

Critics of the film contended that it was a blatant wartime statement from the Roosevelt White House to sell the war. Warner Bros. publicity claimed that its intent was to show the country how working-class ideals shouldered the burden of the last war. And now the children of that generation would not only have to do the same—they would have to do it on two fronts.

This was a syndrome that America's children, in the next generation, would vehemently question.

Metro's *A Yank on the Burma Road*, in 1942, achieved the forgotten distinction of being the first U.S. World War II film released after Pearl Harbor. It was in the theaters less than eight weeks after the attack. The simple plot had Barry Nelson as a cynical, mercenary truck driver who meets Laraine Day, the proverbial suddenly stranded woman in a wartime situation. The triangle is complete when Stuart Crawford enters the plot. In the film, Nelson repeatedly curses Japanese treachery as he helps maneuver a Chinese convoy to its objective. Everyone changes attitudes and pulls together at the end because America has been attacked.

## LIFE IMITATES ART IN COMBAT

After Pearl Harbor, Tyrone Power, under contract at 20th Century Fox, was approached by Darryl Zanuck, who said he would sponsor Power's application as an officer in the Army Signal Corps. Power turned it down, contending that he knew nothing about being an officer.

Before going into production on *Crash Dive* (1943), at the Naval Submarine

Command Center in New London, Connecticut, Power had signed enlistment papers for the Marine Corps and was scheduled to report to boot camp upon the film's completion. Power, who had a pilot's license, was subsequently ordered to Marine Officers' Candidate School at Quantico, Virginia. After being commissioned a second lieutenant, Power was transferred to flight training at Corpus Christi, Texas. During this time, his marriage to the actress Annabella was threatened by rumors of an affair with Judy Garland, who was lobbying for his divorce.

Power then had a series of assignments in Atlanta and Cherry Point, North Carolina, before being sent to the Western Pacific as a transport pilot based on Saipan in the Mariana Islands. He named his plane *Blithe Spirit*, after a United Service Organization (USO) production in which Annabella was appearing. While on Saipan the *Blithe Spirit* was caught on the ground during a daring Japanese kamikaze attack. According to reports, Power was one of the marines on the ground firing back at the Japanese planes as a hangar was blown up, causing the deaths of sixty-nine Americans.

One element that disturbed Power was seeing other actors who, for whatever reason, didn't enlist, yet furthered their film careers. By war's end, Power returned to California with 1,100 logged air hours in a combat zone.

One such Hollywood couple who weren't involved to Power's chagrin was Clark Gable and Carole Lombard. Both had been married to other people but were now enjoying their second married life at Gable's Encino ranch. The Sunday of the Pearl Harbor attack Gable sat in shock while Lombard, notorious for her salty mouth, paced the room shouting obscenities at Japan for the sudden attack.

Gable began vowing to friends that he was "going to get into this thing. I'm certainly not going to sit on my ass!"

However, Gable was scheduled to begin production on *Somewhere I'll Find You* (1942), an MGM war film set in Indochina, about two feuding journalist brothers embroiled in smuggling Chinese babies to safety. Gable and Lombard also became involved with the Hollywood Victory Committee. Clark was named chairman of the Screen Actors Division.

Lombard had just completed the comedy/satire *To Be or Not to Be* (1942). The story had a group of Warsaw actors getting caught up in an underground plot that leads to impersonating the führer himself. Jack Benny did a surprising turn as a straight man. In one scene Benny asks a Nazi officer, played by Sig Ruman, if he had ever heard of a certain Shakespearean actor. Ruman replies, "Yes. What he did to Shakespeare we are now doing to Poland."

Werner Heyman received an Academy Award nomination for his music score. Mel Brooks later remade this movie in 1983, never achieving the level of the original.

Lombard was then asked to headline a War Bond tour in her native state of Indiana. A request for Gable to accompany her was turned down because of the start date for *Somewhere I'll Find You*.

Accompanied by her mother, Bessie Peters, and publicist Otto Winkler, Lombard boarded a train at Los Angeles' Union Station on January 12, 1942. Stops were scheduled in Salt Lake City, Ogden, Utah, and then Chicago.

Lombard gave an inspiring patriotic speech in Indianapolis and sang the National Anthem. Her efforts helped sell $2 million in war bonds.

Now that the bond tour was completed, Lombard opted to make the return trip by plane. Her mother suggested taking the train for the return trip to rest. Lombard then solved the question by flipping a coin. She won the coin toss.

Before leaving, Lombard phoned Gable at the ranch encouraging him to enlist. "Pa, you better get in this man's army." But Gable was already a step ahead. Unknown to Lombard he had already been to Washington to make inquiries about getting an army commission.

On January 16, Lombard, Bessie, and Winkler boarded a plane. Counting the Lombard group, there were a total of twenty-two passengers.

At a stopover in Albuquerque, New Mexico, the Lombard group was told that nine military officers, with orders, had the option to "bump" them. Several of the civilian passengers did get bumped. But Lombard held her ground, contending that she just helped sell $2 million in bonds and had to get back to Los Angeles. The army agreed, and Lombard, Bessie, and Winkler continued on the flight. The plane then made a short, unscheduled stop in Las Vegas. In less than fifteen minutes the pilot, Wayne Williams, had the plane airborne again.

Back in Encino, the dining room table was just about set for a welcome-home dinner when Gable got a phone call from MGM publicity man Howard Strickling, informing him that Carole's plane was reported down near Las Vegas. Strickling then chartered a plane and flew with Gable to Las Vegas.

Lombard's plane had slammed into Table Rock Mountain and burst into flames.

At the base camp, Gable insisted on going up with the search party but was talked out of it. He waited at the base camp for the message. And it came. "No survivors. All killed instantly."

Lombard's body was charred and decapitated.

Gable then accompanied the bodies of Carole, Bessie, and Otto Winkler back to Los Angeles. Devastated and grief stricken, Gable stayed with friends until after the funeral. In the days to come, he would show up on the doorsteps of friends, drunk and in tears.

During this time, Gable received thousands of telegrams. The one that he kept the rest of his life stated: "Mrs. Roosevelt and I are deeply distressed. Carole was our friend, our guest in happier days. She brought great joy to all who knew her and to millions who knew her only as a great artist. She gave unselfishly of her time and talent to serve her government in peace and war. She loved her country. She is and always will be a star, one we shall never forget nor cease to be grateful to. Deepest sympathy."[14]

Gable enlisted in the Army Air Force as a forty-one-year-old private on August 12, 1942. He qualified for Officer Candidate School and survived the rigorous training as one of the oldest candidates.

During this time, Gable confided his fatalistic feelings to friends, still depressed over the death of Lombard. He intended to request combat duty with the Eighth Air Force based in England. Gable often said, "I don't expect to come back. And I don't want to."

By the spring of 1943, Captain Clark Gable was flying missions in a B-17. It was then that the Third Reich announced that Gable had what amounted to a $5,000 price tag on his head.

Upon hearing this Gable quipped, "I'll never bail out. Hitler can have me dead or not at all."

After Jimmy Stewart completed Army Air Force pilot training and got his wings, he was rewarded with a public relations stint, being straight man on radio shows for Edgar Bergen and Charlie McCarthy. After repeatedly requesting a transfer he was finally sent to Kirkland Field in Albuquerque, New Mexico, where he learned to fly the heavy B-24 bomber. After acquiring this new skill, he requested a transfer to a combat command, either in the Pacific or England.

Captain James Stewart ended up in England with the 445th Bomb Group, attached to the Eighth Air Force. Eleven days after arriving, he was on his first bombing mission with the 703rd Squadron on a raid to the German naval base at Kiel. Stewart carried himself well and on many occasions displayed coolness under fire. He flew twenty combat missions before leaving England during the summer of 1945. His personal decorations included the Distinguished Flying Cross, presented by General James Doolittle, and an Air Medal with an Oak Leaf Cluster, indicating a second award.

Stewart outwardly personified the all-American war hero upon his return. He still had the lanky, boyish charm. Hollywood and audiences admired him all the more: an Oscar winner and a decorated bomber pilot.

In reality, his nerves were shot. He subsisted for a while on a diet of sweet, pulpy foods, and he moved in with his old buddy Henry Fonda, who had returned from the Pacific as a naval officer.

Stewart, like Gable and other actors who served in combat zones, simply wanted to get on with his career and didn't think that his combat time with the Eighth Air Force was anything exceptional.

However, Stewart stayed in the reserves and transferred to the air force when it became a separate service branch. Here, he rose to brigadier general. His appointment to the flag rank, when the promotion came up in the U.S. Senate, was opposed by Maine senator Margaret Chase Smith, who set off a firestorm of controversy because she felt that Stewart was being given the rank because he was a movie star.

## THE REAL HOLLYWOOD COMBAT STAR

The most decorated established actor to serve in World War II combat was Wayne Morris, a former Los Angeles City College football player who had won a scholarship to the Pasadena Playhouse. After a screen test at Warner Bros., he got bit parts in several films during 1936 and 1937. Then he was cast in *Kid Galahad* with Bette Davis, Edward G. Robinson, and Humphrey Bogart.

While shooting another film entitled *Flight Angels*, he took an interest in flying. He was then cast in *I Wanted Wings* (1941), which launched Veronica Lake's career. *I Wanted Wings* was Morris's thirty-fourth film. During the summer of 1941 he enlisted in the Naval Aviation Cadet program. The following February he married Patricia Ann O'Rourke, the niece of navy captain David McCampbell, who would later earn a Congressional Medal of Honor.

As a naval aviator, Morris was assigned to McCampbell's Air Group 15 aboard the carrier *Essex* in the Western Pacific. He later flew on missions that included Wake Island, both Philippine Sea battles, Iwo Jima, and Okinawa. After the war, Morris told an interviewer that the second battle of the Philippine Sea was his toughest fight.

Morris flew a total of fifty-seven missions and was credited with shooting down seven Japanese planes. Three of the Hellcat fighters he flew had to be dropped into the ocean upon his return because of bullet holes and flak damage. He was also credited with sinking a Japanese gunboat, two destroyers, and a submarine.

For his bravery, Morris was awarded four Distinguished Flying Crosses and two Air Medals. At the time, he was the most decorated movie actor to serve in combat. His record was exceeded only by army captain Audie Murphy, who had yet to begin his film career.

Morris returned to Hollywood and married life. His roles after the war were relegated to supporting other stars, typically as the loyal best friend. In 1959, while observing flight operations from the bridge of the carrier *Bonhomme Richard*, commanded by Captain David McCampbell, Morris suffered a fatal heart attack. He was forty-five years old.

## PROPAGANDA AND OVER THERE

Memorial Day 1942 was chosen as the New York City release date for Warner Bros.' flag-waving spectacle *Yankee Doodle Dandy*, starring James Cagney in an Oscar performance. The film not only told the life of Broadway showman George M. Cohan; it also celebrated the rags to riches American success story. One of the plot points in the film was using World War I propaganda to develop nationalistic feelings, particularly with the song "Over There."

The film is told with a "bookend flashback" frame, where Cohan visits the White House to tell his life story to President Roosevelt. After the flag-waving musical finale of "You're a Grand Old Flag," the film comes back to present time. And then President Roosevelt presents the Congressional Medal of Honor to Cohan, who neither wore a uniform nor served in combat. Cohan still has the distinction of being the only American civilian to have received the nation's highest military decoration.

In the fade-out scene, Cagney leaves the White House and walks along a file of soldiers heading for overseas. As the troops are singing "Over There," an officer asks Cohan, "What's the matter, don't you know the words to this song?"

Cagney continues walking into the night, softly singing with a smile on his face.

## PACIFIC TURNING POINT

After the Battle of the Coral Sea, the Japanese invasion fleet had headed for Port Moresby but was turned back. Admiral Yamamoto then turned his planning to Midway Island. According to the master naval plan, it was felt that the island could easily be taken with a heavy bombardment, followed by assault troops. The occupation of Midway, the Japanese thought, would deal a final blow to American naval power in the Pacific.

Unaware that the Americans had broken the radio code, the Japanese strike force, under Admiral Nagumo, steamed to a point approximately fifty miles north of Midway. It was then when the Japanese discovered the presence of two American task forces commanded by Admirals Raymond Spruance and Frank Jack Fletcher.

Despite the advantage of being there first, things went badly for the Americans as the battle was joined. It began at 5:30 on the morning of June 4. The next few hours were made up of move and countermove, with American fighter and torpedo planes paying a heavy price. One torpedo squadron's attack resulted in only one survivor, Ensign Gay, who watched the remainder of the battle while floating in the water.

Just when things looked bleakest, a concentrated dive bomber attack, from *Enterprise* and *Yorktown* planes, began to turn the battle. The targets were four Japanese carriers—the *Akagi, Kaga, Soryu*, and *Hiryu*. The latter survived this attack only to be sunk the following day.

By nightfall, Admiral Nagumo had to accept the fact that his most experienced fighter force had been dealt a decisive blow. Once again, the participating ships in the battle never saw each other, owing to improved aerial reconnaissance and radar.

Back in Hollywood, Paramount achieved the distinction of being the first studio to release an honest attempt at depicting the tragic realism of this new war, what the Americans faced on Wake Island, in 1942. In *Wake Island*, Brian Donlevy, Macdonald Carey, Robert Preston, and William Bendix portrayed marines defending the island against overwhelming Japanese numbers for two weeks after Pearl Harbor. They fight to the end, after being notified that help will not be arriving.

The studio used miniatures for the Japanese fleet. On the bridges of the enemy ships, the Japanese officers appeared in dress white uniforms, topped off with visor caps rather than the standard battle dress.

Before they are overrun, Albert Dekker, as a civilian construction worker, and Donlevy, the marine commander, share a final beer and drink a mutual toast to their respective colleges, Notre Dame and VMI (Virginia Military Institute). As they are manning the .30 caliber machine gun against the rushing enemy, the music swells and then the audience hears the patriotic fade-out voiceover about the brave and valiant stand of the marines on Wake Island, implying to audiences that "Americans never surrender." The film was shown constantly at marine bases and army posts all over the country.

In reality, the Wake Island garrison was forced to surrender. Many of those marines died in captivity or sat out the war in a Japanese prison camp.

Alfred Hitchcock used his standard screenplay formula of an ordinary person in extraordinary circumstances in the 1942 espionage thriller *Saboteur* for Universal. When production began the United States was not in the war. During postproduction Pearl Harbor was attacked. And the film was rushed into release.

Robert Cummings plays a Glendale, California, factory worker unjustly accused of sabotage, who is forced to travel across country with a woman he has just met, played by Priscilla Lane. The script shows some comparisons to Hitchcock's 1959 thriller *North by Northwest*. In *Saboteur* the chase ends as Cummings uncovers a Nazi spy ring, with Norman Lloyd falling to his death from the Statue of Liberty.

In early August 1942, the 1st Marine Division landed unopposed on Guadalcanal in the Solomon Islands. Soon the marines found that they had to contend not only with the furious Japanese banzai charges but with tropical conditions that included jungle heat, monsoons, and malaria. It would take the marines and the army six months to secure the island.

## THE EUROPEAN THEATER

The German Wehrmacht in 1942 was at its peak, a fully efficient army, equipped to take on any enemy. Hitler, who had long since envisioned himself as a leader of destiny, now attempted what Napoleon had failed at—the capture and occupation of Moscow. The campaign began well enough but soon fell victim to Hitler's astonishingly contradictory, and often stupid, orders. By the late summer the plan had changed to advance on Moscow after first taking Stalingrad. No one in the Nazi high command thought that the Russians would be able to stop the combined Wehrmacht infantry and tank attack, supported by the Luftwaffe.

But the Russians held on and beat back the Germans. Like Napoleon, Hitler was forced to order a retreat from the Russian front. Some close to the führer contended that he never fully recovered from this defeat. Earlier, the Nazis were forced to stop their western push at the English Channel. And now this.

On November 8, 1942, a hastily trained and inexperienced American landing force, supported by the British, led by General George S. Patton Jr., landed at three points in Vichy-held Morocco. The Vichy French, those who collaborated with the Third Reich, opposed the landings at first but later gave in, allowing the Americans a foothold in the western section of North Africa. The victories, however, were difficult. It was quite evident that the Allies were barely holding on in North Africa.

The following month, in a small building under the football stadium at the University of Chicago, a group of physics professors, among whom were Arthur Compton and Enrico Fermi, produced the first nuclear chain reaction that would set the stage for the Manhattan Project, the development of an atomic bomb. This experiment was classified top secret and continued to have a quiet understanding among those in government service, on a need-to-know basis.

## WELCOME BACK TO THE FIGHT

Probably the most sentimental, and best loved, World War II film came from this period, *Casablanca* (1942). The script, from an unproduced stage play, *Everybody Comes to Rick's*, written by Murray Burnett and Joan Alison, was submitted to the Warner Bros. story department.

Story editor Irene Lee supposedly found the play on a trip to New York. She arranged to have it submitted "for coverage" to the studio. The play arrived the day after the Pearl Harbor attack. Stephen Karnot, a thirty-five-year-old story analyst, gave the play a "good read."

In 1940, twenty-nine-year-old Murray Burnett, a Cornell-educated high school English teacher, had taken a frightening trip to Nazi-occupied Vienna. He was devastated and terrified by what he saw. In the south of France, he frequented a cafe, Le Belle Aurore, that had had a black piano player. These elements found their way into his stage play. The café that the protagonist had owned in Paris and his loyal companion were part of the source material. The role of the piano player would go to Dooley Wilson, who had no piano-playing ability. The 1931 song that became the signature of the film was actually a favorite of Burnett's from his days on the Ithaca, New York, campus.

When Burnett returned, he spent that summer with Joan Alison writing the play about a lonely, tough, morose expatriate who didn't need anyone, surviving in his own fiefdom with Nazis all around. This was a man who hated fascism but was still fighting demons inside himself as a divorced New York attorney.

In 1973 Howard Koch wrote in *New York Magazine* that the film *Casablanca* was actually his: that he wrote it line by line. In her book on the making of *Casablanca, Round Up the Usual Suspects*, Aljean Harmetz quotes Burnett as saying "He [Koch] took credit for everything. He says he took his magic pencil, Eagle Number One, and he wrote it [the screenplay] line by line. But every character in the film is in my play. Every one. Without exception."[15]

Burnett sued the publisher of the magazine and lost. He then sued Warner Bros. to get back the rights to his characters. And he lost again.

After Warner Bros. bought the play, the screenplay adaptation was assigned to a set of screenwriters. Producer Hal Wallis didn't like what they turned in as an outline. The main story line didn't work. And there was no clear-cut antagonist. The rewrite assignment then went to twin brothers Julius and Philip Epstein, along with Howard Koch, with Michael Curtiz as director.

In a Warner Bros. memo, dated December 31, 1941, Wallis stated, "The story that we recently purchased entitled *Everybody Comes to Rick's* will hereafter be known as *Casablanca*."[16]

Casting suggestions began with Ronald Reagan, Dennis Morgan, and George Raft as the enigmatic Rick Blaine who sticks his neck out for no one after being dumped by the love of his life at the Gare du Nord as the Nazis march into Paris.

In his pre-Paris days, Rick ran guns in Ethiopia and fought with the loyalists in Spain.

"And got well paid for it on both occasions," explains Rick.

"The other side would have paid you much more," corrects Prefect of Police Louis Renault. This dialogue exchange between Humphrey Bogart and Claude Rains is the first hint that Rick is always on the side of the underdog.

The reason Rick left New York City is "a little vague" in keeping with his mysterious background.

One of the first things that the Epstein brothers undertook was to clean up the female lead. Lois Meredith, in the stage play, had "been around a while." Rick was just one of her many lovers. Vera Zorina was the initial choice for the love interest. When Ingrid Bergman heard this, as she was waiting for a decision on *For Whom the Bell Tolls*, she became interested. With another quick rewrite, Lois Meredith became Ilsa Lund, an attractive, idealistic, young woman from Oslo.

Humphrey Bogart reluctantly went into the role of Rick. Bogart, who frequently groused about his film assignments while under contract at Warner Bros., had no favor for any script turned down by George Raft. Initially, Bogart was told that Ann Sheridan would be replacing Hedy Lamarr for the female lead.

After more rewrites, with no firm ending, production began in the late spring of 1942 when the Allied war effort was still in the darker-than-dark phase.

It was an extremely difficult "shoot." Bogart played Rick as cynical and hard bitten, lord of his fiefdom. In an earlier draft, the first time Rick is seen, he is sitting at the bar, smoking and pensively staring at a half-filled glass of bourbon.

The first camera angle of Rick Blaine was changed. Bogart would now be sitting at a table, alone, smoking and playing chess—with himself. Without any dialogue, the shot let the audience know that Rick was a contradictory loner looking at one side going up against the other, observing the fray from a distance as he controlled the pieces on the board.

One of *The Maltese Falcon* alums, Peter Lorre, was cast as the sleazy, chain-smoking, black market operative Ugarte, who reveals to Rick that he is in possession of two precious letters of transit that would allow the bearers safe passage. In the first draft of the script, the letters were signed by General Weygand. In subsequent drafts, that was changed to General De Gaulle. Nobody at the time questioned why the Nazis, occupying Casablanca with the Vichy French as Allies, would honor such passes since Germany was at war with the Free French. Still, Ugarte's explanation established screen credibility for the letters.

The other actor from *The Maltese Falcon* was the rotund British-born Sydney Greenstreet as Señor Ferrari, the black market entrepreneur who sees people as commodities.

One difficulty with the production was the choice of the three possible endings. First was the stage play ending where Rick and "Captain" Heinrich Strasser have the act-three gunfight in Rick's café. This gave Victor Laszlo, played by Paul Henreid, and Ilsa time to get off on the night plane to Lisbon. Rick is subsequently wounded, arrested, and taken off in the night for the ultimate destination of a concentration camp.

Another suggested ending was that Ilsa and Rick stay in Casablanca and allow Victor to leave. Another possible ending was for Ilsa and Rick to use the precious letters of transit themselves to get out of Casablanca, leaving Victor behind. This was unacceptable because it compromised Bogart's nobility as the worthy protagonist who conquers his dark side and puts the past to rest. Production continued without the cast knowing which ending would be used. It took a toll on everyone.

Bogart became increasingly difficult. But it was not directly the fault of the confusion on the set. His marriage to actress Mayo Methot had been in shreds before production began. And now Mayo, drinking heavily, was even more upset because she suspected that Bogart was having an affair with his Swedish costar. However, all Bogart did during the breaks was spend time alone in his trailer.

Reportedly, the Epstein twins came up with the film's notable and acceptable ending. One of the better stories surrounding this is that Julius and Philip were riding down Sunset Boulevard, each lost in his own thoughts on script problems. Often, each of the brothers knew what the other was thinking, a phenomenon thought to be common among identical twins. Philip and Julius looked at each other and said in unison, "Round up the usual suspects!"

The line would work because it had been planted earlier in two places.

In the end Rick becomes a patriot, doing the heroic thing while the world is being ripped apart. He not only places his life in danger for an ideal, but he sacrifices any chance he will have with Ilsa. Rick then effects the resolution of everyone around him and therefore becomes the classic protagonist.

As the underground leader Victor Laszlo, Paul Henreid personified the Allied thinking with his departing line to Bogart: "Welcome back to the fight. This time I know our side will win."

As Rick walked off with Louis Renault and Max Steiner's fade-out music swelled, audiences left the theaters with hope. Henreid's noteworthy line said it all for Rick's character.

In her autobiography *My Story*, Ingrid Bergman confirmed that the production started "disastrously." She didn't blame Curtiz. It was the script. Hal Wallis was constantly arguing with the Epstein twins.

Bergman added,

So every day we were shooting off the cuff: every day they were handing out the dialogue and we were trying to make some sense of it. No one knew where the picture was going and no one knew how it was going to end, which didn't help any of us with our characterizations. Every morning we said, "Well, who are we? What are we doing here?" And Michael Curtiz would say, "We're not quite sure . . . we'll let you know tomorrow."[17]

Once the airport sequence was finished, there was talk of shooting "the other ending." According to Bergman, they didn't have to shoot another ending. The studio and Wallis liked the idea of Rick and Louis walking off in the mist with the famous fade-out line, "Louie, I think this is the beginning of a beautiful friendship."

During postproduction, it was suggested that the old Tin Pan Alley tune "As Time Goes By" was too dated and should be cut. To do this they would need "pickup shots" with Bergman and Dooley Wilson. However, Bergman had already cut her hair for the role of Maria in *For Whom the Bell Tolls*. So the song stayed, and a bit of World War II film history was saved for American audiences.

Bergman also wrote, "Perhaps the essential reason why *Casablanca* is now a classic, a cult, and a legend is that it was concerned with *our* war! Rarely, if ever, have an actor and actress had the opportunity to work so dramatically, if unknowingly, on our emotions, when defeat seemed a possibility and victory far away. *Casablanca* had a major impact on the Allied war effort."[18]

The film went into American cinematic history, walking off with Oscars for Best Picture, Best Screenplay, and Best Director.

Years later, in front of a younger generation of aspiring UCLA Extension screenwriters, Julius Epstein would say that *Casablanca* was not one of his favorite films. He added that the film was mediocre at best and was a back-lot vehicle to support the Allied war effort. "And I cannot, for the life of me, figure out why they cast an Englishman, Claude Rains, as a Frenchman when we had a lot of French character actors on the lot."[19]

Another element was the so-called credit for *Casablanca*. Producer Hal Wallis, who ran the studio for Jack Warner, claimed that it was his idea to buy the play. At the Academy Awards ceremony, Jack Warner grabbed the Oscar away from Wallis simply because he owned the studio, giving more credit to the World War II adage "Victory has a hundred fathers while defeat is an orphan."

The film was perfectly timed for release. Very few Americans were aware of where Casablanca actually was. However, one week after the film's release, Roosevelt met Churchill at the famous Casablanca Conference, the results of which exceeded everyone's expectations. It was the first time an American president flew in an airplane for a summit meeting.

This wartime summit outlined Allied strategy, that the European Theater of operations would take precedence over the Pacific Theater. And it was decided that the next phase should be the Sicilian campaign rather than the invasion of the European continent. The German intelligence office, the Abwehr, never suspected that the conference would be held in Casablanca. They thought the word was coded. *Casablanca*, in Spanish, means "White House." Hence, the Nazis thought the conference would be held in Washington, D.C.

The Casablanca Conference also established that only unconditional surrender by Germany and Japan would be acceptable. It was a coincidence: Politics and war merged with film.

## THE WAR THROUGH FILM

Robert Gessner, chairman, Department of Motion Pictures, New York University, wrote in the *New York Times*, in January 1943, that narrative film needed to be used in promoting the war, both in the propaganda films, being produced by Hollywood studios, and in the service training films. "There is no substitute for a [*good*] story. The narrative film packs a whallop [*sic*] all its own. . . . Garnished with [movie] stars the dish is irresistible. In a way this is a war for men's minds and our side needs all the persuasions we can command."

Gessner added, "In 1943 Hollywood should give us stories which will awaken America to the meaning of war, to the social patterns behind the battles. We had no such feature films in 1942."[20]

At the Academy Awards that year, on Wednesday evening, March 3, 1943, producer Walter Wanger presented a letter from President Roosevelt to the members of the Academy over nationwide radio. Roosevelt wrote, "At no time in the history of motion pictures have these awards possessed so much significance. Achievement in motion pictures today means much more than merely having attained the heights in public entertainment.

"In the months to come world conditions may cause the motion picture industry to play an even larger part in the war against the Axis tyranny."[21]

The War Department, the OWI, and the BMP were in agreement about one element of American war films during this time: They should all end with a feeling of hope. Even at the darkest point, in both theaters of war, Americans had to be given the feeling that the one element that the future held was victory. The stirring flag-waving speeches at fade-out continued.

RKO released *Hitler's Children* in 1943 to show what Hollywood thought life would be like in Nazi Germany. Directed by Edward Dmytryk from a script by Emmett Lavery, the film was thought to be another propaganda vehicle, showing the Third Riech as brainwashing its children and sterilizing "unfit women." In the most graphic sequence of the film, Bonita Granville is partially stripped and flogged. The film was thought to be overloaded with anti-Nazi propaganda by critics.

In a 1998 interview, Dmytryk, as an adjunct professor, told how he showed the film to his students at the USC School of Cinema/TV in the early 1990s. "They didn't believe it," said Dmytryk. "And I thought the film was mild compared to what really happened."[22]

Paramount took a play by Lajos Biró about the British attempts to infiltrate

Nazi General Erwin Rommel's desert supply dumps. Just as some of those before it, *Five Graves to Cairo* (1943) straddled the genres of a war film and an espionage thriller. Paramount was banking on the "headlines to the screen" spin, which would attract audiences.

Franchot Tone portrayed a British spy who was able to get information out of Rommel's headquarters to insure victory for Field Marshal Montgomery at El Alamein. Erich von Stroheim gave a signature performance as Rommel, personifying the American image of a Nazi field commander. In one scene, von Stroheim tells Anne Baxter, playing a maid in a North African hotel, that he has an aversion to women in the morning.

*Five Graves to Cairo* was perfectly timed, coming in on the heels of Montgomery's North African push. It did better than expected at the box office.

Warner Bros. continued to grind out propaganda dramas. In 1943, the studio released *Air Force*, starring John Garfield, Gig Young, John Ridgely, Arthur Kennedy, and Harry Carey. The script, written by Dudley Nichols, was requested by the Army Air Force, feeling competition with the navy because of the Midway victory and the emergence of naval air power.

In the film, a B-17 bomber, the *Mary Ann*, arrives in Pearl Harbor on the day of the attack. Actually, on the morning of the attack, radar observers had thought that the Japanese planes were the American B-17 squadron approaching the island from California. The next stop for the *Mary Ann* was Clark Field in the Philippines, where they would take part in defending against Japanese forces. The *Mary Ann* then leaves for Australia and participates in the Battle of the Coral Sea. The filmmakers relied on audiences' suspension of belief for one plane to participate in so many combat situations over an entire theater of operations.

John Garfield played an alienated gunner who washed out of pilot training. Harry Carey, as an older sergeant, was worried for his son, a pilot. Carey later learns that his son's plane never even made it off the ground at Pearl Harbor. FDR is heard on the radio: "The American people will win through!" A colonel says, "We'll teach the Japs that treachery can't win!"

Garfield later becomes furious, explaining, "We're gettin' kicked around all over the place by a lot of stinkin' nips."

The film opened to rave reviews and won Academy Award nominations for Nichols and the photography crew. George Amy won an Oscar for his editing.

The only World War II propaganda film that Jack Warner regretted giving the "green light" to was *Mission to Moscow*, in 1943. Since Warner Bros. was the studio making more World War II films than any other, it reportedly received a phone call from the White House. President Roosevelt suggested using the autobiography of U.S. Ambassador Joseph E. Davies as a tool to keep Stalin in the war by doing something positive with his image to relay to the American audiences.

The result was an outlandish propaganda vehicle that would lay the foundation for a notorious backlash.

The screenplay and direction came, respectively, from two *Casablanca* graduates, Howard Koch and Michael Curtiz. In the cast were Walter Huston, as Davies, Ann Harding, Oscar Homolka, George Tobias, Gene Lockhart, and Eleanor Parker.

Mannart Kippen gave a protrayal of Joseph Stalin as warm and kind, dedicated to the Russian people despite the allegations of mass executions. The purge trials of 1937 were blandly rationalized that those convicted were agents of either Japan or Germany.

Despite the propaganda, historical figures are used in the film. In *Yankee Doodle Dandy* the audience never directly saw President Roosevelt, giving him a God-like presence. Here, the audience actually sees FDR in the opening sequence where Davies gets his diplomatic orders. Certain members of the U.S. Senate came off as war profiteers.

The film was later brought up, during the McCarthy Era, as an example of the Hollywood establishment's flirtation with Moscow and New Dealism. Despite Warner Bros. intention of showing what the Russian people were up against, in World War II, the politics of a subsequent era came back to haunt the studio. And screenwriter Howard Koch was later blacklisted.

While *Mission to Moscow* was in production, Warners also gave the go-ahead to *Action in the North Atlantic* (1943), most of which was filmed off the California coast near Santa Barbara. The film, starring Humphrey Bogart and Raymond Massey, was a propaganda tribute to the Merchant Marines. The plot concerned a ship carrying materiel to Russia, crossing the dangerous Nazi U-boat lanes. The Liberty ship's commander, Massey, orders his ship to ram a surfaced U-boat. In the end, Massey is fatally wounded, and Bogart assumes command, going forward on other voyages.

The best reviews of the film concerned the battle scenes, which used super-large miniatures that had to be transported to the set by railroad flat cars.

Lamar Trotti got another war film assignment to adapt John Brophy's novel *The Immortal Sergeant* for 20th Century Fox. The film, of the same title (1943), was the generic war tale of the battle-hardened master, played by Thomas Mitchell, who teaches his men how to survive in North Africa at the expense of his own life. Maureen O'Hara provided the love interest for Henry Fonda. After the film was completed, Fonda reported for duty in the navy.

In the late spring of 1943, MGM released *Bataan*. The story was about the American defenders who fought to the humiliating end but still managed to delay the Japanese offensive in the Philippines. Robert Taylor led a cast that included George Murphy, Thomas Mitchell, and a young Desi Arnaz. The ending was pure propaganda, with Taylor, as the last man standing, manning the .30 caliber machine gun as his position is brutally overrun by a horde of Japanese troops.

## THE NEGRO AND THE WAR

In addition to the stereotypical ethnic cross section, MGM executive Dore Schary had a black actor written into the script despite the fact that the American armed forces remained segregated.

Schary, willing to take the risk, later said, "I figured to hell with it. We're going to have one black. [And] we got a lot of letters from people complaining."

It was almost as if Schary was responding to a 1942 report from the OWI, "The Negro and the War," which outlined generalizations of American public opinion, abstracts, and analyses from the American media.

This report stated that many American Negroes felt a degree of sympathy for the Japanese "as colored men." The report added that "among all classes of Negroes there is a discernible feeling that the present war is, in fact, a race war.

"The most conspicuous grievance of the Negroes is this: 'If you want the war so badly, why don't you let us fight?' "

The report added that Negroes are denied admission to the Marine Corps; that Negroes are accepted into the navy only in menial capacities; that Negroes are segregated in the army and are often relegated to the less desirable types of service.

The fact that [the] army and navy practice has changed markedly has not sunk home in the Negro part of the population. . . . The issue of military service has a particular significance to Negroes who are asked to die for a country which accepts Filipinos, Chinese, Indians and recent aliens into its armed services without discrimination—but segregates Negroes who have long records of unimpeachable loyalty.[23]

The report was noted and filed. The USO shows continued at army posts and navy and marine bases. Two of the black entertainers at the time were Hattie McDaniel and singer Lena Horne. McDaniel often told of accompanying USO shows to military posts below the Mason-Dixon line. When the show ended for the night, McDaniel was not allowed in the same hotel or in the same restaurant as the white performers.

But Horne created the most controversy. As the war continued, she often bristled at being the token black pinup queen. She resented having to entertain the white soldiers before putting on a show for the blacks.

At Fort Riley, Kansas, her boiling temper came to a flash point. Horne recounted that she had to stay overnight to do a separate show for the blacks. The next morning, in the black mess, she saw a row of white men up front. After asking who they were, she was told that they were Nazi prisoners of war.

Horne stormed off the stage, went to the back of the hall, and gave her show directly to the black soldiers. She then complained to the local chapter of the National Association for the Advancement of Colored People (NAACP) and found out that the army's policy was business as usual.

Upon returning to Hollywood, Horne was reprimanded and told to stop being a troublemaker. She continued with her own independent shows to the segregated black units, financed with her own money and with her own band.

## THE COLONELS

At 20th Century Fox, Darryl Zanuck was commissioned in the Army Signal Corps and produced a documentary about the North African campaign, *At the Front*. Zanuck was a member of a clique known to columnists as "The Hollywood Colonels."

Lieutenant Colonel Darryl Zanuck, Army Signal Corps, was among many Hollywood figures later called to testify in front of the Inspector General Division that was investigating alleged criminal wrongdoing and war profiteering. The Inspector General Division came out of the Truman Committee investigation into alleged misappropriation of wartime government funds. Zanuck was grilled for two days in Los Angeles on January 4–5, 1943, by an army committee of three officers, Major John Amen, Lieutenant Colonel Lucien J. Moret, and Captain Thomas S. Hinkel.

The army panel was concerned with a lack of reporting regarding training film budgets that were being charged to the government. No detailed accounting was done. The films were financed through a loose purchase order system.

As the questions got more pointed and direct, Zanuck, becoming increasingly irritated, proclaimed that he took responsibility for the first three training films that Fox produced in the early days of the war.

"I made the first two or three pictures at 20th Century Fox studio. I took the responsibility then. I take the responsibility now. They [the government] wanted the pictures. If any one is to blame, I and I alone, am to blame."

An officer asked, "For what, colonel?"

Zanuck then began banging on the desk in front of him and shouted, "I am to blame for being a sucker and trying to help my country. That's what I am to blame for!"

Another officer asked, "You said you would take the blame for the whole thing. Just what do you mean?"

Zanuck answered, "When the War Department insisted that they needed these films in a time of war emergency—when the Academy and the producers would not put up the money, I then took the responsibility of accepting the idea of doing it on a purchase order basis and put up the money for it."[24]

The investigation continued, both in Hollywood and Washington. At its conclusion, new guidelines and regulations were put into place.

## HEYDRICH TO THE SCREEN

United Artists called on Fritz Lang to do *Hangmen Also Die!* (1943), the first fictionalized account of the assassination of Nazi General Reinhard Heydrich, starring Brian Donlevy, Walter Brennan, and Anna Lee. This was the strongest indictment of the Third Reich. An actual incident, once again, was being used to re-create another story.

Donlevy plays a Czech doctor whom the Prague partisans assign to kill Heydrich. After being wounded in the attempt, Donlevy seeks refuge in the home of a university professor played by Brennan. As Brennan's daughter, Anna Lee plans to turn Donlevy over to the Nazis after her father, and hundreds of Czech civilians, are taken as hostages. She relents when she realizes the dedication of Donlevy. A traitor, portrayed by Gene Lockhart, is then framed and arrested by the Nazis.

MGM followed suit with *Hitler's Hangman*, also known as *Hitler's Madman* (1943). It was released the same year, about the massacre at Lidice. When the story was published, Eleanor Roosevelt suggested that it be adapted for a film.

The studio acquired the rights and assigned Peretz Hirschbein, Melvin Levy, and Doris Malloy to the adaptation. The cast included Patricia Morison, Alan Curtis, and Ralph Morgan. John Carradine played Heydrich. As previously noted, it was not uncommon for the real-life Heydrich to sign an order authorizing the execution of a group of civilians. Over a period of days, Heydrich would witness their executions and return to his office for a three-course lunch at his desk.

In *Hitler's Hangman*, Czech civilians retaliate with sabotage after several atrocities. After a local priest is killed, several of the citizens assassinate the general. The townspeople are then rounded up and slated for execution. Then the village of Lidice is destroyed.

The poet Edna St. Vincent Millay contributed several verses for the film. At the film's end, the ghosts of those executed recite lines from Millay's poem.

Columbia released *Sahara* on Armistice Day of 1943. The story was based on an incident from the Soviet film *The Thirteen*. *Sahara* was a tribute to the Allies who were left stranded in the desert after the retreat from Tobruk. A mixed Allied group, led by Humphrey Bogart as American tank commander Sergeant Joe Gun, forage for water and then are forced to defend a hill where water is available against a 500–man Nazi infantry and tank battalion. *Sahara* showed the brutality of war against the desert elements where the Allied teamwork brings victory despite overwhelming odds.

One week after *Sahara* was in the theaters, 20th Century Fox released *Guadalcanal Diary*. The film follows members of the famed 1st Marine Division as they prepare to land on the island in early August 1942, through hard jungle fighting to when they are relieved by the Army's American Division, based on Richard Tregaskis's book.

William Bendix, as a former Brooklyn cab driver, gave a believable performance. He won the audience's sympathy in scenes where he shaved with a straight-edged razor with a mirror propped to a palm tree and Betty Grable's pinup photo nearby to remind him what he was fighting for.

In a patriotic speech, reflective of the vicar's sermon in *Mrs. Miniver*, Bendix gives his working-class wartime credo:

I'm telling you this thing is over my head. It's gonna take someone bigger than me to handle it. I'm no hero. I'm just a guy! I came out here because somebody had to come. I don't want no medals. I just want to get this thing over with and go back home.

I can't tell them bombs to hit somewhere else. Like I said before it's up to somebody bigger than me, bigger than anybody. . . . What I mean is . . . I guess it's up to God.[25]

Bendix goes into a rage while listening to the World Series as the radio report suddenly fades into static, robbing him of knowing the final score.

The script departed from the book in an effort to show the war in the Western Pacific from Hollywood's point of view. Much of the brutal and grim reality of Tregaskis's eyewitness account was toned down. The preparation phase of the film came off as documentary real. And the all-male cast gave the audiences what they wanted, a stirring courageous look at American marines in combat. The film was so successful with American audiences that the Marine Corps set up recruiting tables in theater lobbies.

A storm of controversy came about when General Douglas MacArthur and his staff were ordered from the Philippines to set up Pacific headquarters in Sydney, Australia. In addition to leaving the American Philippine Defense Command to the mercy of the Japanese, American nurses were also left behind. Many of them were doomed to horrific ends. In total, more than 200 army nurses lost their lives in World War II.[26]

This was what Allan Kenward had in mind to tell their story, when he wrote the Broadway play *Proof through the Night*. MGM quickly bought the rights to the play and got a script from screenwriter Paul Osborn. The play was retitled *Cry Havoc*. And just as *Guadalcanal Diary* centered around an all-male cast, *Cry Havoc* (1943) went the female route.

In the film, army nurses on Bataan recruit civilian volunteers from the refugees fleeing Manila. Fay Bainter leads the nurses as Captain Alice Marsh. Her second in command is played by Margaret Sullavan as Lieutenant Mary Smith.

The group is brought together as their situation gets more hopeless, knowing that reinforcements will never arrive. The film went for a brutally realistic ending as the women leave their bunker to surrender to the Japanese and the fate that they all dreaded. The film stunned American audiences and added to the anger toward Japanese atrocities in the Philippines.

Two days before Christmas 1943, MGM released *A Guy Named Joe* starring Spencer Tracy, Irene Dunne, and Van Johnson. The director was Victor Fleming (*The Wizard of Oz, Gone with the Wind*).

The title is said to have originated from Army Air Force veterans who claimed that any guy who is a "right guy" is a Joe. Still other veterans claim that the phrase came from Colonel Claire Chennault, who reportedly said, "When you're in the cockpit you're just a guy named Joe."

This romantic war melodrama had Tracy coming back in spirit after he was killed in a spectacular plane crash. He then oversees his ex-girlfriend's new romance with Van Johnson as the latter prepares for a dangerous mission.

Although this film had excellent intentions, it was criticized for the ending, going against the established propaganda premise that victory is to be achieved through teamwork. In the end Tracy steals a plane and flies off solo, grandstanding on a bombing mission. Despite negative reaction from most critics regarding the ending, American audiences bought into this film. And it became an enormous success.

In 1989, Steven Spielberg remade *A Guy Named Joe* under the title of *Always* with Richard Dreyfuss, Holly Hunter, and Brad Johnson. This version never fulfilled its expectations.

When Universal released *Gung Ho!* in 1943, the American forces were in the middle of the Western Pacific island hopping campaign. The 2nd Marine Division was about to engage in one of its toughest battles of the war, Tarawa (which would later be portrayed as the first battle sequence of Republic Pictures' *Sands of Iwo Jima* in 1949).

Lucien Hubbard's traditional flag-waving script was taken from the combat experiences of Marine Captain W.S. LeFrançois, who served with Carlson's Marine Raiders on Makin Island. The title came from an Asian phrase that originally meant "to work together." The rousing patriotic speech delivered by Randolph Scott, as Lieutenant Colonel Thorwald at film's end, contributed to a new Americanized definition of "Gung Ho."

British-born Cary Grant played an American submarine commander in Warner Bros. *Destination Tokyo*, which was released on New Year's Eve of 1943. This was a tribute to the "silent service" and became the godfather of American submarine films.

The script told the tale of the USS *Copperfin*, tasked with picking up a meteorologist in the Aleutian Islands and then to proceed to Tokyo Bay to put him ashore so he could radio weather information for the Doolittle Raid. The boat has to withstand a dive bomber, a Japanese aircraft carrier, and a depth-charge attack. The action was good and provided the needed tense moments. The cast included John Garfield, who offered some humorous moments, Alan Hale, Dane Clark, and Warner Anderson.

The script was written by Delmer Daves and Albert Maltz, from an original story by Steve Fisher. Strangely, when the Academy Awards nominations were announced for that year, Steve Fisher got the only nomination from this film.

"And on they go, these giant killers of the deep" is the beginning of the patriotic fade-out speech at the close of *Crash Dive*, one of 20th Century Fox's 1943 propaganda offerings. The film dishes up every wartime cliché, a love triangle between Anne Baxter and two dashing submarine officers, Tyrone Power (as a Naval Academy alumnus) and Dana Andrews, the boat's captain. The supporting actors cross every ethnic line, leading to the special effects denouement, a night commando raid on a Nazi outpost.

Another commendable account about women's sacrifices in the Western Pacific came from *So Proudly We Hail*, released by Paramount in 1943. It is often compared to *Cry Havoc*, emphasizing the bravery of the army nurses left behind in the Philippines. A photo feature in *Life* magazine was the basis for the script, directed by Mark Sandrich.

The narrative of Allan Scott's Oscar-nominated screenplay was done with a "bookend flashback." Army nurse Claudette Colbert is in a catatonic state on a ship after the harrowing ordeal. An army physician, portrayed by John Litel, attempts to uncover the key to Colbert's psychological state as the story unfolds. Her husband, played by George Reeves, is missing, presumed dead. They had little time, spending their wedding night in a foxhole.

Veronica Lake comes off as the gutsiest heroine when she sacrifices herself to kill a group of Japanese soldiers with a grenade. Lake approaches the soldiers with a knowing smile. And they allow her to approach because they don't fear women. The grenade detonates, and Lake achieves her end, sacrificing herself and attaining revenge for her fiancé, who was killed at Pearl Harbor. Colbert, at film's end, learns that her husband is dead but finds strength to survive.

Although Paulette Goddard won an Academy Award nomination for Best Supporting Actress, it was Colbert who gave the flag-waving voiceover at fade-out. The film, often referred to as a "woman's combat film," was extremely successful at the box office mainly because audiences were well aware of what happened to the American nurses when the Japanese overran the Philippines.

RKO released *Flight for Freedom* in 1943, a thinly disguised film based on the disappearance of Amelia Earhart over the Pacific in 1937. At one point, she was believed to have been executed by Japanese soldiers after being transferred to Saipan following her crash landing. Another version is that Earhart's plane simply crashed into the ocean with no survivors.[27]

The film edges toward the real story when Rosalind Russell, playing the character Tonie Carter, disappears after photographing Japanese outposts with a hidden camera. Also integrated into the film are segments from the aviation career of Jacqueline Cochran, wife of one of the film's producers Floyd Odlum.

Amelia Earhart's disappearance has been unresolved and inconclusive over the years despite many observers contending that the famed aviatrix and her navigator, Fred Noonan, were on a special White House mission.

In 1976, a television Movie of the Week, titled *Amelia Earhart*, written by Carol Sobieski, was aired with Susan Clark as Earhart.

After considerable head scratching, in 1943, Paramount decided to go ahead with the production of *For Whom the Bell Tolls*, based on the Ernest Hemingway classic novel about the passionate, albeit tragic, loyalist fight against fascism during the Spanish Civil War.

Gary Cooper portrayed Robert Jordan, a freelance demolitions expert who joins a group of partisans and falls in love with María, played by Ingrid Bergman. Idealistic and laconic, Cooper dies in the suicidal defense of a strategic bridge at the end.

For the movie, part of California's Sierra Nevada range was transformed for the northern mountains of Spain. Bergman had her hair cut short to play María while her previous film, *Casablanca*, was in postproduction. After *For Whom the Bell Tolls* was released, the "María Cut" briefly became a fashion fad for American women.

Bergman later reflected:

I suppose it had something to do with the war and the difficulties over hairdressing, but they made a terrible mistake. They didn't know I had a hairdresser who followed me around like a shadow and rolled my hair up every minute of the day. It was rolled up in little bobby pins—we didn't have such things as hairspray in those days—and then it was combed out before I shot each scene. But of course the poor women who had their heads done in the María cut in the morning found that after two hours it fell down again and they looked like little rats.[28]

Hemingway believed in the nobility of sacrifice, which is why he chose the title, a quote from John Donne: "Any man's death diminishes me, because I am involved in Mankinde; and therefore never send to know for whom the bell tolls; It tolls for thee."

The film received nine Academy Award nominations. However, only one resulted in an Oscar: Katina Paxinou, who had escaped from Greece after the Nazi invasion, won a golden statuette for portraying the passionate guerrilla fighter Pilar.

Hemingway returned from a journalism trip to China after the Oscars were awarded and met with Bergman. She asked the author if he had seen the film. Hemingway nodded, adding, "Five times."

"Ah, five times! You liked it that much!" she exclaimed.

Hemingway shook his head. "No, I did not. . . . After I'd seen the first five minutes I couldn't stand it any longer so I walked out. They'd cut all my best scenes and there was no point to it. Later I went back again because I thought I must see the whole movie, and I saw a bit more, and again I walked out. It took me five visits to see that movie. That's how much I liked it!"[29]

Paul Lukas won an Oscar for his performance in *Watch on the Rhine* (1943) in which he portrayed an alienated German living in the United States in conflict with himself as to whether he should remain in safety or return home to fight the Nazi menace. The script, by Dashiell Hammett, was adapted from Lillian Hellman's successful stage play. Bette Davis portrayed Lukas's prim wife Sara Muller. The movie was criticized as a good stage play that did not transfer well to film.

One of the most unusual and disturbing war films in this time frame was 20th Century Fox's *Lifeboat* (1944), directed by Alfred Hitchcock. *Lifeboat* mixed a cross-section of Allied survivors of a freighter sunk by a Nazi U-boat. The skipper of the U-boat, strongly played by Walter Slezak, ends up in the lifeboat when the submarine is sunk.

The collection of survivors in this one-set production included Tallulah Bankhead as a self-absorbed reporter, Mary Anderson as a confused nurse, Hume Cronyn as a withdrawn radio operator, John Hodiak as an engaging crew member, Henry Hull as a corporate executive, Heather Angel as the unbalanced mother of a dead baby, a black steward played by Canada Lee, and a wounded crewman portrayed by William Bendix.

The screenplay outline was completed by John Steinbeck on March 26, 1943. Jo Swerling used that outline for the screenplay. Hitchcock employed his staff for wartime research, which included an Armed Forces memo, dated May 25, 1943, on "Instructions for the Shipwrecked." British Information Services sent Hitchcock a memo, June 22, 1943, regarding shipwrecked sailors.

During postproduction, Darryl F. Zanuck sent a memo to Hitchcock and producer Kenneth MacGowan, dated August 19, 1943, that he didn't like the idea of a crazy woman with a baby in the cast. "I now regret that we have Mrs. Higgins and the baby in the picture at all."[30]

However, the woman and the baby stayed. The studio wanted as much realism in the film as possible depicting the Atlantic Ocean horror when a ship is torpedoed and sunk. Further postproduction research came up with a July 3, 1943, story in the *New York Times*, an account of shipwrecked sailors who rescued a Nazi U-boat commander after he was washed into the sea during a crash dive.

As a departure from the standard World War II film, Slezak's Nazi was the only realistic and pragmatic member of the survivors. He had a plan. This left audiences and critics confused as to exactly what the filmmakers were saying. Hitchcock, in a later interview, explained that Slezak's character was made purposefully strong to let American audiences know that Nazis should not be underestimated.

Steinbeck, Hitchcock, and cinematographer Glen MacWilliams all received Academy Award nominations for their work on *Lifeboat*. The film did well on both coasts but not in the heartland. Bankhead won the Best Actress award from the New York Film Critics.

Soon after *Lifeboat* was released, Fox rushed *The Sullivans* (later rereleased as *The Fighting Sullivans*) into the theaters in February 1944. This was the sad, true story of five working-class brothers from Waterloo, Iowa, who joined the navy. They asked for and received an exemption from the navy so that all five could serve on the same ship, the USS *Juneau*, a cruiser that was sunk during the Battle of Guadalcanal.

Ward Bond played the naval officer who called on the Sullivan home to inform the parents, played by Selena Royle and Thomas Mitchell, of the family tragedy.

"How many were lost?" asks Royle.

Bond pauses and then says, "All of them."

Mitchell, as Mr. Sullivan, who had never missed a day of work, then bravely heads off to his job at a railroad yard, painfully aware of the price that his family has paid for the war. Audiences at the time quietly wept, identifying with the family.

The film was initially titled *The Sullivans* and did little box office business.

It was then pulled and reissued as *The Fighting Sullivans* and became a sleeper hit.[31]

The tragic story of *The Fighting Sullivans* led to a policy change by the Navy Department: No more than one family member would be assigned to any one command during wartime.

The film ends with the navy commissioning one of its destroyers the USS *The Sullivans*. That ship has since been retired. In 1997, the navy commissioned a modern Arleigh Burke class guided-missile destroyer, the USS *The Sullivans*.

By 1944, the OWI had undergone a shakeup. The power shifted from the Domestic Branch of the Bureau of Motion Pictures to the Overseas Branch, headed by Ulrich Bell, a former journalist who was known as aggressive and opinionated. When Republic Pictures sent a copy of the script of *The Fighting Seabees*, the Overseas Branch demanded that the Susan Hayward character, Constance Chesley, who is a wire service reporter, be rewritten. She was part of a romantic triangle including John Wayne and Dennis O'Keefe and came off as the dominant character. Once the script, credited to Borden Chase and Aeneas MacKenzie, was rewritten with the war and the two men in the forefront, production began.

*The Fighting Seabees* (1944) was intended to be a tribute to the navy's Construction Battalion, men who were recruited from various building trades. These were the men who built airfields on remote islands that made the primitive Western Pacific bearable for the fighting men. Wayne portrayed "Wedge" Donovan, a hard hat with a quick temper who is the leader of the newly formed Seabee unit. Donovan listens to nobody and, as such, winds up allowing his men to endure unnecessary casualties.

In the end, Wayne redeems himself with a suicide mission, driving a bulldozer into a Japanese position. A reviewer noted that Hayward set a new precedent for female reporters, wearing designer dresses in a combat zone. The film went on to be a hit.

MGM acquired the rights to Captain Ted Lawson's book (cowritten with Bob Considine) to make *Thirty Seconds over Tokyo* (1944), about Lawson's participation in Lieutenant Colonel Jimmy Doolittle's daring 1942 Army Air Force raid on Japan. Lawson was one of the pilots who survived the raid, although he ended up losing a leg to gangrene.

In the beginning, the audience sees Spencer Tracy, as Doolittle, speak to the assembled men. "Boys, you're all volunteers to perform an exceedingly dangerous mission." Tracy then looks around, taking a dramatic pause, adding, "It is so dangerous that it would be best for the safety of all of you not to discuss your destination—even among yourselves."

Audiences sat anxiously waiting for those seconds over Tokyo to see what would happen to the surviving airmen who were forced to crash-land in China after the bombing run. During the actual mission, 133 days after Pearl Harbor, the sixteen bombers were placed aboard the carrier USS *Hornet*. The launch had to be earlier than scheduled because it was determined that Japanese intelligence had suspected something was coming. The B-25 bombers didn't have enough return fuel. All but one of the bombers either crashed or had to be abandoned. Seventy-one of the eighty airmen eventually found their way to safety.

Besides Tracy the cast included Van Johnson, as Lawson, Robert Walker, Phyllis Thaxter, Don DeFore, and Robert Mitchum.

Director Mervyn LeRoy had his editors intercut combat footage of the actual carrier launch with rear projection and flight deck scenes. It was a method that other studios would quickly adopt. The effects worked, and Oscars were waiting for cinematographers Robert Surtees and Harold Rosson.

The irony of the Doolittle raid was that while it did little damage to the targets, it raised spirits in the American psyche. The raid inspired ideas for two other films besides *Thirty Seconds over Tokyo*. Those were *Destination Tokyo* (1943) and *The Purple Heart* (1944).

*The Story of Dr. Wassell* (1944), a Paramount production, took two years to get into production (considered to be a slow time frame for this period). This was Cecil B. DeMille's only war film, the true story of navy doctor Corydon Wassell, stationed in Java, who saved approximately fifteen men from falling into the hands of the Japanese in the days following Pearl Harbor. DeMille heard about the account, which became a book by James Hilton, from one of President Roosevelt's radio fireside chats. The producer wanted to start production immediately, but the navy demurred, preoccupied in two theaters of war. The film was finally put into production in 1944 with a rousing patriotic musical score by Victor Young. In the film, FDR's praise of Dr. Wassell is heard on the soundtrack.

In an unusual move for a noted Hollywood producer, David O. Selznick wrote the screenplay for *Since You Went Away*, in 1944, described as a home front tearjerker. Selznick adapted the screenplay, from a novel by Margaret Buell Wilder, that related the problems of an American family after their father is reported missing in action. The mother, played by Claudette Colbert, realizes that middle-class comfort must surrender to wartime necessity. She then goes to work in a defense plant. Her adolescent daughter, portrayed by Jennifer Jones, falls in love with a soldier played by Robert Walker. The film brought out the problems of American women being forced to live without men during the war's duration. Hattie McDaniel, who had played Mammy in *Gone with the Wind*, gave extended support as the maid.

Home front insensitivity was blatantly thrown to American audiences, almost lecturing them from the screen as to what wartime sacrifice meant. A man on a train tells Colbert that he has a daughter the same age as Jones, but he doesn't know where she is. "You see, she was at Corregidor."

A disgruntled businessman is angered by the train's unscheduled delay because a military transport is given priority. The audience then sees the camera pan to a soldier with a missing limb. Agnes Moorehead, an indulged and spoiled middle-aged woman, is suddenly lectured to by an idealistic Jones. It was as if the younger generation understood and endured wartime sacrifice more than their elders.

Despite being an unusually long film, it received numerous Academy Award nominations, including Best Picture and Best Actress for Colbert and Jones. Shirley Temple added a supporting role as the younger daughter who sells war stamps.

Skip Homeier gave a shocking performance as a fanatical twelve-year-old Nazi who is adopted by an American college professor and his wife, respectfully played by Fredric March and Betty Field in *Tomorrow the World* (1944). What was unusual about this film was that the Third Reich philosophy was being parroted by a member of the new generation, complete with rantings about what to do with "undesirable races." Homeier had a film career through the 1950s but is best remembered for this brutal and chilling 1944 role.

Shortly after the government released information of the Japanese torturing American prisoners, 20th Century Fox distributed *The Purple Heart* (1944), starring Dana Andrews, Richard Conte, Farley Granger, and Kevin O'Shea. Darryl Zanuck tapped Lewis Milestone (*All Quiet on the Western Front*) to direct from a script by Jerome Cady and rewritten by Zanuck himself under his pseudonym Melville Crossman.

The plot centered around eight crewmen of an American B-25 downed after Doolittle's raid. The Americans are brought into Japanese criminal court and charged with "murder." Various tortures are employed to get the airmen to give information about American bomber bases. The men are beaten and tortured but stand together in refusing to reveal any pertinent information.

Chinese-born Richard Loo was at his evil best, smirking as a decorated Japanese officer, complete with shaved head. Andrews emerges as the group's leader at film's end. His fade-out flag-waving dialogue pointed to the nation's anger, again echoing the vicar's speech in *Mrs. Miniver*. "This is your war, you wanted it, you asked for it," says Andrews to the Japanese court. "And now you're going to get it. And it won't be finished until your dirty little empire is wiped off the face of the earth."

David O. Selznick was so gripped by *The Purple Heart* at a private screening that the next morning he wrote a quick note to Lewis Milestone:

Dear Milly,
   Please accept my enthusiastic congratulations on the beautiful job of direction you did on "Purple Heart," which I finally saw last night.
   Cordially
   David[32]

MGM used a poem by Alice Duer Miller as a basis for the 1944 screenplay of *The White Cliffs of Dover*, starring Irene Dunne and Frank Morgan. Critics called the film a tribute to English gentility, as Dunne portrayed an American who marries into a British family, only to lose a husband in World War I and a son in World War II. Others in the cast were Metro contract players including Roddy McDowall, C. Aubrey Smith, and Dame May Whitty. It was Peter Lawford's debut film.

George J. Folsey won an Academy Award nomination for his cinematography.

## OVERLORD IN FRANCE

By early 1944 it had become more apparent that the long-awaited invasion of the European continent was getting closer. Sicily was now in Allied hands. The American Fifth Army was slowly fighting its way toward Rome.

In England, the largest invasion force in the history of Western civilization was being formed under a cloud of secrecy. There were approximately 1,108 Allied camps with 3 million men in uniform waiting for the word to go.

Many observers had long felt that General George C. Marshall, serving at the time as chairman of the Joint Chiefs and President Roosevelt's chief military adviser, would be named as Supreme Commander of the Allied Expeditionary Forces to coordinate the invasion, code-named Overlord.

General Marshall asked President Roosevelt to be relieved of his duties in Washington and be reassigned as the Commander of Overlord. After listening to his plea Roosevelt told him, "General Marshall, I don't think I could sleep at night with you out of Washington."

The Supreme Commander post went to General Dwight Eisenhower, who had commanded the American forces in North Africa and Sicily. During these operations, Eisenhower had demonstrated a remarkable diplomatic ability to get along with the inflated egos of General de Gaulle, Field Marshal Montgomery, General George Patton, and General Mark Clark.

Hitler always felt that the invasion would come at Calais, the closest French landfall to England. British intelligence, deciphering the German code known as the "Ultra Intercepts," had known for some time that Calais was assumed, by the Nazis, to be the site. American army intelligence purposefully had General Patton's Third Army and Sixth Armored Division train at Dover to give the impression that Calais was indeed the invasion point.

The German general staff also felt that the Allies would attempt the invasion under ideal weather conditions at the closest landfall.

On the morning of June 4, Field Marshal Erwin Rommel left his French coastal headquarters ostensibly to visit his wife, in Berlin, whose birthday fell on the sixth. His main purpose was to pay a call at Berchtesgaden to convince Hitler to transfer two additional armored divisions and a mortar brigade to Normandy. Rommel told his staff, on several occasions, that the Allies must be beaten back on the first day. That day, he added, would be "The Longest Day."

A Luftwaffe meteorologist in Paris filed a report that no Allied invasion could be expected within the next two weeks because of heavy weather conditions in the Channel.

The Allied planners purposefully chose to make a wide channel crossing to Normandy, rather than a presumed landing at Calais. Allied intelligence felt that landing at Calais was too obvious and that the coastal terrain between the foot of the Cotentin Peninsula on the west and the line of the Orne River was accessible to the huge logistical problems of men and materiel.

The waiting became nerve–racking. Eisenhower was informed that a break in the weather over the English Channel would come on the night of June 5. He called his staff together, realizing that another delay would place the entire operation in jeopardy. After hearing the pros and cons, Eisenhower turned to Montgomery, whose reply was, "I would say go."

Eisenhower took a long pause and then said, "All right, we'll go."

The Supreme Commander would later confide to friends that he would be history's whipping boy if the Allies were repulsed at the beaches. This dramatic moment was destined to happen from the onset of the North African invasion.

That night, nearly 5,000 ships headed out and moved across the Channel as the most heavily participated and planned military event in the history of modern warfare began to unfold.

The skies filled with 1,200 transport planes and gliders. As dawn broke, the invasion armada approached the five landing beaches on the Normandy coast to which Allied intelligence assigned the code names: Sword, Juno, Gold, Omaha, and Utah. Approximately 12,000 Allied planes participated in the invasion.

In Leesburg, Virginia, General Marshall was taking time off to tend to his garden when a phone call came. It was General Frank McCarthy of the General Staff. He explained to Mrs. Marshall that he had to speak with the general. Marshall came to the phone, listened, and nodded. He then hung up and began walking back to the garden.

Mrs. Marshall wanted to know what was so important that was answered with only a nod and "I see. . . . Well, okay."

Marshall told his wife in a quiet voice, "We landed at Normandy during the night."

She suggested that possibly he ought to go into the office. Marshall shook his head. "No, there's nothing I can do now. Besides, Eisenhower will have to handle it."

The Nazi general staff was informed at 3:00 A.M. that paratrooper and glider landings were taking place in and around Normandy. At Berchtesgaden, General Alfred Jodl felt it was a diversionary attack. The führer headquarters, upon intercepting a dummy Allied intelligence report, was still convinced that the main invasion point would be Calais. Jodl refused to wake the führer for consultation.

Finally, at 9:00 A.M., Hitler was awakened. He emerged from his bedroom in a robe and listened to the reports from his generals. The führer then turned and went back to his bedroom.

The war effort and the American war film had turned a major corner. As the dramatic events began to unfold on the Normandy coast, Hollywood, as always, was listening and watching. Within the next three decades what went on in France during those few days would be reenacted or used as a back story in countless American war films.

## PACIFIC ISLAND HOPPING

On October 20, 1944, General Douglas MacArthur fulfilled his promise "I shall return" when he stepped off a landing craft, with his staff, and waded ashore at Leyte beach in the Philippines. But the battle was far from won. By October 25, it seemed that the Japanese naval forces might succeed in a counterattack through Leyte Gulf. Admiral William Halsey's Third Fleet steamed northward in search of Admiral Jisaburo Ozawa's force leaving the San Bernardino straits with a slim force. The outgunned American navy rose to the occasion and held on. However, Halsey and Admiral Thomas Kincaid of the Seventh Fleet would argue for years as to what might have happened. It has often been said that Leyte Gulf was the most important naval battle since Jutland in 1916.

On February 19, 1945, units from the 3rd, 4th, and 5th Marine Divisions assaulted Iwo Jima in the Bonin Islands. The island was crucial because of the Motoyama airfield, which would be used to refuel American bombers headed for the Japanese home islands. It was the worst landing experience of the war for the marines. Many of the wounded were evacuated to the beach, where they were wounded again by repeated mortar attacks.

After days of constant naval gunfire the marine assault force crossed the lines of departure and headed for the beach. The fighting was brutal, unlike anything the marines had experienced before. The Japanese defenders were steadfast in obeying orders to fight until the last man. The American casualties continued to mount. There were nighttime attacks where Japanese soldiers would emerge from spider holes and caves. As daylight approached, the Japanese would retreat, only to come up again at an opportune time.

Within a week there was grave concern back in the United States as to the price the marines would pay to secure Iwo Jima. On February 27, William Randolph Hearst ran a front-page editorial in the *San Francisco Examiner* contending that the slaughter on Iwo had to stop. He called for General Douglas MacArthur to be placed in command of the entire operation. Hearst had long been an admirer of MacArthur and often praised the general.

Hearst, a product of private schools and a privileged background, had never worn a uniform. An extremely opinionated man, he often gave unsolicited advice to President Roosevelt, on radio, as to the correct way to run the country. And now he was telling the military who to place in command of an invasion thousands of miles away.

Marines at Camp Pendleton, halfway between Los Angeles and San Diego, were enraged at the editorial. Many of them held the belief that General Mac-Arthur was responsible for the lack of prepardness in the Philippines following the Pearl Harbor attack. Camp Pendleton marines were so upset with the Hearst editorial that a convoy departed Camp Pendleton and arrived at the *San Francisco Examiner* offices to protest the publisher's suggestion.

When the island was declared secure, on March 16, some 6,821 Americans had been killed, 20,000 wounded, over one-third of those who had landed. The Japanese defense force on Iwo Jima of 21,000 died almost to the man. When photographer Joe Rosenthal's reenactment photo of five marines and a navy corpsman planting the flag atop Mount Suribachi was released, it added to the public mystique of the battle. It also added inspiration for one of John Wayne's more memorable films.

The marines, who had endured more than their share of gruelling combat at Guadalcanal, Makin Island, Bougainville, Tarawa, Guam, Tinian, Kwajalein, Saipan, and Pelilieu, now went into the hardest fighting of the Pacific war— Okinawa. The island siege began on Easter morning and lasted until June 1945. The U.S. fleet stood off the island and endured repeated suicide attacks from Japanese kamikaze planes that sunk thirty-eight American warships. Like Iwo Jima, the Japanese troops fought to the end, with the senior officers opting for ritual suicide (*seppuku*). Many in the civilian population, who believed that the Americans would kill them when the island was taken, also committed suicide by throwing themselves off cliffs.

The American victory at Okinawa was costly. And it gave the Truman administration a warning of what awaited the armed forces in the upcoming invasion of the home islands—that the Japanese military was committed in a fight to the death.

During this time, the major propaganda phase in American war films began to wind down. War production had approached its peak.

## A MIST CALLED AUTUMN

Approximately six weeks after the Normandy Invasion, a daring attempt on Hitler's life was made by a cadre of Nazi field-grade officers at Rastenberg, his field headquarters in East Prussia. Hitler miraculously survived by a quirk of fate. The briefcase containing the hastily assembled bomb was placed under a heavy oak table. The wooden support, under the table, shielded the führer from the full impact. Hitler suffered a wound to his right arm. However the führer, who was able to keep an afternoon meeting with Mussolini, interpreted his survival as proof of his destiny, to lead the German people to "their former glory."

Like the aftermath of the Heydrich assassination, he retaliated with a string of swift and brutal executions. Anyone remotely suspected of having any knowledge of the July 20 plot was arrested, tried, convicted, and sentenced to death. The first group was simply lined up in front of firing squads. More convicted conspirators were hung with cattle wire. These executions were filmed. Hitler watched the films repeatedly. General Erwin Rommel, whom Hitler privately envied for his popularity, was suspected of being peripherally involved in the plot. Rommel was later permitted to take poison in the back seat of a staff car in order to save his wife and son from any retaliation. He was then given an elaborate state funeral.

In his own mind, Adolf Hitler was far from through. In a September meeting with the general staff, he suddenly came up with a plan to mount an offensive through the Ardennes forest to cut the British off at Antwerp.

In Hitler's vision, it was to be a winter offensive, code-named *Herbstnebel*, Autumn Mist. Many in the general staff felt that the concept was wrong, a combined infantry and armored thrust across arduous terrain during the winter.

Plans for Autumn Mist went forward, proving to be the last gasp of the Third Reich that would be engraved as the Battle of the Bulge. It began in the early dark hours of December 16 and lasted into the first weeks of 1945. The doubting Nazi general officers proved to be correct. The logistics and manpower needed to sustain any drive over the Allies had long since been exhausted.

Many Nazi leaders already knew it was just a question of time before Berlin was taken. But Autumn Mist was nonetheless a jolt to the Allies, reminding them that victory over the Third Reich was far from complete.

Hitler had suspected that the Allies had somehow cracked his intelligence code, the Ultra Intercepts, that employed the Enigma machine. Preparation messages for Autumn Mist bypassed using the Enigma code machine.

The Autumn Mist breakthrough toward Antwerp was swift and deadly, exploding with an artillery barrage in the predawn hours. One of the American infantry units placed along the front was the inexperienced 106th Division. It would surrender 8,000 men to the Nazis, a number exceeded only by the American surrender at Bataan.

Nazis employed English-speaking soldiers to pose as GIs, infiltrating mostly at night. Approximately ninety-five American prisoners were executed in a field outside Malmedy. It was a war crime that would later cause overreaction, with trials and executions, and be portrayed in several American war films.

The civilian population in Belgium began to panic with the very thought of the country being returned to Nazi occupation. A contingency plan was drawn up in the event that Paris would have to be evacuated by the Allies. The 101st Airborne Division, under the temporary command of Colonel Tony McAuliffe, found itself surrounded at Bastogne in the middle of one of the worst winters ever recorded in Western Europe. When the Nazi commander met with McAuliffe, to entreat surrender terms he listened for the translation in German. It was only one word.

"Nuts!" answered McAuliffe.

The fighting continued as the American army fought to take back the ground it had lost. Because of thick fog, air support was nonexistent. General George S. Patton's Third Army broke through to relieve Bastogne. Patton remarked that any man who says "Nuts!" to the Nazis had to be saved.

Finally, by the day after Christmas, the weather broke and air support flooded the skies. On January 3, Field Marshal Montgomery ordered a counterattack along the British front. The Nazi Panzer divisions began to retreat.

The Bulge was costly: 19,000 fatal casualties with 15,000 taken prisoner. The optimism, about the end being near, that had been so prevalent in Washington and London was noticeably shaken.

What the Battle of the Bulge did was to cause a delay in the Allies' thrust into Germany. Again materiel and reinforcements foretold what was to come. Even though the British army had come to the end of reinforcements, the Americans' production peak was in full force. The German army could not keep up, even with daily attrition. All Hitler did was stall for some breathing room.

The European events from the breakout at Normandy through the liberation of Paris and the officers' plot on Hitler to the Battle of the Bulge would serve as backgrounds for many war films through the Korean and Vietnam eras and beyond. The tastes of American audiences changed. But as World War I demonstrated, the audiences always returned to the war film genre.


## A TERRIFIC HEADACHE

On March 30, 1945, a special train pulled into the depot next to the Warm Springs Hotel in Georgia. Dozens of people were there to greet the train and its passengers.

At the rear of the train, from an observation platform, a small elevator descended carrying a wheelchair. In the wheelchair was a big man, in a slouching position, with a hat pulled over his eyes. Several people in the crowd gasped at the sickly appearance of the man whom they had come to know as another neighbor in this village of 600.

The man in the wheelchair was Franklin Delano Roosevelt.

One of the greeters approached Merriman Smith, a UPI (United Press International) White House correspondent. "Is he all right?" she asked.

"Tired to death," replied Smith. "But he'll pull out of it. He always does."

C.A. Pless, the station agent, remarked that Roosevelt was "the worst looking man I ever saw who was still alive."

This working vacation was designed as a recuperation period after the physically punishing trip to the Yalta Conference, held February 4–11, 1945. In addition, the UN conference in San Francisco loomed on the horizon.

Mrs. Roosevelt remained in Washington.

Critics of the Yalta Conference later argued that not enough time was given to discussion before the important decisions were made, such as occupation zones of Berlin and the prosecution of war criminals. Roosevelt was the one who had to travel the farthest. And he did on the condition that the conference be limited to one week.

Ever since Hitler failed to occupy Moscow, Stalin carefully waited for the Soviet Union's time. And now the time had come. Roosevelt's critics would later claim that he "sold out" to Stalin and sealed Eastern Europe and Manchuria to communism.

Many of the people attending the conference, including Churchill, remarked privately about Roosevelt's physical deterioration. For decades afterward many observers felt that the cunning Stalin took advantage of Roosevelt's declining health and maneuvered the postwar fate of Eastern Europe to his advantage.

The staff at the Little White House had never seen Roosevelt look so incapacitated. Lizzie McDuffie, a black maid, remarked that he looked feeble. And it worried her.

By April 12 the president looked much better. Roosevelt began the day by reading the *Atlanta Constitution* that accompanied his breakfast tray.

The *Atlanta Constitution* headlines were not news to him, although they were nice to see:

> 9th 57 Miles From Berlin
> 50-Mile Gain In Day
> Sets Stage For Early
> U.S.–Russ Juncture

The lead of the story stated that armored columns of the U.S. Ninth Army were within fifty-seven miles of Berlin and advancing to the Elbe River.

The news from the Pacific was equally good:

> 150 Superforts Hammer Tokyo
> In Two Hour Daylight Raid

Another story, with a London dateline, carried a report that Adolf Hitler was in broken health and had been forced to give control to SS Reichsfuehrer Heinrich Himmler.

The president came across an account, on the inside pages, that the war to date had taken the lives of 196,669 Americans. The total casualties—killed, wounded, and missing—were 899,390. This was an increase of 6,481 from the previous week.

He knew that the daily mail from Washington was due shortly. Also scheduled that afternoon was a session with Madame Elizabeth Shoumatoff, who was working on a portrait of Roosevelt.

The president then held a short meeting with three reporters assigned to the Little White House. The question came up about a White House announcement concerning the Soviet Union getting three votes in the UN General Assembly.

A reporter asked, "Do you think we'll have the chance to talk with you again on other subjects before you go [to San Francisco], such as the three-to-one vote?"

Roosevelt nodded and said that he would see them several times before the conference.

The president then fiddled with some papers on a card table next to his chair. His 998th press conference had ended.

A little before noon the president was sitting in a leather armchair, his back to the wall of windows that overlooked a broad array of pines out on the lawn. Two cousins, Margaret Suckley and Laura Delano, were in the room. Also in the room was Lucy Mercer, now known as Mrs. Winthrop Rutherford, who had been widowed for the past year.

Aide Bill Hassett entered with Dewey Long, the White House transportation officer. Hassett was carrying the mail pouch from Washington. He noticed that the president was wearing a dark gray suit and a Harvard red four-in-hand tie. He thought that the tie was odd since the president was partial to bowties. Moreover, the president was wearing a vest; FDR was known to dislike vests. Hassett assumed that his boss had acquiesced to the requests of Madame Shoumatoff.

Because of the large volume of mail, Hassett suggested that the president might want to wait until after lunch to begin the reading and signing. Roosevelt shook his head and said he wanted to start right away. Madame Shoumatoff was due shortly.

The first letter Hassett placed in front of the president had a State Department letterhead. Roosevelt read it and then said, "A typical State Department letter. It says nothing at all."

Madame Shoumatoff entered and began setting up her easel near the windows.

Several minutes later Roosevelt gripped the arms of the leather armchair and swung himself into a straight-back Dutch-style chair that had been fitted with rollers.

Madame Shoumatoff placed a navy blue cape on Roosevelt's shoulders and carefully arranged the folds. She then went behind the easel and began working.

The president continued reading and signing mail. Later he glanced at his watch and looked at Madame Shoumatoff. "We've got just fifteen minutes more."

As Madame Shoumatoff continued working she knew it was futile to have the president separate himself from his reading for the remaining time. The president then slid a Camel cigarette into his holder and lit it. Madame Shoumatoff noticed that he raised his left hand to his temple and pressed it. The hand moved around to his forehead. Roosevelt seemed to be squeezing it. Then his hand flopped down.

Miss Suckley thought that he had dropped the cigarette in his lap and was groping for it. She asked, "Did you drop something?"

The president then pressed the palm of his left hand behind his neck. His head was leaning forward. His eyes were closed. Quietly he said, "I . . . have a . . . terrific headache."

He said it so quietly that Miss Suckley was the only one who heard it. It was inaudible to Madame Shoumatoff, who was standing at her easel only six feet away.

The president's arm slipped down, and his head tilted slightly to the left. Then his caped body sagged in the chair. The time was 1:15.

Miss Delano and Miss Suckley quickly approached the slumped president. Each grabbed a shoulder to prevent him from falling out of the chair.

Miss Suckley turned to Madame Shoumatoff and calmly said, "Ask the secret service man to call a doctor immediately."

Madame Shoumatoff left her easel and quickly exited the room.

Miss Suckley then picked up the phone. She announced herself to the White House operator as Daisy Suckley, using a nickname.

At 4:00 that afternoon, Washington time, a black White House limousine dropped off Mrs. Roosevelt at the seventeenth annual Tea and Entertainment of the Thrift Shop, a fashionable Washington charity, being held at the Sulgrave Club. She already was informed that there was a problem at the Little White House.

She sat at the head table between Mrs. John A. Dougherty, chairwoman of the event, and Mrs. Woodrow Wilson. Nobody suspected that the First Lady was putting up a brave front, masking feelings of grave concern.

Mrs. Roosevelt was then notified that she was wanted on the phone. The First Lady seemed surprised, got up, and quickly left the table.

Steve Early, the president's press secretary, asked Mrs. Roosevelt to return at once to the White House. She didn't even ask why, but instinctively she knew that something dreadful had occurred at Warm Springs. Feeling that appearances must be kept up at such a stressful time, Mrs. Roosevelt returned to the celebration. She kept a pleasant look on her face, not giving anyone the slightest clue as to what was really running through her thoughts. At an opportune moment Mrs. Roosevelt stood and apologized for leaving early.

Mrs. Roosevelt later recalled that she sat with clenched fists on the ride back to the White House, feeling that the worst had indeed happened. It wasn't what was said on the phone; it was what wasn't said.

On Capitol Hill that afternoon Vice President Harry Truman was on his way to the "hideaway" office of House Speaker Sam Rayburn of Texas. Rayburn took pride in stocking his second office bar with miniature bottles of the best lines of southern bourbon. The vice president was part of a group that met with Rayburn frequently, as they would put it, "to strike a blow for liberty."

When the vice president arrived at the Rayburn office, glasses were already filled. Besides the Speaker, Lew Deschler, Parliamentarian of the House of Representatives, was present, along with James M. Barnes, a White House legislative assistant. The usual topics at these gatherings were upcoming bills.

Sam Rayburn handed the vice president a glass of bourbon and water upon his entrance. The Speaker added that Steve Early had called from the White House and needed to talk with him right away. Truman immediately picked up the phone. At the White House Early told the vice president to come right over and enter through the main Pennsylvania Avenue entrance. Early added that the vice president was to come up to Mrs. Roosevelt's suite on the second floor.

Truman later said that he assumed the president had returned from Warm Springs.

The vice president's limousine drove through the northwest gate of the White House at 5:25 P.M. An usher then escorted Truman to an elevator that went to Mrs. Roosevelt's second-floor suite. As he entered the room and saw the expression on the First Lady's face, he knew something out of the ordinary was coming. Besides Mrs. Roosevelt and Steve Early the president's daughter Anna and her husband, Colonel John Boettiger, were in the room.

Mrs. Roosevelt then stepped forward and softly placed her arm on Truman's shoulder. Then she quietly said, "Harry, the President is dead."

Truman was speechless for several moments. He remembered reading news reports that the president was recuperating nicely in Warm Springs.

He then asked Mrs. Roosevelt, "Is there anything I can do for you?"

The First Lady replied, "Harry, is there anything *we* can do for *you*? You are the one in trouble now."

Harry Truman would remember those sentences for the rest of his life.

At 5:48 P.M. the first report went out on the International News Service (INS) wires:

FLASH. WASHINGTON—PRESIDENT ROOSEVELT DIED THIS AFTERNOON.

It was later followed up that cause of death was a suspected cerebral hemmorrhage.

In New York City, executives at NBC made a decision. At 5:49 P.M. an announcer broke into the radio drama *Front Page Farrell* with the Roosevelt death announcement. Within the minute ABC broke into the *Captain Midnight* show. The Mutual Network then followed, interrupting *Tom Mix*.

As the first announcements were going across the country Harry Truman went downstairs and into the Oval Office, where he would conduct the nation's business for the next seven years. In the office he attempted to call his wife Bess and daughter Margaret. He had difficulty getting through.

Finally the vice president got through to the Truman apartment in northwest Washington. Margaret answered the phone and gave it to Bess. Margaret then went to her bedroom to prepare for a date.

Several minutes later Bess Truman was standing at Margaret's door. She tried to say something but couldn't. She continued staring at her daughter.

"Mother, what's the matter? What is it?"

"President Roosevelt is dead."

At the White House, Chief Justice Harlan Stone arrived and waited nervously for the beginning of the swearing-in ceremony, which was to take place in the Cabinet Room. Bill Simmons, a staff member, then went from office to office, frantically searching through the Executive Wing for a Bible. Suddenly he recalled seeing one in Bill Hassett's office, an inexpensive red-edged Nelson and Sons Bible.

Returning to the Cabinet Room, with the Bible, Simmons apologized to the vice president for taking so long. Several cabinet members were now in attendance, along with Mrs. Truman (who appeared red-eyed) and Margaret.

There was a hush in the room. A clock on the mantel read 7:09 P.M. as Vice President Harry Truman, under life-sized portraits of Woodrow Wilson and Franklin Roosevelt, raised his right hand to take the oath of office from Chief Justice Harlan Stone as the thirty-third president of the United States. For the first time in a dozen years a man other than Franklin D. Roosevelt would be chief executive. And for the seventh time in the nation's history a man was sworn in as president while the previous one had yet to be buried.

Another flash went out on the wire services. It contained only three words: "Truman sworn in!"

Within moments staff members and photographers shuffled out of the room to allow President Truman to hold his first cabinet meeting.

When the meeting ended, seventy-seven-year-old Secretary of War Henry Stimson remained behind, waiting to be alone with the new president. Grim and choosing his words slowly, Secretary Stimson began to tell President Truman that he should be aware of a top secret project that was being developed of which only a handful of people were aware. He added that it was an explosive of almost unbelievable destructive power.

Truman had long suspected that a top secret project was being developed but had been kept out of the official information loop. He knew immediately that eventually he would have to make a decision about this unbelievable destructive power.

When the first flashes went out on the Armed Forces radio networks servicemen around the world stopped what they were doing, caught by the emotions of disbelief, shock, and bewilderment. Why did this happen now, just when victory seemed so certain? From that moment on members of the World War II generation would recall what they were doing when two historical incidents occurred: Pearl Harbor and the death of Franklin Delano Roosevelt.[33]

## THE GENRE CHANGES

"I wonder whose side God is on?" was a question attributed to a Nazi general after the Normandy invasion. But in Warner Bros. *God Is My Co-Pilot* (1945), there was no room for debate. This was one of the last "propaganda" films to be released in this period. And, appropriately enough, it came from Warner Bros.

The script was adapted from the autobiography of Colonel Robert L. Scott Jr., who attended West Point and later became a highly profiled pilot as a volunteer in General Claire Chennault's "Flying Tigers" before Pearl Harbor in the China-Burma-India theater of operations.

In the American tradition Scott wrote about his boyhood, becoming fascinated with flying. One of his first experiences was jumping off a barn roof using an umbrella as a parachute. The total wartime credit to Scott came to shooting down thirteen Japanese planes.

While he was with the Flying Tigers, Scott downed three Japanese planes, including the famous ace "Tokyo Joe." In the spring of 1942 he transferred to the Army Air Force and commanded a fighter group in the Western Pacific.

The supporting cast included Raymond Massey as Chennault and Alan Hale as "Big Mike" Harrigan, a missionary priest who lectures Scott and restores his faith in religion. Dennis Morgan, as Scott, has to learn that he's not alone up there in the cockpit of his fighter plane. "You've got the greatest co-pilot in the world," explains Father Harrigan.

With the standard cadre of Chinese actors playing Japanese pilots the enemy is routed at film's end. Richard Loo put a new spin on his career as the stereotypical Japanese officer, portraying Tokyo Joe, whose death in flames made American audiences applaud. In another stretch of propaganda imagination, Morgan and Loo have battle conversations, exchanging barbs over the same radio frequency in English.

After Lieutenant Commander John Ford returned from his photographic field assignment, he set out to direct *They Were Expendable* for MGM. The film was in production as U.S. forces were preparing for the invasion of the Japanese home islands. Ford used Frank "Spig" Wead, a decorated navy pilot, to adapt the screenplay from the book of the same name by William L. White.

The book's hero was a character patterned after Lieutenant John Bulkeley whose Motor Torpedo boat, PT 41, in 1942, was assigned with getting General MacArthur and his staff safely out of the Philippines.

In addition to MacArthur's departure, the film also dealt with the Japanese invasion of the Philippines and the fate of the army nurses after the fall of the Philippine Defense Command.

If MacArthur had used any other mode to escape, it is likely that PT boats in the Pacific would have passed through the war in obscurity. But this historical incident left its figurative wake. In 1942 the country needed war heroes. And the Bulkeley image, portrayed in the book, which was excerpted in *Reader's Digest*, gave the PT boat squadrons a national romantic image.

In reality many navy officials felt that PT boats were an anachronism, plywood boats without radar, with four torpedo tubes, two light machine gun emplacements, powered by extremely inflammable fuel. However, they were ballyhooed as the "cavalry of the navy," paralleled to the British Spitfire fighter plane that helped win the Battle of Britain.

As an accomplished public speaker Bulkeley gave inspiring recruiting talks to groups of midshipmen and officers around the country. Bulkeley also talked realistically about the high mortality rate in the Motor Torpedo Boat squadrons.

During one speech he added, "Those of you who want to come back after the war and raise families need not apply. P.T. boat skippers are not coming back!"

One of the ensigns who happened to hear Bulkeley speak at Northwestern

University was twenty-five-year-old John F. Kennedy, who was deeply concerned about forever bearing the stigma of seeing the war at a stateside desk job. Ensign Kennedy, along with many of his peers, flocked to apply for Motor Torpedo Boat training at Melville, Rhode Island. They did so with youthful, romantic, reckless abandon, knowing what the survival rate was.

It could be said that a version of this syndrome was written in the previous war, where Paul Baumer leaves a classroom with his peers to plunge headlong into the fighting in *All Quiet on the Western Front*. And like that story, Kennedy's tour of duty in a Motor Torpedo Boat squadron would first appear in print and then a film.

Before heading to the Solomon Islands, Kennedy wrote to his former Harvard roommate Lemoyne Billings, "So far in the war the fatalities in P.T.'s are ten men killed for every survivor."

When Ford and MGM cast *They Were Expendable*, Robert Montgomery (fresh off active duty) portrayed Lieutenant John Brickley, leader of a small torpedo boat squadron based in Manila, patterned on Bulkeley, who was a friend of Ford's.

John Wayne played Lieutenant Rusty Ryan, Montgomery's executive officer, who is as skeptical about the performance of PT boats as the navy brass, until Pearl Harbor.

The crews, referred to as "expendables," were often assigned dangerous and near-suicidal missions during the war. Many veterans recounted that the only good the torpedo boats did was rescuing downed American pilots.

The major highlight in the film is getting MacArthur (portrayed by Robert Barrat) out of the Philippines. Some veterans, who no doubt recalled the fall of the Philippine Defense Command, felt that Ford went over the top in "deifying" MacArthur.

Donna Reed was Wayne's love interest, a nurse who is left behind on Corregidor.

As propaganda took its much-needed back seat to the stark realism of war, United Artists acquired the rights to combat correspondent Ernie Pyle's tribute to the American infantryman in the Italian campaign. *The Story of G.I. Joe* (1945) was called by General Dwight Eisenhower, "The best war film I have ever seen."

Three writers are credited with adapting Pyle's book: Leopold Atlas, Guy Endore, and Philip Stevenson. United Artists gave the director's job to William Wellman (*Wings*). Pyle, much admired by the infantrymen about whom he wrote, had the deserved reputation of getting the best, and most gripping, combat stories. His method was simple: Get in the foxholes with the men, eat their rations, share their stories, and feel their grief at a buddy's death. Burgess Meredith gave a convincing portrayal of Pyle.

The story line was typical of the war film genre: A group of Americans thrown together in an infantry unit become an efficient combat team as they slug through the difficult Italian campaign, devoid of false heroics. Their loyal company commander is Robert Mitchum in his only Oscar-nominated performance.

When Mitchum dies the warrior's death he is brought out on a donkey, in a biblical metaphor. As Private Dandaro, Wally Cassell's poignant farewell is done in silence, a tribute to a fallen leader.

Pyle and several of his peers, combat correspondents all, gave technical advice to the production. And true to his war film form, director Wellman stripped the story of clichés and propaganda, telling American audiences, "This is what it's like."

After production was completed, Pyle was reassigned to the Western Pacific. On the morning of April 18, 1945, during the Okinawa campaign, Pyle was reporting from the nearby island of Ie Shima.

Fifty-three years after the fact, Bill King, a junior major assigned as an operations officer in a gun battalion attached to the 10th Army, would recall the dramatic last moments in the life of the famed war correspondent.

At the time of the Pyle incident we were on a patrol to select sites to place gun batteries. As our patrol was walking single file we noticed a jeep coming down the roadway (an unpaved oxcart road). As the jeep was adjacent to our patrol the enemy opened fire. . . . Occupants of the jeep and our patrol dove into the ditch on the south side of the roadway. It was a "keep your head down situation."

One of the occupants of the jeep crawled up to me and asked that I move over—I was partially covering a person. He was identified to me as Ernie Pyle. Blood and brain tissue appeared to be in Pyle's helmet. The corpsman in our patrol crawled over and told us what was already evident—Pyle was dead.[34]

King also said that it was possible that the Japanese gun crew thought that Pyle was a general because he was riding in a jeep and wearing a field jacket, which made him stand out in comparison to the troops.

According to King, someone later marked the spot with a hastily painted sign. That was later replaced by a bigger sign. Eventually a monument was erected at the site where the beloved war correspondent, Ernie Pyle, was killed in action.

Right along with these historical incidents, precipitated by President Roosevelt's sudden death, the American war film began to move into its realistic phase. These late World War II films were the vanguard of the coming realistic dramas. For American audiences the wartime propaganda bloom was coming off the rose.

The infantry realism continued as the war began to wind down. In 1945, 20th Century Fox released *A Walk in the Sun*, directed by Lewis Milestone (*All Quiet on the Western Front, The Purple Heart*). Robert Rossen adapted Harry Brown's novel of the same name. Brown, a Harvard-educated soldier, was the editor of *Yank Magazine*.

The story was simple, following an army squad in the Salerno campaign in 1943. Dana Andrews, as Sergeant Tyne, keeps his squad in line as they inch toward their objective in the hot Italian sun, blowing up a bridge and taking a farmhouse where a Nazi machine gun emplacement threatens to halt their advance. Milestone used interesting camera angles, showing the farmhouse attack from the Nazi's point of view. Throughout this production he used camera angles that he had experimented with many times before.

The men in the squad come from everywhere, and they lovingly talk of "back home." Richard Conte reflects on summer holidays in Coney Island. John Ireland is the proverbial Greek Chorus, writing to Frances, his off-screen sister, telling her of the mundane doings that are forced on riflemen, moving forward, overcoming fear and exhaustion. Others in the cast included Sterling Holloway, George Tyne, Richard Benedict, Norman Lloyd, Huntz Hall, and Lloyd Bridges.

Norman Lloyd's fatal wound at film's end was foreshadowed with his character wondering, in the first act, how many would be lost. His view of war was that "nobody dies." When he takes his death wound, those are his last words.

Like *All Quiet on the Western Front*, Milestone made the ending more cinematic with the assault on the farmhouse. After the farmhouse is taken the men enjoy the fruits of a skirmish victory, example, fresh oranges and apples and a bottle of wine. And then they get back to the war.

After *A Walk in the Sun* was released, Sam Fuller, himself a combat veteran with the First Infantry Division, wrote a lengthy letter of surprising disappointment to Lewis Milestone. Part of Fuller's letter stated:

Aside from the fact that you undoubtedly paid no attention to the story of "A Walk in the Sun" or to the shabby, forced, remarks made by riflemen (why is it that every movie has to have a riflemen talk about Brooklyn or Coney Island?) or to the stupidity of making such an epic out of knocking out a bridge—I was startled because the warmth you had in "All Quiet . . ." was so damned sincere.

I still have faith in the man who landed "All Quiet . . ." with such sock, and some day, as I said before, when the people are ready for it I'm going to put a yarn in your hands that will make your mouth water because it will be real with no message; no chatter about letters to Dear Mom, Dear Ruth or Dear Sis; it will show how doggies [infantrymen] went out of their way to get the million dollar wound; it will expose the "you shoot me and I shoot you" routine that made the rounds before every assault.

The day of Tom Mix and the Patent Leather kid are over, I believe. I don't see why people still like to wear those rosy glasses and write such rosy scenes.

     With keen disappointment,
     Samuel Fuller[35]

Fuller would eventually fulfill his prophecy, making the first disturbing and penetrating Korean War film, *The Steel Helmet*, (1951) five years later. He would then go on to make his personal epic, *The Big Red One* (1980) with Lee Marvin in the title role, a tribute to his own army infantry unit.

John Hersey's award-winning novel *A Bell for Adano* was snapped up by 20th Century Fox for a 1945 release with the same title. It came to be known as the first film to deal with end-of-the war effects on Americans as wartime turned to occupation.

The cast included John Hodiak, Gene Tierney, William Bendix, Richard Conte, and Henry Morgan.

Hodiak, as an army major, attempts to secure a bell for an Italian village whose inhabitants are tired of fascism and distrustful of Americans. Tierney plays a young village woman who becomes attracted to Hodiak despite her initial feelings.

An element to the story line was altered because of censorship, portraying the military in a bad light. The novel had a brutally negative American general who had to be convinced that not all Italians were fascists. The general's character was cut from the script with the antagonists simply being referred to as "higher ups" or "the brass."

Despite military bureaucracy Hodiak and Bendix are able to get the village bell, destroyed in the war, replaced.

## THE BUNKER

As the American war films began to take on a more realistic air the circle around Berlin got tighter with the British and Americans advancing from the west, the Russians from the east.

In Italy, Mussolini fled northward to Lake Como, attempting to reach Switzerland. He was detained and turned over to Italian partisans, along with his mistress Clara Petacci. Both were subsequently executed.

By the middle of April the U.S. Seventh Army reached Nuremberg. As the American and British units advanced, shocking reports came back describing the concentration camps.

Hitler and his general staff had retreated to the underground bunker complex beneath the chancellory where the deluded führer imagined himself in command of divisions that no longer existed.

Several staff officers attempted to persuade Hitler to make an escape, which he refused. During the next week he met with staff officers and dictated his last will. On April 30, after a brief marriage ceremony to Eva Braun, his longtime mistress, the führer passed command to Fleet Admiral Karl Dönitz. He then bid his staff farewell, poisoned his dog Blondi, and committed suicide with Braun. The bodies of Hitler and Braun were wrapped in blankets, doused with fuel, and set afire.

Berlin unconditionally surrendered on May 2. The empire that Hitler envisioned to last for a thousand years was in ruins after twelve. Ironically, the Third Reich lasted the same amount of years as the Roosevelt administration.

On May 7, at Rheims, France, General Jodl signed the official surrender of the Third Reich in front of the Supreme Allied Command, ending the war in Europe.

## A SIMPLE DECISION

On his first full day in office Truman met with the four service chiefs. Collectively, they informed the new president that the war in Europe would last for another six months and that the war in Japan would go on for another eighteen months.

In one of the interviews with author Merle Miller, for *Plain Speaking*, Truman recalled that time and quoted Washington and Jefferson, as presidents, warning how wrong generals and admirals can be. "Most of them are like horses with blinders on. They can't see beyond the end of their noses."[36]

He qualified that with an exception: General George Catlett Marshall.

On June 18 Truman met with Admiral William Leahy, his Chief of Staff, and other members of the Joint Chiefs. Leahy explained that army and marine casualties on Okinawa were 35 percent. Truman was disturbed with that figure. A similar percentage could be expected for the first invasion of the home island of Kyushu, Operation Olympic, explained Leahy.

General MacArthur's staff came up with the figure of 105,050 casualties within ninety days after D-Day. More than 50,000 would occur during the first thirty days, likewise disturbing figures.

One stratagem was to continue pounding and strangling Japan by sea and air until an unconditional surrender came.

Strangulation, if it were to be employed, would take months. By mid-July British and U.S. relations with the Soviet Union had deteriorated because of clashing issues over the divisions of postwar Europe. This would overlap to the upcoming Potsdam Conference. Despite repeated requests from the Allies, Stalin held off from coming into the Pacific war.

The long-range White House plans had the Olympic operation scheduled for November 1, 1945. Operation Coronet, the invasion of the main island of Honshu, was penciled in for March 1, 1946. The barometers of the fierce fighting on Iwo Jima and Okinawa gave suggestions that what awaited U.S. forces was a military nightmare.

General Marshall felt that the invasion of Kyushu alone would be no more difficult than Normandy.[37]

No amount of study could actually predict what the true figures would be. On July 16 President Truman was notified, by Brigadier General Leslie Groves, that the atomic bomb test in the New Mexico desert was a success. The objective of the Manhattan Project gave the president another option. Truman chose to wait until after the Potsdam Conference to make the decision.

At Potsdam, Germany, a summit meeting was held between Stalin, Truman, Churchill, and Clement Atlee. A four-power Allied Control Council would rule defeated Germany. An ultimatum was issued to Japan, to capitulate and accept the Potsdam terms of unconditional surrender.

There was no response from the Japanese government.

By the time the conference ended, Truman's mind was just about made up. According to Miller, he was convinced that if an invasion of Japan took place, "half a million soldiers on both sides would have been killed and a million more would have been maimed for life."[38]

On the other side was the never-ending argument of placing the invasion on hold and continue the B-29 raids to simply pound and starve the Japanese into surrender.

So one of the greatest, most monumental decisions in the history of civilization initally came down to numbers.

And then down on the shoulders of Harry Truman.

Truman would later tell Merle Miller, in *Plain Speaking*: "A simple decision. That was all there was to it. And I never lost any sleep over it."[39]

It was definitely the stuff of screenplay, all the elements of a movie. And decades later there would not be just one movie but several, from different angles, telling the same story about the entry into a new age.

## THE BRIDGE

The B-29 raids continued on the home islands. And on an early August morning a flight of three B-29 superfortresses moved closer to their objective in a triangular formation. In the point bomber the pilot checked his airspeed. It was marked at 200 miles per hour. The altimeter read 30,080 feet.

Back in the tail the gunner repositioned himself in his cramped seat. He was to put his armored vest on, but the space was too tight, so he let the jacket drop to his feet.

The clouds were interspaced; it would be a clear day, clear to the target, a T-shaped bridge, which would easily be seen at this altitude. In the nose the bombardier leaned forward and took another look at the reconnaissance photos. The navigator called for a change in the heading. He then informed the pilot that they were at the "initial point."

On the ground the alert was forwarded that three large enemy planes had been spotted. The radio broadcasts went out as they routinely had in the past, top alert.

The triangular formation continued to its target. The bombardier announced that the target was coming into his viewfinder. The pilot warned the crew to stand by for the tone break and the turn.

The bombardier adjusted his eyes from the black-and-white tones of the recon photos. He immediately could see the real-life contrasts below in the greens and the buildings that lined the land over to the edge of the bay. The tributaries of the river appeared brown, while the roads alongside seemed to be a dull gray.

He noticed a slight haze over the city. But it was nothing that would hinder his view of the aiming point, the bridge.

And then he saw it. "I've got it," he said.

He locked in the Aioi Bridge with the cross hairs of his bombsight. Then he made the final adjustments and turned on the tone signal. This started the automatic process for the final fifteen seconds of the bomb run. The bomb bay doors snapped open.

The load was released.

The plane gave a quick lurch forward, about ten feet.

The bombardier called out, "Bomb away!"

The bomb load dropped out of the bay and fell freely, gathering speed. The pilot, Colonel Paul Tibbets, then moved the wheel into a right-hand turn.

The bombardier looked through the plexiglass, getting a final glimpse of the bomb as it continued its fall.

Tibbets, still handling the 155-degree turn, called on the intercom, asking the tail gunner if he could see anything.

Back in the tail the gunner was spread eagled with the gravitational force of the turn. He gave a one-word answer, "Nothing."

Tibbets felt the wind resistance in the yoke, watching his altitude as the plane pulled away from the target area. Tibbets turned but could see nothing. Then he called to the tail gunner once more. The tail gunner again replied that there was nothing to see.

Approximately forty-five seconds after leaving the bomb bay, falling nearly six miles, the bomb was going to miss the aiming point by 800 feet. It detonated approximately 660 feet above a medical clinic.

There was a blinding flash of light. In the years to come, no one would ever agree on the color, whether it was pink, blue, red, or yellow.

The bright, clear, sky began turning a dark yellow as a churning cloud of smoke turned over and over again, spurting upward toward the height of 50,000 feet over the city of Hiroshima.

The tail gunner, Bob Caron, was the first crew member to see the phenomenal mushroom cloud. He tried to shout a warning into the intercom. It was unintelligible. The farthest thing from his mind was that he was the first person ever to witness an atomic bomb's shock wave in a combat zone. He yelled again as the shock wave slammed against the *Enola Gay*, bouncing the B-29 higher. A second shock wave slammed into the plane and jerked it upward again.

Captain Jacob Beser, a staff officer and observer, then moved around to each crew member with a wire recorder to get first impressions. The *Enola Gay* was now at an altitude of 29,000 feet, eleven miles from Hiroshima.

When Captain Beser came to Caron the tail gunner looked at the microphone. He knew he would be recording for history. Caron began his account:

A column of smoke is rising fast. It has a fiery red core. A bubbling mass, purple gray in color, with that red core. It's all turbulent. Fires are springing up everywhere, like flames shooting out of a huge bed of coals. I am starting to count the fires. One, two, three, four, five, six . . . fourteen, fifteen. It's impossible. There are too many to count. Here it comes, the mushroom shape that they told us about. It's like a bubbling molasses. The mushroom is spreading out. It's maybe a mile or two wide and a half mile high. It's nearly level with us and climbing. It's very black, but there is a purplish tint to the cloud. The base of the mushroom looks like a heavy undercast that is shot through with flames. The city must be below that. The flames and smoke are billowing out, whirling out into the foothills. All I can see now of the city is the main dock and what looks like an airfield. There are planes down there.

Many accounts agreed that within a 1,000-yard radius of the impact, granite buildings melted, steel and stone bridges burned, along with the Ota River. Roof tiles boiled; people evaporated, leaving shadows of themselves "photographed" like X-ray negatives on walls and pavements. In a matter of seconds four square miles of central Hiroshima was sent into extinction.

In the cockpit of the *Enola Gay* copilot Robert Lewis was waiting to speak into the wire recorder. He was thinking of something that would be historic and memorable. What he wrote on his notepad was more memorable than what he said to the recorder. It asked a simple question.

"My God, what have we done?"[40]

As with any weapon of mass destruction accounts vary as to the number of casualties. The figure of 130,000 at Hiroshima is the one most people agree upon today.

The Truman White House then called upon the Japanese government to accept the Potsdam ultimatum. If not, Japan could expect "a rain of ruin from the air."

There was no response.

On August 9 another B-29 atomic bomb raid was ordered, this time on Nagasaki, resulting in approximately 40,000 casualties.

Again the White House called upon the Japanese government to accept the Potsdam terms or face complete destruction.

On August 15 in a historic radio address to his nation Emperor Hirohito, against the advice of his military council, announced that his government would accept the Potsdam ultimatum.

However, hostilities had not entirely ended. The Japanese government had to put down a palace revolt where a cadre of army officers, among whom was General Hideki Tojo's son-in-law, attempted to sieze control of the government to continue the fight to the very end. Many of these officers, in the failed coup, chose ritual suicide.

General MacArthur, in his memoirs *Reminiscences*, stated that he was given total control as to the surrender schedule and signing. The Allies wanted the document signed as soon as possible. Lieutenant General Robert Eichelberger, commander of the Eighth Army, was named ranking officer of the advance party into Japan.[41]

The general staff flew on MacArthur's plane the *Bataan*, unarmed, from Manila to Atsugi airfield with a brief refueling stop on Okinawa. Upon reboarding the plane at Okinawa MacArthur noticed that several of his staff were checking their pistols and inserting loaded magazines into the handles of their .45 automatics. MacArthur, accustomed to the Asian culture, told them to put their weapons up, that sidearms will be useless.

"Nothing will impress them like a show of absolute fearlessness," he added. "If they don't know they're licked, this will convince them."

On the leg from Okinawa to Atsugi airfield MacArthur began dictating random thoughts to his aide, Courtney Whitney, priority items for the occupation: destroy the military power, build the structure of a military government, enfranchise the Japanese women, free the political prisoners, liberate the farmers, establish free labor, encourage a free economy, abolish police oppression, disband the secret Kempeitai police, develop a free and responsible press, liberalize education, and decentralize the political power. When he finished, MacArthur settled into a seat and began writing on a pad. After a period of time he set the pad aside and took a quick nap.

Whitney looked at his notes. It was a complete outline of the occupation goals, which would take years to accomplish. Already the chief of the occupying force was outlining steps to rebuild. Whitney would keep the notes for the rest of his life.

With the fanfare of a Hollywood premiere MacArthur's plane touched down on a pocked marked runway at 2:05 on the afternoon of August 30, 1945. MacArthur, with trademark sunglasses, emerged waving from the door of the plane and ambled down the ladder as a band from the 11th Airborne Division struck up a march. MacArthur had previously designated the 11th Airborne to be the lead element in the home island invasion. The general then strolled over to the band leader and said, "Tell the band that that's about the sweetest music I've ever heard."

At the airfield, which was once a training base for kamikaze pilots, MacArthur held a quick press conference and then walked to where a waiting motorcade, cobbled together from available vehicles, stood. Many of them, in a sad state, had charcoal-burning rear-mounted engines. One staff officer remarked that the motley collection of cars looked like "the Toonerville Trolley."

MacArthur and Eichelberger rode into Yokohama in a 1930s model Lincoln sedan that followed a cherry-colored fire engine. It was ironic for MacArthur to enter Japan in a car named after a great American president.

During the ride, as the siren from the fire engine wailed, what the American officers saw brought disbelieving stares and frightful shivers. Lining the road, at various intervals, were a total of 30,000 Japanese infantrymen. They stood at parade rest, bayonets fixed, wearing soft peaked caps. Equally shocking was that they stood with their backs to the motorcade, facing outward.

The site of the surrender had been finalized. It was naturally thought that the USS *Missouri*, the battleship commissioned to be the surrender ship, would be the place. However, it was also suggested to have the document signed in the courtyard of the Imperial Palace. This idea was rejected.

The surrender ceremony would bring the Pacific war full circle. It began on U.S. soil on a Sunday morning. It would end that way. The U.S. soil would be a navy warship. And it would occur on a Sunday morning, in homage to Pearl Harbor.

The Japanese delegation, brought out to the battleship anchored in Tokyo Bay, consisted of Toshikazu Kase; Mamoru Shigemitsu, the foreign minister representing the Japanese government; and General Yoshijiro Umedzu, Army Chief of Staff representing the Supreme Command. When General Umedzu was informed that he would be a delegate, he grew pale with anger and stated that *seppuku* would be his first choice rather than sign the surrender document. It took the intercession of Emperor Hirohito to persuade him to represent the military.

Waiting for the Japanese delegation on the quarterdeck that morning were Allied admirals and generals, all in khaki, in addition to staff officers and ship's company. A special scaffold was constructed for the cameramen. There were only two chairs at the surrender table, placed in the center opposite each other.

Behind a line of admirals was the framed flag that flew from Commodore Matthew Perry's flagship ninety-two years before when he sailed into Tokyo Bay to begin trade between Japan and the world. Admiral Halsey had it flown in.

General MacArthur made an introductory statement. He then invited the Japanese delegates to sign the document. Standing near MacArthur were British General Sir Arthur Percival, taken prisoner at Singapore, and General Jonathan Wainwright, who was flown in from a Japanese prison camp in Manchuria.

Mamoru Shigemitsu was the first to sit at the table, moving awkwardly with a wooden leg. He took a pen and paused, looking at the document. Everyone waited as Shigemitsu appeared as if he was staring blankly at the paper, not wanting to sign. Seconds went by. Shigemitsu continued looking at the paper.

Nearby Fleet Admiral Chester Nimitz was growing impatient. Finally Nimitz growled, *sotto voce*, "Sign! Damn it, sign!"

As if he heard Nimitz, Shigemitsu began signing.

Other representatives, in order, then sat at the table and signed, beginning with the United States: It wasn't noted until later that the representatives from Canada had signed in the wrong place.

Above the *Missouri*'s quarterdeck came the steady sound of approaching aircraft. It was 9:32. The sound got louder as the planes swept through the sky, over the anchored warships. There were 400 B-29 bombers and 1,500 carrier planes parading overhead in a final salute.

The Pacific war was over.

Later, General MacArthur made a speech broadcast across the Pacific and to America. In his resonant voice he stated, "The holy mission has been completed. And in reporting this to you, the people, I speak for the thousands of silent lips, forever still among the jungles and the beaches and in the deep waters of the Pacific which marked the way. I speak for the unnamed brave millions homeward bound to take up the challenge of that future which they do much to salvage from the brink of disaster."[42]

The ultimate twentieth-century experience had ended. Approximately 16 million Americans had worn uniforms during the previous four years.

Europe was now in ruins; so was Japan. Their economies were in likewise shape. Military intelligence teams in Germany and Japan were already conducting preliminary investigations that would lead to war crimes trials, followed by executions and lengthy prison terms, in both countries.

More details about the Holocaust in Europe and brutalities to Allied servicemen in Japanese prison camps were painfully being revealed. Everyone was talking about the "bomb" that ended the Pacific war so quickly. If the United States had developed a weapon with that potential, what was next?

The brave men and women who left to fight the war began to return older, somewhat confused, but determined to resume the lives that Germany and Japan had interrupted. They would carry certain character traits from this time and transfer them to their offspring with mixed results, which would cause further turmoil and controversy in another war.

So as one curtain came down on World War II another was raised with a new president and veterans on college campuses experiencing mixed feelings of curiosity and fear as to where the United States was going.

The next phase of American war films would reflect those traits of curiosity and fear. And to American audiences these films would illustrate the drama and brutal reality of a world facing chaos only to survive it with another set of problems.

# 3

# Postwar Reality

There never was a good war . . . or a bad peace.
—Benjamin Franklin

A bad peace is even worse than war.
—Tacitus

There is an oft told tale concerning a navy admiral and an army general on the afternoon of September 2, 1945, after the Japanese representatives signed the surrender document aboard the USS *Missouri* anchored in Tokyo Bay. According to the story, the admiral turned to the general and wondered, "My God, what will we do now?"

Other Americans in uniform didn't have to wonder. Sooner or later they had to try to pick up the pieces of their lives, resuming long-interrupted careers and relationships. Many were going to finish their education financed by the GI Bill. And like most American postwar periods, the veterans would come to realize that times had already changed.

It is said that World War I gave way to the "Jazz Age" and a generation that Gertrude Stein termed as "lost." A similar comparison could be made about World War II. Another generation had just gone through the trauma of a world war. Japanese domination in the Pacific came to a violent end; the Third Reich folded its bunker and Berlin lay in rubble.

Exactly what sort of men and women were coming back? And how would the nation's changing social structure affect both them and the war films that were to come?

Writing in the *New York Times*, in March 1993, novelist Robert Plunkett observed, "Movies and war have always been naturals with each other (the 1915 '*Birth of a Nation*' is a war movie), but it wasn't until World War II that the war movie came into its own. The cliche (squad) platoon has a farm boy from Iowa, a Jew from Brooklyn, and so on.

"But in the 1950s, with the country at peace and prosperous, Hollywood took another look at World War II. The military was now seen as a thuggish place, fueled by alcohol and run by sadistic superiors with sexual dysfunctions."[1]

Several films already scheduled for release fit right in with the aura of victory. One of these was James Cagney's production of *Blood on the Sun* (1945), directed by Frank Lloyd from a script by Lester Cole. Sylvia Sydney, Wallace Ford, and Rosemary DeCamp were in supporting roles. The time frame was in the 1920s. The script dealt with Japan's design for world conquest when an American editor in Tokyo, Cagney, comes upon the plan.

Twentieth Century Fox set *The House on 92nd Street* (1945) in New York City. Set during the war, it follows the FBI chasing Nazi agents who are pursuing the atom bomb formula. Even though it could be classified as a spy drama, the film had a World War II documentary feel under Henry Hathaway's direction. The script had three credited writers: Barré Lyndon, Charles G. Booth, and John Monks Jr. The cast included Lloyd Nolan, Signe Hasso, and Leo G. Carroll.

Errol Flynn continued his combat bravery in *Objective Burma!* (1945), set in the Pacific theater of war where an American platoon is given a behind-the-Japanese-lines mission. Raoul Walsh's direction came from a script where Lester Cole was again one of the writers. The other two were Ranald MacDougall and Alvah Bessie. The British Allies didn't come off well at all in this film. For that reason, the picture wasn't released in Great Britain until 1952, then only with an apology.

Bessie, who would later be named with Cole as a member of the Hollywood Ten, received an Academy Award nomination for original story.

World War II had placed the United States of America as the dominant nation on this planet. Like the movie stars of World War I, setting the stage for the "actors" of World War II, the proverbial tide seemed to turn when the "Yanks" entered the fray. And when the Yanks came over, the ultimate result was victory. Now, in World War II, victory was not in one theater of war but two.

Writing a reflection on the 1998 passing of Frank Sinatra, author Neal Gabler observed that the singer came to prominence in the 1940s but also presided in the spirit of the postwar period. "He was able to do so because America was riven between two extremes [at the time]. At one end was a sense of angry rue that had been loosed by the traumas of the war and that surfaced in everything from film noir to jazz. At the other end was a new sense of rambunctiousness loosed by the U.S. victory and the economic good times that followed and surfaced in everything from drive-in movie theaters to hot rods."[2]

Even before Japan signed the surrender document, every major Hollywood studio renewed its interest in war films. On July 15, 1945, the *New York Times* noted that release schedules of major studios will bring about a new crop of war films: "Those which are being planned to follow will be factual, for the most part, and minus the phony Hollywood glamor and heroics of those earlier films which brought about the almost universal exhibitor cry of 'no more war pictures.' "[3]

One of the first postwar Warner Bros. dramas about a wounded veteran was *Pride of the Marines* (1945), the true story of Guadalcanal hero Al Schmid, who almost single-handedly turned back a night attack of more than 200 Japanese soldiers, making a heroic stand with hand grenades and a .30 caliber machine gun. In the process, Schmid was blinded.

The fight on Guadalcanal was only the beginning of the film. The real battle was Schmid's homecoming and adjustment to civilian life. Delmer Daves directed Albert Maltz's script, with John Garfield playing Schmid. Eleanor Parker turned in a sympathetic performance as the loyal girl back home who still loves her man and wants a life with him despite his new handicap. Dane Clark and John Ridgley portrayed Garfield's marine buddies. Maltz's screenplay won an Academy Award nomination.

Captain Eddie Rickenbacker's survival of being adrift for twenty-two days in the Pacific convinced 20th Century Fox to bring the story to the screen. Rickenbacker was already a war hero, being awarded the Congressional Medal of Honor and the French Croix de Guerre as a World War I aviator.

Fred MacMurray was cast as Rickenbacker, in *Captain Eddie* (1945), who relives his life in flashbacks showing the progress of American aviation through peace and wartime. Directed by Lloyd Bacon from a script by John Tucker Battle, the film was rushed into production for a 1945 release and ended up being called a flat and overly sentimental account of a true war incident.

The characters in these postwar films were more dimensional and complex than in the previous "propaganda" period. This gave the country a more realistic view and gave rise to new social issues: prejudice, segregation (the military was soon to integrate), combat stress, the questioning of political and military decisions, and military corruption.

These issues were always below the surface.

The war experiences brought back by the American filmmakers and actors ushered in a new era. Because of this syndrome, it was no accident that some of the finest American war films emerged from this period.

Many of these films included actual combat footage that brought a look of brutal reality. It was a time when veterans flocked to college campuses under the GI Bill of Rights. Harry Truman was finishing FDR's last term with his head pointed toward a new legislative program called "The Fair Deal."

Realism was one of the first elements that studios and filmmakers were eager to implement. The actual sights and sounds of a combat situation would be taken to a new level. However, even during this time frame realism was still kept under check.

Movies were designed to entertain and inform. The former usually took precedence over the latter, particularly if a major studio was financing the film.

It was felt at the time that American audiences would be aghast and appalled if they saw young men being decapitated and horribly wounded from an artillery barrage. A round entering through the forehead usually meant a section of the rear skull blown out with the exit.

Combat horrors suffered by U.S. marines on the first days of the invasions of Tarawa and Iwo Jima were graphically told by the survivors afterward. But when these beachhead battles were reproduced, the graphic combat brutality was seriously edited.

The same held true for Anzio during the Italian campaign and Omaha Beach on the first day of the Normandy invasion, where the 1st and 29th Infantry Divisions were landed into a virtual Nazi buzz saw of withering machine gun and pounding artillery fire.

It wasn't until Steven Spielberg's *Saving Private Ryan*, released during the summer of 1998, that American audiences saw the graphic realism of what those Americans waded into on that June morning at Omaha beach.

One of the first battle documentaries was *With the Marines at Tarawa*, a harrowing twenty-minute visual depiction of the bloody Pacific fighting in November 1943 surrounding the island of Betio where units of the 2nd Marine Division were initially pinned down on the beach. British-born actor Louis Hayward, who became a naturalized U.S. citizen the day after Pearl Harbor, was a marine captain with the photographic unit during the fighting. His photo crew of marines had been planning to document what was thought to be a fairly easy operation because of the intense preparatory naval gunfire.

It took four days of intense combat. When it was over, Japanese dead came to more than 4,000. The number of marines killed in action came in under 1,000. The documentary, edited at Warner Bros., not only showed the fighting sequences; it also served as a set design model for Republic Pictures' 1949 marine opus *Sands of Iwo Jima*. Many of the actual shots were re-created on the beach at Camp Pendleton for the Tarawa sequence.

For his actions during the Tarawa operation, Captain Louis Hayward was awarded the Bronze Star by Fleet Admiral Chester Nimitz. The documentary went on to win an Academy Award.[4]

Navy Lieutenant Robert Taylor gave the narration for 20th Century Fox's *The Fighting Lady* (1944), directed by Louis De Rochemont. The color footage by photographer Edward Steichen brought aircraft carrier life in the Pacific to audiences whose previous images had only come from newspaper accounts and letters from servicemen. The action sequences documented the Mariana islands campaign, including a Japanese kamikaze attack.

John Huston's documentary *The Battle of San Pietro* (1945), a forty-minute film about the fierce and brutal fighting with the 5th Army under General Mark Clark in Italy, went through several editing phases. The battle, which was the key to the Liri Valley and the road to Rome, lasted from October 1943 to late December of that year. Huston took two camera crews to cover the arduous uphill fighting. Reportedly, two of the cameramen were killed; all but two were wounded. The camera crews later received a Presidential Unit Citation.[5]

As the battle continued with units from the 142nd and 143rd Infantry Regiments fighting, foot by foot, volunteer patrols were called for. Not one member of these patrols came back alive.

In December, the Nazis pulled back and the town of San Pietro was liberated. When the Americans entered the shattered town, they discovered women and children hiding in caves and in the basements of bombed buildings. The townspeople slowly emerged from the rubble, happy to have survived.

Huston then returned to the United States to begin postproduction and editing his narration. In scoring the music, a Salt Lake City choir was contracted. By the end of the postproduction period, it was decided to change the name of the Salt Lake City Choir. Thus, the Mormon Tabernacle Choir was born, giving a haunting background score to the documentary.

In a War Department memo dated November 3, 1944, Colonel Curtis Mitchell, Chief of the Pictorial Branch, called for a revision to delete the showing of the bodies of recognizable American dead. Colonel Mitchell was thinking of the families of the soldiers killed during the battle.

Postproduction continued as the war in Europe finally began to wind down. In February 1945, Warner Bros. notified Major John Huston that the suggested release date of his documentary would be "on the day the war in Europe ends."[6]

A disclaimer appeared at the end of the documentary, emphasizing that "all scenes in this picture were photographed within range of enemy small arms or artillery fire." Exactly which scenes or how many was not noted. The disclaimer added that "for the purpose of continuity a few of these scenes were shot before and after the actual battle of San Pietro."

Writing in the *Quarterly Journal of Military History*, years later, University of Nebraska history professor Peter Maslowski stated, "Director John Huston staged virtually all the action after the battle."[7]

After postproduction, Huston then went ahead with selected preview screenings. After a preview screening in March, Huston wrote a letter to 20th Century Fox production chief Darryl Zanuck: "I can't say it was a joyous evening. 'San Pietro' is a dolorous goddamn picture, full of hacked up towns and tanks and bodies, but the response from the 200 assorted people present was very gratifying. In other words, I succeeded in making everyone of them utterly miserable which is the purpose of the picture."[8]

The film's release was May 3, 1945, one day after Nazi admiral Karl Dönitz unofficially surrendered to Russian forces in Berlin.

Writing in the *Washington Evening Star*, Jay Carmody noted, "San Pietro never lets you up for breath, just as the actual participants in the battle never found breathing time."[9]

## PULLED FROM RELEASE

Huston's most controversial documentary, *Let There Be Light* (1946), was still in postproduction. He spent weeks at Mason General Hospital at Brentwood, Long Island, in the psychiatric ward to show the traumatic effects that combat had on veterans. In World War I, the expression was "shell shock." By the end of World War II that term had graduated to "battle fatigue," often with clinical symptoms occurring while still in the thick of battle.

After Vietnam, another diagnosis would be termed "posttraumatic stress disorder," or PTSD. Here the symptoms were similar to the maladies of the two previous wars except now there were added elements: geography and time. In the early 1980s, PTSD was recognized as a legitimate psychological malady. It was a throwback to battle fatigue and shell shock. In most cases, the victims' symptoms didn't surface until years later. These included wide mood swings, depression, inability to communicate with family members, flashback nightmares, and night sweats.

At Mason General Hospital, Huston's crew interviewed numerous patients, doctors, nurses, and hospital personnel to show how the army was dealing with treating the men who were extremely emotionally and mentally scarred by the trauma of combat experiences. Many of the patients had problems sleeping, constantly reliving the horrors of war in nightmares. Others completely withdrew from reality, often to a catatonic state, staring blankly at a wall, unable to communicate with another human being.

After postproduction, *Let There Be Light* was scheduled for various preview screenings during the summer of 1946. Dorothy Wheelock, an editor at *Harper's Bazaar*, had the film reviewed by Frances McFadden.

Perhaps the most exciting sequence of all is the scene in which Dr. Benjamin Simon hypnotizes a boy who lost his memory at Okinawa. Slowly, without mechanisms, the veteran is put to sleep. He is told that he will remember everything that has happened to him. Head sunk low on his chest, in halting sentences broken by fits of trembling, he begins to speak. The battery area, the Jap shells coming over, his buddy calling, "Dutch, I'm hit." And then at last his own name, his father's and his mother's—Isabel. When he comes out of his trance and he has remembered, his face is that of a man rescued after having been buried alive.

But here is the brutal god of war unadorned, a monstrous subnormal thing which can twist good looking normal high school boys into shivering frightened wrecks.

"Let There Be Light" should be released throughout the world wherever there is anyone who still thrills to martial music—and presented regularly to the delegates of UNO [United Nations Organization] whenever they show signs of the League of Nations blues.[10]

However, the army did not cooperate with advance press releases. Wheelock wrote to John Huston, "The War Department, as you know, was no help at all, but finally due to Iris Barry's [curator of the Metropolitan Museum of Art] conniving, our photographer was able to snap [still] pictures from the screen while the film was being shown.[11]

"It has given me a good feeling to know that I have outwitted the red tape department," wrote Wheelock.[11] (Because of the sensitive theme of the documentary, still photos were not released to the media.)

The film was scheduled for regular release at New York City's Museum of Modern Art. Shortly thereafter, the army sent a detachment of MPs to the museum and seized the film. No reason was initially given for the seizure. The War Department later released a terse statement stating that it was decided that the documentary should not be shown to the public because of "copyright restrictions."[12]

Brigadier General William C. Menninger, Office of the Surgeon General, wrote to John Huston about the problem that the Department of the Army had in releasing the film.

There are, however, some very grave questions about it. As you may or may not know, when these men signed a permit to utilize their services, that permit only specified that we could show the picture to the military. Much more important, however, is that anyone with legal experience knows that a patient in a psychiatric hospital who signed such a release is going through the motions. The paper he signs is really worthless.[13]

The outcry was swift and furious. Writing in the *New York Post*, Archer Winsten noted in his "Movie Talk" column, "The Army, having shrunk to its unleavened core of pre-war top executives, is re-embarking upon a do-nothing, say-nothing, think-nothing, be-nothing policy.... They would be capable of hiding a great film like a crow with a bright diamond, without ever becoming aware of its real value."[14]

In another column, Winsten added, "This is not the first time in the history of the arts that a great work has been fouled up by contemporary nitwits."[15]

In his autobiography, John Huston noted that twenty-four years after *Let There Be Light* was completed, in 1970, the Archives of American Films in Washington, D.C. scheduled a showing of his documentaries, less one.

Huston added, "To this day I don't know who the opponents of this picture were, or are, but they have certainly been unflinching in their determination that it shall not be seen. The same mentality was at work here as at the first showing of San Pietro. Unfortunately there was no [General] George C. Marshall around to save this one."[16]

It wasn't until the early 1980s that *Let There Be Light* was finally placed into general release.

## FACTS BEING DRAMATIZED

Pulling a documentary from release and sealing it from the public did not stop Hollywood from producing dramas about veterans coming home and adjusting from the trauma of combat. Veterans' readjustment was the main story line in what some critics called the best American film made about the effects of World War II, Samuel Goldwyn's *The Best Years of Our Lives* (1946).

According to the accepted version, Goldwyn was made aware of a 1944 *Time* magazine story about marines on leave who were finding it difficult to adjust to the home front. He was taken with it and saw film potential.

Goldwyn then contacted novelist MacKinlay Kantor and asked for a screenplay outline for a novel. Kantor had flown missions with the Eighth Air Force as an overseas correspondent. This was the beginning of his novel *Glory for Me*. It was the realistic and believable story of three returning veterans—one, a spastic named Homer Parrish—making valiant attempts to pick up their interrupted lives.

After *Glory for Me* was published it stayed on Goldwyn's shelf until December 1945. He then became absorbed with a film biography on the life of General Dwight Eisenhower, which was never made. The postwar focus still remained on the problems of returning veterans and in these times stayed away from flag rank characters being the center of film biographies.

Another war biography about General Billy Mitchell was placed on the back burner when the subject of Mitchell's controversial court-martial came up. One of the members of that tribunal was General Douglas MacArthur, also a talked-about subject for a biography. It would be another decade before the Mitchell film was put into production with Gary Cooper in the lead.

After a period of back and forth thinking Goldwyn finally decided that it was time to adapt Kantor's *Glory for Me* into a screenplay. His choice for the script assignment was Robert Emmett Sherwood, who by that time had already collected three Pulitzer Prizes for playwriting.

Goldwyn arranged for Sherwood and his wife, Madeline, to reside as guests in the producer's Beverly Hills home on Laurel Lane. The book presented a difficult task for Sherwood to adapt. It wasn't long before he was confronting writer's block. After a frustrating period, Sherwood came up with a structure that would intertwine the stories of the three returning veterans, departing somewhat from the narrative of the novel.

In regard to casting, Goldwyn first went to his own contract players, Dana Andrews and Virginia Mayo. The part of the veteran infantry sergeant, Al Stephenson, was initially offered to Fred MacMurray. Olivia de Havilland was approached to play Milly, the loyal wife. MacMurray and de Havilland both turned down the offers, which opened the doors for Fredric March and Myrna Loy.

Farley Granger was set for the role of the spastic veteran Homer. Again, reality set in, and a casting change came about. Kantor's book dealt with Homer's character being rendered clinically spastic because of combat trauma. For the screenplay, it was felt that American audiences of the day would be repelled by watching a spastic on the screen.

The director's nod went to William Wyler, an Army Air Force veteran of three and a half years. Wyler, still under contract to Goldwyn, was already experienced in veterans' readjustment problems.

While in the Army Air Force, Wyler directed a forty-three minute documentary on the last mission of a B-17 bomber and its effect on the crew. In concept the documentary was to be an "on the spot" film that depicted what an Eighth Air Force bomber crew went through in flying the final of its required twenty-five combat missions. During postproduction it was decided to name the film after the name of the bomber, the *Memphis Belle* (1944). His footage provided the stock film to be used later in other war films.

Wyler then did another documentary, *Thunderbolt* (1945), about the fighter plane that was so crucial in the Italian campaign. It was during this filming that Wyler suffered ear damage that would plague him for the rest of his life.

When Wyler got the Sam Goldwyn assignment for the film of *Glory for Me*, he drew on some of his own experiences in the service and of the coming home experience.

Two of Wyler's anecdotes that survived the final cut of the film were Wyler meeting his wife, Talli, when, after a long wartime separation, the two ran for each other in a hotel lobby, embracing emotionally. Wyler put a similar scene in the film when Sergeant Al Stephenson comes down a corridor in his home to embrace his wife Milly.[17]

Another scene concerned Wyler confronting anti-Semitism from a bellman at the Statler Hotel in New York City on March 10, 1944. Wyler got into a confrontation with the bellman while waiting for a cab. The argument escalated when the bellman referred to another guest as "One of those goddamn Jews."

"Whaddya mean?" asked Wyler.

The bellman shook his head, pointing to the other guest. "I wasn't saying it to you. I meant him."

"You're saying this to the wrong guy," responded Wyler. The director then punched the bellman, "sending him down in a sagging heap."[18]

Another army officer witnessed the melee and reported Wyler who was in uniform. Wyler ended up getting a letter of reprimand for conduct unbecoming, which, according to many combat veterans, is better than no mail at all.

Still, the experience stayed with Wyler, as did the scene where Homer sends a man crashing into a drugstore display booth for voicing offensive remarks. The scene rang true to many veterans.

In his noted *Goldwyn, a Biography*, A. Scott Berg mentions how Sherwood and Wyler toured veterans hospitals in search of deep background and character traits. Wyler then recalled seeing an army documentary, *Diary of a Sergeant*, about a former meat cutter, Harold Russell, who lost both hands as a result of a TNT explosion. Russell was fitted with a prosthetic device of the time: a set of steel claws controlled by a shoulder harness and moved by elastic bands.

After a screen test, Russell, who had no formal training as an actor, landed the part over Farley Granger because, it was felt, his physical disability would be more believable and sympathetic to American audiences than the spastic.

Wyler noted that Homer's character, despite the disability, made a better adjustment than the other two veterans who returned with emotional disturbances.

The film begins at war's end where three combat veterans—a sailor, an Army Air Force bombardier, and a middle-aged infantry sergeant—return to Boone City, a mythical city set in the Midwest, with a new set of values and problems. Homer, Harold Russell's character, is a navy signalman second class. Dana Andrews portrayed Fred Derry, the neighborhood soda jerk who became a flashy Army Air Force captain, returning to the wreck of a hasty marriage to party girl Virginia Mayo. March, as Al Stephenson, attempts to resume his routine duties as a bank loan officer, slowly realizing not only what the war robbed him of but the way in which the country came to discard the men who bravely served. March, Russell, and Andrews individually realize the emotional price that they have paid when they see the advancement made by others who managed to avoid wearing a uniform.

Years later, members of Vietnam veterans' support groups would openly weep when viewing *The Best Years of Our Lives*, identifying with the readjustment problems of their fathers' generation.

Besides Russell's award for Best Supporting Actor, Oscars went to March for Best Actor, Sherwood for screenplay, Daniel Mandell for editing, and Hugo Friedhofer for musical score. Wyler got another Oscar as Best Director (his first was for *Mrs. Miniver*).

Another 1946 film about veterans readjusting to civilian life was partly overshadowed by *The Best Years of Our Lives* This was RKO's *Till the End of Time*, directed by Edward Dmytryk from a script by Allen Rivken. The story was the same, three veterans: Guy Madison, Robert Mitchum, and Bill Williams return to a small town and find romance along with problems.

Alan Ladd and Geraldine Fitzgerald teamed up in 1946 as American agents who parachute into occupied France on the eve of the Normandy Invasion in *O.S.S.*, from Paramount. The actual agency, the Office of Strategic Services, was founded by General "Wild Bill" Donovan and became the forerunner of the Central Intelligence Agency (CIA) during the Truman administration. Directed by Irving Pichel, the film had Patric Knowles and Don Beddoe in supporting roles. The story, concerning American agents infiltrating France before the invasion, was based on rumors. The exact documentation was still classified at the time.

In Merle Miller's oral history of Harry Truman, *Plain Speaking*, Truman was quoted as saying that the organization and chartering of the CIA "was a mistake." Truman added that had he known what was going to happen, he never would have authorized the agency. He also chided the Eisenhower administration for letting the CIA get out of hand.[19]

Henry Hathaway directed *13 Rue Madeleine* in a documentary style for a 1946 release. The film's title was the Gestapo headquarters at Le Havre, France. The script had two writers, John Monks Jr. and Sy Bartlett, the latter fresh from

Army Air Force duty. The story has James Cagney leading an OSS commando team into occupied France to locate a Nazi rocket site.

Paramount used the war background for two veteran flyers hunting down the murder of a friend in the backstreets of *Calcutta* (1947). Alan Ladd and William Bendix seemed to re-create their roles from their 1943 film *China*. Playing the woman was Gail Russell. John Farrow directed from a script by Seton I. Miller.

Metro-Goldwyn-Mayer released *The Beginning or the End* (1947), a semi-documentary drama about American scientists producing the atom bomb despite fears of ultimate destruction. Brian Donlevy, Robert Walker, Hume Cronyn, and Tom Drake played the men making the decisions, with Beverly Tyler as a love interest. Godfrey Tearle gave a supporting role as President Roosevelt.

During this time, MGM gave a big 1948 fanfare to *Homecoming*, a Clark Gable and Lana Turner melodrama about a self-absorbed society doctor who gets called up in the war and is changed after a brief affair with a nurse nick-named "Snapshot." Turner played the nurse, while Anne Baxter portrayed the long-suffering wife.

The semidocumentary style took another turn with MGM's release of *The Search* (1948), starring Montgomery Clift. It was a heart-gripping story of an American soldier in Germany caring for a war orphan. Richard Schweitzer and David Wechsler shared the Oscar for Best Screenplay, while director Fred Zin-nemann and Clift each received Academy nominations. Ivan Jandl got a special award for playing the young orphan.

The transformation of college boy to fighter pilot worked well for Warner Bros.' *Fighter Squadron* (1948). The young men going up against the German Luftwaffe are Edmond O'Brien, Robert Stack, John Rodney, and Tom D'Andrea. This also served as one of Rock Hudson's earlier films. Actual combat footage was used making the aerial scenes more realistic.

Paramount came up with a comedy about postwar Germany with *A Foreign Affair* (1948), starring Jean Arthur, Marlene Dietrich, John Lund, and Millard Mitchell. The story concerned a congresswoman, Arthur, who journeys to Berlin on a fact-finding tour, only to come into a love triangle with an army captain, Lund, and his German girlfriend played by Dietrich. Director Billy Wilder had some help on the script from Charles Brackett and Richard Breen. The screen-play received an Academy Award nomination along with Charles Lang Jr.'s cinematography.

Social issues continued coming to the screen in different dramas during these postwar years. The film noir thriller *Crossfire* (1947), set in New York, directed by Edward Dmytryk, starring Robert Young, Robert Mitchum, Paul Kelly, and Robert Ryan, had three soldiers accused of killing a Jew in a New York hotel. Young played the homicide detective assigned to the case. In a later interview Dmytryk recalled that the film was reflective of the era. "There was a cooling off period from the traditional war films. In this time, we were the enemy."[20]

Richard Brooks's novel used the issue of homophobia as the motivation for the killing. But this was considered too controversial even for this period. So

John Paxton's script substituted anti-Semitism for the homophobia. The film was shot entirely at night in the film noir mode of tight settings and angled shadows.

The victim, played by Sam Levene, was originally thought to be a draft dodger and war profiteer, but it is ultimately revealed that he served honorably. He was killed simply because he was a Jew.

Oscar nominations came in for producer Adrian Scott, Dmytryk, Paxton, Ryan, and Gloria Grahame.

*Crossfire* and 1947's *Gentleman's Agreement*, which 20th Century Fox bought from the Laura Hobson novel, both dealt with anti-Semitism in the post-war years and caused RKO'S *Home of the Brave* (1949) to go to another social issue—racism.

Arthur Laurents's hit Broadway play dealt with a Jewish soldier having to suffer the taunts and cruelty of the men in his unit. When RKO and Stanley Kramer gave the screenplay assignment to Carl Foreman, they decided to go for the racist angle despite the fact that the American armed forces were segregated throughout World War II.

James Edwards portrayed the black soldier who is psychosomatically paralyzed following a reconnaissance mission to a Japanese-held island. The other soldiers in his unit are played by Frank Lovejoy, Lloyd Bridges, Douglas Dick, and Steve Brodie. Jeff Corey portrayed the army physician who attempts to get to the root of Edwards's mental block. Corey eventually realizes that it wasn't the effects of combat that caused Edwards's malady but the torment of racism.

Warner Bros. had Gary Cooper cast in 1949's *Task Force*, a history of naval aviation told in flashback on the day of "Admiral Cooper's" retirement. The realistic, and redeeming, element in this drama was the civilian resistance to the prewar navy modifying its fleet to include aircraft carriers. The character actor Stanley Ridges personified the conservative element that refused to believe that carriers would have any effect in war. Naturally, when Pearl Harbor is attacked and the Pacific island–hopping campaign begins, the criticism is silenced. Jane Wyatt and Walter Brennan had supporting roles along with real-life combat pilot Wayne Morris. Delmer Daves directed from his own script.

## THE NOVEL COMES FIRST

Like the aftermath of previous wars the experiences of World War II continued to stay around because the books and plays became riveting, each adding a realistically new angle to the ageless mythological struggle of men and women getting caught up in a war.

In certain quarters during these postwar years, people went up and down in their affection for war films. Nonetheless, war novels and plays continued to be, respectively, published and produced.

For Sy Bartlett and Beirne Lay Jr., even though the war was several years in the past, the Army Air Force memories weren't. Their life and death experiences, coupled with the passage of time, were the motivations for a novel.

Bartlett and Lay's friendship began during the war when they met in England at Thurleigh Field while assigned to the Eighth Air Force. Both men knew and were impressed with the exploits of Colonel Frank Armstrong, commander of the 306th Bombardment Group. Armstrong led several of the early Eighth Air Force missions across the English Channel during the so-called dark days at the beginning of what came to be known as "daylight precision bombing."

Both men knew that they were enduring a memorable lifetime experience and that one day the war would end. If something wasn't to come of this, then nobody would remember what they did. Bartlett and Lay agreed to tell a story that people would remember.

The story would take place at an airfield like Thurleigh and have a central character patterned after Colonel Frank Armstrong and one of the Army Air Force's hard-driving and more colorful flag officers, General Curtis LeMay. As commander of the 305th Bombardment Group in 1942, LeMay developed bomber formations and techniques, such as low-level daylight bombing, that were followed throughout the European Theater. The same formations and procedures were later used in the Pacific Theater during the B-29 raids on the home islands of Japan, many of which LeMay himself led.

The two writers would begin by outlining a novel. When the novel was completed, Bartlett explained, they would start on a screenplay. "It will be the best war film ever." (How many times has that been said?)

After Lay rotated stateside, Bartlett remained with the Eighth Air Force. Bartlett then joined Frank Armstrong's staff. Like LeMay, Armstrong had now been promoted to a flag rank, brigadier general, and was transferred to the Pacific Theater after the Normandy Invasion.

By the spring of 1946, Bartlett and Lay were civilians. Lay was getting work as a freelance writer. Bartlett was now a contract screenwriter at 20th Century Fox. Lay invited Bartlett to his home in Santa Barbara, where the two planned to talk further about their definitive World War II story.

Lay had given the project a lot of thought but also felt that it was too soon after the war. He also felt that American audiences were tired of war films.

Bartlett shared his friend's opinion about American audiences and contemporary war films. They decided to concentrate on writing the novel. At this point they began not by outlining the story but by writing the protagonist from the traits of Frank Armstrong and Curtis LeMay. LeMay was known as an "ass kicker," going back to the old Army Air Corps (pre–June 1941). In September 1947, the Army Air Force was designated as a separate service branch: the U.S. Air Force.

The central character's name would be Brigadier General Frank Savage. He would command the fictional 918th Bombardment Group. They came to this figure by multiplying Armstrong's 306th Group by three. The bomber command headquarters kept its code name of Pinetree. And Thurleigh Airdrome was changed to Archbury.

The title of *Twelve O'Clock High* came from a phrase common among the Army Air Force crewmen, meaning life-threatening danger. Fighter pilots of the German Luftwaffe figured out that the best way to attack the American B-17 bombers was at the front and from a high angle. Using the points on the clock, a B-17 was at its most vulnerable when attacked from twelve o'clock high.

The conflict begins when the 918th's original commanding officer, Colonel Keith Davenport, becomes overly identified with his men, which leads him to lose his sense of command and focus of the mission. Davenport, already carrying a command load of stress, is headed for a breakdown. Davenport is then replaced by General Frank Savage, who is forced to take a unit that calls itself a "hard luck group" and turn it into an efficient and courageous group of bomber crews. Savage then isolates himself, slowly moving to the breakdown that Davenport was headed for. The relief of command sequence came from an actual incident where Frank Armstrong took over command of the 306th Group at Thurleigh.

Bartlett accompanied Armstrong when they drove to Thurleigh. According to author Steven Jay Rubin, in *Combat Films*, they were allowed to drive right through the main gate without being challenged by the sentry. Armstrong, a stickler for military protocol and discipline, got out of the staff car and "blew his stack," a scene so impressive that it ultimately ended up in both the novel and screenplay.

Upon seeing the group and the staff, Armstrong could see the appalling situation, a rudderless military unit with "no pride whatsoever."[21] It was no coincidence that both Armstrong and LeMay had to take such groups and turn them around into units that could handle their assigned missions.

The novel was a classic collaboration, a perfect complementary balance between the authors. Bartlett brought his studio experience of screenplay structure and pacing to the manuscript, according to Rubin, while Lay added his "sense of realism and the actual experience of command responsibility." Lay's clear writing style was devoid of tactics and aerial strategy. He concentrated on characters he had known who were in life-threatening situations, facing death every morning and returning to the base wondering what would happen tomorrow. The main story line was Savage's struggle after taking over command of the 918th. For subplots, there were the daily radio-transmit intercepts that were drawn from actual incidents and valued intelligence that helped plan various missions such as the Schweinfurt/Regensberg raids (led by LeMay in real life). And there was military jealousy from the general staff at Pinetree. Another subplot was a love story between Savage and Patricia Mallory, an attractive flight Leftenant, a British Wren. Still another subplot was Savage's personality clash with a playboy officer, Ben Gately, third-generation West Point.

As the novel progressed and rewriting was being done, Bartlett began using his Hollywood contacts. One of his first was Louis Lighton, who, according to Rubin, worked as David O. Selznick's story editor at MGM. Lighton's objective was to come aboard as producer and get Darryl F. Zanuck interested in it at 20th Century Fox.

The authors were correct about the current war film market, that American audiences were turning to other genres. However, as the novel's publication date approached, more people heard about the manuscript and the background of the authors. Elements that attracted the Hollywood curious were a war film written by two combat veterans.

Bartlett then called upon William Wyler, who now was under contract at Paramount. Again, everything fit. Wyler, the director of *Mrs. Miniver* and *The Best Years of Our Lives*, plus his credits as a combat documentary filmmaker, was instantly drawn to the novel as a film. When Zanuck was told that Wyler was hot for the project, he immediately changed his mind about the war film market. A bidding war commenced between 20th Century Fox and Paramount. In the end *Twelve O'Clock High*'s screenplay rights sold to Fox for $100,000, an enormous price at the time.

The novel was published by Harper & Bros. in late 1948. It would be almost two years before the film was released.

Next came the adaptation. Zanuck decided to stay with the authors of the novel instead of calling in a contract screenwriter. Since Fox owned the screenplay rights, Lighton felt that the subplots in the novel watered down the main story line: Savage's conflict to turn the group into an effective unit.

The first subplot to be jettisoned was the jealousy at Pinetree. In the novel, the general staff resent Savage's methods and make several attempts to have him transferred back to the States. It conflicted too much, according to Lighton, with the main story line. The authors, with much reluctance, agreed.

The next item on Zanuck's hit list to become a creative casualty was the love story subplot with Leftenant Patricia Mallory. But not without a fight.

Lay was adamant about the love story subplot remaining. Lighton contended that the main story line was building Savage into an isolated and strong leader who carries everything on his shoulders. Here, Lighton felt, the love story allowed Savage to have "a convenient release." Lay argued that the release was the exact element that contributed to Savage's eventual breakdown.

Lay reminded Lighton what Savage says at his first briefing at Archbury. He tells his men to write themselves off. "Tell yourself you're already dead. Once you accept that fact, it will be easier to fly those missions." This was Savage's combat philosophy. With Mallory, he had a diversion; he was no longer isolated. Lay reasoned that this distraction "would eventually destroy him."

Lighton accepted Lay's argument, and the love story remained. However, the screenplay draft came in way too long, forty pages too long. So ended Leftenant Patricia Mallory and the love story subplot.

Likewise, scenes went on too long and had overwritten dialogue, the usual beginning draft problems with screenplay adaptations. There was now a problem with the confrontation between Savage and the Ben Gately character. The dialogue became an ongoing puzzle, to the point where Zanuck felt that these men in war were turned into "nonstop chatterboxes." Zanuck felt that something decisive had to be done from the studio's point of view.

Lighton was fired from the project, and the screenplay was shelved. The writers and Zanuck could not agree on rewrites. Nothing was done for six months.

The escalating conflict between Savage and Gately was seen as the key to the resolution of the story. In the beginning Savage sees Gately, the air executive, as personifying what is at the lethargic nub of the 918th Group. Savage calls him a coward and demotes him to an airplane commander. Gately is then told his crew will be made up of misfits and aptly named "The Leper Colony," to be painted on the nose of the ship.

As Savage tells Gately, "If there's a navigator who can't find his way to the men's room he'll be in your crew. If a bombardier can't hit his dinner plate with a fork, you'll get him."

Gately's character arc begins to turn when Savage later learns from the group medical officer, Major "Doc" Kaiser, that Gately is in traction after being rescued from the Channel. Gately, who seriously injured his back, continued to fly three missions despite the worsening pain. When Savage learns of this he visits Gately in the hospital. It's an awkward moment for both men but in the end resolves their clash. Gately learns from the nurse that Savage now thinks very highly of him because of his demonstrated bravery.

Savage then witnesses another of his B-17's getting hit while negotiating through enemy flak. He yells to the airplane commander, Major Joe Cobb, "Get out, Joe! Jump!"

However, Cobb, another officer with whom Savage had a personality clash, dies with his crew. This greatly affects Savage and takes his emotional load to a higher level.

Preparing for the next mission, Savage endures his complete breakdown, not being able to hoist himself into the nose hatch as the collapse goes from mental to physical. He is pulled away by the adjutant, Major Harvey Stovall, and Davenport. The airplane commander taking Savage's place is Ben Gately, the man he once called a coward. What Savage did, in his own resolution, was prepare the next leader for the lonely responsibility of command.

With the script problems being resolved, Zanuck called in director Henry King, who was also an Army Air Force veteran. King had just come off four tough months in Italy filming *Prince of Foxes* (1949), starring Orson Welles and Tyrone Power. King's photographer on the film was Leon Shamroy, who would also come aboard on *Twelve O'Clock High.*

While location scouting went on, so did casting. King then got in touch with Colonel John H. deRussey who was the operations officer of the 305th Bombardment Group in Chelverton, England, during the war. The film got Pentagon cooperation, and after several busted attempts, Eglin Field in Florida was selected because it looked like the small Archbury Airdrome.

During this time, Bartlett returned to Hollywood and began the shooting draft of the script. The revised screenplay was turned in on June 10, 1949. For the Frank Savage character, Zanuck settled on Gregory Peck. Zanuck admired Peck's performances both as the priest in *Keys to the Kingdom* (1944) and as Lionel Barrymore's unruly son in David O. Selznick's adaptation of Niven Busch's novel *Duel in the Sun*, an epic 1946 western that went through four directors.

Gary Merrill, an Army Air Force veteran, was signed to play Colonel Keith Davenport, while Hugh Marlowe got the part of Ben Gately. The supporting character of the Adjutant Major Harvey Stovall went to the professorial-looking Dean Jagger as the film's "Greek Chorus" of the 918th Group. Jagger's role was to maintain the structure and balance of the "bookend flashback," the way the film is told. It begins and ends from his point of view. There was only one female cast in the film, the army nurse portrayed by Joyce Mackenzie.

The film begins with American attorney Harvey Stovall in London on business in 1948. After purchasing a derby hat, he passes an antique store and notices a cracked Toby mug in the window. He instantly recognizes it as the same mug that once rested on the mantle of the Archbury Officers' Club. The next scene has Stovall on a train out to Archbury. He then visits the airdrome, walking up and back on the empty runway as steers jostle playfully in the field behind him. Slowly he hears the laughter and the voices from the abandoned Nissen huts. And then the audience hears the barrack room ballads "Don't Sit Under the Apple Tree" "Bless 'em All," and "The Whiffenpoof Song." The middle-aged man begins to stand more erect, reliving his most memorable life experience. The sounds of propellers warming up for the day's mission are then heard as prop wash blows through the field.

And suddenly, up in the air, the B-17s of the 918th Group are approaching for the landings. And the audience is now transported back to that life-and-death time frame.

In the novel, after the action is played out, Harvey Stovall returns the Toby mug to the mantle of the Nissen hut, where it was a metaphor for the dangerous missions that they flew. In the film, Stovall merely walks back to the fence, gets on his rented bicycle, and rides back to the train station as the music swells and ending credits roll.

The studio gave King and his cast and crew a fifty-nine-day shooting schedule. As the dailies began to form, it was clear that an exceptional war film was in production.

The film was previewed at the Fox Theatre in Riverside, California, on October 20, 1949. The audience response echoed Darryl Zanuck's feelings. In a confidential memo to Henry King, dated November 3, 1949, Zanuck wrote: "This is a big picture—big in every way and should be a contendor [*sic*] for top honors when the ballots are tallied [at the Academy Awards]. . . . Peck does a stand-out job as the tough commanding officer who dislikes what he has to do but goes ahead. Gary Merrill and Dean Jagger trail closely behind him in performance."[22]

The critics were equally impressed. The *New York Times* called it: "Integrity all the way down the line." The *Daily Mirror* went even further: "The best war film since the fighting stopped."

Sy Bartlett and Beirne Lay's instincts, along with Zanuck's and other studio executives', proved correct. The film was nominated for Best Picture; Peck got nominated for Best Actor. But it was Dean Jagger who walked off with the golden statuette for Best Supporting Actor.

The film lost in the Best Picture category to *All the King's Men*. Broderick Crawford won Best Actor in that film for portraying Willie Stark, patterned after Louisiana's legendary Huey Long.

Forty-nine years later, sitting in the living room of his spacious Los Angeles home, eighty-two-year-old Gregory Peck reflected on *Twelve O'Clock High*.[23] He said that he had read the novel first and recalled the decision to drop the love story subplot along with the radio transcript intercepts.

"I do remember that Zanuck and Beirne Lay agreed to drop the love story," said Peck. "We ended up with only one woman in the film [Joyce Mackenzie]."

For the climactic breakdown scene, under the nose hatch, Peck added, "Between Henry King and I, we worked out what looked like a breakdown from fatigue and nervous tension and exhaustion."

Peck then reflected on Savage's path toward the breakdown, including when the group commander sees Major Joe Cobb's B-17 taking a direct flak hit. "No matter what the circumstances, he [General Frank Savage] would be affected by the terrible event that he had just witnessed. At that point he was both paternal and fraternal about his men."

At the time of his casting, Peck believed that he was the only actor to be considered for the role of Frank Savage. "Later on I heard the part had been offered to John Wayne, but he turned it down." Peck added that he had no proof of that. "It's hearsay. I have no idea why he turned it down."

Peck was asked if it was possible that he and John Wayne canceled each other in the Academy's voting, allowing Crawford to win. Wayne was nominated for playing the tough marine squad leader Sergeant John Stryker in *Sands of Iwo Jima*.

Peck laughed and replied. "I never thought of it in those terms. Somebody else won. That year they thought he [Crawford] was better than I was. I never got involved with any aftermath of it. I lost to Fredric March when he did *The Best Years of Our Lives*. I didn't have any quarrel with that. . . . I was nominated four times before I carried away the little statue [as Georgia attorney Atticus Finch in *To Kill a Mockingbird*, 1962]. I always felt that somebody was better than I was."

Peck paused and commented on later Oscar controversies. "I really can't understand today the way people seem to resent it when they don't walk off with the award."

Peck also acknowledged that for years *Twelve O'Clock High* was shown at business management seminars as an example of how a leader handles stressful situations. After the screening, the seminars would break out into discussion groups to hear opinions on business leadership as opposed to wartime leadership.

As Oscar nominations unfolded for 1949, John Wayne got his first nod for Republic Pictures' *Sands of Iwo Jima*, directed by Allan Dwan, who began his career under the tutelege of D.W. Griffith. It was the most expensive film, to date, that Republic had produced. Kirk Douglas was first mentioned for the lead, but negotiations broke down. That's when John Wayne stepped up and lobbied Herbert Yates, president of Republic, for the part.

At the age of forty-two, Wayne portrayed twenty-seven-year-old John M. Stryker, a Guadalcanal survivor. He's a flawed career marine, a buck sergeant busted from sergeant major. Stryker's job is to take a squad of inexperienced marines and drive them beyond their limits, sometimes "butt stroking" them into obedience.

As Stryker tells them at the first meeting, "I'm gonna make marines out of you. One way or another I'm gonna get the job done."

The film uses a "Greek Chorus" structure, so common in war films, where one of the survivors, Corporal Robert Dunne (Arthur Franz) tells the story.

The original story and first draft screenplay is credited to Harry Brown (*A Walk in the Sun*) with second writer James Edward Grant. Stryker's off-screen wife Mary divorced him for reasons unknown. His only connection with her is their five-year-old son. Whenever mail call arrives and there is nothing for Stryker, he goes into town to drown himself in booze. These character flaws gave John Wayne's combat image a new turn. He's a doomed man, with an alcohol problem, incapable of a lasting relationship with any woman. But he is also a taskmaster, grooming younger men to be survivors.

The script takes poetic license with the squad being both at Tarawa and Iwo Jima, unlikely occurrences for such a unit. The intercut combat footage gave the film brutal realism, for which editor Richard L. Van Enger received an Academy Award nomination.

The squad members were the usual cross section of young warriors: feuding brothers, boys off the farm and from the city. John Agar portrayed PFC Pete Conway, the alienated son of posthumously decorated marine officer Sam Conway (a Navy Cross at Guadalcanal), who served with Stryker in the back story.

In the second act, Stryker learns that another marine, Al Thomas (Forrest Tucker) didn't return promptly on a Tarawa ammunition run, causing one wounded and another dead. Stryker then confronts Thomas, resulting in a fistfight. Both characters are marine boxers.

An earlier screenplay draft called for Stryker getting beat by Thomas. Thomas then goes off to cry next to a tree, knowing what happened was his fault. In the revised draft, Thomas is forced to take his lumps from Stryker until a passing officer stops the fight.

Three of the participating marines were from the second Iwo Jima flag-raising team, Rene A. Gagnon, Ira H. Hayes, and navy pharmacist's mate John H.

Bradley. Hayes, the tragic Pima Indian, later had his story told in the 1962 Tony Curtis film *The Outsider*.

The film received complete Marine Corps cooperation, from Los Angeles to Washington, D.C. In Los Angeles marine Captain Leonard Fribourg was appointed as technical adviser. A major portion of his liaison job was to insure military accuracy and attention to detail. A section of White Beach at Camp Pendleton was re-created for the Betio landing on the Tarawa atoll.

According to biographers, Wayne took the preparation very seriously, taking everything in, asking questions about character and Marine Corps training.

Fribourg held a "mini boot camp" for the supporting actors, emphasizing military dress and bearing, close order drill, and the proper handling of an M-1 rifle. Captain Harold G. Schrier, the platoon leader who actually led the original patrol up Mount Suribachi on February 23, 1945, portrayed Wayne's platoon leader for the Iwo Jima sequence.

One of Fribourg's major protests was the horizontal butt stroke scene. A squad member, Choynski, has a difficult time coordinating his feet in bayonet training. Stryker then challenges him to thrust, parries it, and smashes Choynski in the jaw with the rifle. Fribourg objected all the way back to Headquarters Marine Corps but was overruled. He argued that a sergeant like Stryker would never resort to that tactic. But the scene stayed, being followed up with Choynski eventually learning the coordination to the tune of the Mexican hat dance. It came off as the most humorous scene in the film.[24]

A major script change came in the Mount Suribachi assault (most likely for the sake of historical accuracy). In an earlier draft, Stryker leads five marines up Suribachi to raise the flag (with photographer Joe Rosenthal waiting to take his reenacted prize-winning shot). Stryker is then killed by a machine gun burst on the way down. Clutched in his hand are an unfinished letter and a package of cigarettes. As the marines look at the letter, Stryker's voiceover is heard, apologizing to his son for past mistakes. On the actual patrol, led by Schrier, there were no casualties.

After script revisions, giving allowance to the actual incident, Stryker's squad goes up the mountain only to provide cover for the six. Just before the dramatic flag raising, Stryker is shot in the back by a sniper, killing him instantly. Thomas then reads the unfinished letter to the rest of the squad. After the letter is read, Conway takes it, vowing to finish it for Stryker.

The taskmaster's job is done. He has molded these men despite their initial dislike of him. As the mantle is passed (like the Toby mug in *Twelve O'Clock High*), the marines then walk back down the hill, getting back into the war, to the rousing Marine Corps hymn against one of its bloodiest encounters.

After the West Coast preview in Studio City, *Daily Variety* wrote, "Now and then a motion picture comes along which by virtue of subject matter is predestined to live. No tom-toms are needed to herald its coming. It bears [a] mark of greatness."[25]

In 1976, when Vietnam marine Ron Kovic published his emotional and angry autobiography *Born on the Fourth of July*, he wrote about sitting in a theater with neighborhood friend Bobbie Castiglia, watching John Wayne.

Castiglia and I saw *Sands of Iwo Jima* together. The Marine Corps hymn was playing in the background as we sat glued to our seats, humming the hymn together and watching Sergeant Stryker, played by John Wayne, charge up the hill and get killed just before he reached the top. And then they showed the men raising the flag on Iwo Jima with the Marines' hymn still playing, and Castiglia and I cried in our seats. I loved the song so much, and every time I heard it I would think of John Wayne and the brave men who raised the flag on Iwo Jima that day. I would think of them and cry. Like Mickey Mantle and the fabulous New York Yankees, John Wayne in *Sands of Iwo Jima* became one of my heroes.[26]

In James Bradley's book *Flags of Our Fathers* (cowritten with Ron Powers) different feelings emerge about the film after the passing of years. Bradley, the son of one of the flag raisers, knew very little about what his father did on Iwo Jima, or the fact that John Bradley was awarded the Navy Cross for heroism under fire. With Powers, James Bradley set out to research the story of the three survivors and how their lives turned out after the war.

According to James Bradley, Republic Pictures hatched a plan to get the three surviving flag raisers to California for cameo appearances in the final sequence. Each was led to believe that if he didn't appear, it would ruin the film.

Bradley returned to his hometown of Antigo, Wisconsin, feeling saddened and used. Later, he wrote to a friend, "If you think you will see real action like Iwo Jima by seeing the picture I really think you will be sadly disappointed. Chief [Ira] Hayes says they have the picture so fucked up he isn't even going to see the movie."

Bradley added that his father had it right. "The flagraisers' roles in the movie were minuscule. Their two scenes—one bunched around John Wayne as they receive orders, the other a quick glimpse of them pushing up a flagpole—required a total of about thirty minutes of filming."[27]

The war's realism took another bent as William Wister Haines's Broadway play *Command Decision* was turned into a novel, dedicated to his brother John Wister Haines and fellow POW (prisoner of war) Grant Barney Schley. John Haines and Schley were killed on a prisoner of war ship while being transferred from the Philippines to Japan when the prisoner ship was attacked by American planes.

MGM acquired the rights to both the stage play and Haines's novel and cast Clark Gable as an Army Air Force general who finds himself in the moral dilemma of sending bomber crews on high-risk missions to knock out Nazi jet factories or to bow to the pressure of visiting congressmen who are more concerned with voters' reactions to the high losses. Gable knows that if he lets up on the missions the losses down the line will be even greater.

The 1949 film, directed by Sam Wood from a screenplay adaptation by William Laidlaw and George Froeschel, was unique in this postwar period not because it had an all-male cast but because it was a war film with no combat scenes. The conflict centered behind the closed doors of a general staff that had to make decisions where young American airmen would die.

Supporting Gable were Walter Pidgeon, Van Johnson, Brian Donlevy, John Hodiak, and Charles Bickford. Edward Arnold turned in his signature performance as the scheming politician.

The syndrome of a screenwriter reflecting on firsthand wartime experiences repeated itself with Robert Pirosh and the Battle of the Bulge. Unlike the conflict in *Command Decision*, the men who met the brunt of the Battle of the Bulge were the infantrymen, the "dogfaces," who slept in the foxholes.

The feeling at many studios was that the fickle American moviegoing public was tired of war films once more. As a comedy screenwriter, Pirosh had worked on several films before the war. His army service took him to Europe, where he pounded the ground during the Bulge. Pirosh was with the 35th Infantry Division, part of which was assigned a section to relieve the surrounded 101st Airborne Division commanded by Colonel Anthony McAuliffe at Bastogne in December 1944.

Like many combat veterans, Pirosh kept a diary, writing down anecdotes, situations, and character traits of the men in his unit. In 1949, back at RKO, he approached McAuliffe, who was in Hollywood at the time. Pirosh explained that he still wanted to do a screenplay about the 101st, Bastogne, and the Bulge. McAuliffe agreed and supported the project.

Pirosh then went back to Belgium and, as a civilian, walked through the very woods where he endured combat. He even found one of his own foxholes. The sights and sounds were once again alive with him. The movie would center around a typical squad, in this case the second squad, third platoon of I Company.

However, the project was not an exact fit for the climate at RKO, which was headed by Howard Hughes. Dore Schary, the executive running operations at RKO, felt that the time was right for another war film. The good news was that Hughes felt the same way. But the bad news was that Hughes wanted an Army Air Force film. He felt that the public was tired of infantry movies.

The argument between executive and studio chief escalated between the army infantry and the air force. Schary soon found it impossible to work with Hughes. After resigning from RKO, Schary was quickly grabbed by Louis B. Mayer at MGM. And after a period, Pirosh's Bulge project found a new home.

Mayer felt that the story was too depressing and grim for audiences so soon after the war. But, to his credit, Mayer allowed Schary to proceed in developing a screenplay.

Despite the nervous tension surrounding the project, now known as *Battleground* (1949), Schary chose William Wellman as a director. Wellman (*Wings* and *The Story of G.I. Joe*) was an opinionated man who had his own feelings about soldiers in combat.

During the script development stage, Wellman and Pirosh worked well together, shaping the outline that would become the screenplay. But the creative
honeymoon soon ended.

Schary made Pirosh associate producer on *Battleground*. This immediately
caused a conflict with Wellman, who eventually had Pirosh barred from the set
as casting continued. Pirosh was also replaced as the technical adviser by Lieutenant Colonel Harry W.O. Kinnard Jr. (West Point 1939), who was on Mc-
Auliffe's staff and organized the defense of Bastogne.

For additional realism, soldiers from the 101st Airborne Division were flown
to Hollywood and put up in a Culver City motel. While this was happening,
casting changes were continuous. Because of contract negotiations and availability dates, Robert Taylor, Bill Williams, Robert Ryan, and Keenan Wynn
were forced to leave the project.

Taylor was replaced by Van Johnson, as Holly, the wisecracking playboy
who eventually becomes a squad leader. Johnson was joined by John Hodiak,
another alum from *Command Decision*.

James Whitmore (who became a staple in American war films) was cast as
Sergeant Kinny, the tobacco-chewing platoon sergeant who holds the unit together.

Wellman had the actual 101st Airborne soldiers mix with the actors during a
two-week training sequence where a nine-to-five schedule was rigidly employed
(similar to what Captain Leonard Fribourg did in preparing the actors for *Sands
of Iwo Jima*). This included daily wearing of the infantry uniform, close order
drill, weapons firing, grenade throwing, bayonet training, firing positions, combat movement, and scouting. These actor training sequences became models for
subsequent war films in another generation, such as *Platoon* (1986) and *Saving
Private Ryan* (1998).

The close order drill training included a "jive drill" that several black drill
instructors had employed during the war when the service branches were segregated. One of these instructors was Master Sergeant Samuel Jaegers, a Southern University graduate.

When Wellman felt that the actors finally were marching like an army platoon,
he felt it was time to begin production. The "jive drill" sequence opened the
film.

Another difficulty was censorship. In 1949, any kind of swearing or four-
letter words were unthinkable. Only ten years before was Clark Gable allowed
to say the word "damn" in his farewell to Vivien Leigh in *Gone with the Wind*.

When the 101st Airborne found out that they were surrounded and that the
overcast and heavy snow made air support impossible, the option of surrender
was mentioned in one of McAuliffe's staff meetings. Several days later the Nazis
sent a truce party to Bastogne, wanting the Americans to entreat surrender.
McAuliffe wondered aloud what his answer should be.

Kinnard reportedly asked, "Why not tell them what you said earlier?"

McAuliffe forgot what he had said at the staff meeting. Kinnard reminded him that he said "Nuts!" That one word became McAuliffe's answer to the Nazi surrender request. Since "nuts" was on the censor's list, Schary and Wellman had to convince the censor board that the actual word was needed because, in keeping with the realism of the time, that's the way it happened. In their wisdom the censors agreed to go along with history.[28]

The film opened to favorable and memorable reviews in December 1949. When the Academy Awards were announced for that year, *Battleground* received six nominations, including Best Picture (Schary), Best Director (Wellman), Best Supporting Actor (James Whitmore), and Best Editing (John Dunning). When the Oscars were announced, the winners were Robert Pirosh for story and screenplay and Paul C. Vogel for Best Cinematography.

It was not surprising that the year 1949 had three classic American war films nominated for Oscars in various categories: *Twelve O'Clock High, Sands of Iwo Jima*, and *Battleground*. The American war film had turned a new corner into realism with actual events in both theaters of war being depicted in films that will be remembered for generations.

## A DARK EPIC

It is both tragic and ironic that one of the more productive and memorable periods for American war films was also one of the most divisive for the country. What began as a period of victory and peace deteriorated into political suspicion and paranoia, giving rise to demagogues that ruined lives and ended careers.

Today it is called the "Blacklist Era."

Like most political events, it didn't happen overnight. It was a three-act drama with a deep back story.

The back story of the Blacklist Era began in the silent film era, 1917. America had entered World War I on the Allied side. The Russian aristocracy, headed by Tsar Nicholas II, was criticized as being too rigid with its court being populated with irresponsible political favorites.

When soldiers in several of the Russian army units threw down their arms at the front, turned, and began the walk home to partake in the coming civil war, the entire world watched. Some Russian army units steadfastly remained at the front as the split in the service branch widened.

Many observers simply viewed this revolution as a reaction to an oppressive aristocracy, recalling the American and French Revolutions. The two revolutions in Russia in 1917 (in March and November) brought more instability and uncertainty. For eight months, following October, a provisional government struggled vainly to stabilize the situation. The provisional government toppled quickly because it failed in two major respects: not being able to take Russia completely out of the war and being unable to capitalize on peasant land reform.

The instability and civil war continued from December 1917 to November 1920. It was during this period after World War I when certain progressive and liberal Americans became intrigued with communism and the events taking place in Russia. The Romanov dynasty, after 304 years, had lost its power and brutally ended in a family execution in 1918.

The Americans, initially attracted to the Communist Party, were drawn to it because of the apparent quick reform element, to change society in a comparative short period of time. But this was not without contradictions. Many Americans simply ignored the violent outfall of the Russian Revolution and the subsequent civil war.

The fascination continued. This resulted in the formation of two American political parties, the Communist Labor Party and the Communist Party of America. They were united in 1921 as the "Workers Party." By 1929, it was renamed the Communist Party of the USA. Its leader was William Z. Foster.

During the 1930s and 1940s, American Communists were denied freedoms that European Communists enjoyed. They had to meet in secret, whereas their European counterparts could fully attend meetings, vote for candidates, and march in demonstrations.

The late 1920s and early 1930s saw a marked rise in the Communist Party USA membership. This was further fueled by the Great Depression and the rise of fascism in Europe. Many young people and college students showed interest because, they felt, the Communist Party USA was one of the few organizations actually fighting fascism and racism in America, plagued with lynchings in the South.

As the depression continued, established playwrights and novelists came to Hollywood, attracted by the enormous salaries of the day, the glamour, and the sun. Accompanying these creative newcomers, many of whom were liberals and progressives, were their ideals, hopes, and dreams.

As noted, America, entrenched in isolationism, remained aloof toward the European incidents. Civil war erupted in Spain in July 1936 when the Popular (Republican) Front was elected.

Foreign volunteers saw the Spanish struggle as fascism against the free world. Progressive and liberal factions in the United States, including some members of the Communist Party, joined the "Lincoln Brigade" and went to Spain to support the Popular Front. Just when Franco's forces were about to crush the Republicans, the Soviet Union sent them aid, which continued the fighting until the Franco forces prevailed in 1939.

The Third Reich began its reclaiming campaign in Europe, headlined by annexing Austria in the Anschluss in 1938. That same year, the U.S. House of Representatives authorized and chartered the temporary House Un-American Activities Committee (HUAC) to investigate alleged subversive organizations. The chairman was Congressman Martin Dies (D–Texas). Dies had a reputation of being tough on witnesses to the level of harassment.

Much of the prewar attention of HUAC was directed toward the bureaucracies created by the New Deal. It was felt at the time that many of these bureaucracies were populated by Communists, socialists, and "crackpots."

The HUAC charter was changed after World War II when it became a permanent committee. With that change, the curtain was raised on the Dark Epic.

Originally HUAC's purpose was to investigate suspected individual Communists and alleged Communist front organizations. There was a period of investigating Communist infiltration in the labor unions on the East Coast. And then HUAC began to look west.

In the spring of 1947, the HUAC committee came to Hollywood, investigating alleged Communist influence in the film community. These first postwar preliminary hearings were geared toward "friendly" witnesses and recognized studio heads. All voiced alarm and concern about films being released in Hollywood with a Communist point of view that seemed sympathetic toward the Soviet Union.

Any film that was remotely felt to be sympathetic to the Soviet Union came under close scrutiny, regardless of when it was released. Films like *Mission to Moscow* (1943), *The North Star* (1943), and *None but the Lonely Heart* (1944) were produced when Russia was on the Allied side, fighting Nazis. But in the committee's eyes, there was an element of subversion with these films and with the people who wrote, directed, and produced them.

Another example was MGM's release of *Song of Russia* in 1944. The wartime story line had an American symphony conductor witnessing the Russian war effort with admiration. But now, in 1947, the climate had changed. The writers of this film, Paul Jarrico and Richard Collins, came under committee scrutiny, along with director Gregory Ratoff. Robert Taylor, the male lead in the film, testified to the committee as a "friendly" witness.

By this time the faces of the HUAC had changed. The committee was now chaired by J. Parnell Thomas (R–New Jersey), a diminutive man who was given to sitting on phone books to elevate his height. Thomas's character traits were similar to those of Dies's. However, Thomas carried with him a particular hatred of Eleanor Roosevelt and anything that had to do with New Deal legislation.

The committee members were John McDowell (Pennsylvania), Richard Vail (Illinois), John S. Wood (Georgia), and Richard M. Nixon (California). The committee's chief investigator was Louis Russell, accompanied by counsels Robert Stripling and Frank Tavenner.

Follow-up hearings were scheduled for Washington in October 1947. By then, the Capitol curtain began to rise. On September 21, 1947, subpoenas were issued to forty-three people.

During this time, many film-connected people, in Hollywood and New York City, failed to see exactly what was coming: an inquisition on a scale that had never been seen before. Or since.

The creative people in films and stage, many of whom were at their career strides, suddenly found themselves being accused by people they did not know, discovering that their names were on a list with other people who were thought to be subversive. One of the more noted lists was "Red Channels: The Report of Communist Influence in Radio and Television."

In many cases, people were named simply because they went to a gathering at someone's house. In other cases, they were named because in college years they had joined the Communist Party USA. Some continued with that membership, while others left the party after a short period because of disillusionment, political disagreement, the demands of marriage, or service in World War II.

The fact that membership in the Communist Party USA was not illegal at the time was largely ignored. Just being associated with alleged party members, attendance at a meeting or a social gathering, was enough to place a name on a list of suspects.

It wasn't until 1954 that membership in the Communist Party USA was outlawed. In 1966 the party began open membership again.

Many of those subpoenaed were "friendly" witnesses and had already given testimony. As history's coincidences would have it, two future presidents would take part in these hearings: Richard Nixon as a committee member and Ronald Reagan as a friendly witness.

Out of this group emerged eighteen people who initially became known as "unfriendly." There would be more to follow over the years. The unfriendly witnesses used various amendments of the U.S. Constitution to decline to answer certain questions concerning past political memberships or whoever might be a member of an organization that would conspire to overthrow the United States.

From the original eighteen, ten witnesses were ultimately held in contempt by the committee and sentenced to one year in prison. The appeal process would take up three years before they had to actually begin serving their sentences.

The ten were: Dalton Trumbo, John Howard Lawson, Adrian Scott, Alvah Bessie, Albert Maltz, Herbert Biberman, Ring Lardner Jr., Lester Cole, Samuel Ornitz, and Edward Dmytryk.

The other eight were: Richard Collins, Howard Koch, Lewis Milestone, Larry Parks, Irving Pichel, Robert Rossen, Waldo Salt, and Gordon Kahn.

As the Washington hearings continued that fall the progressives and liberals in Hollywood decided to react quickly. A group of actors, writers, and directors known as the Committee on the First Amendment was formed by Philip Dunne, John Huston, and William Wyler. It included June Havoc, Danny Kaye, Marsha Hunt, Humphrey Bogart, Lauren Bacall, Evelyn Keyes, and Paul Henreid. After arriving in Washington the group found itself unprepared for the hard-edged, tough questions that awaited them. Embarrassed, the First Amendment Committee quickly returned to Hollywood to lick its wounds, realizing exactly what was taking place in Washington. Bogart later lamented that the trip was "ill advised and foolish."[29]

Another group gathered, this time on November 24–25, 1947, in New York City's Waldorf-Astoria Hotel. It was a reaction of fear that gave actual birth to the blacklist. This group of forty-eight studio and network chiefs and executives vowed to support the HUAC and cited the "Hollywood Ten" as being in contempt and stated that they would fire anyone who would disgrace filmmaking by citing a morals charge. This two-day meeting, from which there are no known notes or minutes, became known as "The Waldorf Conference."[30]

The witness numbers quickly grew—friendly and unfriendly—as the series of HUAC hearings continued. The officeholders were responding to the rising wave of hysteria. The parade of witnesses seemed endless. Each person had to prepare to answer the basic question: "Are you now or have you ever been a member of the Communist Party?"

As noted by actor Robert Vaughn in *Only Victims*, the answer posed a dilemma for the witness. If the witness was a Communist and denied it before the committee, the witness went to jail for perjury. If the witness admitted to being a Communist, the witness was then asked to inform on his or her friends. If the witness refused, a jail term was waiting because the witness had already waived protection of the Bill of Rights when answering the affirmative to the first question.[31]

As the HUAC investigation went on in various phases into the creative rolls of Hollywood and New York, people began to realize the long-term punishment that was approaching. Lifelong friendships were permanently severed as friends turned on friends. An element of betrayal surfaced. Film studios, television networks, and production companies refused employment to anyone who was suspect.

The blacklist grew. Many unknowing victims of this list found out about it through an agent or friend. When the obvious question came, "Who gave my name?" it was often met with a shrug and silence.

Screenwriter Carl Foreman, basking in the success of *Home of the Brave* (1949) and *The Men* (1950), was subpoenaed to appear on May 20, 1952, along with many other writers, directors, and activists. Foreman notified the committee that he would be coming in as an unfriendly witness. Foreman was a member of the American Communist Party (ACP) from 1938 to 1942. During the war he served as a Tech Sergeant in Frank Capra's film unit. While in the army he came to the conclusion that upon discharge he would resign from the party. "I felt it [the ACP] had no independence and no viewpoint and had become a kind of awkward appendage to the Russian party."

Years later, in an interview, Foreman would recall walking down a street only days before he was to appear. Up ahead he noticed an old studio friend coming his way. Upon seeing Foreman approaching, the studio friend quickly crossed the street and hurried off in another direction. It foreshadowed what was to be repeated.[32]

After his testimony as an unfriendly witness Foreman completed work on the western classic *High Noon* (1952). He then settled in London attempting to get his writing career back on track. His conflict was an example of the times. He later wrote:

I couldn't write. When I sat down at the typewriter to do a screenplay, my impulse was to write a letter to the Times. "Dear Sir: Do you know what they are doing to me?" That sort of thing. The world had rocked that much, you see, and suddenly we didn't know where the hell we were. We were blacklisted. For that kind of thing to happen in America . . . I mean we couldn't work in our own country. It took me three years to be able to write again. It took some fellows longer. I know some guys who never recovered.[33]

Numbers have been thrown out through the years as to the number of creative people blacklisted at the height of their careers. The total number of people directly affected hovers somewhere around 350. But that figure does not take into account family members who were likewise affected, many of whom were sons and daughters in grammar school. Many actors, writers, and directors of American war films were caught up. And many of them had even served in uniform with distinction during World War II. In this era, their service mattered very little.

The Hollywood Ten continued with the appeal process. Other unfriendly witnesses left the country after testifying. A few settled in Mexico. Another group of writers, actors, and directors went to England and France. Several of these expatriates then began having problems with their passports.

The blacklisted writers who remained were driven underground. Many of them had to fall back on a pseudonym or a "front" (someone who had an acceptable name while the blacklistee did the actual writing). The blacklist continued to be honored as the suffering continued.

In 1950, their appeals exhausted, the Hollywood Ten reported for their prison terms. They served their terms in different prisons, mostly in the East. By now, many people were realizing the actual toll that the hearings had taken. But it was too late, as the proverbial wheels of justice were slowly moving.

It was at this time when Lester Cole and Ring Lardner Jr. were sentenced to the Federal Correction Institution at Danbury, Connecticut. One of the inmates at that facility just happened to be a former member of Congress who was convicted of taking salary kickbacks from nonworkers on his staff. That felon was New Jersey Republican J. Parnell Thomas, former HUAC chairman.

The issue of communism swelled so much that in February 1950 Joseph Raymond McCarthy, a little known U.S. senator from Wisconsin, speaking in front of a Republican Women's Club in Wheeling, West Virginia, announced that he had a list of 205 Communists presently working in the State Department. Two weeks later McCarthy claimed he had more names, prompting the Senate to name a subcommittee to investigate.

The ripple effect of the Blacklist Era spilled into the McCarthy Era, which thrived throughout the mid-1950s. The war in Korea set the background for the ever-present Soviet threat that under every rock, behind every bush, lurked a Communist whose motivation was to overthrow the country. In a Catholic grammar school in Chicago, students were called upon to pray for the success of Senator McCarthy.

Howard Suber, a retired UCLA film school professor and recognized authority on the Blacklist Era, explained how the paranoia of those times grew. "The paranoia that led to the blacklist created a paranoia of its own. This secondary paranoia created a situation where everybody could imagine their own worst fantasies. And there was absolutely no denial or corroboration of those fantasies—so secret was the operation of the blacklist."[34]

McCarthy's investigations into Communist subversion in almost every aspect of American life escalated and was largely unchecked by the Eisenhower administration, then in its first term. The climactic moment came when McCarthy accused the army of aiding the Communists. Thereafter, McCarthy's charges deteriorated into the ridiculous and often sparked laughter. His influence went downhill quickly. After all of his claims of lists McCarthy never produced any documentation. He was subsequently censored by the U.S. Senate. McCarthy died in May 1957 of acute hepatic failure caused by cirrhosis of the liver.

But the blacklist reverberations continued throughout the 1950s. Carl Foreman and Michael Wilson were never given the appropriate credit on the Academy Award–winning screenplay of Pierre Boulle's novel *The Bridge on the River Kwai* (1957). Boulle, who didn't write in English, admitted publicly that he didn't write the film. On March 26, 1958, actress Kim Novak accepted the Oscar for Boulle and quickly left the stage.[35] Wilson, who adapted *A Place in the Sun* (1951) from the Theodore Dreiser novel, was also denied credit for his work on *Lawrence of Arabia* (1962). After being blacklisted, Wilson and his wife Zelma (who also lost her job as an architect) took their two small children and left for Paris.

Foreman would remain based in London for years, where he worked with the British film industry. In 1967, he returned to the United States and Columbia Pictures to produce *MacKenna's Gold*, a star-packed action western that he adapted from the Will Henry novel.

In 1956, Robert Rich was announced as the Oscar winner for the screenplay story of *The Brave One*, a drama where a boy saves the life of his pet bull when the animal is sent into the ring. The Academy audience did not find it surprising that Robert Rich was not present. Days later, it was learned that Robert Rich was actually Dalton Trumbo working under a pseudonym.

Albert Maltz's name was kept off the screenplay for *The Defiant Ones* in 1958, which had the earlier writing credits given to Nathan E. Douglas and Harold Jacob Smith. Douglas was the pseudonym for blacklisted writer Ned Young.

In 1960, producer and director Otto Preminger gave the okay to hire Trumbo to write the screenplay adaptation of *Exodus*, based on the Leon Uris novel about the formation of Israel. That hiring helped break the blacklist. In the same year *Spartacus* was released, also written by Trumbo.

But in its time, the wake that the blacklist left was strewn with hundreds of ruined careers and ruptured friendships and in some cases contributed to premature deaths. Another wound in this political battle was the number of witnesses who turned and named names. This gave way to conflicted feelings that would span the rest of the twentieth century.

In the summer of 1957 Carl Foreman was still living in London, where he worked on *The Bridge on the River Kwai* and *The Guns of Navarone* (1961). He was still writing letters to the editor. In a letter to the *London Daily Express* in July 1957 he wrote, "Don't sell us short. We're a young nation, inclined at times to take ourselves too seriously, to be headstrong and impatient, to be both overconfident and insecure. But the love of freedom and fair play, which we have inherited from you [Great Britain] will always be our link with you and our most precious possession. Yes, I am a proud American today, and I don't particularly want to be quiet about it."[36]

Finally, Dalton Trumbo and Albert Maltz had their names, respectively, added to the screenplays of *Roman Holiday* (1953) and *The Robe* (1953).

It wasn't until 1975 that Dalton Trumbo was finally presented with the Oscar for his work on *The Brave One*. On March 16, 1985, the Academy of Motion Picture Arts and Sciences presented to the widows and families of Carl Foreman and Michael Wilson Oscars for their work on *The Bridge on the River Kwai*.

Today the threatening times and hysteria of the Blacklist and McCarthy Eras are bitter and distant memories.

But as the widow of Hollywood agent George Willner, of one of those black-listed, so succinctly put it, "I can forgive . . . but not forget."[37]

# 4

# Korea: A Disturbing War

The boast of heraldry, the pomp of power,
And all that beauty, all that wealth e'er gave
Awaits alike the inevitable hour:—
The paths of glory lead but to the grave.

—Thomas Gray

Six months into the second half of the twentieth century, the United States suddenly found itself in another war. What had happened?

When World War II ended, the United States and the Soviet Union agreed to split Korea along the 38th parallel. The Soviet Union would occupy the northern half, whereas the United States had the South. Almost from the start, the Soviet Union set up a Communist government in the North. Tensions between the North and the South escalated, paralleling a growing conflict between the United States and the Soviet Union.

On June 25, 1950—with Soviet approval and armed with Russian weapons— the North Korean Army crossed the 38th parallel and invaded South Korea. The South Korean Army was unprepared and quickly overrun. The North Koreans continued to push southward and occupied Seoul.

The United Nations condemned the invasion and quickly established a fighting force made up of sixteen UN member nations, including the United States.

General Douglas MacArthur (headquartered in Tokyo to supervise the reconstruction of Japan) was named to head the UN force. During that summer, the retreat continued as UN forces fell back to what was called the Pusan Perimeter at the tip of the peninsula.

It was at this point where MacArthur pulled off one of the boldest maneuvers of his long career. On September 15, an "end run" invasion at Inchon caught the North Koreans flat-footed and outgunned. Instead of using army units, Mac-Arthur chose the marines as the initial invasion force because of their being accustomed to Asian amphibious operations. Within eleven days, Seoul was retaken. By September 29, the North Koreans were pushed back across the 38th parallel. On October 7, UN forces invaded North Korea.

## REALITY CONTINUES

During this time two films, respectively, about World War II and Korea, were released. They were *The Men* (1950) and *The Steel Helmet* (1951).

When Carl Foreman began researching the project about wheelchair veterans adjusting to a new life, it was called *Battle Stripe*. For assistance, Foreman called on the staff at the spinal ward of the Birmingham Veterans Administration (VA) Hospital in Van Nuys, California. Fred Zinnemann came in as director for producer Stanley Kramer. The three worked well on *Home of the Brave* and would work again on the western classic *High Noon* a year later.

During the development phase, the title was changed to *The Men*. Foreman's script centered around the double-edged conflict that paraplegic veterans faced after World War II: conquering self-pity and adjusting to the dispassion and denial of society. Foreman used the societal syndrome of letting the other guy go over and get wounded or killed.

What happened next was Stanley Kramer's coup of signing a little-known Broadway actor to a one-picture contract, unheard of at the time. The actor would have to convince the audience that he actually was a paraplegic veteran. When the actor read Foreman's completed first draft, he was impressed and felt that *The Men* was the perfect vehicle for his first film.

The actor was Marlon Brando, coming off his stage play success in *A Street-car Named Desire*.

Kramer and Zinnemann cast Teresa Wright as the loyal and loving fiancée and Jack Webb as another wheelchair veteran. Twenty-six-year-old Arthur Jurado, injured in a plane crash as an Army Air Force lieutenant returning to the United States, brought his real-life predicament to the screen as one of the veterans on the spinal ward. Everett Sloane was cast as the physician in charge of the ward.

In one of the first scenes Sloane informs the veterans' wives and family members that their condition is permanent and that relatives will have to adjust as much as the patients.

Like Foreman, Brando went to Birmingham Veterans Hospital. But Brando, going for authenticity, checked himself in as a patient and stayed there for three weeks. In his autobiography, Brando explained, "A few patients and members of the staff were informed, but most of the patients didn't know I was an actor and because it was my first movie, no one recognized me."[1] The first thing he learned was that the wheelchair veterans hated pity.

Brando gave a stellar performance as Lieutenant Ken Wilocek who was shot by a German sniper in the closing days of the war. As a patient on the spinal ward, Wilocek goes through the phase of self-pity. Brando calls off his engagement to Wright because they won't have a "normal life." Again, the reality of sexual problems broke new ground in this war film. Brando is steeled by Webb to get a grip and adjust to his new life.

Brando's character does adjust, and he makes the ultimate decision to marry Wright (whose parents have already cautioned her about the "problems"). Wright then brings Brando home to begin their life together. Foreman's powerful script resulted in an Oscar nomination.

Former infantryman Samuel Fuller fulfilled his promise to Lewis Milestone (made in the letter following the release of *A Walk in the Sun*) to turn in a realistic war film. The difference was that this one was not about World War II—there was a new war. The Korean War was only months old when Fuller finished the script and began production. He based the scenario on what was coming out in the news.

Fuller cast a struggling actor, Gene Evans, who was a former army sergeant, as the grizzled, middle-aged Sergeant Zack in *The Steel Helmet* (1951). Fuller shot the film in and around Los Angeles' Griffith Park on a shoestring budget of $104,000, remarkable for the time.

Evans's helmet is already pierced by a bullet as the opening credits roll. As Sergeant Zack, Evans is befriended by a Korean boy after surviving a POW massacre by playing dead. Evans then puts together a makeshift squad to get back to UN lines. Evans also has problems with a green officer who hasn't seen any combat. James Edwards (*Home of the Brave* [1949]) portrays a black soldier constantly aware of the prejudice. One of the interesting scenes for Evans is when he tracks the line of fire from an enemy sniper and zeroes in on his position, showing survival skills in a combat zone that others do not have.[2]

Rounding out the cast were Robert Hutton, Steve Brodie (*Home of the Brave*), and Richard Loo.

Upon release the film became the sleeper hit of the year. Writing in the *Los Angeles Daily Mirror*, entertainment writer Dick Williams noted that *The Steel Helmet* was written, produced, and directed by a "former infantryman—Samuel Fuller—which may account for its real feeling."

Williams also noted the box office success of *Sands of Iwo Jima*, number eight in the gross at $3.9 million; *Twelve O'Clock High* was tenth, with $3.22 million, moneymakers of the time. The bottom line was evident, according to Williams. "This trend has not escaped the attention of a single Hollywood producer from the majors to the smallest independents. Hence the big boom in all types of war pix."[3]

After *The Steel Helmet* was released, Fuller gave the pierced helmet to Evans as a present. Decades later, Evans returned it to him at a film retrospective at USC.

Lewis Milestone's next combat outing centered around the marines in the

Pacific with *Halls of Montezuma* (1950), from a script credited to Michael Blankfort. Richard Widmark portrayed Carl Anderson, a high school teacher who is called to active duty as a platoon leader. One of his students, Robert Wagner, ends up in his unit. The mission is to advance on a Japanese-held island to knock out rocket-launching sites. Widmark's platoon has the usual cross section of American guys. Karl Malden is a navy corpsman who bootlegs pills to Widmark for his crushing headaches. Skip Homeier is "Pretty Boy" Riley who carries an obsessive hatred for the Japanese because his sister married one. Reginald Gardiner, with a clipped British accent, comes in as a quirky intelligence type attached to the platoon as a translator. Gardiner's uniqueness is shown by his shoulder holster that houses a pearl-handled revolver. Jack Webb is a combat correspondent who follows the platoon as background for the war novel he intends to write. The Marine Corps hymn blasts from the sound track as the marines head toward the beach in the early going.

Studios were becoming more content with World War II films. And the situation in Korea was becoming such that more films would come from this new and complex war.

In a memo to director Henry King at 20th Century Fox, Darryl F. Zanuck wrote, "All of the better war pictures released to date have been enormous successes. *Twelve O'Clock High, Battleground, Sands of Iwo Jima* have been big money makers. I believe this field is a fairly safe risk providing the industry as a whole does not overdo it and flood the market."[4]

John Huston wrote and directed the adaptation of Stephen Crane's Civil War classic novel *The Red Badge of Courage*, released in 1951 by MGM. As soon as it was announced in the Hollywood trade papers that Huston was preparing the adaptation, he was deluged with offers from established and unknown actors begging to audition for the lead.[5]

For the part of Henry Fleming, Huston cast the most decorated World War II army infantryman, Audie Leon Murphy. This was Murphy's third film but first as the lead character.

Murphy was brought to Hollywood by James Cagney. The war hero hadn't given Hollywood the slightest thought until Cagney saw the *Life* magazine cover story on Murphy. After repeated phone calls Murphy decided to at least come to California and meet with Cagney. That meeting was the start of war hero to movie star. But first came the proper training. And Cagney supplied that: acting lessons.

Raised among a large Texas family in poverty, Murphy never finished grammar school. Because of his slight frame (112 pounds at the heaviest) he was rejected by the marines.

MGM didn't want to produce the script because executives felt it had a thin main story line, no love story subplot, and no name star in the lead. But Huston prevailed on a low budget and shot the film at his own ranch and other locations in Chico, California. He saw the project as showing the ironically thin line between cowardice and heroism while the Korean War appeared every day in headlines.

Murphy portrayed Henry Fleming as naive about the horrors of combat. And when his first action is thrust upon him, Fleming cuts and runs like many other young Union soldiers. But the young man is able to come to terms with his faults and redeems himself on the field by leading a charge of his 304th Regiment with the "Battle Hymn of the Republic" stirring on the sound track.

Several actors were mentioned to record Crane's narration from the novel. First suggestions were Spencer Tracy and Gregory Peck. Huston finally settled on James Whitmore.

Supporting Murphy were Bill Mauldin, Douglas Dick, Royal Dano, Andy Devine, Arthur Hunnicutt, and John Dierkes as the "Tattered Soldier."[6]

In a series for *The New Yorker* magazine Lillian Ross wrote an account of production and postproduction entitled "The Red Badge of Courage—Saga of a Monster and a Movie." The series was later expanded into the book *Picture*.

After a test showing the studio determined that audiences could not get the plot. The film was then pulled and reedited after Huston left the country to scout locations for *The African Queen*. According to Lillian Ross, after a studio screening, William Wyler remarked about the Civil War, "It was the bloodiest war. No Red Cross. Nothing."[7]

Some reviews were complimentary to the film but still voiced reservations. Writing in the *Los Angeles Collegian*, Vic Heutschy commented, "Murphy appears in his finest role to date and his characterization is perfect. . . . But still one wonders why in these troubled times Huston would film a picture that shows cowardice, fear, raw emotion, and terrors of war—even if it is the Civil War. . . . Judging by the direction and acting it is pictorially a good movie, but due to its realism and general material content the film should appeal to a limited audience."[8]

Huston was upset upon seeing the recut version and was never able to sit through another screening of the film.

Coming off the success of *Battleground*, screenwriter Robert Pirosh initially got *Go for Broke!* (1951) set up at 20th Century Fox, with him as the director. This was the memorable story of the 100th Infantry Battalion that was later merged with the noted 442nd Regimental Combat Team whose motto was "Go for Broke!"

The units, made up of Nisei (second-generation) Japanese in Hawaii and California whose relatives were "interned" in relocation camps after Pearl Harbor, took a major part in the Italian campaign and emerged as World War II's most decorated regiment. By the war's end the 100th and the 442nd had amassed a total of 18,143 personal decorations, including 9,468 Purple Hearts. Some 650 of these Americans were killed in action.

Reacting with the strong feeling about Japanese in the United States after Pearl Harbor, California Attorney General Earl Warren convinced the Roosevelt administration to "re-locate" 110,000 Americans of Japanese descent to guarded camps. Many of the sons and brothers of these citizens ended up as soldiers in the 100/442nd.

Another prejudicial scar inflicted on the Nisei soldiers was the military combat award syndrome. A record number of Distinguished Service Crosses, fifty-two, the second highest combat medal, was awarded to these soldiers. Many of those decorations were posthumous. In many instances, when the initial award was recommended as a Congressional Medal of Honor, somewhere in the army chain the surname on the recommendation was noted. The award would then be "knocked down" one grade and returned to the individual as a Distinguished Service Cross. In other cases the award was taken down again to a Silver Star.

Other combat awards were: 560 Silver Stars (with 28 Oak Leaf Clusters), 22 Legions of Merit, 4,000 Bronze Stars (with 1,200 Oak Leaf Clusters), and eight Presidential Unit Citations.[9]

The only Congressional Medal of Honor awarded to a soldier in the 100/442nd bypassed the army chain of command. This was awarded to Sadao S. Munemori, who threw himself on a live Nazi hand grenade, thereby saving the lives of several of his comrades. In addition to recognition and the Congressional Medal of Honor a Los Angeles freeway bridge was named after him years later.[10]

As development of the script continued at 20th Century Fox, the project suffered its first setback. Darryl Zanuck suddenly decided that he didn't want to risk making the picture. In a letter to Earl Finch at the 442nd Veterans Club in Honolulu, May 23, 1950, Anthony Coldeway, a studio executive, stated,

Just a note to tell you that I was notified this morning that Mr. Zanuck had decided not to make the picture.

Naturally I am quite disappointed, particularly as I am still convinced that a story along the lines we discussed would not only have been commercially successful, but a real and important influence towards a better understanding and appreciation of all that the boys of the 442nd experienced.[11]

Once again Dore Schary at MGM came in to rescue a project written by Robert Pirosh. Pirosh and the script found a home on the Culver City lot. The team from *Battleground* was rounded out when Van Johnson came aboard as the young lieutenant who is frustrated when he discovers that his new platoon is made up of Nisei soldiers from Hawaii and California. The Nisei leads were given to Lane Nakano, George Miki, and Akira Fukunaga. Approximately 350 applicants were interviewed; 100 were auditioned for speaking and bit parts.[12]

Like any film, *Go for Broke!* had its production and personal problems. On October 17, 1950, Akira Fukunaga wrote:

We're beginning to feel the pressure of being actors. Every little thing seems to bother us. Mainly because we feel we are not receiving the "star" treatment" any actor wants to get. After learning what the bit player get [*sic*] for a few lines we feel we are underpaid and plan to hit Dore Schary for a raise or a bonus. The 375 a week we pull down don't seem so big now. Especially after the indignities we have to tolerate. You really take a lot of shit here.

Everyone seems to be tightening up. The director Pirosh swore at Lane Nakano yesterday. Lane got so mad he threw down his rifle and walked away. Pirosh apologized to him during the lunch hour.[13]

In the film, Johnson, an initial racial skeptic, comes to understand and be impressed with the bravery and courage of the Nisei soldiers under his command. The climactic sequence centered around the 100/442nd's relief of "The Lost Battalion" of the 36th Infantry Division in a four-day battle up rugged terrain, fighting from tree to tree. Approximately 800 casualties were suffered, including 200 killed.

The unit's resolution, using actual footage, comes when President Harry Truman pins the final Presidential Unit Citation on the 100/442nd colors. Truman added, "You fought not only the enemy but you fought prejudice—and you won."

It took decades for the Medal of Honor slights to be corrected. After years of lobbying, including many setbacks, it finally happened. On June 22, 2000, in a White House ceremony, President Bill Clinton awarded the Medal of Honor to twenty-two members of the 100/442nd. Only seven of the twenty-two were present. The others, in posthumous honors, were represented by surviving relatives.[14]

After passing on *Go for Broke!* 20th Century Fox produced *The Desert Fox* (1951), the first post–World War II film about an enemy officer, Field Marshal Erwin Rommel, who earned the nickname from his North African campaign against the British Eighth Army in 1942. The script, Nunnally Johnson's adaptation of a book by Desmond Young, parallels a Greek tragedy. An ethical and educated man, who is the consummate leader, is caught up on the wrong side of a conflict and pays the ultimate price. Henry Hathaway directed James Mason, who turned in a touching performance as the doomed general. Jessica Tandy played his loyal wife, while Luther Adler did a spiteful turn as the jealous Adolf Hitler. Rounding out the cast were Everett Sloane, Leo G. Carroll, Richard Boone, and Desmond Young.

Rommel was brought to occupied France to help organize the "impregnable" Atlantic wall against the coming Allied invasion. He is reported to have told his staff that the Allies must be stopped on the first day—"that day will be '*The Longest Day.*' "

The real-life tragic ending in the film comes when Rommel is connected to the July 20, 1944, failed plot to assassinate Hitler. One of the objectives of the attempt was to oust Hitler and negotiate a truce with the Allies, keeping Germany from being invaded. Rommel was allowed the option of suicide, by taking cyanide in the back seat of a staff car on the promise that his family would be protected.

Arthur Kennedy received an Academy Award nomination for his performance as a bigoted GI who is blinded in combat in Universal-International's *Bright Victory* (1951). He is then befriended by another sightless GI, a black played by James Edwards. The friendship causes Kennedy's character to "see" what blindness his bigotry actually was. Peggy Dow played Kennedy's faithful girlfriend. Kennedy was named Best Actor by the New York Film Critics.

More sympathy toward Germany was brought out in *Decision before Dawn*, for 20th Century Fox. The story is really a spy thriller set against the war. Oskar Werner leads a group of anti-Nazi POWs who parachute back into Germany to spy for the Allies. As the disillusioned group makes it way through Nazi-held territory, they see the ravages that the Third Reich has inflicted. Supporting Werner were Richard Basehart, Gary Merrill, and Hildegarde Neff. The film was nominated for Best Picture of 1951. Also nominated was Dorothy Spencer for Best Editing.

After appearing as the star-crossed lovers in *Sunset Boulevard* (1950), Warner Bros. brought William Holden and Nancy Olson together, in 1951, for *Force of Arms*. The script, credited to Orin Jannings from a story by Richard Tregaskis, was loosely structured on Ernest Hemingway's *A Farewell to Arms*, where a wounded soldier falls in love with his nurse. This updated version took place during the Italian campaign in 1944, with Frank Lovejoy, Gene Evans, and Paul Picerni in supporting roles.

One of John Wayne's buddy screenwriters, James Edward Grant, turned out *Flying Leathernecks* (1951), the story of marine fighter pilots on Guadalcanal. The routine RKO story line had Wayne in conflict not only with the missions his men must fly but with his executive officer, Robert Ryan, whose leadership style was different. The film is saved by aerial combat footage involving hellcats and corsairs. Jay C. Flippen portrayed the "scrounger" sergeant, who comes up with much-needed war materiel from a variety of illegitmate sources. Rounding out the cast were Don Taylor, Janis Carter, William Harrigan, and James Bell.

Samuel Fuller wrote and directed a second Korean War outing with *Fixed Bayonets* (1951), which was garnered from the headlines for 20th Century Fox. Fuller used the background of the disastrous 1950–1951 winter offensive. Richard Basehart, Gene Evans, and Michael O'Shea played soldiers fighting a winter rear-guard action.

John Huston hit his stride with distant locations by taking James Agee's adaptation of C.S. Forester's *The African Queen* to Africa. Humphrey Bogart's Oscar-winning performance as the gin-soaked Charlie Allnut was balanced by Katharine Hepburn's spinster rendition of Rose Sayer. The unlikely pair are caught up in the beginning of World War I in East Africa as the German and British colonists square off. Bogart and Hepburn then concoct a hairbrained scheme to sink a German gunboat with a homemade torpedo as they venture down a dangerous river. Obstacles overcome included going over rapids, a mosquito attack, and bloodsuckers being peeled off Bogart's upper torso.

The entire production was plagued with problems right from the start. The heat, the distant location, and direction problems with Hepburn all took their toll. Huston then suggested to Hepburn that she play Rose Sayer as Eleanor Roosevelt, which filled in for some needed comedy relief.

Decades later Hepburn wrote a memoir of the entire production experience: *The Making of* The African Queen: *Or How I Went to Africa with Bogart, Bacall, and Huston and Almost Lost My Mind* (1987).

As difficult as the experience was, it resulted in Oscar nominations for Agee, Hepburn, and Huston.

One of the more intriguing scenarios of World War II was the true-life espionage case of Elyesa Bazna, who was the valet to Sir Hughe Knatchbull-Hugessen, the British ambassador to Turkey. Bazna set up a deal with Nazi agents because he had access to decoded, classified, Allied information about the Casablanca and Moscow conferences. He was given the code name "Cicero." The Third Reich paid his high rates without hesitation in British pounds. Even though his information was deemed doubtful by the Nazis, Bazna continued to give over facts about Allied movements including the actual site for the cross Channel invasion. However, the Abwehr (Nazi intelligence) discounted much of Cicero's decoded information. After the war, it was concluded that Cicero was actually a double agent, working for the British giving information to the Nazis that the British approved.

James Mason's performance as Bazna, in *Five Fingers* (1952), came from Michael Wilson's *taut* adaptation of *Operation Cicero*, by L.C. Moyzische at 20th Century Fox. The supporting cast included Michael Rennie as the ambassador, Danielle Darrieux, Walter Hampden, and Oscar Karlweis. Wilson and Joseph Mankiewicz both received Oscar nominations.

The Nazis got one up on Bazna when he later discovered that he was paid in counterfeit British currency. After the war he continued to cause legal problems for the West German government because of alleged monies owed. This continued until Bazna's death in 1971.

Colonel Paul Tibbets's story as the pilot of the *Enola Gay*, the B-29 that dropped the atom bomb on Hiroshima, was set up for a 1952 release at MGM. Beirne Lay Jr. (*Twelve O'Clock High*) got story credit with a script titled *Above and Beyond* by Melvin Frank and Norman Panama.

In his combat life, Tibbets was a pilot with the Eighth Air Force in Europe and had amassed an enviable record. He piloted the first B-17 to cross the English Channel. As a major, Tibbets flew General Mark Clark to secret meetings in North Africa. On November 5, 1942, he transported General Dwight Eisenhower to Gibraltar prior to the North Africa invasion. As the European war was winding down, he was placed on a draft to the Pacific Theater. However, Tibbets and other airmen were detoured to Wendover Field, Utah, for training on the top secret B-29 mission.

Part of the conflict in the film is the way that the secrecy affected the Tibbets marriage. Robert Taylor portrayed Tibbets with Eleanor Parker as Lucy, his stuggling and confused wife, who had no idea what her husband and his crew were being groomed for. Others in the cast were Jim Backus as Curtis LeMay, James Whitmore, and Larry Keating.

Tibbets named the bomber *Enola Gay*, after his mother (*Enola*, ironically, is *alone* spelled backwards). The night before the mission, as the bomb is being loaded, Tibbets wrote a letter to his mother, putting down his thoughts against the historical impact.

Lay received an Academy Award nomination along with Hugo Friedhofer for musical score.

RKO came to the Korean War starting line with *One Minute to Zero* (1952), starring Robert Mitchum and Ann Blyth. Mitchum comes into the film as a World War II combat veteran advising Republic of (South) Korea troops when the war begins. He is then given command of a regiment and is forced to call in artillery on a refugee column being used as cover by Communist guerrillas. The Army Signal Corps added documentary footage for realism. Backing up Mitchum were William Talman, Charles McGraw, Margaret Sheridan, and Richard Egan.

20th Century Fox decided on a remake of *What Price Glory?* (1952). James Cagney and Dan Dailey were cast as the dueling marines, Captain Flagg and Sergeant Quirt, respectively, in war-torn 1918 France. The film played up the macho pranks of the two rivals for Corinne Calvet's favors as Charmaine. The brawling and drinking sequences are fun to watch, but it still comes in second next to the original, which was based on the 1924 play by Laurence Stallings and Maxwell Anderson. In supporting roles were Robert Wagner, James Gleason, and William Demarest.

## DECISIVE ACTION

Shortly after the Inchon invasion it was necessary for President Truman to meet with General MacArthur to outline further strategy in Korea. MacArthur had not been back to the United States in approximately fourteen years. The meeting place selected was Wake Island. It would be exactly one month to the day after the Inchon invasion. Tensions between the general and his commander in chief began almost immediately when there was some hesitation as to which plane would land first and who would be waiting for whom.

When the meeting finally began Truman expressed his intense anger with MacArthur over an August message to the annual convention of the Veterans of Foreign Wars where the general explained that he wanted a defense line from Vladivostok to Singapore protected by U.S. forces, presumably with himself as commander. Truman reprimanded MacArthur for bypassing the chain of command. MacArthur apologized and said that it wouldn't happen again.

MacArthur added that in his opinion, and as a result of current intelligence, China definitely would not come into the war. The general also said that he would be able to end the war by Thanksgiving. He added that American troops would be back in Tokyo by Christmas. Before the meeting ended, the president warned MacArthur not to issue any public statements that had not been approved by the White House. MacArthur assured Truman that he would follow the chain. Truman returned to Washington, while MacArthur went back to conducting his offensive.[15]

At this point, China condemned the invasion of North Korea and warned that if the UN forces did not withdraw, they would take immediate action. MacArthur, viewing this as an idle threat, pressed the attack. Despite severe weather predictions, MacArthur divided his force, going up two sides of the peninsula. On November 6, two days before the congressional elections, MacArthur sent a message for permission to bomb the bridges along the Yalu River where Chinese troops were massing. He added, "Every hour that this is postponed will be paid for dearly in American and other United Nations blood."

MacArthur's request was rejected. By November 8 nothing had occurred from the enemy side. MacArthur requested permission to bomb certain bases in Manchuria. Again, he was rejected. However, the elections brought about a resounding defeat for congressional Democrats.

By November 20, UN forces reached the Yalu River, the North Korea/China border.

Six days later, more than 200,000 Chinese troops charged across the Yalu, sending UN forces into a massive retreat. Army and marine units found themselves surrounded. At night, the temperature plummeted to minus thirty degrees. The 1st Marine Regiment, under the command of Colonel Lewis B. "Chesty" Puller, slowly came out of the Chosin Reservoir, giving birth to the time-honored phrase "The frozen Chosin during the freezin' season." The U.S. Army retreated southward, while the marines trudged eighty miles eastward to the port of Hungnam, where they were evacuated to the south.

Marine General O.P. Smith then explained, "We're not retreating; we're merely advancing in another direction."

MacArthur was stung. Reacting to his most monumental defeat, he placed blame on the Truman administration's restrictions on his command.

As 1951 began, MacArthur established a defense around Seoul and planned for a counterattack. The Truman White House described what was happening in Korea as a police action. But what Americans saw, in the headlines and in newsreels, was a full-fledged war. The subplot drama between Truman and MacArthur broke full stride into its third act.

MacArthur, still reeling from the defeat of the winter retreat from the Yalu, proposed to bomb key targets in China, blocking the Chinese coast and using Chiang Kai-shek's Nationalist Army in Korea to stage an invasion of South China.

Truman and his advisers felt that this plan, an all-out invasion of China, spelled chaos for the world. General Omar Bradley told Truman that it would be the wrong war at the wrong place at the wrong time with the wrong enemy.

Years later Truman would reflect that these times (the beginning of the Korean War and his troubles with MacArthur) were his most difficult time as president.

He was also becoming concerned that MacArthur, now seventy years old, was not a balanced man.

Truman and the Joint Chiefs ordered MacArthur to hold at the 38th parallel. With South Korea back in UN hands, it was hoped that a cease-fire could be negotiated.

MacArthur paid no attention to the advice from either the Joint Chiefs or the White House. Instead, MacArthur issued a statement that he was ready to meet with Red China to discuss a Korean settlement. He again threatened an all-out attack against China. MacArthur suggested that if North Korea were to be surrendered, it should be surrendered to him personally.[16]

Truman and the Joint Chiefs were rightly concerned that MacArthur's plan would lead to an outright third world war against Red China, Russia, and North Korea, with the destruction of a large portion of the world hanging in the balance. Again, MacArthur was ordered to hold the line.

On April 5, House minority leader Joseph Martin (R–Massachusetts) read a letter from MacArthur contending that if the war against communism in Asia fails, the fall of Europe is inevitable. MacArthur implied that it was difficult for some (the White House and the Joint Chiefs) to realize that Asia is where the Communists have "elected to make their play for global conquest."

His letter made a profound impact with Congress and the American public in light of the escalating hysteria over Communist influence in the United States. Moreover, the letter violated MacArthur's Wake Island promise to Truman that the chain of command be followed. With this letter, MacArthur gave Truman and the Joint Chiefs what they needed, a documented reason to relieve him of command.

Truman met several times with advisers who were often called his "war cabinet." He wanted to fire MacArthur immediately. Everyone in the war cabinet agreed, save one holdout: Secretary of Defense George Marshall, who was mainly concerned with congressional reaction. Truman had Marshall read the White House correspondence with MacArthur going back two years.

The following morning Marshall was waiting for Truman outside the Oval Office. He told Truman that he spent most of the night on the letter file, adding, "Mr. President, you should have fired the son-of-a-bitch two years ago."

With complete agreement of the Joint Chiefs, it was arranged to have the UN command turned over to General Matthew B. Ridgway, who was presently commanding the U.S. Eighth Army. Ridgway, a combat veteran of the Normandy and Bulge campaigns, had impressively transformed the Eighth Army from the chaos of the winter retreat into an effective fighting unit.

On the morning of April 11, MacArthur's dismissal was announced in the American press. The outrage and uproar were immediate. Millions of Americans, unaware of the closed-door background, were violently angered at Harry Truman for firing one of the most celebrated heroes of World War II.[17]

The world, in a short time, was clearly a different place.

MacArthur returned to the United States for the first time since 1937. It was a hero's welcome in many cities, climaxed by the now-famous "Old soldiers never die" speech to a joint session of Congress on April 19. The general was ending fifty-two years of military service.

Public reaction swelled to greater heights. Popular crooner Vaughn Monroe recorded the "Old Soldiers Never Die" ballad to huge sales.

Matthew Ridgway continued with his duties as commander of the UN forces, while MacArthur went on a speaking tour, presumably to capture the 1952 Republican presidential nomination.

By June, the situation in Korea was such that there was no more talk of a Communist victory. The Red Chinese and North Koreans were using diplomatic channels to begin truce talks.

In the meantime, congressional hearings were scheduled regarding Korean War decisions and MacArthur's dismissal. MacArthur was the first witness, giving testimony that lasted three days. He admitted to no mistakes, no errors of judgment. The failure to anticipate the invasion of 200,000 Chinese troops across the Yalu River, causing the devastating winter retreat, was the fault of the CIA, explained the general.

When members of the Joint Chiefs testified, over a nineteen-day period, MacArthur's case seemed to falter. Truman's military advisers were in complete agreement that the general be relieved not only for attempting to widen the war but for repeatedly violating the chain of command. The Joint Chiefs were unanimous that MacArthur's firing was an absolute necessity.[18]

On July 10, 1951, truce talks between the United Nations and the Communist Chinese began at Kaesang. On May 12, 1952, General Mark Clark was named to replace Matthew Ridgway, who was transferred to be supreme commander of allied troops in Europe, replacing General Dwight Eisenhower.

The war in Korea continued as UN forces held the line at the 38th parallel.

On July 7, 1952, the Republican National Convention, meeting in Chicago, nominated Dwight Eisenhower on the first ballot. California Senator Richard Nixon was chosen as his running mate.

Watching the nomination on television that night, MacArthur was asked by his wife, Jeanne, what kind of a president Eisenhower would make. Eisenhower had served as MacArthur's chief of staff, in the 1930s, posted in the Philippines.

"He'll be a good president," answered MacArthur. "He was the best clerk I ever had."

MacArthur's legend did not pass unrecognized in relation to film mythology. In a 1979 interview in his office, at Universal Pictures, producer Carl Foreman was informed that an East Coast film studies teacher told his students that the 1952 western classic *High Noon* was director Fred Zinnemann's tribute to Douglas MacArthur.[19]

The courageous marshal, Will Kane, was supposedly patterned after MacArthur. The back story of Kane making the town of Hadleyville safe was MacArthur's performance in World War II. The four outlaws (the Frank Miller gang) represented the North Korean Communists. The indifference of the town and the cowardice of the former deputies were alleged metaphors on MacArthur's enemies in Congress, the Joint Chiefs, and the White House. The protector saying good-bye (Old Soldiers Never Die) was depicted at the end when Gary Cooper, as Kane, removes the star from his vest and throws it to the ground. He protected the people from the forces of evil, saving the town. And he resents how he was treated.

Foreman listened to the comparison, shook his head, and hit the desk with a closed fist.

"Fred Zinnemann's tribute to MacArthur! Fred Zinnemann came aboard *after* the script was finished!" boomed Foreman in a loud voice. He looked away for a moment and softly said, "My God, I've got to write that book."

Foreman, of course, died before completing his autobiography, *Away from Home*.

The fierce fighting continued in Korea, from one hill to the next, as America saw Eisenhower defeat Democrat Adlai Stevenson for president. The president-elect then kept a campaign promise, making a fact-finding trip to Korea. On July 27, 1953, at Panmunjom, Korea, the United Nations and North Korean officials signed a truce agreement, keeping the peninsula divided, close to where it was before hostilities began. The price the United States paid in this complex war was high: more than 50,000 Americans killed, another 8,000 missing, and 100,000 wounded. The question was often asked, "What was this war about?" Years later Korea became known as "The Forgotten War."

The 1st Marine Division experience in Korea at the Chosin Reservoir served as background for Warner Bros.' *Retreat, Hell!* (1952). Frank Lovejoy served as a company commander, backed up by Richard Carlson and Russ Tamblyn. Producer Milton Sperling gave some personal input based on his service in the corps during World War II.

# 5

# After Effects: The 1950s

Heroic men can die upon the battlefield in vain, because of what occurs after a war, as well as because of what happens during a war.

—Harold Edward Stassen

Even as World War II was winding down in the Pacific, its impact was already being recorded through books and plays.

The first notable work at this time was John Hersey's *A Bell for Adano*, which won the 1945 Pulitzer Prize for fiction. The film was released that same year. *Home of the Brave* (1949) and *Command Decision* (1949) were already Broadway successes and quickly found open cinematic arms in Hollywood.

In 1947, a young army veteran from Massachusetts, John Horne Burns, published his collection of short stories, *The Gallery*. These stories were a recollection of the Galleria Umberto, an arcade off the Via Roma. Through the gallery came men and women whose lives were deeply affected by the war. At the time of its publication, *The Gallery* was acclaimed to be the best book about World War II. The unusual element about Burns's stories was that there was no actual combat. The emphasis was on the people, and their struggles, with the war ever present in the background.[1]

One year later, Norman Mailer burst upon the literary war scene with the publication of *The Naked and the Dead*. This was a fictionalized account of Mailer's army experiences in the Pacific. The novel was a critical and commercial success and opened up new territory with four-letter words and graphic descriptions of combat situations. It would not be until 1958 when the film adaptation was produced.

James Albert Michener, who was a staff officer in the Pacific, did the same as John Horne Burns: He published a collection of short stories based on his war experiences. But there were two distinctions. The first was that Michener's collection, *Tales of the South Pacific*, came from his navy background. The second was that Michener's collection won the 1948 Pulitzer Prize for fiction.

One of the stories in the collection ended up on Broadway as a musical, *South Pacific*. Another Pulitzer was granted to the musical in 1950, with the collaboration of Richard Rodgers, Oscar Hammerstein II, and Joshua Logan.

In 1947, a young army veteran and survivor of the Pearl Harbor attack who aspired to get his war novel published journeyed from Robinson, Illinois, to New York City to enroll in writing classes at New York University. During this time, the young veteran, James Jones, prevailed upon renowned editor Maxwell Perkins of Scribner's to criticize his manuscript, which was titled *They Shall Inherit the Laughter*. Jones took Perkins's notes and returned to Robinson for a rewrite. When the rewrite went back to Perkins, the editor was disappointed. In his opinion, the novel still didn't work.

But Perkins saw raw talent in the young man and was impressed with Jones's idea about another novel. This project was about the peacetime army in Hawaii on the eve of World War II, what was sometimes referred to as "the pineapple army." After the proposal was accepted, Scribner's gave Jones a $500 advance to complete the novel *From Here to Eternity*, based on the author's experiences when he was assigned to the 27th Infantry Regiment at Schofield Barracks in the months before the Pearl Harbor attack. Jones plucked selected characters and incidents from his experiences at several army posts and laid them down at Schofield.[2]

Perkins guided Jones through the first drafts, making suggestions and cuts. However, Perkins, in ailing health, never saw the novel published. After his death the editing was turned over to Burroughs Mitchell.

The novel was published in 1951, along with generally favorable reviews. It caused an instant controversy. Like other novels before it, Jones's work was called the greatest first novel to appear in years. Others were offended and called it "From Here to Obscenity." What had to be realized here was that something was happening in the literary world. And it would soon be reflected in the cinematic world. The next generation was making its statement. And as legend would have it, the older generation didn't like it. The returning warriors were bringing about a change, a change caused by what they had experienced.

Like Mailer's novel, *From Here to Eternity* had the raw, bawdy serviceman's latrine language. It also had whores (Alma), a sadistic stockade sergeant ("Fatso" Judson), and an ambitious, uncaring company commander (Captain Dana Holmes), who gave his wife (Karen) gonorrhea. In retaliation, Karen has affairs with soldiers in Holmes's company.

There's also a rebellious soldier (Robert E. Lee Prewitt) who loves the army despite its persecution of him. Prewitt is a noted bugler and middleweight boxer who transfers to Holmes's infantry company but refuses to join the unit's boxing team, as Holmes desperately desires. Prewitt then falls in love with Alma, a dance hall girl. Because Prewitt refuses to box (he blinded an opponent at his previous unit), he is given the "treatment," constant harassment by the company boxers. Prewitt's buddy (Angelo Maggio) is a male hustler who earns extra money in the back streets of Honolulu and eventually ends up in Sergeant Judson's stockade.

The company first sergeant (Milton Warden) begins a torrid affair with Karen. The fates of these vividly drawn characters mesh on the fateful December 7, 1941, weekend that turned the twentieth century upside down.

That Sunday morning, like most of the soldiers at Schofield Barracks, Jones was at breakfast. The fare was eggs or pancakes with syrup and a bonus ration of a half pint of milk.

Explosions, suddenly heard at Wheeler Field two miles away, were thought to be construction blasting. Later, when low-flying aircraft came in on strafing runs, the troops rushed outside, some still holding their pints of milk to keep them from being stolen.

It was at this moment that Jones became aware "with a sudden sense of awe that we were seeing and acting in a genuine moment of history."

Jones later wrote that they were able to see another Japanese fighter plane on a strafing run preceded by two lines of machine gun fire across the quadrangle. "As he came abreast of us, he gave us a typically toothy grin and waved, and I shall never forget his face behind the goggles. A white silk scarf streamed out behind his neck and he wore a white ribbon around his helmet just above the goggles, with a red spot in the center of his forehead. I would learn later that this ribbon was a *hachimake*, the headband worn by the medieval samurai when going into battle."

The legendary Harry Cohn at Columbia Pictures went all out to grab the film rights to the graphic and controversial war novel. Once again, a historical incident colored with a personal combat account became the foundation for a classic American war film.

Jones went to Hollywood in the spring of 1951 after the screenplay rights were negotiated. He began an acquaintanceship with Cohn and began work on a treatment (narrative outline) for the screenplay. In the Jones treatment, like the novel, the non-coms performed the harassment on Prewitt. Captain Holmes wasn't even aware of it.

But Jones's treatment was never used as a basis for the script. One of the many problems faced by the studio was how to sanitize the graphic and sexual elements of the novel for American movie audiences in the early 1950s. Jones then returned to southern Illinois to begin work on another novel, the return of a disillusioned soldier to his midwestern roots, which was to become *Some Came Running*.

Cohn quickly lined up his people. He needed a workable script, one that showed the strong impression and spirit of the novel. And it had to pass through the production code office. For that he went to Daniel Taradash. Buddy Adler had already been named as producer. Taradash identified with the book, having served in the infantry himself. He was acquainted with the tough sergeants and the regimentation. Taradash had read the novel upon publication. When he got the screenplay assignment, he read it again. In a 1998 interview, Taradash explained that he didn't see *Eternity* as a war film, per se. He saw the story as a character-driven tale set on a peacetime army post.[3]

Regarding the male hustler, Angelo Maggio, Taradash took the male away and left the hustler. "They didn't used the term *gay* back then." In the novel, Alma, using the pseudonym of Lorene, was employed in a Honolulu bordello that passed itself off as a dance hall. For the script, the brothel was changed to the New Congress Dance Club.

The cleanup continued. In the novel the captain's wife, Karen Holmes, had shut her husband out of their bedroom because he gave her gonorrhea at Fort Bliss. They already had one child. Taradash then substituted a miscarriage for the novel's venereal disease.

Here, the script relied on "back story" dialogue. This was combined with the steamy "beach scene," with Karen and Milt Warden in a passionate kiss (her on top), legs intertwined as the evening waves lap over them. Later, in a reflective moment, Karen tells Milt that when labor began, her husband had passed out from a drunken night at the Fort Bliss Officers' Club. Captain Dana Holmes, afterward, agreed to her choice of separate bedrooms to prevent the scandal of a divorce so he could be considered for promotion to major.

In the novel, however, Holmes is promoted to major, a development that reinforced Jones's belief that the military system always wins out, corrupt or otherwise, over the individual. This is further emphasized when Prewitt (AWOL after he kills Judson in a back alley knife fight) tries to get back to his company and is killed by the very people he is attempting to rejoin. The soldier who loved the army is killed by it.

Taradash knew that the film's army advisers would object to Holmes's promotion to major in the film. Taradash later explained, for the Academy of Motion Picture Arts and Sciences' oral history, "It was a splendid idea for the novel [the irony], but I felt it would be ruinous if we tried to cope with that. However, the army did make the suggestion that Prewitt be killed by a Japanese plane instead of American sentries.

"The changes I made [cleaning up the novel] was one of the reasons I got the job," added Taradash. He also said that Jones's treatment was unusable because he (Jones) was excessively worried about censorship and sanitized the book *too* much.

When Taradash turned in a first draft the army got involved, going over each scene and giving extensive notes, criticisms, and suggestions. The army's cooperation was needed since the location of the film was to be Schofield Barracks.

Later, Fred Zinnemann, coming off the successes of *A Member of the Wedding* and *High Noon*, was given the director's assignment.

Other changes came about with the setup of the Robert E. Lee Prewitt character. In the first script draft the only time that "Prew" plays the bugle is for "Taps," when Maggio dies after escaping from Sergeant "Fatso" Judson's stockade. It's a dramatic "day for night" barracks scene where the entire company silently and reflectively listens to the mournful notes.

Taradash explained that Cohn wanted Prewitt to play the bugle once before that to properly set up the taps scene in the quadrangle. A scene was then written to take place at Choy's (the nearby "slop shute") where Prewitt grabs the bugle out of a soldier's hands and plays some virtuoso notes.

Cohn was right, added Taradash. "It turned out to be an excellent scene."

The casting came with many ins and outs before production began in Hawaii. The first roles mentioned were those of Karen Holmes and Milt Warden, the conflicted lovers. Among the names initially mentioned were Joan Crawford and Robert Mitchum.

According to Taradash, Fred Zinnemann was surprised that Crawford wanted the role. Zinnemann told Taradash, "She said she won't glamorize herself and she seems to understand the part, and it's possible."

Taradash added, "So we all said 'okay, let's take her.' And then, within a few days, she was calling from Palm Springs asking for a particular cameraman, and for a certain makeup person and stuff like that. And that was the end of Joan Crawford."[4]

Other casting suggestions included Glenn Ford as Warden with John Derek as Prewitt. Oscar-winner Broderick Crawford (*All the King's Men*) was also mentioned.

The first suggestion for the Angelo Maggio role went to Eli Wallach. The second was Frank Sinatra, whose career, as everyone knew, had taken a downturn. Both actors read for the part.

Taradash explained, "Wallach had the part hands down when you compared the two." However, the bottom line weighed heavily in the outcome.

"Wallach's agent asked for twice what Wallach had made in his last picture. That was the last we heard of Eli Wallach," said Taradash. "Sinatra's slight physical condition swung it over for the part. Sinatra, stripped to the waist, looked like a plucked chicken! You know, he just looked like a pitiful physical speciman," laughed Taradash. "And that helped him enormously in the characterization. It was all there . . . and that's when we decided to go with Sinatra."

Through the years, there has been the repeated implication that Harry Cohn was coerced by certain members of the New York crime families to cast Sinatra as Maggio, which ultimately brought about the crooner's astonishing comeback. Some observers contended that the search for Maggio was fictionalized in Mario Puzo's 1969 best-seller *The Godfather*, as the Johnny Fontane character who gets a supporting role in a war film, based on a best-seller, after a studio chief discovers a thoroughbred's head in his bed one morning. Zinnemann always held that no such coercion was used, that Sinatra was cast, as Maggio, based on his reading after Eli Wallach was eliminated.

In his book, *The Godfather Papers*, Puzo explained that he wrote the Fontane part with sympathy for the man and his hang-ups. He wanted to catch the innocence of show business people and their despair at the corruption. "I thought I had caught the inner innocence of that character. But I could also see that if Sinatra thought that the [Fontane] character was himself, he might not like it—the book—or me."[5]

The final casting for *Eternity* (1953) proved to be on target with Burt Lancaster as Milt Warden, Deborah Kerr as Karen Holmes, Montgomery Clift as Prewitt, and Donna Reed as Alma. "Fatso" Judson's character went to Ernest Borgnine. In the novel, "Fatso" didn't bang on the piano at the New Congress Club. That was Taradash's idea, adding more crassness to his character.

Taradash said that Clift worked like a dog to learn how to march and simply act like a soldier. "He couldn't box at all. We had to use a double in most of the stuff, which is obvious, I'm afraid."

A crucial script decision had to be made about the end. Dramatically, Taradash felt that the film's end should be the beginning of America's entry into World War II, which would be an identifying point for the nation's audiences. "I felt that the picture should end with the two women on the ship leaving Hawaii [after the attack]. That scene is in the book, but the book went on for another hundred and twenty pages or so after that, but I thought it was the logical ending."[6]

The film came away with eight Oscars, including Best Picture, making it one of the most memorable World War II films ever. Holding the statuettes at ceremony's end were Fred Zinnemann, Daniel Taradash, Frank Sinatra, and Donna Reed. Also getting Oscars were Burnett Guffey for cinematography and William Lyon for editing.

Deborah Kerr lost, for Best Actress, to Audrey Hepburn in *Roman Holiday*. It was felt that Burt Lancaster and Montgomery Clift canceled each other, as Best Actor, allowing William Holden to win for *Stalag 17* (1953).

In 1979, Columbia Pictures reprised the film with a six-hour miniseries starring William Devane as Milt Warden and Natalie Wood as Karen Holmes. But, with most remakes, the adage held true that "a soufflé only rises once."

After seeing the stage play *Stalag 17*, written by Donald Bevan and Edmund Trzcinski, William Holden had to be talked into playing the part of Sergeant J.J. Sefton, the army POW scrounger thoroughly disliked by the men in his barracks. American audiences saw Holden as a romantic figure, the way he came off as Joe Gillis, the struggling screenwriter, in *Sunset Boulevard*. Gil Stratton played Sefton's loyal assistant Cookie. Structurally, Cookie is the "Greek Chorus"; he tells the story of the memorable imprisoned gang who endure the unfair odds.

The film rights were acquired by Paramount with Billy Wilder attached as director. Wilder rewrote the play with Edwin Blum. This united Holden again with Wilder. Audiences supported the film because of the comedy mixed with wartime tragedy in the most trying of circumstances. The rough language and sexual overtones that were in the play had to be diluted for movie audiences of the day.

The tragic tone is set from the opening when two GIs, Manfredi and Johnson, are attempting to escape. They walk into a deadly trap, a rake of Nazi machine gun fire. With this serious element set, the Wilder and Blum script then went after the comedy.

There's Animal and Shapiro, the proverbial comedy team. Animal is obsessed with the image of Betty Grable, while the only mail Shapiro gets is from a stateside finance company that wants back payments for his car. As the comic Animal, Robert Strauss received an Academy Award nomination for Best Supporting Actor, along with Billy Wilder, for Best Director.

Sefton is thought to be the Barracks informer, while the actual betrayer is Price, a Nazi agent, played by Peter Graves. Otto Preminger is the Nazi commandant, and Sig Ruman does a turn as the likeable German camp sergeant Schulz.

Trzcinski, one of the playwrights, was cast as "Joey," severely traumatized by a horrific bomber incident that left him unable to communicate verbally with anyone. His only solace is in playing a plastic flute.[7]

The drama proceeds as a wartime mystery in guessing the identity of the Nazi informer, while the high-jinks continue with mouse races and a raucous attempt to get into an adjoining compound where Russian female prisoners are housed.

As Sefton, Holden is able to expose the true culprit, Price, and redeem himself to the admiration of all as the likeable American prisoners win a moral victory at fade-out.

The role that William Holden was reluctant to play became the one that resulted in an Oscar for Best Actor.

Holden was cast again in a war film, this time in Valentine Davies's screenplay (1954) adaptation of James Michener's novel *The Bridges at Toko-Ri*, a drama of naval aviators in Korea who prepare to knock out a set of bridges against antiaircraft fire and enemy planes.

Directed by Mark Robson, the film's back story has Holden as a decorated World War II naval aviator and a Denver attorney. He was called back to active duty, flying F9F Panther missions off an aircraft carrier. As Holden's wife, Grace Kelly has problems understanding what her husband is experiencing in this sudden and complex war.

Supporting Holden is an alum from *Stalag 17*, Robert Strauss, as the landing ship officer who guides the fighters back aboard; Mickey Rooney turns in a colorful performance as the helicopter rescue pilot. Charles McGraw played "Cag" (Commander, Air Group), whereas Fredric March supervised the operations as the paternal skipper of the carrier.

Rooney rescues Holden when his jet is hit by antiaircraft fire. The two are forced down when the helicopter is hit. After Holden and Rooney are killed by enemy troops, March asks himself a rhetorical question, "Where do we get such men?"

In a switch for history following art, the line was later used by President Ronald Reagan in a speech commemorating the fortieth anniversary of the Normandy invasion.

Alma Macrorie received an Academy Award nomination for Best Editing.

A World War II experience again held forth resulting in another Pulitzer Prize, this time for Herman Wouk. His 1952 novel *The Caine Mutiny*, based on experiences aboard the destroyer minesweeper USS *Zane*, caused controversy not because of sexual overtones and four-letter words. The novel challenged the ascent of a man to a wartime command position who is neither mentally nor emotionally capable of handling the profound responsibility. In Wouk's novel, Lieutenant Commander Philip Francis Queeg was such a man, burned out and drained from patrol duty in the treacherous North Atlantic.

Queeg is then reassigned to the USS *Caine*, staffed by reserve officers and assorted "90-Day Wonders," such as Ensign Willis Keith, an Ivy League mama's boy who matures into a man during the novel. He also has a love story subplot with a cabaret singer, May Wynn.

Other reserve officers that Queeg encounters in his new command are Steven Maryk, his executive officer, and Tom Keefer, an eastern intellectual and aspiring novelist who already knows that combat tales offer potential for best-sellers.

Even though Queeg is a Naval Academy graduate and career officer, his previous North Atlantic duty started his descent into instability and paranoia. In the novel, Wouk's rising action brings out individual reactions from the officers and crew. Keefer is one of the first to note the instability and contradiction in Queeg's character, suggesting that the commanding officer is unfit for command. Keefer then begins keeping a log book account of Queeg's behavior, citing various articles of naval regulations of the era.

As the personality conflict escalates, Queeg's behavior becomes more contradictory. Often, in stressful situations, Queeg would pull two steel balls from his pocket and finger them in his hand, much like a security blanket.

Nature then plays its violent hand as the *Caine* is caught in a Pacific typhoon. Queeg then issues contradictory orders on the bridge and is relieved of command by Maryk, with the other officers in support of the decision. Upon return to San Francisco, the junior officers find themselves named as defendants in a court-martial.

The second half of the novel deals with the court-martial, which later became a successful Broadway play directed by Charles Laughton.

Balancing Queeg's contradictory character is Barney Greenwald, a naval aviator and attorney, who reluctantly defends the accused officers. Greenwald, a Jew who is aware of the global Nazi threat, secretly feels for Queeg and understands what caused the commander's breakdown.

"He was defending us from Hermann Goering, while you, Willie, were still on the playing fields at Princeton," Greenwald later explains.

Greenwald gets the officers acquitted and then is invited to Keefer's publishing party at a posh San Francisco hotel. Greenwald shows up drunk, angered by what he did to break Queeg on the stand, thereby ending the commander's career. Greenwald then throws champagne into Keefer's face, observing that the wrong man was on trial, telling the group that Keefer orchestrated the entire scenario, staying safely in the background while allowing the others to stick their proverbial necks into the noose.

Columbia Pictures once again grabbed screenplay rights to *The Caine Mutiny* (1954), with Stanley Kramer as producer. Edward Dymtryk was assigned to direct from a screenplay adaptation by Stanley Roberts. Even though the novel and stage play were considered extremely controversial, the Navy Department cooperated in the production, allowing filming aboard navy ships and shooting at Pearl Harbor.

Humphrey Bogart received another Academy Award nomination for his portrayal of Queeg. Van Johnson was cast as Steve Maryk, while Fred MacMurray played the arrogant Tom Keefer. Also in the cast were Tom Tully (in an Oscar-nominated performance) as Commander DeVriess, the first skipper of the *Caine* at the film's beginning. José Ferrer played the troubled Barney Greenwald. Lee Marvin and Claude Akins portrayed two enlisted men who testify at the court-martial.

Strangely, the actress cast as "May Wynn" changed her name to that character. After the film's release May Wynn dropped out of sight.

As in most film adaptations, story elements had to be surrendered. In the film, after the court-martial, Willie Keith (now a lieutenant junior grade) is transferred to another ship and coincidently discovers that he has to serve under his original skipper, DeVriess. The sympathy for Queeg at the end of the novel was mostly lost in the film. Greenwald's rationale at the party added the intriguing element of complex men in life-and-death situations.

In the novel Tom Keefer becomes skipper of the *Caine* and shows his true character by leaping from the ship during a kamikaze attack. He lands in the water, clutching the pages of his manuscript, rounding out his character not only as a coward but also as a hypocrite. It is the younger officer, Willie Keith, who coordinates damage control and saves the ship.

Sitting in his Encino, California, living room, years later, director Edward Dymtryk said that he saw the film "simply as a young man's coming of age story," that the central character was Keith and not Captain Queeg.[8]

Offering a different angle, Wouk, in a letter from his Palm Springs home, wrote that the novel "is not 'simply' about anything. Nor is the film, which is a thin rinse of the novel, redeemed by some excellent acting. I agree that the cutting of the last sequences loses the thrust of the work."

Wouk added that there were no U.S. Navy mutinies on the high seas during World War II. "There were three courts of inquiry about reliefs of the commanding officer at shore bases, on the basis of Articles 184, 185, and 186 of the then current Navy regulations."[9]

The film was nominated for Best Picture, Best Screenplay, Best Musical Score (Max Steiner), Best Actor, Best Supporting Actor, and Best Editing.

Max Steiner received another Academy Award nomination for composing the musical score for Leon Uris's screenplay adaptation of his novel *Battle Cry*, the story of a marine communications battalion, their lives, and their sexual escapades.

Uris served in combat with elements of the 2nd Marine Division. When he returned to civilian life he began outlining a war novel that "mirrored" the collection of "grunts" with whom he served. Again, the barracks language and the sexual scenes (through dialogue and off-screen implications) were the closest that director Raoul Walsh could come to Uris's graphic novel combining the actions of marines in bed and marines storming a Pacific island.

The "Greek Chorus" was used again. Mac, the "top kick," served as narrator. In the novel's opening, Mac has a classic description of what it was like to be a career and combat marine. Cast as Mac, James Whitmore gives battle-tempered opinions as to the price paid by "the cocky kids in green." Mac also gives new meaning to Abraham Lincoln's famous Civil War observation, "Politics and war make for strange bedfellows."

*Battle Cry* (1955) has standard American war film elements, bringing young men together from their prewar environments: the all-American boy, the street kid, the Pacific Northwest lumberjack, the self-read intellectual (who wants to write that war novel), and the pride of the Navajo nation. Once their training is complete, they ship out, and the combat sequences begin, intertwined with sex and love.

Tab Hunter was cast as Danny Forrester, the all-American boy; Aldo Ray as Andy Hookans, the lumberjack; and John Lupton as "Sister Mary," the intellectual; Perry Lopez played "Spanish Joe," his nemesis who becomes his friend through combat. Van Heflin portrayed Lieutenant Colonel Sam Huxley, the tough but caring battalion commander.

For love story subplot triangles, Hunter has an affair with a "more experienced" Dorothy Malone, while Mona Freeman, his high school sweetheart back in Maryland, loyally waits for him. Anne Francis does a turn as Rae, a party girl with low self-esteem.

Visionaries, particularly military ones, are always controversial. And so is the heavy price that they often pay. General William L. "Billy" Mitchell was no exception.

Born in Nice, France, in 1879, his father, John Lendrum Mitchell, became a U.S. Senator from Wisconsin. Mitchell was commissioned a second lieutenant in time to serve in Cuba during the Spanish-American War. In 1915, he was transferred to the aviation section of the Army Signal Corps. As a qualified pilot, he went to France as an adviser. Upon America's entry into the war Lieutenant Colonel Mitchell was named air officer of the Allied Expeditionary Force (AEF). He then became the first American officer to fly over enemy lines. As a brigadier general, he led a bombing mission behind enemy lines in the Meuse-Argonne offensive.

The dangers of combat were one thing; the tightrope walking of peacetime politics was quite another. And it was here, in a succession of incidents, that led to Mitchell's fall from grace.

In March 1919, Mitchell began a campaign to make the air service a separate service branch. The navy took umbrage to his claim that the aeroplane made the battleship obsolete. Mitchell was challenged to back up his position. He not only accepted the challenge but proved his point by sinking a former German battleship in a war games exercise. The air bombardment of the battleship lasted just over twenty minutes. This ultimately led to the navy creating aircraft carriers as offensive weapons.

Mitchell's constant criticism of the military's failure to recognize new weapons and innovative warfare led to charges of insubordination, resulting in his demotion to colonel and a court-martial. He was convicted in 1926 and sentenced to five years' suspension from active duty without pay. He resigned from the army the following year. Among Mitchell's 1923 predictions was the theory that a carrier-based air strike by Japan against the Hawaiian Islands was entirely possible. The conservative military establishment at the time laughed at this suggestion.[10]

*The Court-Martial of Billy Mitchell* (1955) was directed by Otto Preminger for Warner Bros., with Gary Cooper cast as Mitchell. The film uses the court-martial as the centerpiece, with flashbacks providing the back story. Rod Steiger played crusading army prosecutor Allan Gullion who engineers a brutal cross-examination of Mitchell's theories and arguments. In supporting roles were Charles Bickford, Ralph Bellamy, Elizabeth Montgomery, and James Daly.

One of the officers on the court-martial board was a World War I friend of Mitchell's, General Douglas MacArthur.

The defense testimony of such Army Air Corps figures as Carl Spaatz, Hap Arnold, and Eddie Rickenbacker failed to move the court. President Calvin Coolidge called for a swift end to the trial to prevent further embarrassment to the army. Mitchell then spent the rest of his life writing and furthering his arguments about the future of air power. He died in 1936. Today he is considered the father of the U.S. Air Force.

Another Warner Bros. war film of 1955 had the combined director efforts of John Ford and Mervyn LeRoy in *Mister Roberts*. The studio bought the film rights to the stage play by Thomas Heggen and Joshua Logan, based on Heggen's novel. The conflict occurred on the USS *Reluctant*, a cargo ship that never saw any action. This brought out the bitter rivalry between the regular navy and the reserve navy.

James Cagney was cast as the skipper of the cargo ship with Henry Fonda as the smarter, more logical Lieutenant Junior Grade Douglas Roberts, a reserve officer who increasingly becomes the classic thorn in Cagney's side. Cagney is a time-serving regular officer waiting for promotion to full commander. He also hates the "smart college guys who think they know it all." As an unfeeling commander of a support ship, all Cagney cares about is his palm tree, which has to be watered daily. The palm tree then becomes a metaphor of wartime indifference.

Jack Lemmon supported Fonda as Ensign Frank Pulver. Ensign Pulver is a lazy college type, always figuring a way out of a difficult assignment, which usually backfires. Lemmon won an Oscar for Best Supporting Actor. William Powell also lends his advice to Fonda as the ship's physician.

Both of these 1955 Warner Bros. films depicted the mindless military authority where one man has to go against the entire system, at his own price, to achieve something honorable.

In Fonda's case as Mister Roberts, he gets his long-awaited transfer to a destroyer "in the real navy" that results in his doom. The film was nominated for Best Picture.

## A BOY, THE WAR, AND HOLLYWOOD

Historically, wars open doors of opportunity, both while taking place and after they end. In this, World War II was no different. One of those doors opened for a young Texas man who had a limited education.

Several weeks before his twenty-first birthday, First Lieutenant Audie Murphy was awarded the Congressional Medal of Honor. Murphy personified the link between American twentieth-century history and the American war film. World War II brought the young soldier to Hollywood, opening doors that otherwise would have been closed to him. It also brought him to a life for which he was in no way prepared.

Audie Leon Murphy was one of nine children born to Emmett "Pat," an itinerant Texas sharecropper, and his wife, Josie, who went through twelve pregnancies before she died at age fifty-one.

Hunt County, Texas, suffered as much as any "Dust Bowl" community in the 1930s. As Murphy's father drifted from job to job, Audie struggled through the primary grades, stopping at the fifth grade. He earned a reputation for being a "scrapper," who was excellent hunting rabbits with a .22 rifle.

When Pearl Harbor was attacked, Murphy, like many Americans, didn't even know where the naval base was. But he was just as outraged. He went down to the Marine Corps recruiting office but was turned away for being underweight and underage. Undaunted, he immediately went to the army airborne. Same response. On his eighteenth birthday the army finally relented upon seeing an enlistment petition with local signatures. Because of his small build the scrapper became known in basic training as "baby," a nickname he didn't care for.

After completing advanced training, he was assigned to B Company, 1st Battalion, 15th Infantry Regiment of the noted 3rd Infantry Division. His company landed in North Africa but did not see combat until the Sicilian campaign. Murphy fit right into the role of a combat soldier. He distinguished himself several times, and his reputation grew within the company and battalion. He was awarded his first Bronze Star, near Cisterna, for leading a patrol that pre-

151

vented a tank from being retrieved by German soldiers. Soon thereafter, he was
awarded the Combat Infantryman's Badge and an Oak Leaf Cluster in lieu of a
second Bronze Star.

The 15th Infantry Regiment landed in France, near St. Tropez, on August 15,
1944. And the scrapper from Hunt County, Texas, who was rejected by the
airborne and the marines, began amassing one of America's most impressive
combat records.

One of Murphy's closest friends, Lattie Tipton, was killed during a fake
surrender by German infantrymen. Murphy "went beserk" according to biographer Don Graham in *No Name on the Bullet*. Murphy charged the German
position with two rifles. "He raked them again and again," wrote Graham, "and
did not stop firing while there [was] a quiver left in them."[11]

For this action, Murphy was awarded the Distinguished Service Cross, the
second highest combat award. A month later, he was wounded in a mortar
barrage. He was then offered a battlefield commission to second lieutenant.
Murphy turned down the offer for two reasons: He felt his fifth-grade education
would work against him in the officer ranks, and the promotion would mean he
would be transferred to another platoon.

During this time, the nineteen-year-old Murphy became even more hardened.
He was made platoon sergeant and did not attempt to make friends with any of
the new replacements because of being emotionally hurt as he was with the
deaths of Tipton and several other soldiers.

Murphy was then awarded a Silver Star for saving a patrol from a withering
ambush. At Cleurie Quarry, he led a patrol that stalked and killed a German
sniper who had killed several Americans.

He won another Silver Star while leading a patrol down a creek bed. When
the patrol came under fire, Murphy took a radio, maneuvered to an advanced
position, and doubled both as a sniper and artillery forward observer. He shot
two enemy snipers and, for almost an hour, called in mortar fire that resulted
in fifteen German soldiers killed and approximately thirty-five wounded.

In addition to his second Silver Star, he was once more recommended for
promotion to second lieutenant. This time he was still reluctant but took the
commission with two other enlisted men. Of the three men receiving battlefield
commissions that day, Murphy was the only one to survive the war. According
to biographer Graham, the rank of infantry second lieutenant had the highest
officer casualty rate of the war.

After Murphy suffered his second combat wound, a nine-inch rip along the
right buttock, he was evacuated to a hospital at Aix-en-Provence near Marseilles.
As if acting out an Ernest Hemingway novel, he fell in love with his army
nurse, Carolyn Price.

Lieutenant Murphy returned to B Company in January 1945, where he was
wounded a third time in a mortar barrage. Recovering quickly, he was made
company commander as a first lieutenant.

On January 26, 1945, in an area known as the Colmar Pocket, his company was in position to defend against a coordinated German infantry tank attack. Two American tank destroyers were in an exposed position as two companies of Wehrmacht infantry, with tanks, advanced. One of the tank destroyers was hit. The Germans continued in what looked like a certain rout for B Company. Murphy then ordered his company to fall back. He then grabbed a radio, ran for the tank destroyer, and mounted it. Here, he saw that it had a functioning .50 caliber machine gun with several ammunition cans. With the radio, he directed artillery fire on the advancing Germans and used the machine gun for cover. Several times the enemy soldiers got as close as fifty yards.

As the American artillery fire zeroed in on the Germans, they began to pull back. Murphy continued firing the machine gun and was later knocked off the tank destroyer (which caused an old leg wound to open). The action lasted less than an hour, but in those minutes Murphy's life became emblazoned into the annals of American combat heroes. After several eyewitness accounts were verified, First Lieutenant Audie Leon Murphy was recommended for the Congressional Medal of Honor.

The day of the presentation, June 2, 1945, Murphy had twenty-nine medals. After several postwar awards, his total medal count (including campaign medals and unit citations) came to thirty-seven. Of these, eleven were for valor in combat situations. He was also credited with killing approximately 240 German soldiers.

The celebrity circus began even before Murphy returned to the States. The American public found a combat hero that personified World War II patriotism. Here was a small young man, who was initially rejected by several service branches, who persisted to get into the war and returned as the nation's most decorated soldier. (Coincidently, Neville Brand—also soon to be an actor—was listed as the nation's fourth most decorated soldier.) *Life* magazine ran a cover story on Murphy in its July 16, 1945, issue.

James Cagney saw the cover story and quickly made several attempts to get in touch with Murphy. By this time Murphy was a stateside infantry officer who was preparing to write a book about his combat experiences. Eventually, Murphy did respond to Cagney's queries. Cagney requested that the nation's most decorated soldier come to Hollywood immediately. And Cagney's request was not just to tour the film capital. Cagney saw a movie star in the making.

Murphy arrived in Hollywood in a profoundly exhausted state, recovering from more than two years of relentless combat situations. Initially, he and Cagney got on. Cagney quipped that they had a lot in common. "We're two short Irishmen."

Under Cagney's tutelege, Murphy was enrolled in the Actor's Lab, a progressive acting school of the era. He began serious study, educating himself in both novels and screenplays. This intensive reading agenda included the outlining of his autobiography. Eventually, this would become *To Hell and Back*. Cagney even tutored Murphy in dance steps, explaining how important walking is to an actor's persona. Cagney had noticed Murphy's loping walk, which he called "a hayshaker's walk."

Murphy also became aware that certain people, at the lab, thought he was a guy cashing in on a war record. At first he took this criticism lightly, believing that, at best, his acting was mediocre. After several film roles fell through, he landed a supporting role as Alan Ladd's best friend in a 1948 West Point story, *Beyond Glory*. During this period Murphy had become more sensitive to his acting potential. But he still had that hair-trigger temper that often took control. In Hollywood, as on the battlefield, when he got mad, he acted out, sometimes offending people. On the set, Ladd took Murphy aside and counseled him, advising him not to let little things get to him.

After much rewriting with a Hollywood friend, David "Spec" McClure, Murphy's scrapper autobiography was published and sold well, climbing up the best-seller lists. He also married an ingenue, Dixie Wanda Hendrix, a Texas girl who dropped her first name upon arriving in Hollywood.

Murphy's next role was in *Bad Boy* (1949), with Lloyd Nolan and Jane Wyatt, a family drama about a young man who goes down the wrong path. After that came *The Kid from Texas*, a 1950 updated version of the Billy the Kid story. This film began a string of Hollywood B westerns for Murphy with Universal-International.

He even played a young Jesse James in the film *Kansas Raiders* (1950), with Brian Donlevy as William Clarke Quantrill, the outlaw Confederate guerrilla leader. Then came John Huston's casting of Murphy as Henry Fleming in *The Red Badge of Courage* (1951). By this time his marriage to Wanda Hendrix had failed.

Murphy's autobiography *To Hell and Back* was set up at Universal, adapted by Gil Doud and directed by Jesse Hibbs. Supporting roles went to Marshall Thompson, Charles Drake, and Jack Kelly, playing members of Murphy's squad.

The unique publicity hook to *To Hell and Back* (1955) was that the story was written by the nation's most decorated combat soldier played by the man himself.

The film did considerable business and received favorable reviews, which made Universal look at Murphy not through an acting lens but as someone with box office potential with a young audience. With the release of his filmed autobiography, Murphy was at the peak of his career.

After his marriage to Hendrix ended, he went through a series of female relationships, including one with Jean Peters, who later became Mrs. Howard Hughes. In 1951, he married Pamela Archer, a Braniff Airlines stewardess. Despite producing two sons, the marriage was a roller coaster, laced with separations and reconciliations.

As Murphy's film fees grew, so did his tastes. He bought a ranch near Riverside, California. He also took flying lessons and bought a small plane. He began dabbling in horse breeding, particularly thoroughbreds, which led to a big-time gambling habit that eventually escalated into millions of dollars.

Because of his bread and butter B western roles, Murphy missed out on roles that could have expanded his career into more respected A list films. These included the Oscar-winning role that Red Buttons got in *Sayonara* (1957), as the air force Sergeant Joe Kelly, who befriends Marlon Brando, playing a Korean War jet ace. Murphy was also considered for "The Man with No Name" for Sergio Leone's *The Good, the Bad and the Ugly* (1966), a role that went to a little-known television actor named Clint Eastwood.

Murphy hung out with prizefighters and became a known boxing fan. He also hung out with police officers. At one time, he worked as an undercover narcotics agent with the Tucson, Arizona, police department. He made numerous drug contacts that resulted in several arrests.

But he was never able to shake the posttraumatic effects of combat. He was haunted by nightmares, sweats, and uncontrollable fits of temper. Rarely was he able to get a full night's sleep. When he did go to bed, he slept with a loaded .45 automatic nearby or under his pillow.

Murphy came full circle from his role in *Kansas Raiders* when, in his last film, he did a cameo as an older Jesse James in a 1969 western ironically titled *A Time for Dying*.

By 1971, America's most decorated soldier was bankrupt, caused by faulty business deals, bad management, and compulsive gambling. His income was now reduced to celebrity appearances. He also got involved in a business combine that manufactured prefabricated houses. On May 28, 1971, Murphy was a passenger in an Aero Commander with several other businessmen. The flight was scheduled from Atlanta, Georgia, to Martinsburg, Virgina. The plane ran into fog and rain and was diverted to Roanoke. On the way, it crashed into a mountain. It took four days to recover the bodies.

Audie Murphy's death was announced over the Memorial Day weekend. He was buried with full military honors at Arlington National Cemetery. Today his grave is one of those mentioned on the cemetery tour.

## MEN WITH FLAWS

Realism took another turn in 1957 with Stanley Kubrick's *Paths of Glory*. Based on one of World War I's most tragic incidents, the Battle of Verdun, Kubrick took Humphrey Cobb's novel and worked on the script with two writers, Calder Willingham and Jim Thompson. The battle itself served the background. The issues Kubrick sought to portray were cowardice and military corruption at the highest level.

In February 1916, the Germans launched a concentrated offensive at the fortified salient of Verdun. The French felt that they could not abandon the position and vowed to hold it at all costs. To achieve this end, the French committed themselves to massive suicidal attacks against the Germans. Wave after wave of French infantrymen were ordered into enemy artillery and flanking machine gun fire. Each time a French unit received an attack order, death was obvious to all. The attack orders continued. By December, total casualties came to 700,000 with no significant gain by either side.

In the United Artists film, the French troops ultimately rebel and refuse to go. The general staff considers this a mutinous act. The staff retaliates by selecting three enlisted men to stand in front of a court-martial. The men are subsequently convicted and sentenced to execution as an example for refusing to obey orders that, ironically, meant certain death.

Kirk Douglas played the officer who defends the accused soldiers, portrayed by Joe Turkel, Ralph Meeker, and Timothy Carey. George Macready and Adolphe Menjou personified the corrupt generals, occupying a spacious castle and dining in splendor while planning the next suicidal attack on a position known as "the ant hill." As the soldiers are slaughtered in the attacks they've ordered, the generals watch through binoculars from a safe distance.

Juxtaposed to the opulence of the general officers' lifestyle, the enlisted men live in mud-paneled trenches. Georg Krause's cinematography of the living conditions in the trenches vividly added to the claustrophobic feeling that the general officers consistently avoided.

Douglas's character, Colonel Dax, put up a valiant, although futile, defense, as the verdicts stood and winced as the selected soldiers were executed.

The director's statement had its effect. After the film was released, it was initially banned on American military bases. It is still considered an insult in France and is rarely shown there. Even though "it's just a movie" there is a nagging element: It is based on a true story.

United Artists continued releasing disturbing war films at this time. Another was the adaptation of *Fragile Fox*, a stage play by Norman Brooks. James Poe wrote the script. The title was changed to *Attack!* with Robert Aldrich directing. The cast was headed by Jack Palance with two decorated World War II veterans in support, Eddie Albert (Tarawa) and Lee Marvin (Saipan). Again, war's ugly dark side was examined. Palance played a vengeful platoon leader who suffered needless losses because of the cowardice and ineptitude of the company commander portrayed by Albert. Marvin, the battalion commander, refuses to do anything about the situation because the resulting investigation would damage his political ambitions after the war.

In the end moral justice prevails—but not without a price, as Albert's death is quietly camouflaged as heroic. Palance also pays with his life as the war continues.

The Department of Defense refused cooperation in the production. When the film was screened at the Venice Film Festival, the American ambassador walked out.

However, World War I continued to be portrayed with different angles in American films of the 1950s. But it was not without egos and personalities. These are what marred the 1957 remake of Ernest Hemingway's *A Farewell to Arms*, starring Rock Hudson and Jennifer Jones, produced by David O. Selznick and released by 20th Century Fox. The 1932 version with Gary Cooper and

Helen Hayes is considered one of the best adaptations of a Hemingway novel. When rights to the remake were acquired by Selznick he gave the director's assignment to John Huston.

However, Selznick just happened to be the husband of Jones. Huston saw the film as a young man's coming of age story set against a war with the subplot of the young American, serving in the Italian ambulance service, falling in love with his British nurse. Selznick felt that Ben Hecht's screenplay should emphasize the love story more than the war. Selznick collaborated with Hecht in several quick rewrites, feeling that this would be the best film adaptation of any Hemingway novel.

Rudy Behlmer's *Memo from David O. Selznick* quotes a detailed March 19, 1957, memo to John Huston.

I never concealed from you, John, that even your best friends thought I was out of my mind to cast you on a romantic love story of this kind. It was predicted over and over again that your interest would be in military matters, to the detriment of the love story, with the war as a background to the extent—but only to the extent—that Hemingway made it a background, the military emphasis is going to throw the picture way off balance and to frustrate even readers of the book. The book is a romance; the book is a love story; the book is almost a fantasy as a love story, born out of some cockeyed concept of Hemingway's about a girl and boy that is far from being realistic, or even neo-realistic.[12]

Forty-eight hours before principal photography was to begin, Huston left the production. He was replaced by his assistant, Andrew Marton. Later, on location in the Italian Alps, Selznick called in Charles Vidor.

On March 23, 1957, the *London Daily Express* reported that John Huston walked out on David O. Selznick. It mentioned reports in the "Rome film world" that Jones and Huston "had a row." Staff writer David Lewin wrote, "The reports also say that Huston and Selznick disagreed on how the story was to be treated. Selznick wanted strong emphasis on the love story between Jennifer Jones, who plays an English nurse, and Rock Hudson, an American serving with the Italian Army in the First World War."

The film received mostly negative reviews. The film also played a role in the end of Hudson's marriage to Phyllis Gates. Hudson later reflected that the decision to play Frederic Henry in *A Farewell to Arms* was one of the worst in his career.

Huston overcame the unfortunate experience by staying with the same studio but going to another war film, *Heaven Knows Mr. Allison* (1957). It was a two-character piece, the story of a rugged marine corporal and a nun who find themselves stranded on a Japanese-occupied island. Huston worked with screenwriter John Lee Mahin, from Charles Shaw's novel. The interesting element was Robert Mitchum's tough marine persona going against Deborah Kerr's proper attitudes as a religious woman. In a scene where he is drunk, Mitchum is barely able to control his lust, becoming aware that nuns are beyond the love line. The screenplay (Mahin and Huston) and Kerr both received Academy Award nominations. The film had some similarities to *The African Queen*: two contrasting people trying to survive against the background of a war in a remote location.

William Wellman went back to the combat well with the biography of William Orlando Darby, the commander of the 1st Ranger Battalion that won the nickname Darby's Rangers. Guy Trosper adapted the screenplay for *Darby's Rangers* (1957) from Major James Altieri's book.

As a lieutenant colonel, Darby organized and trained the 1st Ranger Battalion in northern Ireland in 1942. His battalion was in the forefront in North Africa, Sicily, and Italy. By the time Rome was liberated, in 1944, there were only 199 soldiers left from the original roster of 1,500. Darby refused several promotions to brigadier general because he would have to transfer to another unit. He was killed on April 16, 1945, during an artillery barrage in the Po Valley. Darby was then promoted to brigadier general posthumously.

Wellman cast James Garner as Darby. Jack Warden, as the first sergeant, was the "Greek Chorus" who narrates the story, much like James Whitmore in *Battle Cry*, Arthur Franz in *Sands of Iwo Jima*, and Gil Stratton in *Stalag 17*.

With such films as *The Steel Helmet, From Here to Eternity, The Caine Mutiny, The Court-Martial of Billy Mitchell, Paths of Glory*, and *Attack!* the American war film began to reveal the dark side of the war experience, compassionately sharing that men in combat are still men with flaws who often make mistakes costing lives, a heavy burden to bear.

The above films were released after the Blacklist Era had begun, while Senator Joseph McCarthy was still making outrageous charges about Communists working in the State Department. Americans also saw a president, standing on constitutional principle, confronting one of the most popular war heroes of the century—only to fire him. History has proven that that five-star general was also a flawed man with an enormous ego. And it took a president, risking public opinion, to enforce the Constitution and remind the American people about democratic principles and the chain of command.

But the country still liked American war films and war heroes. Audie Murphy was accepted as a movie star. Dwight Eisenhower, hero of Normandy, was now president. And another combat veteran of World War II—a former PT boat skipper—was making a move for Eisenhower's job.

The Blossom Room, May 16, 1929. The first Academy Awards banquet, held in the Blossom Room of the Hollywood Roosevelt Hotel. Seated in the middle of the left speakers' table is Douglas Fairbanks, who distributed the Oscars. At the table in front of the left speakers' table sit (*left to right*) Mr. and Mrs. Louis B. Mayer; Irving Thalberg and Norma Shearer; unidentified man and Sid Grauman, original owner of Grauman's Chinese Theater, a Hollywood landmark; and Mr. and Mrs. Cecil B. DeMille. At middle table, *left*, sits actor Adolphe Menjou. To his *far right* sit Al Jolson and Ruby Keeler. Copyright Academy of Motion Picture Arts and Sciences.

The Boys of *Wings* (Paramount, 1927). From *left*, Charles "Buddy" Rogers, Richard Arlen, and Gary Cooper in one of his first roles. The battle scenes were filmed on location outside of San Antonio, Texas. This war film won the first Academy Award as Best Picture, directed by William A. Wellman, a World War I veteran. Photofest.

Valentino as an Infantryman. Rudolph Valentino (born in 1895 in Italy as Rodolfo D'Antonguolla) quickly became a Jazz Age heartthrob with his role as Julio Desnoyers in *The Four Horsemen of the Apocalypse* (Metro, 1921), directed by Rex Ingram, based on the novel by Vincente Blasco-Ibáñez and adapted by June Mathis. Valentino became the target of worship for thousands of American women. When he died unexpectedly of peritonitis in 1926, the overwhelming majority of the 50,000 people attending his New York City funeral were sobbing women. Photofest.

Doughboys to the Front. Renée Adorée, *right*, says a tearful farewell to John Gilbert as Karl Dane and Tom O'Brien march side by side in *The Big Parade* (MGM, 1925). This film, one of the first to show the harsh realities of World War I, had the largest gross in the Silent Era. Tragically, sound pictures affected both Gilbert and Dane, the former a victim of alcohol, the latter a suicide. Photofest.

Flower of the Confederacy. The wounded and dying in *Gone with the Wind* (MGM, 1939) are grouped in the Atlanta railroad yard under the Confederate "Stars and Bars" battle flag. This famous crane shot visually captured the tragic price that the Southern states paid in the Civil War. Photofest.

USS *Arizona* Memorial. Daily visitors flock by the hundreds to Pearl Harbor to see where the sunken battleship rests on "Battleship Row" following the Japanese attack on December 7, 1941. That morning brought the country and the war film genre into a new era. McAdams.

Attack on Tokyo. Lieutenant Colonel James Doolittle (Spencer Tracy), U.S. Army Air Force, points to the battle map of Tokyo aboard the flight deck of the USS *Hornet* in *Thirty Seconds over Tokyo* (MGM, 1944). The *Hornet* transported the B-25 bombers to their launch point in April 1942. Doolittle's bomber was the first off the flight deck. Photofest.

*Twelve O'Clock High* (20th Century Fox, 1949) Briefing. Brigadier General Frank Savage, U.S. Army Air Force (Gregory Peck), briefs the pilots, navigators, bombardiers, and gunners of the 918th Bomb Group in England in 1943. Major Harvey Stovall, Group Adjutant (Dean Jagger), is to the *left* of Savage. The seriousness of the grim situation is on the face of every man. Peck and the film won Oscar nominations, while Jagger won for Best Supporting Actor. Screenplay credit went to two USAAF veterans, Sy Bartlett and Beirne Ley Jr. Today the film is shown in management seminars as a primer for leadership. Photofest.

Nuts! Colonel Anthony McAuliffe was persuaded by his operations officer, Lieutenant Colonel Harry Kinnard Jr., to use this American idiom as the reply to the Nazi surrender request at Bastogne during the height of the Battle of the Bulge, where the 101st Airborne was surrounded by German infantry and Panzer divisions. The scene was reenacted in *Battleground* (MGM, 1949), with Ian MacDonald portraying McAuliffe. Kinnard was the technical adviser on the film. In the *rear, left to right*, are the airborne infantrymen of the 3rd platoon, I Company, Jarvess (John Hodiak), "Pop" Stazak (George Murphy), and Kippton (Douglas Fowley). The film received several nominations, with Robert Pirosh (a Bulge veteran) and Paul C. Vogel being awarded Oscars, respectively, for Best Screenplay and Best Cinematography. Photofest.

Window to the Pacific. Another memorable 1949 World War II film was *Task Force* (Warner Bros.), directed by Delmer Daves. Here, *left to right*, Julie London, Wayne Morris, Jane Wyatt, and Gary Cooper glance out a window on Christmas Eve 1941, wondering where the new war will take them. Morris, a former California junior college football player, flew some fifty-seven combat missions, earning four Distinguished Flying Crosses. He was also credited with sinking two Japanese destroyers. Morris became one of the most decorated navy fighter pilots and Hollywood's first ace with seven Japanese planes shot down. At age forty-five in 1959, he died of a heart attack aboard the carrier USS *Bonhomme Richard*, which was commanded by his wife's uncle, another decorated navy fighter pilot, Captain David MacCampbell. Photofest.

Surviving Flag Raisers. Republic Pictures' release of *Sands of Iwo Jima* (1949) garnered John Wayne his first Academy Award nomination as the tough, but flawed, Sergeant John Stryker. Here, in cameo roles, the three surviving 5th Marine Division flag raisers of Joe Rosenthal's Pulitzer Prize–winning photo receive the flag from Sergeant Stryker. *Left to right*, Ira Hayes, John Bradley, John Wayne, and Rene Gagnon. Author and marine veteran Ron Kovic wrote in *Born on the Fourth of July* (1976) that he not only cried at the end of this film, but it also motivated him to join the Marine Corps and serve in Vietnam. Both Bradley and Hayes had negative feelings of being exploited in their cameo roles. Filmed on location at Camp Pendleton, California, the movie was the most expensive Republic picture made to date. National Archives.

Cast and Crew. With the Camp Pendleton location scenes on the *Sands of Iwo Jima* (Republic, 1949) completed, the cast and crew posed for this group photo. The crew members are lined up in front with the cast in the middle, in front of the extras from a marine infantry company. Among the cast line are, *left to right*, Wally Cassell, James Brown, John Wayne, Forrest Tucker, Captain Leonard Fribourg, U.S. Marine Corps (technical adviser), director Alan Dwan, and John Agar. The Leonard Fribourg Collection.

*Iwo* Reunion in Vietnam. Colonel Leonard Fribourg, U.S. Marine Corps, met with John Wayne in Danang in 1966 during one of the actor's USO tours. Despite the seventeen-year time gap after the *Sands of Iwo Jima* (Republic, 1949) was released, the two—actor and marine officer—stayed in touch. At the time of this photo Wayne was preparing production on the adaptation of Robin Moore's *The Green Berets*, the only Vietnam War film produced while the war was still taking place. The Leonard Fribourg Collection.

The Bridge of the *Caine*. Former naval officer Herman Wouk won the 1952 Pulitzer Prize for his novel *The Caine Mutiny*. The novel was the basis for the Broadway play *The Caine Mutiny Court Martial*, directed by Charles Laughton. The book was also adapted into a 1954 screenplay by Stanley Roberts and directed by Edward Dmytryk (Columbia Pictures). Here, the officers of the *Caine* observe a gunnery exercise. From *left* are Lieutenant Tom Keefer (Fred MacMurray), Ensign Willis Keith (Robert Francis), Lieutenant Steve Maryk (Van Johnson), and Lieutenant Commander Philip Francis Queeg (Humphrey Bogart). Even though the film received six Oscar nominations, Wouk termed the adaptation "a thin rinse of the novel." Photofest.

Sefton in the Stalag. William Holden reportedly had to be talked into the role of Sergeant Sefton, U.S. Army Air Force, which won him the 1953 Oscar for Best Actor in *Stalag 17* (Paramount), directed by Billy Wilder. Based on a Broadway play, the screenplay was written by Billy Wilder and Edwin Blum. From *left* are Price (Peter Graves), Sefton, and actors Neville Brand and Richard Erdman. Brand, an infantryman during World War II, was listed as the army's fourth most decorated soldier. Photofest.

Marching at Schofield. Robert E. Lee Prewitt (Montgomery Clift) gets the "treatment," marching around the Oahu quadrangle at Schofield Barracks, from one of the company sergeants (Claude Akins) in *From Here to Eternity* (Columbia, 1953). James Jones's 1951 novel, based on his army experiences, broke new ground both in wartime characters and story. Photofest.

Schofield Today. Schofield Barracks, the Hawaiian location for *From Here to Eternity* (Columbia, 1953), is still an army post today. One of the changes to the "new" army are racks for the soldiers' bicycles and motorcycles. The barracks sustained numerous hits from Japanese fighter planes during the December 7, 1941 attack, as described by James Jones in his letters. McAdams.

War Film Oscars. Fred Zinnemann's direction of Daniel Taradash's adaptation of James Jones's novel *From Here to Eternity* resulted in Oscars for the supporting actors. Here, Donna Reed (Alma Burke/Lorene) and Frank Sinatra (Angelo Maggio) pose with their statuettes at the 1953 awards ceremony. Eli Wallach and Joan Crawford were initial favorites for the respective roles of Maggio and Karen Holmes (given to Deborah Kerr, who was also nominated). Crawford and Wallach withdrew for different reasons. Zinnemann and Taradash also won Oscars, and the film was named Best Picture. Copyright Academy of Motion Picture Arts and Sciences.

Overlord Decision. Supreme Allied Commander General Dwight Eisenhower (Henry Grace) hears the opinions of British Field Marshal Bernard Law Montgomery (Trevor Reid) on the decision to cross the English Channel to the Normandy coast, June 1944, in *The Longest Day* (20th Century Fox, 1962). Producer Darryl F. Zanuck quipped that he had more problems with the logistics of the war epic than Eisenhower had at the actual invasion, code-named Operation Overlord. Eisenhower also had a statement drafted to be released in the unlikely event that the Allies were defeated and pushed back into the Channel. Photofest.

Returning Veterans. The Samuel Goldwyn production of *The Best Years of Our Lives* won Oscars (1946) for Best Picture; William Wyler, Best Director; Frederic March, Best Actor; Harold Russell, Best Supporting Actor; and Robert E. Sherwood, Best Screenplay. Russell was cast as Homer Parrish specifically because he was a double amputee, with arms lost in an accidental explosion. In this scene Captain Fred Derry (Dana Andrews), U.S. Army Air Force, and Sergeant Al Stephenson (Frederic March), U.S. Army, wonder where their lives will go now that the war is over, as Homer naps. The bars on their left sleeves each denote six months of overseas service. Above Stephenson's top ribbon is the combat infantryman's badge. Courtesy of the Academy of Motion Picture Arts and Sciences and the Samuel Goldwyn Company.

Fighting the Forgotten War. Director Samuel Fuller filmed the exteriors of *The Steel Helmet* (Lippert Pictures, 1951) in and around Los Angeles' Griffith Park while the Korean War was in its first year. Here, *left to right*, James Edwards, William Chun (Short Round), and Gene Evans check out an enemy position. Years later at a film retrospective Evans gave the "dinged" helmet he wore in the film back to Fuller. Both Fuller and Evans were World War II combat veterans. Photofest.

Coming off Pork Chop Hill. Army Lieutenant Joe Clemons (Gregory Peck) leads his men down from the controversial hill where indecision almost cost the battle as the Korean War peace talks entered a stressful phase. The United Artists film (1959) brought out the complex decision-making process that went from a black-and-white World War II mentality to the contradictions of the Cold War, foreshadowing what was to come in Vietnam. Photofest.

Early Vietnam. In *Go Tell the Spartans* (Avco Embassy, 1978), burned-out army regular Major Asa Barker (Burt Lancaster) gives orders to his men, *left to right*, Dennis Howard, John Megna, Craig Wasson, Evan Kim, Jonathan Goldsmith, Joe Unger, and Marc Singer. Directed by Ted Post from a script by Wendell Mayes, the low-budget film used locations near Magic Mountain, north of Los Angeles. Comparing two wars, Lancaster tells Singer, "World War II, now there was a war . . . this one's a sucker's tour going nowhere." Photofest.

Caged Combat Soldiers. Michael and Steven (Robert De Niro and John Savage, respectively) stare out of their watery cell in *The Deer Hunter* (EMI/Universal, 1978). Directed by Michael Cimino with screenplay credit to Deric Washburn and story credit to Michael Cimino, Deric Washburn, Louis Garfinkle, and Quinn K. Redeker, the film told the story of three young men from a Pennsylvania mill town before, during, and after their return from the Vietnam War, casualties all. The film was awarded Oscars for Best Film; Best Director, Cimino; and Best Supporting Actor, Christopher Walken. The controversial sequences centered around Russian roulette forcefully played out in the POW camp. Some veterans saw this as a metaphor for America putting a gun to the head of its youth. Photofest.

Between Good and Evil. Chris Taylor (Charlie Sheen) stands between the good Sergeant Elias (Willem Dafoe) and the evil Sergeant Barnes (Tom Berenger) in Oliver Stone's *Platoon* (Hemdale, 1986). Even though Stone was an army Vietnam combat veteran, he still came under fire from some veterans for a negative treatment of the war. The film won Oscars for Best Picture; Best Director, Stone; and Best Editing, Claire Simpson. Photofest.

Revolutionary Enemies. South Carolina colonist Benjamin Martin (Mel Gibson) faces the brutal Colonel Tavington (Jason Issacs) in *The Patriot*, directed by Roland Emmerich from a script by Robert Rodat (Sony/Tri-Star, 2000). Colonel Tavington was based, in part, on real-life British officer Banastre Tarleton, who acquired the nickname "Bloody Ban." Martin's character was a composite of several Revolutionary War figures including Daniel Morgan, Elijah Clark, and Francis "Swamp Fox" Marion. Photofest.

Approaching Omaha Beach. Tom Sizemore and Tom Hanks prepare to lead their men out of the Higgins boat and into the battle buzz saw of Omaha Beach on June 6, 1944. When *Saving Private Ryan* (Dreamworks, SKG) was released in the summer of 1998, American audiences were not prepared for the graphic realism depicting what actually happened at Normandy on that morning. Structured in "bookend flashback," many World War II veterans released emotional reactions that had been suppressed for decades because of the opening twenty-four minutes of the film, which won an Oscar for Steven Spielberg as Best Director. Photofest.

Combat Veteran. Audie Murphy's combat record with the 3rd Infantry Division in Europe gave him the celebrity of the most decorated soldier of World War II. A grammar school dropout from Hunt County, Texas, he was initially rejected by the army airborne and the Marine Corps. Murphy received a battlefield commission and is credited with killing or capturing approximately 240 German soldiers. He was awarded the Congressional Medal of Honor and twenty-seven other combat-related medals, including the Distinguished Service Cross, three Silver Stars, and three Purple Hearts. James Cagney brought Murphy to Hollywood and was an influence in getting the young man's acting career launched. His better performances were as Henry Fleming in *The Red Badge of Courage* (MGM, 1951) and as himself in *To Hell and Back* (Universal-International, 1955), based on his autobiography. His often difficult life came to an abrupt end in 1971 when he was killed in a plane crash during the Memorial Day weekend. Today he rests in Arlington National Cemetery. Courtesy of The Audie Murphy Research Foundation.

Pearl Harbor Aftermath. Admiral William F. Halsey, Jr. (James Whitmore) learns of the full impact of the Pearl Harbor attack from Admiral Husband Kimmel (Martin Balsam) in 20th Century Fox's 1970 docudrama *Tora! Tora! Tora!* Kimmel and army General Walter C. Short were finally exonerated of blame for the attack by a U.S. Senate vote in May 1999. Photofest.

Approaching X-Ray. Mel Gibson, as Lieutenant Colonel Harold G. Moore scans the "Valley of Death" as his Huey helicopter nears Landing Zone X-Ray where the three-day battle for the Ia Drang Valley would take place. Moore later observed that Secretary of Defense Robert McNamara's feelings toward the U.S. involvement in Vietnam changed because of his briefing following the Ia Drang battle. The Paramount film, written and directed by Randall Wallace, was based on Moore's book, co-authored with Joseph L. Galloway, *We Were Soldiers Once . . . and Young*. Photofest.

# 6

# Only Great Challenges

Mankind must put an end to war,
Or war will put an end to mankind.

—John Fitzgerald Kennedy

Often in the war film genre a "turning point" film begins with a source from another medium, usually from a book or a play. Such past examples are *The Birth of a Nation, What Price Glory?, All Quiet on the Western Front, A Walk in the Sun, The Best Years of Our Lives, Twelve O'Clock High, From Here to Eternity, The Naked and the Dead, The Caine Mutiny*, and *Stalag 17*. The film adaptation of *Gone With the Wind* turned its source novel into an epic film.

And like *Gone With the Wind*, it took a producer with an epic attitude and philosophy to bring *The Bridge on the River Kwai* (1957) to the screen. The *Kwai* story began when French producer Henri Georges Cluzot optioned the screenplay rights to Pierre Boulle's novel *Le pont de la rivière Kwai*.

Boulle spent two years as a prisoner in Indochina during World War II. His novel told the story of a group of British prisoners interred in a Japanese camp. The Japanese prison commandant, Colonel Saito, and the British commander, Lieutenant Colonel Nicholson, combine efforts when the prisoners are assigned to build a railway bridge across the River Kwai. The bridge becomes an obsession to Nicholson, as it goes into construction. As construction nears completion, the British prisoners secretly plan to destroy it. However, Nicholson learns of this and exposes their sabotage to the Japanese. He then dies in a mortar barrage triggered by a demolitions expert who is one of his own men. Boulle's ending had the bridge standing at the end.

Cluzot had great difficulty getting the project set up. Frustrated, he sold the

option for a mere U.S. $850. The buyer was blacklisted screenwriter Carl Fore-
man, now living in London and working with the British film industry.

British producer Alexander Korda knew of Foreman's American credits and
wanted to work with him. Unfortunately, Korda did not like the character of
Lieutenant Colonel Nicholson. Beyond that, he felt that British audiences would
view Nicholson as a madman.

According to author Steven Jay Rubin, in *Combat Films*, Foreman was then
approached by Columbia Pictures producer Sam Spiegel, who saw the potential
of the Boulle novel.[1] Spiegel had just completed producing *On the Waterfront*
(1954). A quick meeting was set up in England.

Spiegel and Foreman discussed changes if the novel was to work as a screenplay. British Major Shears, a commando in the novel, would be changed to an
American. But the main story line would essentially remain the same: the madness and hypocrisy of war and the thin line between enemies.

Initial casting suggestions were Jack Hawkins and Charles Laughton for Warden and Nicholson, respectively. Columbia Pictures then agreed to finance the
film with Spiegel as producer. David Lean, at the top of his form, was signed
on as director.

Next was construction of the bridge, which alone cost a reported $250,000.
Location work, in Ceylon, continued through the fall of 1956. Spiegel's planned
destruction of the bridge took up two years of effort.

Spiegel then signed the Japanese actor Sessue Hayakawa to play Colonel
Saito.

In the meantime, Foreman was able to deliver a first draft screenplay. He
then began having problems with Lean over many details. The major problem
was the ending. Spiegel had already taken the position of rejecting Boulle's
ending where the bridge is left standing at the end. The producer saw the demolition of the bridge as an epic cinematic event. The question now was how
to develop character and motivation that climaxes in the bridge being blown up
as the first train approaches. In the revised script, as Nicholson becomes more
obsessed with building the bridge as a monument to British will and determination, under the most trying of wartime conditions, he forgets his original
objective as a military officer. A brave man, and a onetime forceful leader, he
deteriorates into self-centered madness caused by war. It's an old story with an
update for the time.

Foreman had a compromise ending where the bridge was partially blown up.
Lean held to Nicholson's end where the British colonel falls on the plunger
detonating the explosive packs set on the bridge. Foreman disagreed with that
ending, feeling that it would be a "copout."

In August 1956, Foreman was granted a reprieve interview with the HUAC
committee. After the hearing, it was rumored that Columbia was offering him
a production deal. This gave Foreman a chance to leave the film and his problems with Lean's ending. But before he left, Foreman recommended Michael
Wilson, another blacklisted screenwriter living in Paris. Spiegel then hired Cal-

der Willingham (*Paths of Glory*), who immediately developed an adversarial relationship with Lean. This forced Spiegel to take Foreman's recommendation.

With Wilson aboard rewriting Foreman's last draft, more work was needed in developing Shears's American character, along with Warden. Wilson made many suggestions and was able to get along with Lean. In September 1956, Laughton asked for his release because of a play commitment. Spiegel then approached Alec Guinness for the second time. This time Guinness accepted.

Spiegel then flew to Hollywood to nail down the Shears role. He submitted scripts to Cary Grant and William Holden. Holden responded first, identifying with the American prisoner of war similar to his Oscar-winning role of Sefton in *Stalag 17*.

Later that fall, production began when the bridge was finally completed. The production now resembled an enormous military operation, complete with logistics and extras wearing uniforms of the era. The jungle location provided the backdrop that both Spiegel and Lean felt was one of the hallmarks of the film. But it was not without more disagreement.

In the pivotal scene, where Nicholson discovers the cables running from the plunger to the explosive packs, Guinness disagreed with the way it occurred. In the script, Nicholson, standing at the railing, drops his baton. The baton lands beside Shears, who is placing an explosive pack on one of the supports. Guinness objected because he felt that a British officer like Nicholson would never, ever, drop his baton! It took some convincing, and Guinness eventually did the scene, under protest.

On March 12, 1957, the onetime-only take of the bridge demolition scene took place, engineered by a team selected from Imperial Chemical in London.

The final scene in the movie is the ultimate statement about war. It was given to the British character actor James Donald, playing Major Clipton, the medical officer. With Shears and Nicholson dead, the bridge blown, and the train in the river, Clipton surveys the horrific carnage, repeating one word, "Madness . . . madness!"

The film swept the 1957 Academy Awards with Oscars for Spiegel (Best Picture), Lean (Best Director), Jack Hildyard (Best Cinematography), and Malcolm Arnold (Best Music).

As previously noted, it took the Academy until 1985 to correct the screenplay credit to Carl Foreman and Michael Wilson.

Another look at racial problems set against war provided United Artists' 1958 film *Kings Go Forth*. Merle Miller's adaptation of Joe David Brown's novel was directed by Delmer Daves. The twist of the love story triangle between Natalie Wood, Frank Sinatra, and Tony Curtis is that Wood's late father was a black millionaire who emigrated to the south of France before the war. Both men come to accept her as she is. The triangle is resolved when Curtis is killed on a mission. In supporting roles are Leora Dana and Karl Swenson.

Irwin Shaw's novel *The Young Lions* was released by 20th Century Fox with Edward Dmytryk directing from Edward Anhalt's adaptation (1958). Shaw's novel intertwined the lives of a German ski instructor, a young Jewish man, and a man of the world who suddenly finds himself drafted into the army.

Marlon Brando portrayed the ski instructor who becomes a Nazi officer and is soon disillusioned. Montgomery Clift has to contend with the army system, much as he did in *From Here to Eternity*, along with anti-Semitism. Dean Martin was cast as the man of the world who suddenly doubts his bravery in combat.

In a 1998 interview, Edward Dymytrk said that he felt he got one of Martin's best performances and had absolutely no trouble with Brando. The production was hit with heavy weather problems caused by one of the worst rainy seasons ever in Europe. Dmytryk added that Irwin Shaw became extremely upset with the screenplay adaptation, causing an estrangement between the two men.[2]

In supporting roles were May Britt, Barbara Rush, Hope Lange, Maximilian Schell, and Lee Van Cleef.

Burt Lancaster's production company developed *Run Silent, Run Deep* in 1958. Lancaster worked with John Gay on an original screenplay about conflicting personalities aboard the tight living quarters of a World War II submarine. Directed by Robert Wise, the script had Lancaster as the executive officer who is in line for a submarine command. Headquarters assigns Clark Gable, a former submarine commander, who was working at a desk but also had extensive knowledge of the submarine patrol areas. Immediately Gable and Lancaster become adversaries who have to work together to accomplish the mission.

Supporting the major stars were Jack Warden, Brad Dexter, and Nick Cravat, Lancaster's longtime friend and acrobat associate.

Having directed two previous major war films, *All Quiet on the Western Front* and *A Walk in the Sun*, Lewis Milestone ventured into the Korean War in 1959 with a brutally realistic script by James R. Webb. The script came from the book *Pork Chop Hill* by S.L.A. Marshall.

The film took on the controversial issues of indecisiveness and politics. Pork Chop Hill was an actual event in April 1953, paralleling the truce talks at Panmunjom.

Gregory Peck portrayed the real-life Joe Clemons. Clemons, as a first lieutenant, commanded King Company. Overnight, Pork Chop is lost. King Company is assigned to retake it and hold it until relieved. Believing that his higher headquarters will support him, Peck accomplishes the objective, but not until after a bloody assault. Peck also has to confront a reluctant black infantryman, played by Woody Strode, who sees the futility and questions whether taking the hill is worth dying for. The enemy uses psychological warfare, loud speakers topped off with dreamy music ("Autumn in New York") interrupted by blaring bugles in the night, preceding their human wave attacks.

King Company holds the hill through a series of Chinese counterattacks. It is here where the military chain shows signs of breaking. Peck's continued requests for reinforcements are met with staff meetings and indecisiveness at the highest level. The army becomes concerned that reinforcing Pork Chop would place the peace talks in jeopardy. Peck and his men are within an eyelash of being pushed off the hill as the peace talks drone on. When it appears that new troops have arrived, they turn out to be a photo-journalist team on an assignment from *Pacific Stars and Stripes*.

The final fight has the company retreating into the command bunker where they make a stand against enemy flame throwers. Reinforcements arrive at the last moment. As King Company is relieved, Peck comes off the hill, shaken by the experience but knowing that his company held the objective in spite of the indecisiveness. And that made all the difference.

In voiceover, we hear Peck observe that there are no monuments on Pork Chop. "Victory is a fragile thing and history does not linger long in this century." This seems to be another way of asking, What do we learn from history?

Supporting Peck were Harry Guardino, George Shibata, Rip Torn, George Peppard, James Edwards, and Robert Blake.

In a 1998 interview, Gregory Peck discussed the complex and thorny issues surrounding the actual battle. "The Truman administration called it [Korea] a police action. And, of course, the American public was not one hundred percent behind the war.

"It [the conflict] was a problem with the chain of command," Peck added. "The company commander [Joe Clemons] got to the top of the hill despite losing forty to sixty percent of his men."

Peck also said that *Pork Chop Hill* was one of the first Korean War films to make a comment on the military's treatment of black soldiers with the Woody Strode character. "I had no problems with the script expressing that. It was a say for the black infantryman," said Peck.[3]

MGM's 1959 release of *Never So Few* took on the issue of corruption, namely, the Chiang Kai-shek Nationalist Chinese government selling U.S. weapons to Japanese and local officials. Tom Chamales's novel, adapted by Millard Kaufman, fictionalized an account of the OSS Unit 101 operating in Burma at the peak of World War II. The Americans recruited local Kachin tribesmen who developed into creditable jungle fighters against the Japanese.

It is not surprising that this tactic was perfected and taken to another level by the army's Special Forces in Vietnam.

The leader of the guerrilla unit is Frank Sinatra, supported by Steve McQueen in his first important role, as Ringa. Gina Lollobrigida is Sinatra's love interest, while Brian Donlevy portrays a General William Donovan–type character who supports Sinatra in exposing the corruption of the Nationalist Chinese. Also in the cast were Peter Lawford and Paul Henreid.

Gary Cooper's eighth and last American war film, *They Came to Cordura*, was released in 1959. Cooper played an army officer, in 1916 Mexico, accused of cowardice who is given the assignment of finding five men who are worthy of the Congressional Medal of Honor. In pursuit of this goal, Cooper discovers the true meaning of courage under fire. Ivan Moffat and Robert Rossen, who also directed, adapted the script from a novel by Glendon Swarthout. The title song was sung by Frank Sinatra.

Supporting Cooper were Rita Hayworth, Van Heflin, Richard Conte, Tab Hunter, Michael Callan, Dick York, and Robert Keith.

Perhaps the ultimate historical statement against fascism in Europe came from the heart of a young girl, Anne Frank. Her real name was Anneliese Marie. She was born in Frankfurt, Germany, to a middle-class Jewish family. When Hitler became chancellor of Germany in 1933, Otto Frank and his family emigrated to Amsterdam, where he transferred his business and eventually began looking for a hiding place, just in case. By 1940, the Nazis seized the Netherlands and were issuing anti-Jewish decrees. In July 1942, Anne's older sister Margot was named for deportation, causing Otto Frank to put his hiding plan into effect. The family then packed their belongings and entered an attic, a few rooms above Frank's business. They stayed there for two years, sharing the cramped quarters with four other people. The attic became a prison only a few feet from the outside world.

During these two years, Anne Frank kept a diary, the daily writings of a young girl. Not only was she looking at herself with the emotions and contradictions typical of someone her age, but she viewed the outside world fighting with itself. And she was aware that her family was in a life-and-death struggle.

Because of the situation, the inhabitants of the attic could not speak above a whisper. Their only link to the outside world was a crystal radio and members of Frank's staff who periodically brought them food and clothes.

In August 1944, the group's hiding place was discovered when four Nazi policemen stormed the attic in an attempt to confiscate the group's jewels and money. The policemen rifled through everything, not even noticing the journals kept by the young girl. The group was taken into custody and ended up in various concentration camps. Otto and Mrs. Frank were confined in Auschwitz, where Mrs. Frank died of exhaustion. Margot and Anne were sent to Bergen-Belsen. Margot died in March 1945. Anne succumbed to typhus one month later.

After Otto Frank returned to Amsterdam, he was given the diary of his younger daughter. Frank made a few copies and gave them to friends as a memorial to his family. He was then advised to get the diary published. Two major Dutch publishing houses rejected it. However, a third house accepted it. Soon it was translated into twenty languages.

Frances Goodrich and Albert Hackett were then contracted to adapt the diary into a stage play. Frank soon retired and dedicated the rest of his life to Anne's legacy. On March 17, 1957, 2,000 people traveled to Bergen-Belsen to place flowers on the mass grave where Anne rested. It was at this demonstration in Europe, coupled with the Broadway play, that the world once again realized what horrors the Third Reich had caused. And it came to pass through the diary of a thirteen-year-old girl who would never see womanhood but who would become one of the many true heroes of World War II.

20th Century Fox retained the writing team of Goodrich and Hackett for the screenplay adaptation, produced and directed by George Stevens. Millie Perkins played Anne, while the part of Peter, her first and only boyfriend, went to Richard Beymer. The supporting cast included Ed Wynn, Shelley Winters, Lou Jacobi, and Diane Baker.

The film won Oscars for William C. Mellor, Best Cinematography; Shelley Winters, Best Supporting Actress; and Lyle R. Wheeler for Art Direction. Also nominated were Stevens for Best Picture and Best Director, Alfred Newman for Best Music, and Ed Wynn for Best Supporting Actor.

Combat veteran and screenwriter Beirne Lay Jr. was again called upon for the 1960 United Artists release of *The Gallant Hours*, an account of Admiral William F. Halsey's toughest fight during the Guadalcanal campaign and making the decision to bring down Admiral Isoroku Yamamoto and his staff in 1943. Lay got cocredit on the screenplay with Frank Gilroy. James Cagney played Halsey with Robert Montgomery directing. Both men produced.

Supporting Cagney were Dennis Weaver, Richard Jaeckel, Ward Costello, and Carl Benton Reid as Admiral Robert L. Ghormley.

One of the negative elements of the film was that it came off as a black-and-white stage play with the Roger Wagner chorale in the background interspersed with Montgomery's narration. The combat occurred off camera and through dialogue.

One of the better dialogue exchanges was between Cagney and Jaeckel, a squadron commander who lost almost his entire unit on one mission. Jaeckel requests that Halsey relieve him of command, that he will fly combat, but that he has had it with suffering the losses of a squadron commander, "because it takes a great man."

Cagney responds in a fatherly tone. "There are no great men. There are only great challenges which ordinary men are forced, by circumstances, to meet."

Racial issues and the Korean War butted heads again with the Columbia Pictures release of *All the Young Men* (1960), starring Alan Ladd and Sidney Poitier as marines set poles apart. The script and direction were from Hall Bartlett.

Poitier is forced to take command of Ladd's squad during the winter retreat of 1950–1951. He has to face the attitudes and taunts of marines who refuse to be led by a black man but eventually have to for the good of the mission. Heavyweight champion Ingemar Johansson (fresh off his defeat of Floyd Patterson) was in a supporting role vainly trying to launch an acting career. Glenn Corbett and James Darren also played marines in the squad. One of the best scenes in the film was a monologue by Mort Sahl as Corporal Crane, giving his sarcastic views on the military mentality.

## FILMING THE LEGEND

In 1948, while scouting locations for the western *Three Godfathers*, John Wayne was photographed at the Alamo holding a rifle that once belonged to Davy Crockett. Through the years Wayne became obsessed with filming the story of the Alamo. A great American historical incident had the potential to be a cinematic monument to himself.

However, Walt Disney's television production of *Davy Crockett, King of the Wild Frontier*, starring Fess Parker, in 1955 put Wayne's Alamo efforts on hold. For a while the country became crazed with Davy Crockett, the title song, and "the coonskin hat."

By 1959, Wayne began preparing his Alamo project—released as *The Alamo* (1960)—with himself as director. His production company, Batjac, chose the area around Fort Clark, Texas, for principal locations.

James Edward Grant's screenplay took a wide poetic license with facts. Grant made it an American story set against tyranny and the fight for Texas independence.

In June 1835, American settlers in Texas, citing land grants and the Texas constitution of 1824, declared themselves independent from Mexico. A group of these settlers, many of them immigrants, made a stand by occupying an abandoned mission known as the Alamo. Leading these settlers was twenty-seven-year-old William Barrett Travis, who had left a failed marriage in South Carolina and was looking for a new life. Travis's group was joined by Davy Crockett and twenty-three followers.

Crockett was a colorful, albeit semiliterate, frontiersman who could tell a good story despite being careless with the facts. He previously served two terms in Congress before being defeated. Crockett had opposed several of President Andrew Jackson's programs. And now he was looking for new challenges and saw the Texas revolution as an opportunity. Likewise was the thinking of Jim Bowie, who gained fame as a knife fighter, land speculator, and slave trader. However, Bowie arrived in a sickly condition. His wife had died of plague three years prior.

The Mexican government, with General Antonio López de Santa Anna as president, voided the land grants and quickly acted to put down any movement that would mean losing territories north of the Rio Grande. In December 1835, Santa Anna sent General Martín Perfecto de Cos to San Antonio to enforce Mexican law. Cos was quickly driven back across the Rio Grande.

General Santa Anna, who possessed an inflated ego, and often referred to himself as "The Napoleon of the West," led his Mexican army across the Rio Grande to prove that the Texas territory was a Mexican province and that the rebels would be pushed out of the Alamo and subjected to his law.

The only way for the Alamo defenders to succeed would be through reinforcements, mainly from General Sam Houston. When Santa Anna's army arrived, he demanded that the defenders stand down. When they refused the die was cast. Thus began a siege that lasted thirteen days and ended in the predawn darkness of March 6, 1836. Santa Anna lost almost 2,000 troops in order to take a fortress occupied by 183.

It is documented that Houston had earlier sent orders that the Alamo be abandoned. Tactically, Houston preferred to conduct a hit-and-run campaign, that in maintaining mobility, a smaller force could defeat a larger one.

Travis, however, held on, believing that the defenders could win, despite orders to abandon the mission. He made numerous appeals for reinforcements. Houston was totally unavailable at the time, having taken leave of his command to pursue a diplomatic mission.

It is here where legend has it that Travis assembled the defenders and explained that reinforcements were no longer a possibility. Standing in front of the church, he supposedly drew a line on the ground with his sword and asked each man, who was willing to give his life for independence, to step over the line. It is left to interpretation whether this event actually occurred, although there is an account of one man, Louis Rose, who left after Travis's appeal. Rose, a mercenary from Napoleon's army, felt that he would not throw away his life for someone else's cause. He consulted Bowie and Crockett before taking his belongings and going over the wall. He managed to slip through Mexican lines and headed north. For the rest of his life he lived with the stigma of being the sole survivor of the Alamo. He died in Louisiana in 1850.

Today, the Alamo mission, in the heart of San Antonio, has a gold inlay over the ground in front of the church where Travis is said to have drawn the line.

Before the final charge, Santa Anna ordered the "Deguello" to be trumpeted before the defenders. This dated back to the Moorish wars in Spain. The notes meant no quarter; prisoners will not be taken. The attack began at 4 A.M. The mission was completely overrun before sunrise. Travis reportedly went down defending the north wall, firing a shotgun before taking a fatal head wound. Bowie, who had grown worse with fever, was bayoneted in his bed.

There is an account of several defenders surrendering to a Mexican officer. One of these defenders is alleged to have been Crockett, according to José Enrique de la Peña, who was on Santa Anna's staff and later published his memoirs of the fight. According to de la Peña, Crockett and several others surrendered to General Manuel Castrillon, who turned the prisoners over to Santa Anna. In keeping with the Deguello, all of the captives were summarily executed.

Whether Crockett died fighting or was executed in captivity is still a contested subject for Alamo historians.

To ensure that there would be no graveyard monuments, Santa Anna ordered the defenders' bodies burned in a massive pyre.

Texas history uses the rationale that the thirteen days at the Alamo allowed Sam Houston time to raise an army to defeat Santa Anna and finally claim independence. In fact, Houston's army was, for the most part, already standing. In numbers, the Texans were less than 800 with the Mexican army massed at approximately 2,000.

Less than two months later, Sam Houston used his hit-and-run strategy to perfection. On April 21, 1836, at the mouth of the San Jacinto River, Houston saw that Santa Anna's defensive perimeter was porous. The Mexican army was literally caught napping, with Santa Anna enjoying a siesta and the troops cooking a meal. With shouts of "Remember the Alamo!" Houston's troops easily broke the perimeter, killing 600. Santa Anna fled during the battle. He was captured the next day, hiding in long grass, dressed in a blue shirt, white trousers, and red carpet slippers. While a prisoner, he signed a treaty recognizing Texas independence.

With the film, Wayne was forced into casting himself as Davy Crockett, solely for box office draw. Initially, he opted to play the cameo role of Sam Houston to allow himself more time for directing. For the part of Jim Bowie, Richard Widmark was cast. The two grated against each other but made themselves get along. Completing the male triangle was Laurence Harvey, as Travis, in spite of his being a South African native. Richard Boone, known for his television role as Paladin in *Have Gun, Will Travel*, was eventually cast as Houston. Pop singer Frankie Avalon was cast to attract the teenage audience.

In other supporting roles were Chill Wills, Denver Pyle, and Linda Cristal as Wayne's love interest. The Wayne family was well represented with son Patrick cast as Captain James Butler Bonham. Patrick's older brother, Michael, was an assistant producer. Other family roles went to wife Pilar and daughters Toni and Aissa.

James Edward Grant's script altered history on several points. Jim Bowie (Widmark) shows up with a slave in tow, Jethro. Although Bowie did slave trading, Travis was the one who came with a slave, Joe. Santa Anna's predawn final assault was changed to an afternoon artillery barrage, followed by the Mexican infantry overwhelming the mission with scaling ladders. In dying a hero's death, Crockett (Wayne), mortally wounded, throws a torch into the Alamo's magazine, taking out himself and numerous Mexican soldiers. The stacked bodies being burned at the end was deemed unnecessary.

As with any distant location the production was laced with problems, including a visit from one of Wayne's mentors—the "Coach" himself—John Ford. Ford was given several action sequences to direct, but none made the final cut. Despite the teacher–student relationship between Wayne and Ford, they shared different visions.

Many local businessmen buzzed the set in private planes for a quick look-see. On one occasion, Wayne took a rifle (loaded with a blank cartridge) and fired at the plane.

Wayne wrote the "Republic Speech," his directorial statement: "Republic—I like the sound of the word . . . one of those words that make you tight in the throat. . . . Some words can give you a feeling that makes your heart warm. Republic is one of those words."

The film was nominated for Best Picture. Chill Wills got nominated for Best Supporting Actor, and William H. Clothier received a nod for cinematography. Dimitri Tiomkin's score and Stuart Gilmore's editing were also nominated.

## THE ORPHAN OF DEFEAT

On the first Wednesday of November 1960, Americans learned that John F. Kennedy, the junior Catholic senator from Massachusetts, defeated Vice President Richard Nixon by a hair-breadth margin of 113,057 popular votes. Nixon was advised to contest that count, based on voter fraud allegations in Cook County, Illinois, and other counties in Texas.

Nixon decided to let the vote count stand and immediately made plans for a return to California. Although they were political adversaries during the historic presidential election, Nixon and Kennedy were closer than many people knew at the time. Both were freshman congressmen in 1946 and established a bonding as wartime naval officers in the Pacific.

It was ironic that, after Eisenhower, the next four American presidents were World War II naval officers: Kennedy, Johnson, Nixon, and Ford. And they all began their careers in Congress during the 1946–1948 period. Their attitudes, beginning to form, would eventually cause a reversal of monumental proportions in terms of history later reflected in war films.

Among Eisenhower's legacies was the Diem regime in Vietnam. After World War II, the French reoccupied Indochina. In 1946, Ho Chi Minh became president of a separatist government headquartered in Hanoi, while Bao Dai was reinstalled as king in the South. Fighting broke out between the two factions and resulted with the French suffering a major defeat at Dien Bien Phu in May 1954. An armistice partitioned the country at the 17th parallel. Ngo Dinh Diem became premier of South Vietnam, with France granting full sovereignty. After 1956, fighting escalated as the National Liberation Front, with northern Viet Minh support, continued its guerrilla attempts to overthrow the Diem regime. By 1960, the situation had become extremely brittle despite U.S. adviser support.

Another legacy that demanded immediate attention was only ninety miles off shore—Cuba.

Shortly after the election was confirmed, President Eisenhower called Kennedy to the White House. They reportedly took a walk in the Rose Garden where the president-elect was informed of a CIA-planned invasion of Cuba at a little-known point, the Bahia de Cocinos (Bay of Pigs). The invasion force, a brigade of Cuban exiles, was completing training in Guatemala. The objective was to storm inland and set up a counterrevolutionary force aimed at the overthrow of the Fidel Castro regime. Eisenhower told Kennedy that the final decision on the upcoming invasion would be his alone.

On January 20, 1961, as the youngest president was sworn in with the oldest president leaving, a vigorous and charismatic John Kennedy told a freezing inaugural crowd that "the torch has been passed to a new generation of Americans born in this century. . . . In the long history of the world, only a few generations have been granted the role of defending freedom in its hour of maximum danger. I do not shrink from that responsibility, I welcome it."

He also welcomed new allies to the ranks of the free, not always expecting these nations to accept the U.S. view. He then warned "that, in the past, those who foolishly sought power by riding the back of the tiger ended up inside."

Kennedy added that "with a good conscience our only sure reward, with history the final judge of our deeds, let us go forth to lead the land we love."[4]

Relying heavily on military advisers and classified CIA reports, Kennedy approved the invasion with the condition that there would be no trace of U.S. involvement. On April 17, the Cuban brigade stormed ashore from landing boats and was confronted on the beach with intense artillery and mortar fire. Pinned down with nothing but the water to their backs, the brigade's request for air support from nearby U.S. Navy ships went unheeded.

The frantic requests for air support were bumped directly to the White House, late in the evening. Richard Bissell of the CIA entered the Oval Office and informed President Kennedy that although the situation was bad, it "could still take a favorable turn if the president would authorize sending in aircraft [from the USS *Boxer*]."

Kennedy, Secretary of Defense Robert McNamara, and Secretary of State Dean Rusk were in white tie and tails. They had just left the East Room where the annual congressional reception had concluded. Also in the Oval Office, in military evening dress, were General Lyman Lemnitzer, chairman of the Joint Chiefs of Staff, and Chief of Naval Operations Admiral Arleigh Burke.

Burke felt that the invasion could still be salvaged with air cover. "Let me take two jets and shoot down the enemy aircraft," he urged.

Kennedy said no and reminded the officers that he had said "over and over again" that U.S. forces would not be committed to combat in this invasion.

Burke then opted for sending in a destroyer to render naval gunfire support. At that point Kennedy exploded and dropped all formality. "Burke!" he snapped. "I don't want the United States involved in this."

Burke came right back at his commander in chief: "All in all, Mr. President, we are involved."[5]

Arriving at the scene, Castro supervised the defeat and capture of the brigade survivors. The U.S. ships hoisted their anchors and steamed away. Those who survived and got off the beach in the landing boats or anything else that floated were left to the elements. Many drowned in the succeeding days.

It was ironic that Kennedy, as the American commander in chief, denied support to a group of military men who were caught on an island beach. One can only wonder at the emotions he must have felt, having lived through a somewhat similar military experience in 1943 after his motor torpedo boat was rammed by a Japanese destroyer. He and his crew ended up on a beach, left to the elements and presumed lost at sea.

At first, the U.S. State Department denied any involvement in the Bay of Pigs invasion. Days later, Kennedy accepted full reponsibility for the disaster, quoting the Italian Count Ciano, "Victory has a hundred fathers while defeat is an orphan." In private, Kennedy reportedly cried in front of his wife Jackie.

The Soviet Union and the Communist bloc nations reacted immediately, castigating the United States and its new inexperienced president. The fiasco caused a high-echelon shakeup at the CIA where the director, Allen Dulles, resigned.

The following month, Kennedy made a commitment to the space program predicting that by the end of the decade the United States would land a man on the moon and return him safely to earth. Many political observers scoffed at the idea.

That spring and summer, Kennedy journeyed to Paris to meet with President de Gaulle and then to Vienna for a difficult two-day meeting with Soviet Premier Nikita Khrushchev. It was at this summit where Khrushchev made the assumption that Kennedy was inexperienced and a pushover. It would set the stage for the Cuban Missile Crisis.

In May, renewed fighting in Laos prompted the United States to send naval and ground forces to support local troops against Communist insurgents. American military advisers were increased in Vietnam where the Diem regime was still being bitterly opposed from several sides.

While the 1962 World Series between the New York Yankees and the San Francisco Giants was taking place, increasing evidence, including reconnaissance photos revealing that Russia was building missile bases in Cuba, brought Kennedy to secret meetings with his advisers and the Joint Chiefs.

Kennedy rejected an outright military invasion, based on his experience with the ill-fated Bay of Pigs attempt. Instead, he ordered a naval quarantine of Cuba to block the island from receiving any further missiles. On October 22, Kennedy revealed to the nation the international drama that was taking place on the high seas. The conflict increased for four days until a communication was received that the Soviet Union would dismantle their missile bases in exchange for the promise that the United States would not invade Cuba. A follow-up letter, the next day, called for the United States to remove its missile sites in Turkey. Kennedy ignored the second communication, and the Soviets accepted the first offer. The Cuban Missile Crisis averted an outright nuclear confrontation but also resulted in a telephone "hotline" between Washington and Moscow. In July 1963, a nuclear test ban treaty was signed between the two superpowers.

Also, in the summer of 1963, President Kennedy was welcomed by 2,000,000 citizens in West Berlin where he gave his famous "Ich bin ein Berliner" speech.

As the situation in Vietnam worsened a civil rights march on Washington had 200,000 people hear Dr. Martin Luther King Jr. give his "I have a dream" speech.

The military bickering and political instability continued in Vietnam. It was felt that the Diem regime, an elitist oligarchy, had distanced itself from the villages and hamlets.

The United States brought in what was termed the U.S. Military Advisory Group (Military Assistance Command Vietnam—MACV). What the American military advisers found was a poorly trained Army of the Republic of Vietnam (ARVN) with antiquated equipment. The officer corps was uneducated; promotion was based on loyalty rather than merit. And the ARVN doctrine was geared toward a conventional rather than a guerrilla war. Despite an infusion of American aid the situation became darker. The Diem regime, clearly riding the back of the proverbial tiger, did not share American values. Democracy was an alien form of government. The oligarchy, consisting of Diem's brother and his wife, Madame Nhu, continued to impose its will on a disenfranchised people. Anyone suspected of opposing Diem ended up in the hands of the secret police and then jail. The bitterest enemies of the Diem regime were the Buddhist monks.

At first Kennedy placated Diem while steadily increasing the numbers of advisers and amount of aid. When the Laos crisis erupted in 1961, the Vietnam situation became even shakier. It was felt that if Laos fell to the Communists, Thailand, Cambodia, and South Vietnam would be in worse positions. If the United States did not draw the line it would have to write off Southeast Asia.

In one of his last interviews with Walter Cronkite, held in Hyannis Port, Massachusetts, Kennedy emphasized that the Vietnam situation would be confined to that country. "It's their war. They will have to win it," said Kennedy.

It soon became clear that if U.S. military advisory assistance was to continue, the Diem regime would have to go, willing or otherwise. The next question was who would be the replacement?

In early November, South Vietnam President Ngo Dinh Diem and his brother Ngo Dinh Nhu were arrested in a coup. The two brothers were then transported outside of Saigon and assassinated in the back of a truck. When Kennedy was told of their deaths he was visibly shaken. Kennedy had assumed that Diem and his brother would be replaced and sent into exile.

Three weeks later, Kennedy was himself assassinated while riding in an open limousine in Dallas, Texas. Local police arrested Lee Harvey Oswald, a former marine and expatriate, in a movie theater where he fled after shooting a policeman. The title of the film playing in the theater, ironically, was *War Is Hell*.

Lyndon Johnson was sworn in as president by federal judge Sarah Hughes.

Two days later, on November 24, Oswald was shot by nightclub owner Jack Ruby.

By the end of the turbulent month, Johnson appointed Chief Justice Earl Warren to head a commission to investigate the Kennedy assassination.

## A NEW ANGLE AT VICTORY

The basic war theme of a gang of heroes for a noble goal was seized upon with many angles in the American war films of the 1960s. History again was the foundation with poetic license running a close or distant second, depending upon one's perspective.

Carl Foreman, still operating out of London, used his Columbia Pictures deal to acquire the screenplay rights to Alistar MacLean's World War II novel *The Guns of Navarone*. The film (1961) unfolds the story of a commando mission where specialists are recruited, in 1943, to destroy two massive Nazi artillery pieces emplaced on a Turkish island.

In the cast were Gregory Peck, David Niven, Stanley Baker, Anthony Quinn, Anthony Quayle, James Darren, Gia Scala, James Robertson Justice, Richard Harris, and Irene Pappas.

In a 1998 interview, Gregory Peck referred to the film as "a swashbuckler with a World War II background. We all played it tongue in cheek. We couldn't have played it dead straight."

However, a problem developed with the initial director, Alexander McKendrick. Peck described a personality clash between Foreman and McKendrick over several elements in the script. "There was another problem," added Peck. "It happened that McKendrick had a fondness for the bottle."

After McKendrick left the project Foreman made an attempt to direct. "He called up Quinn and Niven," said Peck. "But he was already one of the producers. With a film with distant locations, special effects, and logistics, it was too much for one man to write, produce, and direct."

Columbia then called in J. Lee Thompson. He was handed a script to read on the plane. "We got adequate preparation time and soon we saw that we were in good hands," explained Peck.[6]

The film received mixed reviews but was a box office success. Academy Award nominations came in for Best Picture; Carl Foreman, Best Screenplay; J. Lee Thompson, Best Director; and Dimitri Tiomkin, Best Musical Score. Bill Warrington and Vivian C. Greenhan got nominations for Best Special Effects.

Abby Mann's play *Judgment at Nuremberg* was brought to the screen, produced and directed by Stanley Kramer (1961). It was a fictionalized version of the 1948 Nazi war crimes trials. The film begins as the American legal team arrives in Nuremberg. The chief judge was played by Spencer Tracy. Burt Lancaster was cast as the Nazi Ernst Janning, after Laurence Olivier dropped out.

The documentary style of the film contributed to heart-rendering performances by Judy Garland and Montgomery Clift, giving accounts as victims of Nazi horrors.

Richard Widmark and Maximilian Schell opposed each other, respectively, as prosecutor and defense counsel. Marlene Dietrich played the wife of a dead Nazi general who disliked Hitler but was still loyal to Germany. Dietrich does a turn as Tracy's "tour guide" through the German culture and, in one scene, explains what the ballad "Lili Marlene" meant to soldiers of the Afrika Corps.

In reality, twenty-two Nazi leaders were tried at Nuremberg. Twelve were sentenced to hang, among whom was Reichsmarshal Hermann Goering, whose Luftwaffe was supposed to dominate the skies over England. Goering was able to swallow a cyanide pill smuggled to him before execution. Seven Nazis were sentenced to long prison terms, and three were acquitted.

The film was nominated for eight Academy Awards in 1961. Schell and Mann were the two to receive Oscars.

History and tragedy came together with Tony Curtis playing the doomed Pima

Indian Ira Hamilton Hayes, one of the three celebrated surviving Mount Suribachi marine flag raisers on Iwo Jima. Delbert Mann directed *The Outsider* for Universal-International, in 1961, from a penetrating script by Stewart Stern.

The February 23, 1945, flag raising mixed fact with legend. In his 1965 book *Iwo Jima*, author Richard F. Newcomb explained that Associated Press photographer Joseph Rosenthal's Pulitzer Prize–winning photo was actually a reenactment of the first flag raising.

First Lieutenant Harold G. Schrier was executive officer of E Company, second battalion of the 28th Marine Regiment. His battalion commander gave him the order to take a patrol of forty men to the rim of Mount Suribachi. The commander handed him a flag. "And put this up on top of the hill."

As the patrol started out they were plainly visible to all the marines on the southern end of the island. Slowly they made their way up. At 10:15 that morning they arrived at the rim. It was the highest point on the island, 550 feet above sea level. There was no opposition.

That Friday Rosenthal just happened to be in the southwestern section of Iwo Jima. He had heard that a patrol was going up to the top of Suribachi Yama to place a flag. Rosenthal was also told that he was late; the patrol had already gone up. But he decided to take a chance and go up anyway. Even though the fiercest Iwo Jima fighting had yet to occur, it was decided that the flag be put up on the highest point for morale purposes.

When Schrier's patrol reached the rim of Mount Suribachi, they began looking for a staff. Someone found a long pipe, and they attached the flag to it. Besides Schrier, five other marines took up positions along the pipe. They were: Platoon Sergeant Ernest I. Thomas Jr., Sergeant Harry O. Hansen, Corporal Charles W. Lindberg, PFC James R. Michaels, and Private Louis Charlo, a Crow Indian from Montana.

As soon as the flag was up and flapping it was visible to the marines down on the beach, a thrilling sight. Whoops and cheers were heard repeatedly. The morale element worked.

One of those observing the first flag raising was Secretary of the Navy James Forrestal, who turned to marine General H.M. "Howling Mad" Smith and said, "This means a Marine Corps for the next five hundred years."

It was determined that the flag now had the status of a war souvenir. The order then went out to find another flag, get it up there, and bring back the original for historical safekeeping.

As Rosenthal reached the rim of the Suribachi volcano the first flag had been taken down. The second patrol, carrying a ship's flag from a tank landing ship (LST), had just about reached the rim. This flag was bigger and the staff longer. Rosenthal tried to get a shot of the two flags crossing but didn't get into position in time. The second patrol was also comprised of marines from the 2nd battalion of the 28th Regiment, 5th Marine Division. The second flag was attached to the staff, and the marines got in line.

From left to right, they were: PFC Ira Hayes (Arizona); PFC Franklin Sousley

(Kentucky); Sergeant Michael Strank (Pennsylvania); navy corpsman John H. Bradley (Wisconsin); Private Rene Gagnon (New Hampshire); and Corporal Harlon Block (Texas).

Rosenthal quickly made a stand for himself with some bricks as the 2nd battalion marines attached the larger flag and got in line. The camera speed was set at 400 with the f-stop between 7 and 11.

As the flag was at an angle, Rosenthal unknowingly snapped the prize-winning photograph that was to personify the World War II marines in the Pacific Theater. This onetime shot was to become one of the most recognized wartime photos of the twentieth century.

With the second flag secure on the rim, the marines had more important duties other than posing for pictures. Rosenthal likewise went back down the mountain and took more photos. At the end of the day he went back aboard ship and sent the day's film rolls to Guam for processing.

As soon as the images came up in the developing tray the marines knew what they had. No words were needed to express this wartime work of art. Strangely, the faces of the six marines were not identifiable. It took several days to back-track and determine who the marines were in the second flag raising that Rosenthal photographed. The first group was relegated to historical obscurity. Because of the prize-winning photo, the three survivors of the second raising were given celebrity status, whether they liked it or not. The Marine Corps public relations office didn't waste any time in enhancing its battlefield image. The three survivors of the second flag raising were brought back to the States and used for appearances for morale, recruiting, and the seventh war bond drive.

The survivors of the second group were: Hayes, Gagnon, and Bradley. The story of *The Outsider* was of Ira Hayes, treated afterward as a war hero. But Hayes never thought of himself as such. His true battle would emerge after war's end.

Hayes's conflict was his background, reared on a Pima Indian reservation at Bapchule, Arizona, coupled with his inability to adjust to postwar society, traveling in a white man's world. This led to a downward spiral into alcohol, which caused an early death in 1955 at age thirty-two. Hayes was found along a road where he had drowned in his own vomit.

Supporting Curtis, in one of his best performances, were James Franciscus, Gregory Walcott, Bruce Bennett, and Vivian Nathan. It is left to argument as to whether a Native American would be cast in the title role if *The Outsider* were to be made today.

Leo Rosten's novel *Captain Newman, M.D.*, the story of an Army Air Force psychiatrist's struggle to cure traumatized soldiers and airmen, was adapted by Richard Breen along with the writing team of Phoebe and Henry Ephron. The film (1963) was derivative of *The Men* and the John Huston documentary *Let There Be Light*. Rosten's novel was a thinly disguised wartime biography of Dr. Ralph Greenson, who later became Marilyn Monroe's noted psychiatrist.

Eddie Albert and Bobby Darin portrayed veterans diversely affected by the horrors of combat. Albert was an operations officer, while Darin played Corporal Jim Tompkins, who was affected by the deaths of his buddies, wondering why he survived.

Gregory Peck played Captain Josiah Newman, supported by Angie Dickinson and Tony Curtis. Peck is stymied in his efforts to find the keys to both Albert's and Darin's maladies. Too late does Captain Newman discover that Albert had been suppressing his guilt for sending young fliers to their combat deaths while he sat at his group headquarters supervising more missions. Darin is eventually cured and requests to rejoin his squadron, somewhat of a victory for the hospital staff.

The guilt, however, is too much for Albert. Unable to live with seeing the faces and names of the dead, he climbs to the railing of a reservoir tower and takes his own life.

The poignant climax comes when Peck and Dickinson learn that Darin was killed in action. Academy nominations came in for the screenplay and Bobby Darin.

The effects of war continued to take a deeper, penetrating turn in 1962. World Wars I and II and Korea were included. And as the wars grew in distance the view became more complex.

Novelist Richard Condon combined the background of the "McCarthy Era" and the Korean War to make a Cold War statement about both in *The Manchurian Candidate* (1962), directed by John Frankenheimer. George Axelrod adapted Condon's novel about a manufactured Korean War hero, portrayed by Laurence Harvey, who is psychologically programmed to assassinate a presidential candidate upon a given subliminal signal.

Condon worked the McCarthy angle into the novel with the character of Senator John Iselin, played by James Gregory, a bufoonish tool of the right wing—and vice presidential candidate—who spouts in the Senate well about false numbers of Communists working in the State Department. Behind the senator is Angela Lansbury as the ambitious, evil wife who is actually calling all the shots. Lansbury, it turns out, is working with the other side to get her son to assassinate the presidential candidate. For her portrayal, Lansbury received an Academy Award nomination for Best Supporting Actress.

Frank Sinatra, playing Ben Marco, was a captain and an infantry patrol leader in the latter stages of the Korean War. After the patrol ventures into enemy territory they are silently set upon and captured. When the soldiers wake up, they are prisoners in a "psychological" camp. It is here where each is programmed and tested in a different way. This leads to Harvey being falsely awarded the Congressional Medal of Honor.

After the war, Sinatra, now promoted to major, slowly begins to figure out the plot, which culminates in a Madison Square Garden shootout.

Sinatra's love interest is Janet Leigh. Reportedly, Sinatra broke his hand while filming the well-choreographed karate fight with Henry Silva.

The film used the Korean War to take Cold War politics to another level.

One year after its release, out of respect, Sinatra (who held the film rights) had the movie pulled because of the JFK assassination. It wasn't until years later when the film was rereleased.

John Hersey's novel *The War Lover* was brought to the screen (1962) by Columbia Pictures with Steve McQueen doing a turn as Buzz Rickson, a B-17 pilot who really loves the danger and excitement of his job: dropping bombs on Nazi targets. Even though McQueen is the best airplane commander in the group, his associates come to despise him. But they tolerate him because of his unusual good luck. Robert Wagner plays his copilot who takes exception to the way McQueen treats his girlfriend Daphne, played by Shirley Anne Field. McQueen's arrogant attitude about war and women eventually spells doom, making him realize that his time is limited. After ordering his crew to bail out, resulting from a flak hit, McQueen aims his bomber right at the white cliffs of Dover. Knowing that he wouldn't be able to function without the excitement of a war, McQueen opts to take himself out.

Philip Leacock directed from a script by Howard Koch. Actual combat footage of Eighth Air Force missions contributed to the realistic black-and-white look.

Men using war to randomly kill was used as a theme in United Artists' *War Hunt* (1962), Robert Redford's debut film set in Korea. John Saxon plays a kill-crazy soldier who is good at his job. Directed by Denis Sanders, from a script by Stanford Whitmore, the unpleasant realities of war are brought out in the ugly business of killing the enemy by whatever means possible. When the squad finally realizes that they have a psychotic soldier in their midst, they take it upon themselves to rectify the situation and have him written off as a combat death. Supporting Saxon and Redford are Sydney Pollack, Charles Aidman, and Tommy Matsuda as a war orphan.

History reflecting itself came full circle with *The Longest Day* (1962). Naturally, when the international star-studded black-and-white epic was released in 1962, most American audiences had no idea what it took to get the novel published, the film rights sold, and the film produced.

At the time of the Normandy Invasion, correspondent Cornelius Ryan was covering the event for the *London Daily Express*. Afterward, he found it difficult to write about the meaning of it, the planning, the ships, the planes, and the people who made it happen, the "sung" heroes along with the unsung.

After the invasion, Ryan was assigned to cover General George Patton's Third Army. When the war in Europe ended, Ryan was transferred to the Pacific.

In 1949, while employed at *Collier's* magazine, Ryan returned to Normandy for a correspondent's reunion. Observing the beach he saw the flotsam of that June day still littering the shore. The sight moved him to make the attempt to tell the whole story. He was motivated, but others were not. Nobody at the editor's desk was interested. Some felt that the story had been told and retold. Besides, the war was over.

With his own money, Ryan began the research. He read every book on Operation Overlord. He sent out thousands of questionnaires to military men who had served on both sides. These led to hundreds of interviews.

By 1956, *Collier's* was bankrupt and Ryan found himself $20,000 in debt for his *The Longest Day* efforts. Despite this setback, he began the manuscript. He submitted the first chapters to Simon & Schuster. This resulted in an acceptance along with a $7,500 advance.

Three years later, the manuscript was finished. Ryan did get additional financial help from *Reader's Digest*, but was about $60,000 in debt by the time of completion.

The *Reader's Digest* condensation was published in the spring of 1959. The Simon & Schuster publication came one month later.

Raoul J. Levy, a French producer, acquired the first option on the book, with Ryan attached as the screenwriter. Levy hoped to get the production under way by March 1961. Ryan's first draft screenplay included more than 300 speaking parts.

Levy, however, was unable to get American cofinancing and thus went into a deal with Associated British Picture Corporation. All the while, Darryl Zanuck, at 20th Century Fox, was keenly watching from afar.

The executives at Associated British Picture Corporation were unable to finance the film's proposed $6 million budget. When Zanuck saw that the Levy deal had fallen apart, he stepped up and bought out Levy's option.

At the time, 20th Century Fox was hemorrhaging red ink because of the astronomical overruns on *Cleopatra*, being filmed in London and Italy. That production was garnering daily scandalous publicity not just because of the budget problems but owing to the love affair that developed between two of the married actors, Richard Burton and Elizabeth Taylor. In the middle of this, Taylor fell ill with pneumonia and almost died. The studio needed a blockbuster to offset the obvious looming financial disaster on *Cleopatra*.

*The Longest Day* deal was not without its own risks. Zanuck was the first to say that the production would be a massive undertaking, much like the cross Channel invasion itself. He later quipped that Eisenhower had had an easier time planning Normandy.

Ryan had structured the book and screenplay as an epic docudrama, telling the story from both the Nazi and Allied sides, a style that would lay the foundation for later war epics. Technical advisers were unlike any other previous war film, French, British, German, and American.

Elmo Williams and Frank McCarthy began working on the logistics in different areas, while Ryan started the next screenplay draft. McCarthy, a VMI graduate who had served as an aide to General George Marshall, was a retired brigadier general who knew his way around the D.C. beltway. The script would need army and Department of Defense approval if the use of battalions of extras and materiel such as ships, planes, and landing craft were to be loaned.

Zanuck came up with the idea of using a "team" of directors instead of loading everything on one man. He also would control this team much like an army commander controls his divisions. This team consisted of Andrew "Bundy" Marton (American exteriors), Ken Annakin (British exteriors), and Bernhard Wicki (German episodes). In addition, four cinematographers would be needed.

Based on Ryan's screenplay, Elmo Williams began designing the major battle sequences including the American beaches at Omaha and Utah, the assault of the 2nd Ranger Battalion at Pointe du Hoc, the French commando attack at Ouistreham, the tragic American paratroop drop at Ste. Mere Eglise, and the glider assault on the Orne River bridge by the British 6th Airborne Infantry.

Zanuck, insisting on realism at every turn, had to find a substitute for the British landing area, Sword Beach. The actual beach now butted up next to a bird sanctuary, and the environment maintained its priority over a film production, no matter how epic.

When Zanuck saw Ryan's latest draft, it resembled the size of a metropolitan phone book. A page-one rewrite was called for, adding and cutting, causing a strain on both men.

McCarthy came back from Washington with a plus. They would be able to use the U.S. Sixth Fleet's amphibious maneuvers at Saleccia Beach in northern Corsica. The beach would be fortified along a two-mile stretch that would resemble Omaha Beach. A reinforced Marine Corps battalion would be outfitted with camouflaged net helmets and World War II–type leggings.

The Americans were joined by a flotilla of French vessels resulting in a combined fleet of 22 ships that would substitute for the 5,000 that were actually used on D-Day.

And just like the army troops on D-Day, when the marines left the landing boats and trudged through the water, many were seasick and had already thrown up. The nauseated looks on the marines' faces as they hit the beach contributed to the realism of getting through the deadly Nazi machine gun and artillery fire.

Zanuck followed a casting suggestion of using popular American teenage heart throbs. Fabian and Tommy Sands took the roles of 2nd Battalion rangers at Pointe du Hoc. Also cast as a ranger was Paul Anka, who would also write the title song. The scaling of Pointe du Hoc, on the right flank of Omaha Beach, would be almost as dangerous in film production as the actual event. The sheer cliffs went to an eighty-foot drop down to a gravel beach. As Paul Anka's character observes, "Three grandmothers with brooms could sweep us off there like flies off a sugar cane."

William Holden was initially cast as Lieutenant Colonel Benjamin Vandervoort, a battalion commander in the 82nd Airborne who has to lead his unit despite a broken ankle. After Holden left the film John Wayne replaced him. This was followed by the casting of major American actors including Robert Mitchum, Henry Fonda, Robert Ryan, Edmond O'Brien, Rod Steiger, Jeffrey Hunter, Eddie Albert, Robert Wagner, Red Buttons, and George Segal.

The international casting included Leo Genn, John Gregson, Irina Demich, Bourvil, Jean-Louis Barrault, Christian Marquand, and Arletty.

The Nazi casting included Curt Jurgens as General Gunther Blumentritt, Paul Hartmann, Gert Frobe, Wolfgang Preiss, Peter van Eyck, and Richard Wattis. The international star list came to forty-two.

There was no need to cast Hitler. The führer was intentially off camera, on the phone, or asleep. It wasn't that no actor wanted to play Hitler. It was simply felt that the story was about the characters caught up in the actual event.

An MGM set designer, Henry Grace, was cast as Dwight Eisenhower because of his resemblance to the general. Richard Burton and Roddy McDowall, still at work on *Cleopatra*, came in when needed. Sean Connery was cast as a sarcastic British soldier landing at Sword Beach. Advising the British actors and sequences were D-Day veterans Lord Lovat and Major John Howard (for the Orne River sequence), who was portrayed by actor Richard Todd, also a Normandy survivor.

In one of the more visual scenes, reflecting the history of the event, is Rod Steiger, as a naval officer who walks into the bridge of a ship crossing the Channel. Steiger looks at the crowded dots on a radar scope. "Impossible to believe," he says. "Every dot represents a ship . . . the biggest armada the world has ever known. . . . [W]e are on the eve of a day people are going to talk about long after we are dead and gone. . . . [I]t gives me goose pimples just to be part of it."

When the credits for final screenplay draft were approved Cornelius Ryan received first billing. Backing him up, with rewrites, were Romain Gary, James Jones, David Pursall, and Jack Seddon.

The premiere festivities of *The Longest Day* were held in Manhattan, over two days, complete with a star-drenched banquet and a Broadway parade that featured the Fordham University marching band. Besides the cast were Senator Jacob Javits (D–New York) and Francis Cardinal Spellman.

However, when the Academy Award nominations came in, the film only received two, for Best Picture and Cinematography. The latter category won the Oscar, with the team of Henri Persin, Walter Wottitz, Pierre Levent, and Jean Bourgoin.

In any other year *The Longest Day* would have swept the Oscars. But it was to be the year of *Lawrence of Arabia* (1962). The Columbia Pictures *River Kwai* team of producer Sam Spiegel and director David Lean combined on another blockbuster. The multitiered sweeping story of the historic Normandy invasion placed second to a desert drama centered around an unusual character.

Thomas Edward Lawrence was called a warrior–poet in the obituaries following his untimely death. He was forty-seven when he died of injuries suffered in a freak motorcycle accident in 1935. But when Lean began working with Robert Bolt on the screenplay, they decided to concentrate on the two years of what came to be known as "the Arab revolt in the desert."

Born out of wedlock, to Sir Robert Chapman and his daughter's governess Sara Maden, Lawrence graduated from Oxford and already had a reputation as a scholar and archeologist when World War I broke out. After being commissioned, he was assigned as a cryptographer attached to the British military intelligence section in Cairo. In the fall of 1916 he was assigned as a liaison officer with Prince Faisal's army, which had faltered in its insurrection against the Turks. Lawrence then changed the direction of the flagging Arab revolt. He immediately began the centuries-old difficult task of uniting the nomadic tribes. He also began harassing the Turkish supply lines. He then led an unprecedented overland thrust that resulted in the capture of the strategic port of Aqaba. The attack, from the landward side, caught the Turks totally unprepared. This resulted in his promotion to major and established his reputation as a guerrilla leader. As his fame steadily grew so did the jealousy among his British superiors.

Lawrence won another surprising victory at Tafila in January 1918 and was promoted again. As a lieutenant colonel, Lawrence planned a campaign to capture Damascus that gained him even more notoriety. It was here where the renowned guerrilla leader found that celebrity, even in combat, carried a big price.

After war's end, Lawrence became disillusioned with the politics of the Versailles conference. He later served as an adviser on Arab affairs in the British Colonial Office but resigned his commission in 1922.

Barely five feet six inches, Lawrence was a loner and a man of extreme neuroses and contradictions. Seeking to escape the fame that consistently followed him, he enlisted in the Royal Air Force under an assumed name. He later resigned that post when a newspaper uncovered his identity. Lawrence then joined the Royal Tank Corps under the new name of T.E. Shaw, which he later adopted legally.

In 1926, he published his wartime memoirs, *The Seven Pillars of Wisdom*, in a limited edition. Two years later, he released a condensed version under the title *Revolt in the Desert*. His memoirs are considered one of the best to come out of World War I.

Albert Finney was the first choice to play Lawrence. But when negotiations broke down, Lean decided to take a chance on six-foot-three-inch unknown Irish actor Peter O'Toole, who in no way resembled Lawrence's physique. Supporting O'Toole were Omar Sharif as Ali, Anthony Quayle, Claude Rains, Alec Guinness, Anthony Quinn, and José Ferrer.

Arthur Kennedy played a journalist loosely patterned after Lowell Thomas, who wrote his own account in *With Lawrence in Arabia*. Thomas later characterized the film as distorted: "They only got two things right, the camels and the sand."[7]

A controversial Turkish sequence made implications about Lawrence's alleged homosexuality. In another sequence, Lawrence orders an attack on a Turkish column with the secondary command of "no prisoners." The entire Turkish column is slaughtered to the man. At this point in the script, Lawrence realizes the horrific barbarism that accompanies combat situations. He also becomes aware that he likes it.

Oscar nominations came in for Robert Bolt, Peter O'Toole, and Omar Sharif. Michael Wilson did several screenplay drafts for Lean but remained uncredited because of his being blacklisted.

The film won Oscars for Best Picture, Best Director, Best Musical Score (Maurice Jarre), and Frederick Young for photography.

In the Best Actor category Peter O'Toole watched Gregory Peck get the statuette for *To Kill a Mockingbird* (1962).

While *The Longest Day* was in production, another director, John Sturges, began the location shooting for still another World War II epic, *The Great Escape* (1963), based on the true story of the Great Escape from Stalag Luft III on the night of March 24–25, 1944. For Sturges, this was the result of a thirteen-year journey.

The Great Escape was initially planned for approximately 200 Allied prisoners, mostly British and Canadian airmen, who worked on three tunnels to break out of Stalag Luft III, which was designed for hardened POWs who were known for repeated escape attempts. One of them was Roger Bushell, a thirty-year-old Royal Air Force (RAF) pilot who was shot down during the beach defense at Dunkirk. Bushell had been in and out of several stalags. He now found himself, with the nickname of "Big X," in the newly constructed Stalag Luft III with other Allied flyers. His reputation preceded him.

As soon as Bushell was incarcerated, he began supervising an escape committee, the requirements of which were astounding in wartime terms. This would not be just three or four men going out under a wire. Bushell, known for his intense hatred of Nazis, wanted an Olympic record in the Allied POW books. His requisitions to the escape committee left jaws hanging. According to author Arthur Durand, in *Stalag Luft III: The Secret Story*, Bushell wanted shoring boards for the three tunnels, each descending 30 feet and extending out toward the woods 300 feet or more. He also wanted an underground railway and a workshop.

Durand added: "two hundred forged passes; two hundred civilian outfits; two hundred compasses; and one thousand maps. When the chief forger, Tim Waleen, heard the request for two hundred passes, all properly dated, his only reply was 'Jesus.' Bushell reportedly answered, 'Maybe he'll help you.' "[3]

The planning was coordinated, efficient, and intense. The tunnels were code-named Tom, Dick, and Harry. On the night of the attempt, 80 prisoners managed to get through tunnel Harry before the Nazis found the hole outside of the wire. This impacted on Bushell's intent of breaking out 200. Eighty Allied POWs got through the tunnel; 4 were captured at the wire; but 76 cleared the Stalag Luft area.

The Nazis then issued a *Grossfahndung*, a priority search bulletin. All German units were to set up an extensive search of the area. Bushell did accomplish part of his Herculean objective: The breakout of seventy-six Allied prisoners led to great embarrassment. His attitude was guerrilla in nature: to cause confusion and mess up the works. In addition, the camp commandant, Colonel von Lindeiner, was relieved of command.

Hitler then issued the infamous Sagan Order. In the tradition of Lidice, and the July 20, 1944, attempt at Rastenberg, Hitler demanded deadly retaliation.

It came swiftly. Fifty of the seventy-six prisoners were rounded up during the succeeding days. Instead of returning them to Stalag Luft III, they were executed in small groups. Roger Bushell was among the fifty. Three of the escapees eventually made it back to England.

On April 6, 1944, the Allied prisoners at Stalag Luft III were informed that fifty of the prisoners in the escape attempt were captured and shot. According to Durand, "The prisoners were numbed by the news, and believed the camp administrators when they said the Luftwaffe could not ensure the prisoners' safety outside the wire and that the men must realize that escape was no longer a game."

Paul Brickhill's account of the famed breakout, *The Great Escape*, was published in 1950. For more than a decade, Brickhill refused to give up the film rights to his book. In the meantime, another British POW book by P.R. Reid, *The Colditz Story*, about a mass escape from a Saxony castle, was produced and released in Great Britain in 1955. Still, *The Great Escape* (dedicated to the fifty) was out there, unproduced as a film, a tribute to the will and fortitude of the British and Allied cause. Ever since he first read the book, the story stayed with Sturges. To him, it was an American war film that had to be made.

Eventually, Sturges managed to get a meeting with L.B. Mayer at MGM. When Mayer and the Metro executives read the "script coverage" of the book, they balked. In their collective opinion, it was anything but a great escape because of the executions. There were also too many subplots and supporting characters. The meeting ended, and Sturges realized that he didn't even have the rights to Brickhill's book.

Sturges, an Army Air Force veteran, convinced Brickhill to at least fly from his home in Australia and meet in California. From that meeting Sturges was able to acquire the film rights to the book. The two hit it off, and Brickhill sold the film rights to the book to Sturges and became a partner in the production. There was no cooperation from the military in Hollywood. And after a confrontation with the Screen Extras Guild, Sturges took the production to Europe.

The location shooting took place in the Bavarian countryside, near the Geiselgasteig Studios. A Stalag Luft prison camp had to be constructed, complete with wire, guard towers, and barracks.

After several rewrites from W.R. Burnett and James Clavell (who was a World War II POW), Sturges began shooting. For legal reasons, Roger Bushell's name was changed to Roger Bartlett, played by Richard Attenborough. Camp commandant Colonel von Lindener's name was changed to von Luger, played by the noted German actor Hannes Messemer.

Weather became a factor. When that cleared up, egos entered into the mix. Steve McQueen, as Captain Virgil Hilts the "Cooler King," felt that his character had lost importance through the initial rewrites. With his friend Bud Ekins, a professional motorcycle rider, McQueen came up with a chase sequence. It was poetic license since a motorcycle chase never occurred in the original escape. However, there was documentation that escaped Allied prisoners stole German motorcycles.

Sturges liked the idea, and the chase was blocked out with McQueen not only doing his own stunt work but also playing the German chasing him. The motorcycle chase sequence was to become one of the most famous in American film annals.

## PRESIDENTIAL LIFE AND PRESIDENTIAL ART

Naval Lieutenant (j.g.) John F. Kennedy's experience in the Solomon Islands was chronicled in *The New Yorker*. Upon his election, Kennedy's World War II experience moved to the cover of the *Saturday Evening Post*. After his inauguration, Warner Bros. got the idea for a theatrical feature, titled *PT 109* (1963), with a script written by Richard Breen. Kennedy even approved the casting of Cliff Robertson as himself, despite the obvious age difference. Kennedy was twenty-six at the time. Robertson, the actor, was thirty-eight.

The 1963 production had problems from the start. Lewis Milestone was replaced as director after problems escalated.

The original experience, however, was not without controversy. Kennedy's boat was one of several groups assigned to patrol the Kolombangara Straits on the night of August 1, 1943. Their mission was to observe and intercept Japanese troopships nicknamed "the Tokyo Express." There were thirteen aboard the *109*. In addition to Kennedy and his executive officer, Ensign Leonard Thom, Lieutenant (j.g.) Barney Ross went along to observe.

Each boat was equipped with a VHF radio. But only the lead boat in each division had radar. The boats became separated in the moonless, foggy darkness.

*PT 109* and *PT 162*, both without radar, continued patrolling, while the other boats returned to the base. It was after two in the morning, and still there was no sign of the Tokyo Express, which was expected to be returning from its earlier troop run with destroyer escorts.

In a sudden flash, a Japanese destroyer, the *Amagiri*, heading at approximately thirty knots, appeared out of the night fog, bearing down on the *109*. It rammed into the boat on the starboard bow and ripped it lengthwise. Kennedy, who was knocked to the side in the cockpit, ordered everyone into the water. The *Amagiri* continued on course.

Two crewmen, Marney and Kirksey, were immediately lost, never to be found. That left eleven in the water. The bow hulk was still afloat, so Kennedy ordered everyone back aboard.

At dawn they found themselves on the bow, a fifteen-foot section of the eighty-foot boat still above water. Another crewman, "Pop" McMahon, was badly burned. The far side of the strait—Kolombangara Island—was occupied with approximately 10,000 Japanese troops.

They waited all morning, hoping to be sighted by an American patrol plane. By noon, it was apparent that no such patrol plane would be coming. Compounding the situation, it was also apparent that the hulk was not going to stay afloat much longer. They headed for a small island nearby.

Kennedy led the way, towing McMahon, holding the straps of the burned crewman's life jacket in his teeth. Thom was behind him, alternately pushing and pulling a wooden log with four crewmen clinging to it.

They had no food, only several pistols, including a flare gun, and a battle lantern from the boat. Landing on the island they discovered that there were no Japanese troops.

In addition to McMahon being badly burned, a second crewman, Bucky Harris, had a badly injured leg. A third, Johnston, was also in bad shape, coughing and retching.

Kennedy then took the battle lantern and went back out into the water, toward Ferguson Passage. If the remaining PTs were still patrolling, he could signal one of them. He stayed out all night until realizing that the PT boats had left the area.

From another island, Australian coastwatcher Reg Evans radioed to his supervisor that he had earlier sighted an "object" drifting in the strait.

Back at Kennedy's squadron headquarters, it was determined by his CO (commanding officer) Lieutenant Commander Thomas Warfield that the boat, with all hands, was lost. No search parties would be ordered. This became a bone of contention among many of the officers who felt that a search party should have been ordered.

The next night, Barney Ross went out into the water. Again, no patrol boats were sighted. Worse than that, Ross lost the lantern.

The next day, Kennedy then had the crew back in the water to a nearby island named Olasana, which had coconut trees in abundance. Kennedy and Ross then went on a forage mission, swimming to nearby Naru Island.

Here they were spotted by two natives who immediately took flight in a canoe. Kennedy and Ross then returned to the crew. That night Kennedy went out into Ferguson Passage again. It was another futile attempt.

Back on the island, Kennedy found his crew mingling with the two natives he and Ross saw earlier. From this meeting Kennedy dispatched the two natives with a coconut. Carved on the coconut was Kennedy's message that stated, "Naru Island Native knows posit He can pilot 11 Alive Need small boat Kennedy."

On the night of August 6, Kennedy and Ross made another vain attempt to flag down a PT in Ferguson Passage. However, the water was too rough.

The next morning a large canoe with natives appeared. One of them had a message from Evans, the coastwatcher. Kennedy then left with the natives, hiding under several palm fronds to avoid detection by Japanese planes.

The next day, a rescue PT picked up the crew. In quick time they were treated at a hospital on Tulagi.

Kennedy's next command was the *PT 59*, refitted to be a gunboat. In November, he rescued a unit of marines at Choiseul Island, commanded by Lieutenant Colonel Victor Krulak.

In December 1943, Kennedy was ordered back to Melville, Rhode Island, the PT training base. A personal decoration recommendation had already gone into the chain. It was felt that Kennedy would probably be awarded a Silver Star, the nation's third-highest combat medal.

After taking one month's leave, Kennedy reported to Melville but was subsequently transferred to Miami, Florida. During this time, he met author John Hersey (*A Bell for Adano*), who indicated interest in the *PT 109* story. Hersey began work on a piece intended for *Life* magazine. He got Kennedy's account of the incident, then began contacting other crew members who were now stateside. The *PT 109* piece was rejected by *Life*. After some thought, the article was then submitted to *The New Yorker*, which surprisingly agreed to publish it. Ambassador Joseph Kennedy then came up with the idea of approaching the *Reader's Digest* to publish a condensation.

Before Kennedy entered a hospital for surgery on an aggravated back injury, in June 1944, he was awarded the Navy-Marine Corps Medal for heroism in the Solomon Islands. The award recommendation had been "knocked down" from the Silver Star. Still, he was being decorated for heroism in a combat zone.

The publicity surrounding Kennedy's PT boat found its way to England where JFK's older brother, Joseph Kennedy Jr., a naval aviator, was patrolling the English Channel as the pilot of a B-24 Liberator. The intense brotherly rivalry dated back to grammar school days and thrived at Harvard, through athletic teams and debutantes. Now, Joe Kennedy Jr. had to face the fact that he might have to stand in his younger brother's shadow in terms of an enviable war record.

After flying the required thirty patrol missions, Lieutenant Joe Kennedy Jr. was eligible to rotate stateside. Instead, he not only volunteered to fly ten more but persuaded his crew to follow him. The additional ten missions proved uneventful.

It was during this period when Kennedy volunteered to be considered for Operation Anvil. This was a special classified operation that required a TNT-laden bomber to fly over the Channel to a target near Calais. At a prescribed point, over the Channel, the pilot and copilot were to bail out. The Liberator would then be controlled as a drone by a trace aircraft, through Nazi flak, to its target.

Kennedy was selected as the pilot. Undoubtedly, his motivation for volunteering stemmed from the assumption that anyone who undertook this mission would be recommended for either a Silver Star or a Navy Cross (second to the Congressional Medal of Honor).

At 6 P.M., August 12, 1944, the Liberator took off. Following it was a photo-reconnaissance Mosquito plane. In the Mosquito was President Roosevelt's son Elliott, who was assigned to photograph the Liberator.

Twenty minutes after takeoff, Kennedy's Liberator disintegrated in two horrific explosions. Neither Kennedy's body nor that of his copilot was ever recovered.

The TNT package was reconstructed, with better wiring, and another Liberator was fitted for the special mission. This time, the mission came off as planned. But, in the end, it proved all for naught. The target was a bunker that housed a Nazi secret weapon, the V-3 "London Gun." The bunker hadn't even been completed, and the gun was never installed because it tested defectively.

However, Lieutenant Joseph Kennedy Jr., in death, achieved part of his plan. He was posthumously awarded the Navy Cross, a combat decoration ranked higher than the Navy-Marine Corps Medal.

In 1977, Peter Strauss portrayed Joe Kennedy Jr. in a television Movie of the Week entitled *The Lost Prince: Young Joe, the Forgotten Kennedy*, based on Hank Searls's 1969 book of the same title.

By 1964, the country was still getting used to the Lyndon Johnson administration. As the summer unfolded, it proved to be pivotal, both for American history and for American war films.

## MORE PT BOATS

In July, Arizona senator Barry Goldwater won the Republican nomination for president at the San Francisco convention. Congressman William Miller (New York) was named as his running mate. Less than three weeks later, two U.S. destroyers, the *Maddox* and the *Turner Joy*, patrolling in the Gulf of Tonkin off the North Vietnamese coast, were allegedly attacked by PT boats. Two of the PT boats were sunk. The United States responded further with planes from the attack carrier *Ticonderoga*, on August 5, bombing the nearby bases. Two days later, Congress passed the Gulf of Tonkin Resolution, giving President Johnson the power "to take all necessary measures to repel any armed attack against the forces of the United States and to prevent further aggresion." In an interview after he retired, Johnson admitted to Walter Cronkite that he had been given a "blank check" to do exactly what he wanted as far as troop commitment went in Vietnam.[9]

On August 26, President Johnson was nominated at Atlantic City, New Jersey, with Minnesota senator Hubert Humphrey as the vice presidential candidate.

## A NEW LOOK TOWARD WAR

Carl Foreman adapted *The Human Kind*, a novel by Alexander Baron, into the screenplay *The Victors* (1963). Foreman, who also directed the film, admitted in a later interview that he got a little heavy-handed to tell this war story.

Filmed in Europe under the Columbia Pictures banner, the story follows an infantry squad through the European campaign to the end of the war.

Eli Wallach was cast as the squad leader. Backing him up were George Peppard, George Hamilton, Albert Finney, Vince Edwards, James Mitchum, Peter Fonda, and Michael Callan. The women who come in and out of the soldiers' lives were played by Jeanne Moreau, Rosanna Schiaffino, Elke Sommer, and Senta Berger.

Foreman wanted to take on the issue of the brutality of war—that nobody really wins. Even in victory, innocence is lost. In a June 1979 interview at Universal Studios, he reflected, "I probably used a sledgehammer approach at the time. But I felt it needed to be done. I'm proud of what that film said."

In a painfully realistic scene, Wallach's squad sits by a roadside, watching a French infantry unit attack a Nazi bunker. After shots are fired, a white flag is waved by the Nazis. But the Frenchmen refuse to accept it and fire back, forcing the Nazis back into the bunker. The bunker is then circled with plastic explosive and blown up with the Nazis inside. The Americans are shocked at what they think is a war crime since the Nazis attempted to surrender. Their protests are met with sardonic looks.

One of the Frenchmen looks over at the Americans and warns, "If you have to report this, pray that your country is never occupied."

The Eddie Slovik execution is also portrayed here. In January 1945, Slovik, a soldier in the 29th Infantry Division, was executed for desertion. Foreman initially intended to have the scene filmed, without dialogue, as Slovik is led out in the snow to the execution pillar, while Bing Crosby is heard singing "White Christmas." Negotiations with Crosby, over the song rights, broke down. That forced Foreman to approach Frank Sinatra, who agreed to let Foreman use "Have Yourselves a Merry Little Christmas."

In the final scene, George Hamilton confronts a young, drunk Russian soldier. A mild exchange turns into a blind argument as neither can speak the other's language. A shoving match then forces Hamilton to pull out a switchblade knife. He's surprised when the Russian brandishes his own knife. Hamilton then calls an end to it. But the Russian doesn't understand and lunges forward. The two grapple, roll over, and fatally stab each other.

As Baron wrote in the novel, "The two young victors, who had come so far to meet each other, lay dead among the ruins."[10]

The Slovik execution, based on a story by William Bradford Huie, was made into the 1974 TV movie *The Execution of Private Slovik*, with Martin Sheen playing Eddie Slovik and Ned Beatty portraying Father Stafford, an army chaplain. The army never intended to carry out the execution. The original purpose was to make an example of Private Slovik. However, through a series of military and bureaucratic foul-ups, the 29th Infantry Division found that it had to carry out the sentence. Slovik was the first American soldier to be executed for desertion since the Civil War.

*The Thin Red Line*, James Jones's sequel to *From Here to Eternity*, was produced as a realistic black-and-white 1964 release. Jones followed the 27th Infantry Regiment through the Pearl Harbor attack at Schofield Barracks to the brutal Guadalcanal campaign, in which Jones actually participated, for which he garnered a Purple Heart. He also described his feelings about killing a Japanese soldier.

The novel was adapted by Bernard Gordon for Andrew Marton's direction. In the cast were Keir Dullea, Jack Warden, James Philbrook, and Kieron Moore.

Amid mixed reviews, the film was often compared to its classic predecessor, but it didn't stand a chance, despite its realism.

It was remade in 1998 under the same title with Terrence Malick directing. This cast included Nick Nolte, John Travolta, and Sean Penn. Despite competing with *Saving Private Ryan* (1998) the film was well received, with Malick receiving an Academy Award nomination.

Service rivalry and the insanity of war set against the Normandy invasion is what Paddy Chayefsky brought out in *The Americanization of Emily* (1964), from the William Bradford Huie novel. The love story subplot between James Garner, a navy staff officer, and Julie Andrews (as Emily Barham), a British Wren officer, gets complicated when it is decided, for public relations purposes, that the first American to land on Omaha Beach should be a sailor and not a soldier.

Garner, as Charlie Madison, proclaims himself to be a practicing coward and proud of it. Chayefsky, a wounded World War II veteran, risks getting too preachy in driving home his points about war in his screenplay drafts.

In a scene with Andrews and the British character actress Joyce Grenfell, Garner observes that it's not necessarily war that's insane. It's what happens to ordinary people when they are placed into it by fumbling politicians and warmongering generals. "It's always the generals with the bloodiest records to shout what a hell war is. It's always the widows who lead the Memorial Day parades . . . we wear our widows weeds like nuns . . . and perpetuate war by exhalting its sacrifice." Garner goes to the invasion as a "handcuff volunteer" and emerges as a true hero in spite of himself.

Directed by Arthur Hiller, the supporting cast included Melvyn Douglas, James Coburn, Liz Fraser, Edward Binns, Keenan Wynn, and William Windom.

Garner always held a singular affection for *The Americanization of Emily*, calling it his favorite film. Many writers felt, through the years, that it was the first antiwar film of the Vietnam era.

Just as America was increasing its military adviser strength in Vietnam, Columbia Pictures released the godfather of all black comedies: *Dr. Strangelove, Or: How I Learned to Stop Worrying and Love the Bomb* (1964).

Working from his time-honored formula of taking a book and making it cinematic, director Stanley Kubrick went from the corruption and hypocrisy of *Paths of Glory* to the contradiction and insanity of a nuclear holocaust.

The film was based on the novel *Red Alert* by Peter George. It begins with a psychotic American Air Force general, played by Sterling Hayden, dispatching a squadron of B-52 bombers to various Russian targets because he feels that the Soviets are plotting to take away his precious bodily fluids. He suddenly became aware of this "plot" during the physical act of love. Naturally, in Hayden's twisted mind, this coincides with the international Communist conspiracy to dominate the world.

The script, adapted by Kubrick and Terry Southern, also did an unusual turn with the characters' names. Hayden's character was Jack D. Ripper; George C. Scott played Air Force General "Buck" Turgidson; Slim Pickens was Major "King Kong," the country-western airplane commander whose bomber gets through the fail-safe net. The Soviet premier's name is Kissoff.

The only female in the cast is Tracy Reed, who plays General Turgidson's bikini-clad "personal secretary."

As different options are explored in regards to recalling the squadron, General Turgidson urges that the attack press forward, now that it has been set in motion. "Mister President, I don't say we wouldn't get our hair mussed, but I do say that no more than ten to twenty million people killed—tops!"

The best character statement in the film comes from Peter Sellers doing a triple turn as the demented Nazi-trained, wheelchair-bound Dr. Strangelove himself, who is given to forgetting that he is now developing weapons for America. Dr. Strangelove cannot help himself from raising his right arm in an instinctive Nazi salute. Sellers is also British Group Captain Lionel Mandrake who recognizes General Ripper's madness and placates him. His third character is the ineffective U.S. President Merkin Muffley. (A merkin is a pubic wig.) Army officer Keenan Wynn is the right-wing army Colonel Bat Guano.

The installation from which the squadron is launched is Burpleson Air Force Base where "Peace Is Our Profession." Except that, in the film, there is anything but peace. The film begins with the standard Cold War precautions and ends with nuclear devastation where everyone is rendered useless.

As Pickens's rogue bomber continues to its target, negotiations between the president and Premier Kissoff begin and predictably break down, signaling total miscommunication with the superpowers. General Turgidson then attacks the Soviet ambassador, who attempts to photograph the war room's "big board."

President Muffley quickly admonishes the general for the assault. "You can't fight in here, this is the war room!"

The bomber arrives on target, but Pickens has trouble with the wiring in the bomb bay. After jury-rigging the wiring, Pickens then rides the bomb down, bronco style, waving his cowboy hat, signaling nuclear victory over the godless commies.

The resolution is that the United States is forced to hibernate in middle earth for the next generation. The only person cured is Dr. Strangelove, who stands to announce the film's last line, "Mein führer, I can walk!" The madman is the only one cured.

The final sequence is the nuclear holocaust with British singer Vera Lynn crowing "We'll Meet Again."

*Dr. Strangelove* won Academy nominations for Best Picture, Best Director, and Best Actor (Peter Sellers).

Like other sections of the country, Hollywood followed the buildup in Vietnam. And subsequent American war films would make contemporary statements using the background of previous wars.

# Vietnam:
# The Emerging Counterculture

You may kill ten of my men for every one I kill of yours,
but even at those odds, you will lose and I will win.
                                                —Ho Chi Minh, 1948

It is ironic that America's longest and most divisive war had to wait until after its bitter end for any major films to be produced, with one exception: *The Green Berets* (1968). It is not surprising that these films were, in tone, angry and disturbing, reflecting the haunting Vietnam experience.

Frank Wetta and Stephen Curley, in their book *Celluloid Wars*: *A Guide to Film and the American Experience of War*, observed: "The Duke of Wellington is reported to have said that the Battle of Waterloo was won on the playing fields of Eton; it has also been suggested that the Vietnam War was lost in the Hollywood jingoism of World War II films."[1]

The true guilt from Vietnam did not manifest itself until long after the war. Political apologies didn't emerge from the leaders until years later. The effects of World War II predisposed its military and political leaders who formed a doomed, anachronistic, mind-set on the Vietnam generation.

There was guilt across the board with the first American generation burdened to lose a war. Many of the vets came home with guilt, whereas many of those who stayed home were riddled with guilt for not going.

When Americans refer to World War II, it is often called "The War" with a sense of pride. Conversely, when the word *war* is mentioned, preceded by the condemning qualification "Vietnam," scarring images come to mind.

The Vietnam War seared the nation's conscience and psyche so much that it caused one president to decline to run again and began a chain of events that led to his successor's resignation. No other war in America can make that claim.

Because of the deep-rooted foundation in the World War II mentality, Vietnam was initially looked upon as yet another chapter in the twentieth-century wartime chronicles.

## IN WARTIME ORDER

This film era began with the identifiably safe ground of World War II: clean-cut good guys against the bad. In 1965, Paramount released *In Harm's Way*, directed by Otto Preminger, adapted by Wendell Mayes from a novel by James Bassett. The title came from the noted Revolutionary War John Paul Jones quote, about taking a ship and going "In Harm's Way." The film was a black-and-white epic, fitting for World War II, but out of place in the Vietnam Era. In the lead was John Wayne as Admiral "Rock" Torrey. Supporting Wayne were Kirk Douglas, Burgess Meredith, Dana Andrews, Brandon de Wilde, and Patricia Neal as Maggie Haynes, Wayne's love interest. Wayne and Neal had similar roles in the 1951 release of *Operation Pacific*.

The main story line dealt with the sudden confusion following the attack on Pearl Harbor. Wayne is relegated to a minor desk job, while Andrews, an ineffective admiral, is in command of a misdirected fleet. Subplots include Wayne's estranged father–son relationship with de Wilde, who is the product of a privileged Ivy League upbringing. Wayne's off-screen ex-wife is replaced by navy nurse Neal. Henry Fonda, as a task force commander, eventually sees that Andrews's lack of leadership has to be replaced by Wayne's. The enemy is defeated, at a cost, and peace is preserved for the next generation. An interesting comparison to *PT-109* is that de Wilde's torpedo boat is slashed by a Japanese destroyer. The major difference is that de Wilde, as the skipper in this film, is killed. Franchot Tone portrayed a fictionalized Admiral Husband Kimmel, blamed for the navy's lack of preparation.

While the Vietnam War escalated, it was ignored in favor of epics from "The War." These included *Is Paris Burning?* (1966) This was Hitler's question to his staff after realizing that the Allies were soon to retake the city in the late summer of 1944. If the Third Reich could not occupy the city, it was to be set afire, at the führer's command. Francis Ford Coppola and Gore Vidal wrote a script from the book by Larry Collins and Dominique Lapierre. Again, an international cast had to prop up a ponderous conglomeration of subplots and anecdotes.

The cast included Leslie Caron, Gert Fröbe, Charles Boyer, Yves Montand, Orson Welles, Alain Delon, Jean-Pierre Cassel, Jean-Paul Belmondo, Kirk Douglas, Glenn Ford, Anthony Perkins, and Robert Stack. Marcel Grignon received an Academy Award nomination for his cinematography.

Twentieth Century Fox decided to adapt Richard McKenna's acclaimed novel of the 1926 Yangtze river wars, *The Sand Pebbles* (1966). The script was written by Robert Anderson, directed by Robert Wise.

It was a troubled production from the start, and the film almost didn't get made. Part of the production problems stemmed from gunboats of the era, which were nonexistent. And then there was the lead, Steve McQueen, who had a reputation for being difficult.

McQueen portrayed Jake Holman, a career navy machinist's mate who becomes the victim of changing times in "gunboat diplomacy" in Southeast Asia. In the end, McQueen is confronted and outflanked in a special guerrilla operation. As escape is within easy reach, McQueen is shot by a sniper. Before he dies, McQueen asks a rhetorical question: "What happened? What the hell happened?" The question and the implied American interference in Asian troubles, leading to tragedy, had direct parallels to Vietnam in 1966.

Supporting McQueen were Richard Attenborough (an alum from *The Great Escape*), Candace Bergen, and Richard Crenna as the skipper of the USS *San Pablo*. The film was nominated for Best Picture.

Mako, the Asian actor, won an Academy nomination for Best Supporting Actor. McQueen lost in the Best Actor category to Paul Scofield in *A Man for All Seasons*.

"War films had been utterly unfashionable through the 1970's, a sufficient distance from Vietnam made them the rage again for several years. . . . Just the same, *The Magnificent Seven* in 1960 may have partly been about imperial America's ideas about policing the Third World, and Westerns like *The Wild Bunch* and *Little Big Man* were about Vietnam," wrote Todd McCarthy, commenting in his column "The Back Lot" in *Daily Variety* on June 18, 1993.

In a conversation in 1959, novelist E.M. "Mick" Nathanson spoke with independent filmmaker Russ Meyer, who had been a combat cameraman in World War II. Meyer told Nathanson a tale of convicted army felons who were recruited for a special mission before the Normandy invasion. Most of the men were awaiting execution for either rape, murder, or both. According to Stephen E. Ambrose, in his 1998 book *The Victors: Eisenhower and His Boys*, the Allies placed the maximum sentence for these crimes in the European Theater of Operations. The total number of executions for rape and murder in that theater in World War II was forty-nine.

Meyer was assigned to film the group at the felons' training base in the south of England and was told that the men had taken an oath not to bathe or shave until the classified mission was completed. The guards had thus given them the moniker "The Dirty Dozen." Meyer told Nathanson that he later heard all the men had perished in the mission.

The mystery was that nobody really knew what their mission was.

Nathanson was haunted by the story. "The hackles on the back of my neck went up. I was excited by the dramatic possibilities of *those* men in *that* situation," he said in a later interview.[2]

One year later, Nathanson submitted an eight-page outline to the West Coast editor of Random House and Dell Publishing. Nathanson then discovered documentation showing that high-ranking Nazi officers were ordered to a Kriegsspiel, German war game exercises, on the eve of the invasion, at an R&R (rest and relaxation) château in Rennes, France.

"At that time I didn't know what the hell the mission was. But I continued doing the research, playing it out as if I were allied intelligence," explained Nathanson. "I had to play Eisenhower. What would he have done had he known of this?"

Nathanson then made up an OSS operation, where the mission would be to kill as many high-ranking officers as possible. The unit would jump in and raid the officers' R&R château.

Nathanson had access to the Pentagon's law library, researching court-martial convictions in England during World War II. He never came across an actual "Dirty Dozen"–type mission.

A partial manuscript was submitted, separately, to Frank Sinatra and Tony Curtis. In 1963, with the manuscript two thirds completed, MGM took an option. There was no ending at this point. In Nathanson's original book outline, Captain John Reisman, the OSS unit commander, is flying over the area observing the fires down below. He never finds out what happened to the men he trained. Nathanson then changed that ending to where Reisman actually goes on the mission. After the final fight, Reisman is last seen going back in, disappearing into the night to look for any U.S. survivors. The novel ends with a staff officer reading the after-action report.

Before the novel was published, Nathanson was commissioned to write the second screenplay draft. The shooting script was written by Nunnally Johnson and Lukas Heller. Robert Aldrich got the director's assignment and a budget of $6.5 million.

Reisman's character was promoted to major in the screenplay and was cast with Lee Marvin after John Wayne passed on the role. Ernest Borgnine was General Worden, with Robert Ryan playing Colonel Everett Breed, who Reisman refers to as "a stuffy West Point bum!" Richard Jaeckel took the role of Reisman's training NCO (noncommissioned officer).

The main members of the unit were: Charles Bronson, John Cassavetes, Jim Brown, Donald Sutherland, Telly Savalas, Clint Walker, and Trini López. Supporting them in lesser roles were Ben Carruthers, Stuart Cooper, Tom Busby, Colin Maitland, and Al Mancini.

In the film, the OSS operation was changed to an army operation, thought to be suicidal. "I'm not really sure of the thinking that led to the change of the mission from OSS to the army," said Nathanson.

The script has Major John Reisman as a rogue officer who has an instinctive dislike for the army establishment and the West Point officer system. Reisman (Marvin) has a meeting with General Worden (Borgnine). Reisman accepts the mission, adding, "This plan must have been thought up by a stark raving lunatic."

John Cassavetes, portraying the social degenerate Victor Franko, received an Academy Award nomination.

As America began expanding into Vietnam, lunacy and mental instability reached new heights. Like Kubrick's *Paths of Glory*, a decade before, leadership on the American side was being questioned even more closely through film.

World War II was now being used to exploit not just the dark side of war but the Machiavellian thinking of a special operation where a group of felons—some awaiting execution—are recruited for a heroic mission to give them redemption.

Nathanson agreed that there was an antiestablishment feeling in the novel. "Some of the criminal activity was morally justified. And that the staff officers came off as political opportunists." Also in the novel Reisman couldn't say positively if the surviving Dirty Dozen would be pardoned. The film implied that the capital sentences would be commuted if the soldiers made it back.[3]

The film had an added sequence where the high-ranking Nazi officers and their women are ushered into the R&R cellar. Gasoline is then poured through ventilation shafts, each topped off with several hand grenades to ensure a mass execution. The grisly sequence gave audiences a graphic contrast to the Third Reich gas chambers.

The same year MGM released *The Dirty Dozen*, Columbia came out with *The Night of the Generals*, (1967) produced by Sam Spiegel. Peter O'Toole portrayed General Tanz, a Nazi panzer commander who is a favorite of the führer. General Tanz is also a psychotic serial killer who preys on prostitutes.

The screenplay, by Joseph Kessel and Paul Dehn, was adapted from a novel by Hans Helmut Kirst. Anatole Litvak directed.

Omar Sharif played Lieutenant Colonel Grau, the Nazi investigator who rightly concludes that O'Toole is solely responsible for the deaths of the victims. It comes down to a detective thriller set against Nazi atrocities where fascism intersects with homicidal mania. General Tanz becomes even more aware of his descent into madness with prolonged looks into Vincent van Gogh paintings in Paris art galleries.

Bits of Nazi history are brought out, such as Lieutenant Colonel Klaus von Stauffenberg and the July 1944 "Generals' Plot" on Hitler at Rastenberg. Tom Courtenay and Joanna Pettet have a love story subplot. One interesting twist is that General Tanz doesn't get his due until long after the war at a panzer reunion.


## THE VIBRATION

The only major Vietnam War film released while the war was still being fought was the Batjac Production of the Robin Moore book *The Green Berets*, with John Wayne starring and directing with Ray Kellogg. *The Green Berets* (1968) was Wayne's second and final effort at directing.

Moore, Harvard educated and a friend of Robert Kennedy's, took the John

Horne Burns and James A. Michener example, writing a collection of short stories set against a war background. Initially, it was thought to be classic timing.

In the early days of his administration, John F. Kennedy wanted to make the Green Berets an elite unit. Founded by Colonel Aaron Bank, an OSS veteran of World War II, the unit originally had red berets. Because of his Irish roots, Kennedy had the color changed. By 1965, when *The Green Berets* was published, the intent in Vietnam had the majority approval of the American public. When Staff Sergeant Barry Sadler, a Vietnam veteran, went on the *Ed Sullivan Show* in 1966 singing "The Ballad of the Green Berets," it gave the film a title song. The song also produced a brief boost to enlistments.

The army was not totally pleased with the stories. Wayne, writing for Department of Defense approval, agreed to certain changes. After the army and the Department of Defense gave script approval, Fort Benning, Georgia, was selected for location shooting, during the summer of 1967.

But time, once an ally, was quickly becoming an enemy. On the other side of the country, the Vietnam generation was launching the "summer of love," centered in the Haight-Ashbury section of San Francisco.

As Scott McKenzie noted in the popular ballad "San Francisco," "If you're going to San Francisco, be sure to wear some flowers in your hair . . . all across the nation, there's a big vibration."

The World War II generation was oblivious to this "big vibration" until it was upon them. The World War II generation had been born in the sunrise of the twentieth century, tempered by a hard but justifiable war, and was proud of its global defeat of fascism.

But the times, they were a-changing, as Bob Dylan sang. The Vietnam generation agreed. The World War II generation did not, and they held on to their hard-earned, established beliefs—all the way to the White House.

By the time of the release of *The Green Berets*, the Tet Offensive had taken its toll, the country had been numbed by two more assassinations (Martin Luther King Jr. and Robert Kennedy), and the rioting at the Chicago convention left the Democratic Party in shreds.

At one army compound in Vietnam, where *The Green Berets* was being shown, troops threw beer cans at the screen as Barry Sadler's famed ballad swelled up at fade-out.

An ill-fated omen of the final scene in *The Green Berets* was not only noted but ridiculed. In the scene, Colonel Kirby (Wayne) is walking on a beach against a sunset with a Vietnamese orphan nicknamed "Hamchuck." Hamchuck asks Kirby what will happen now. Kirby reassures the boy that he will be taken care of. "You're what this is all about," says Kirby. What was wrong with the scene, technically, was that the sun was setting in the wrong place for that part of the world. The first Vietnam combat film ironically became a metaphor for the war, being in the wrong place.

Wayne's patriotic feelings about Vietnam had crystallized several years prior. No doubt this contributed to his motivation for making a film statement about the war. In August 1965, Wayne returned to the USC campus where he once was a student and a member of the varsity football team. He and his secretary, Mary St. John, were taking a stroll on Trousdale Parkway, near the Doheny Library. A student antiwar group had set up tables and posters. Wayne watched as a young marine, in uniform with combat ribbons on his chest, walked by and the students at the table began heckling him. The marine continued walking, not paying any attention to the jeering students.

Wayne became unnerved when he suddenly noticed that the right sleeve of the marine's shirt was neatly folded and pinned to keep it from flapping. The young veteran was on the campus to inquire about the GI Bill. Wayne followed the marine to the parking lot where he learned that the marine had lost his arm from a Viet Cong booby trap. The actor then gave the marine an autographed card and thanked him for serving.

Then the Duke turned and jogged back to the student table. Mary St. John followed him, knowing that all hell was about to be unleashed on the Trojan campus.

When Wayne got to the table, he slammed both fists on it, barely controlling his raging anger. He growled, "You stupid bastards! Blame Johnson if you must; blame that sonofabitch Kennedy; blame Eisenhower or Truman or goddamn-fucking Roosevelt, but don't blame that kid. Not any of those kids. They served! Jesus, the kid's arm is gone!"

Wayne walked away from the table, muttering to himself, "What the hell is happening to this country?"[4]

What had happened was that the vibration had taken hold. Vietnam was not just nudging into the World War II thinking; it was confronting and replacing it. This was exacerbated by the argument that the United States was intervening in a civil war whose orgins went back centuries.

## THE WATERSHED YEAR

Prior to 1968, many Americans believed that U.S. forces would eventually prevail in Vietnam and that the objective of a stable South Vietnamese government would eventually be in place, spelling defeat for the North and the Viet Cong (VC). However, stability was the only thing that did not unfold in 1968.

If any one year stands out as a major plot point in the Vietnam experience, it has to be 1968, from fade-in to fade-out. When it ended, the country would never be the same. Values, ethics, and morals from the previous era collided head-on with the rebellious and complicated present. The damage would still be unending as the twentieth century drew to a close. It was a year never to be forgotten, forever etched in the memory of everyone who participated in the events or even just read about them vicariously.

Three weeks into the year, the marine base at Khe Sanh, eleven kilometers from the Laotian border, southwest of the demilitarized zone, was reinforced and came under attack. Several days later the USS *Pueblo*, a navy intelligence ship with an eighty-three-man crew, was captured by North Koreans in the Sea of Japan.

Many observers initially felt that the siege of Khe Sanh was General Vo Nguyen Giap's reenactment of Dien Bien Phu. The French outpost fell to the Viet Minh in May 1954, ending the era of French colonization. President Johnson insisted that Khe Sanh be defended at all costs. General Westmoreland reinforced it with 6,000 soldiers and marines. Johnson, adamantly explaining how he felt, said, "I don't want any damn Dinn Binn Foos!"

The North Vietnamese bombardments intensified as the American press made more references to Dien Bien Phu. Like Dien Bien Phu, the base was ringed with a mountain range and completely encircled by enemy units. The only way in and out was by air. The heavier C-130 cargo planes were quickly scratched in favor of the lighter C-123's, which didn't demand as much runway space.

Marine Colonel David Lounds, the commander of the 26th Marine Regiment, carried out the order to defend the base at all costs. The artillery shelling became one of the worst nightmares in Marine Corps history. It turned young American boys into old men overnight, much like the trench warfare in World War I. On the worst days more than 1,000 enemy artillery rounds pounded the outpost.

In his noted book *Dispatches*, Michael Herr made a Civil War comparison in the eyes of the young marines at Khe Sanh. "If you take one of those platoon photographs from the Civil War and cover everything but the eyes, there is no difference between a man of fifty and a boy of thirteen."[5]

On the same day that Robert McNamara was replaced by Clark Clifford as Secretary of Defense, January 30, the North Vietnamese launched the offensive that not only would change the course of the war but would affect the United States into the end of the century.

The planning for the Tet Offensive began with a July 1967 conference in Hanoi. The objective was to carry new fighting into South Vietnamese urban areas. This coincided with a presidential election year in the United States. At the center of the offensive would be a coordinated strike on Saigon and the very heart of American diplomatic and military presence: the embassy.

Comparisons have been made to the 1944 Nazi winter offensive in the Ardennes that caught the Allies by surprise. The same stealth in movement and preparation took place in the days and weeks before Tet 1968. Men and weapons moved into urban areas, getting through checkpoints and security checks. The usual rumors swirled in these areas. Military intelligence did detect that an enemy buildup was coming. One telling action, in urban areas, was when the shop owners began replacing storefront windows with plywood.

South Vietnamese President Thieu issued a thirty-six-hour cease-fire for the Tet holiday. Many South Vietnamese soldiers were granted leaves to visit their families.

On January 30, General Westmoreland's headquarters (MACV) issued a warning order placing all troops on full alert. The previously scheduled cease-fire was canceled upon commencement of the holiday.

At 2:47 on the morning of January 31, a truck and taxicab unloaded a group of Viet Cong sappers (a suicide squad) in front of the American embassy. They were noticed by several Saigon police officers, who immediately fled the scene without giving any warning. A section of the front embassy wall was blown open.

Tet had begun.

The sappers gained entrance to the embassy lawn, firing in every direction. Rifle and rocket grenades exploded in the embassy lobby. Sporadic fighting continued on the lawn as Viet Cong soldiers took up positions behind oversized flower tubs.

American reinforcements began to arrive. But the fighting continued; it was a standoff until morning.

Attacks began throughout Saigon and the Delta region. Further north, Nha Trang, Qui Nhon, Pleiku, and Danang came under attack.

The largest Tet attack in the northern I Corps area was the ancient imperial city of Hue. The stone walls of Hue were built by the French in the nineteenth century, modeled after Peking's "Forbidden City." Towering over the citadel in Hue was the tallest flagpole in South Vietnam. It was an open psychological target. As soon as the North Vietnamese occupied the city, a Viet Cong flag was flapping over Hue.

The Viet Cong flag flew over the Citadel of Hue for twenty-five days. During that time, intense house-to-house fighting resulted in mounting casualties for the 1st Marine Division, battalions, and units of the army's 1st Cavalry Division. The Americans and the South Vietnamese marines quickly realized how entrenched their enemy was. As soon as the Americans advanced, the North Vietnamese Army (NVA) came back with counterattacks. The bloody fighting continued, street by street. American heroism was common in every unit. Countless wounded marines and soldiers opted to stay with their units, refusing to be evacuated.

On February 26, American troops came across freshly turned earth in the yard of Gia Hoi High School. What they uncovered was both disgusting and shocking: a mass grave of bound bodies, civilians, intellectuals, and students. The total number came to 2,810, with another 2,000 missing.

To this day, the Hue City Massacre remains one of the most unexplored controversies coming out of the Vietnam War. It was touched on by Stanley Kubrick in his adaptation of Gustav Hasford's novel *The Short Timers*, the basis for the film *Full Metal Jacket* (1987).

In a 1987 essay in *The Village Voice*, Leo Cawley, a former member of the "Vietnam Veterans against the War," wrote about a "proposed" network documentary contradicting the Marine Corps claim that the Hue dead were victims of VC/NVA executions. Cawley wrote of the counterallegations, that the massacre victims were actually killed by army and marine air strikes and artillery during the twenty-five-day siege. As the VC/NVA units continued to hold the

Citadel, the corpses became a health hazard and the dead were dumped into mass graves.

Cawley added that the network (CBS) had taken a great deal of heat over the My Lai cover-up and that it was impossible to go with a similar story of another alleged cover-up of an atrocity. Nothing further was done to correct the explanation, according to Cawley.[6]

On the other side of the controversy are the journalists. Richard Pyle, Associated Press correspondent, covered the excavation of the graves (at several sites, which took place over a three-day period) in 1969. Pyle recalled that there were as many as 3,000 bodies uncovered. "That artillery theory is a new one on me," said Pyle. "I certainly didn't hear it at the time, and to my recollection there was nothing about the bodies, massive damage, mutilations, etc., that would seem to support it. But for every mass atrocity committed by the communist side there seemed to be somebody in the American peace/anti-war movement ready to deny that and blame it on the GI's, ARVN [Army of the Republic of Vietnam] or natural calamity."

Pyle added, "I recall the bodies being reasonably intact for the conditions, many with bullet head-wounds, wires around the necks, hands tied behind backs, all giving rise to the accepted theory of executions."[7]

George Washington University historian Ronald Spector, a marine Vietnam veteran, former director of naval history for the U.S. Navy, and author of *After Tet: The Bloodiest Year in Vietnam* (1993), spoke at a symposium in April 2000 at the College of William & Mary, titled "Rendezvous with War: A Reflection on the Vietnam War Twenty-five Years After." Spector contended, "The real war was being run by committee, not [General] Giap or Ho Chi Minh. It was a gamble, with Tet, to inflict more casualties."

Peter Arnett, speaking at the same symposium, supported the Hue execution theory. Arnett, a Pulitzer Prize winner who covered the war for Associated Press from 1962 to 1975, always felt that the Hue victims were executed by the VC and NVA. "You have to remember, they came to Hue City with lists of people. They took them out and mass executed them."

Spector added, "The U.S. (MACV) employed a round of offensives from January to August '68 through January '69 [after Richard Nixon was inaugurated]. Nixon began withdrawing troops while these rounds of offensive continued. The Saigon government [at this time] was corrupt and ineffective."[8]

The 1st Cavalry units cut off the North Vietnamese supply lines, while the marines made a final push to retake the Citadel. A political decision was then made to allow the South Vietnamese Army's "Black Panther" company to make the final assault. This rankled many soldiers and marines who felt that they carried the workhorse part of the battle.

Militarily, the 1968 Tet Offensive was an Allied success. Nationwide, the North Vietnamese suffered approximately 40,000 to 50,000 battlefield deaths. In contrast, Americans killed and wounded came to 4,000. This does not include various Viet Cong hard-core cadres that ceased to exist as fighting units.

Politically, the Johnson administration and the country learned a sudden, painful lesson. The casualty figures seemed meaningless. Just when the American public began to feel that the war was turning, they saw the televised battles around the embassy in Saigon and the fierce street fighting in and around Hue City. Urban areas in South Vietnam were supposed to be safe. What had happened?

The graphic realism was in living rooms every evening. The reporting was downbeat and pessimistic. The images were devastating to Americans at home.

Associated Press's Eddie Adams's January 1968 photo of Saigon Police Chief General Nguyen Ngoc Loan executing a handcuffed Viet Cong prisoner shook America to its proverbial roots. General Loan, who harbored an obsessive hatred for the Viet Cong and North Vietnamese because of family members killed, reacted out of instinct and emotion. His execution of the Viet Cong prisoner recalled the sequence in the 1964 Carl Foreman film *The Victors*: "Pray that your country is never occupied." Adams's photo was awarded the 1969 Pulitzer Prize for spot news photography.

Despite the numbers, the 1968 Tet Offensive was not looked upon as an allied victory. It simply raised new questions. Why and how did this happen when we were supposed to be winning? Why did it take twenty-five days to retake the Citadel? When and where was all of this killing going to end?

While the country was still reeling from the effects of the Tet Offensive, another plot point occurred. On the night of February 27, 1968, CBS news anchor Walter Cronkite narrated a nationwide spot that touched the very heart of the fallout from the Tet Offensive.

Cronkite concluded by stating: "To say that we are closer to victory today is to believe, in the face of the evidence, the optimists who have been wrong in the past. . . . To say that we are mired in stalemate seems the only realistic yet unsatisfactory conclusion. . . . It is increasingly clear to this reporter that the only rational way out will be to negotiate, not as victors, but as an honorable people who lived up to their pledge to defend democracy, and did the best they could."[9]

Cronkite's speech and its effect went straight to President Johnson in the Oval Office. Johnson came to realize that the speech carried with it an end to his administration.

"If I've lost Walter Cronkite, I've lost Mr. Average Citizen," said Johnson.[10]

Changes came quickly. Another casualty was General William Westmoreland, destined to be replaced by General Creighton Abrams. The argument could be made that both Johnson and Westmoreland were unable to respond directly to a guerrilla enemy. Both were brought up on the conventional tactics of World War II. The leadership credibility, militarily and politically, had been severely damaged despite a victory in the field and the unquestioned heroism and bravery of American troops. Vietnam had turned into the proverbial double-edged sword with the point being held at the American psyche, firmly grounded in past wars.

After the assassinations, the debacle at the Chicago Democratic National Convention, and the narrow Richard Nixon victory, the war escalated. And so did the demonstrations. The World War II generation was losing its children. And many of the World War II generation failed to realize that the current Washington, D.C. rationale, and implied nobility, was exacting an ongoing terrible, tragic price.

## NO FRONT LINES

Hollywood added to the national confusion in delaying the recognition of the Vietnam War Film. As chronicled, every other war clearly defined, quickly produced, and released these films. The dramatic lines of conflict were clear in the Civil War and World Wars I and II. Korea was a harbinger of the approaching complexity that would meld into the vagueness of Vietnam. From the start, the Vietnam War film hit a wall before it even began. It was the classic finger in the air, to test the prevailing winds.

There were many people in America, conditioned by past war films, who blindly accepted Vietnam combat operations as business as usual. Despite the war being in everyone's living rooms on the six o'clock news, ignorance persisted in many quarters. After the 1968 Tet Offensive, however, Americans took a harder look at the war.

In the early 1970s, the furor over the release of the Pentagon Papers was marked by daily headlines. Los Angeles radio talk show host Michael Jackson was fielding questions about the issue when a caller came on the line and offered his opinion, explaining that he had completed a full combat tour in Vietnam. The talk show host then asked, "Were you in the front lines?"

The veteran responded with a chuckle. "That's a World War II question. Vietnam has no front lines."[11]

In 1986, advice columnist Abigail Van Buren was taken to task for making assumptions about Vietnam veterans. She recommended the *Vietnam Vet Survival Guide* to a reader. "Realizing that the average Vietnam veteran did not get past high school, the authors use plain language and short sentences," she added.[12]

Van Buren later apologized when corrected by another reader, obviously a Vietnam veteran. This reader noted statistics from the *National Vietnam Veterans Review* (November 1982), debunking the myth that high school dropouts formed the largest proportion of U.S. forces in Vietnam. Quite the contrary to this misperception, and quite unlike any war before it, figures showed that approximately 80 percent of those who served in Vietnam had a high school diploma, or better, when they entered military service. This figure was compared to Korean War veterans, 63 percent, and World War II veterans, 45 percent. Thus, Americans reporting for service were increasingly better educated.

There were other surprising veteran statistics that came out of the Vietnam War:

• There were more Medal of Honor winners in Vietnam than in World War I or the Korean War.

- There were more casualties in Vietnam than in Korea.
- Volunteers, not draftees, accounted for 77 percent of Vietnam combat deaths.
- Proportionately, three times as many college graduates served in Vietnam as in World War II.
- While 30 percent of Vietnam casualties came from the lowest third of the income range, 26 percent came from the highest third.[13]

Despite the above statistics, myths surrounding Vietnam veterans persisted. As late as the March 2000 California presidential primary, Republican candidate John McCain, a former naval aviator and Vietnam POW for five and a half years, was being portrayed as a freaked-out head-case, a coiled spring ready to snap.

Responding to this portrayal was Thomas Doherty, author of *Projections of War: Hollywood, American Culture and World War II*, writing in the *Los Angeles Times*. Doherty pointed out:

The casting of McCain as a head case draws upon two deep-seated fears Americans seem to harbor about the ex-warrior in their midst. The first finds expression in the stereotype of the Vietnam veteran as a wounded animal come back from the jungle to lash out at his countrymen. The second taps into an ancient prejudice toward the redeemed captive, an individual repatriated back into a community that now looks upon him as tainted by prolonged contact with the enemy. Both bespeak a kind of native xenophobia, a suspicion of one's own kind for having survived an experience that should have been lethal.[14]

## REFLECTING THE CULTURE

The year 1968 and the Tet Offensive seemed to launch Hollywood into re-inventing itself. Previous restrictive sexual mores and four-letter words were being tossed aside in favor of social and graphic realism. But these were cast-off social restraints. Outright political statements would remain in the proverbial closet until unlocked by a combination of time and events. At first the counterculture opted for subtlety.

The first group of counterculture films to have an impact on the Vietnam generation were *Easy Rider, Alice's Restaurant, They Shoot Horses, Don't They?*, and the Academy Award–winning *Midnight Cowboy*. It is no small coincidence to historians that all four were released in 1969.

Distributed by Columbia, *Easy Rider* was written by the two lead actors, Peter Fonda and Dennis Hopper, with a rewrite by Terry Southern. The main story line, about two alienated dropouts who ride across America on motorcycles, instantly connected with the Vietnam generation. In their travels, Fonda (wearing a Captain America helmet) and Hopper (shoulder-length hair, topped off with a cowboy hat) meet a disenfranchised attorney, played by Jack Nicholson, who comes forth with a new liberal philosophy on contemporary American politics. As a reward for making his counterculture views known, Nicholson is set upon by a group of local bigots and pummeled to death. In the end, Hopper flips off a southern redneck, who advises him to "get a haircut," and is likewise rewarded with a shotgun blast to the face. The message was clear, that if you didn't adhere to the establishment's rules, it had the right to kill you. The younger generation felt that nobody was listening to them.

Arthur Penn, fresh from directing the pop antihero opus *Bonnie and Clyde*, received an Academy Award nomination for *Alice's Restaurant*, a United Artists film that followed the adventures of musician Arlo Guthrie and his hippie band, who go to any lengths to avoid being drafted. The group hangs out at a local restaurant managed by the good-natured Alice. The draft board scene was designed to ridicule the establishment sending young men off to fight in an immoral war.

Gig Young's portrayal as the slimey master of ceremonies in a six-day depression-era marathon dance contest won him an Oscar for Best Supporting Actor in *They Shoot Horses, Don't They?* Based on Horace McCoy's novel, the theme of the film was that no matter how hard young people tried, their efforts would be futile in a corrupt world. Again, the establishment will win. As Young's character states, "There can only be one winner folks, but isn't that the American way?" Academy nominations were in store for Jane Fonda and Susannah York; James Poe and Robert E. Thompson for their screenplay adaptation; and Sydney Pollack as Best Director.

The Vietnam generation's frustration and alienation continued with *Midnight Cowboy*, adapted by Waldo Salt from James Leo Herlihy's novel about a naive Texan who comes to New York presumably to become a stud for wealthy Manhattan ladies. Instead, the Texan Joe Buck (Jon Voight) meets Enrico Salvatore "Ratso" Rizzo (Dustin Hoffman), an unkempt, gimpy, tubercular con man. Joe Buck then moves in with Ratso and lives a hard winter amid the Manhattan squalor of pathetic lowlifes in a condemned apartment. Even when they plan to relocate to Florida and a better life, it results in Rizzo's death.

Despite the "down theme" of the film, it illustrated the generational split. Like *Bonnie and Clyde*, the young audiences flocked to *Midnight Cowboy*, nominated for Best Picture. Also nominated were both lead actors, director John Schlesinger, screenwriter Waldo Salt, and supporting actress Sylvia Miles.

The film went up against *True Grit*, with John Wayne getting his only Oscar, a World War II screen hero meeting the antihero era, a conflict of distinct generations. Many felt that Voight and Hoffman, in the same film, canceled each other out. On the other side, *Midnight Cowboy* won for Best Picture, with Salt and Schlesinger also getting Oscars.

The 1969 Oscar contenders clearly showed that there was a serious generational gap caused by the Vietnam War.

In 1970 two more films made generational appeals: *The Strawberry Statement*, where college students take over a campus building, and *Getting Straight*, which showed idealistic political activism on a college campus with the older generation depicted as clowns, ruling the faculty long past their effectiveness. Clearly, the ways of the previous generation were not working.

*Johnny Got His Gun* (1971), originally written by Dalton Trumbo as a novel in the 1930s, was resurrected for a major release, written and directed by Trumbo. A World War I soldier, Timothy Bottoms, somehow stays alive after losing both arms, both legs, and his eyes. Bottoms eventually finds a way to communicate with his nurse, begging to die. The film's message, about the horrible price war takes, had been sitting on the shelf for years. And with the antiwar mode in Hollywood, the time was right for its production.

With trepidation, Hollywood began to make war film statements about Vietnam. Antiwar films about Vietnam emerged, with the main story line safely set in previous wars and centuries.

One of the first was *Little Big Man* (1970). Dustin Hoffman, in age makeup, played 121-year-old Jack Crabb who tells his story of being adopted by the Sioux Indians in the 1870s. Crabb's narrated tale, told in "bookend flashback," accounts alleged U.S. Cavalry atrocities culminating with Custer's Last Stand.

It is documented by several biographers that Civil War hero Lieutenant Colonel George Armstrong Custer (last in his class at West Point) was reckless, driven by vanity, ambition, and a thirst for glory. The film took these traits over the top to make a contemporary antiwar statement.

Richard Mulligan, as Custer, rendered Custer as a raving megalomaniac. Surrounded by Sioux warriors in his final stand, between the Little Big Horn River and the Rosebud Creek in southern Montana in June 1876, Mulligan descended into delusions of grandeur as he imagined himself giving a presidential address to Congress before going down.

According to several Sioux accounts brought out in Evan Connell's biographical book *Son of the Morning Star*, Custer took a mortal wound through his right side before going down that Sunday afternoon. He died in a cluster of other cavalrymen who were using their dead horses as a shield. Afterward, a group of Sioux warriors attempted to mutilate Custer's body. But they were put off by several squaws, one of whom was known as Kate Bighead. Two squaws then punctured Custer's eardrums with a sewing awl to improve his hearing, according to Bighead. Seven years before, at a treaty conference in Oklahoma, the squaws contended, he did not listen. Now he would listen.

Extreme violence came about the same year with *Soldier Blue* (1970), again set in the west of the 1800s with a U.S. Cavalry detachment being attacked by victimized Indians. The message that the victims in the villages were being plundered by a powerful military force from the outside world was obvious.

Joseph Heller's 1961 military satire novel *Catch-22* finally became a film in 1970, adapted by Buck Henry and directed by Mike Nichols. The novel was met with mixed reviews. It dealt with the themes of the insanity of war and the bizarre state of people who not only are caught up in the fighting but are managing it.

But now it was perfectly timed for the increasing alienation of the children of the World War II generation.

Like so many wartime authors before him (James Jones, Irwin Shaw, Leon Uris, James Michener, Harry Brown, Sy Bartlett, Beirne Lay Jr., Norman Mailer, Herman Wouk, and Kurt Vonnegut Jr.), Heller drew on his personal experiences as an Army Air Force bombardier in Italy where he flew sixty combat missions.

The protagonist, Captain John Yossarian, is a bombardier who can no longer take the insanity of war. Yossarian goes to the squadron surgeon, Doc Daneeka, to get himself declared unfit for combat because he's crazy. Doc Daneeka listens to Yossarian's plea and then cites regulations, specifically Catch-22. Daneeka explains that anyone who wants to get out of combat duty "isn't really crazy." It's a normal reaction. Yossarian is then pronounced sane and fit for duty. Despite the black humor, graphic realism was not spared. A mortally wounded crew member on a bombing run futilely attempts to pull in his exposed intestines. In another scene an airman is cut in half by a plane's prop.

According to Heller's obituary, the novel was set in World War II, but he "actually was anticipating a future war" when he first thought up the main story line.[15]

*Catch-22*'s supporting characters included Milo Minderbinder, who creates M&M Enterprises, manufacturing a chocolate-coated cotton ball that made enormous profits in the European Theater of Operations. Balancing Minderbinder was Major Major, a staff officer who allowed visitors into his office only when he wasn't there.

The group commander was General Dreedle, an overweight flag officer, sadly ineffective and out of his time but who had with him a shapely WAC, doubling as his mistress. The WAC mistress parallels Tracy Reed in *Dr. Strangelove* as General Buck Turgidson's "personal secretary."

The Catch-22 phrase later became a dictionary entry, "a paradox in law, regulation, or practice that makes one a victim of its provisions no matter what one does."[16]

The original title was *Catch-18*. The title was quickly changed when Leon Uris's novel *Mila-18* was published first.

Alan Arkin was Yossarian, with Jon Voight as Minderbinder. Jack Gilford was Doc Daneeka, with Orson Welles as Dreedle. In other supporting roles were Bob Newhart, Paula Prentiss, Richard Benjamin, and Martin Sheen.

Military incompetence and diplomatic bungling were brought out in 20th Century Fox's 1970 re-creation of the Pearl Harbor attack in *Tora! Tora! Tora!*, the codeword that Commander Mutsuo Fuchida, the Japanese flight commander, relayed to the carrier *Akagi* that total surprise had been achieved at Pearl Harbor.

Even though the script brought out how the debacle could have been avoided, that Sunday morning nonetheless brought the United States into World War II. As noted, the U.S. Navy had been given warnings of an impending attack, yet failed to fully heed them. The army, particularly the U.S. Army Air Force, inadvertently contributed to its own near-complete destruction in the islands by parking the fighter and bomber aircraft close together.

Martin Balsam portrayed Admiral Husband Kimmel, while Jason Robards performed as General Walter C. Short. (Ironically, Robards, a navy veteran, was at Pearl Harbor and served on several ships that were either damaged or sunk. He was awarded the Navy Cross.) Both flag officers were subsequently relieved by President Roosevelt and spent the rest of their lives defending themselves as scapegoats. It wouldn't be until the end of the century when the two commanders were finally exonerated by an act of Congress.[17]

The film was a combined effort between the studio and Japanese filmmakers, much as Darryl Zanuck had done with *The Longest Day* in the early 1960s. However, the Vietnam War protest was at its peak, and the film never did clear a profit. Four directors were utilized from both sides: Richard Fleischer and Ray Kellogg from the United States and Toshio Masuda and Kinji Fukasaku in Japan.

The combat photography and special effects won an Oscar for A.D. Flowers and L.B. Abbott.

The message at the film's end was clear: America was ill prepared despite warnings, and the military leadership at the time was suspect, something not lost on the younger generation who were faced with a new kind of war.

Ring Lardner Jr.'s adaptation of Richard Hooker's novel *M*A*S*H* won an Oscar in 1970 for the portrayal of an army Korean War Mobile Hospital, the 4077th. It was a biting, sarcastic, and irreverent look at the contradiction of repairing wounded men so that they could return to battle and either be wounded again or killed.

Hooker was the pseudonym for Dr. H. Richard Hornberger, who wrote the book as a memoir to his time with the 8055th Mobile Army Surgical Hospital in Korea.[18]

Again, a story set in a previous time was designed to make a contemporary statement. But in this outing, the story would advance to the outrageous, offending many in "the establishment." This made the college students and war protestors love it all the more.

Helicopter shots bring the audience into the compound, giving a prologue over the confusion, "And then there was Korea."

Army surgeons Hawkeye (Donald Sutherland) and Trapper John (Elliott Gould) arrive at the 4077 fresh out of medical school, where they were conscripted for Korean service. The pair then embark on a personal mission: to create a Far East fraternity party, complete with an intramural football game where the players sit on the bench and pass around joints of marijuana.

Traditional values take a generational drubbing as the higher military authorities come off as clowns. Robert Duvall's hypocritical character, Major Frank Burns, believes in traditional values, despite conducting an affair with a likewise believer, Sally Kellerman as Major Margaret "Hot Lips" Houlihan, the chief nurse. Burns and Houlihan get their justified lunacy awards. Duvall suffers a complete breakdown and is taken away by the military police in a straitjacket.

Kellerman is rendered completely nude in an exposed shower for the entire unit to watch. She then barges in on the commander, Lieutenant Colonel Henry Blake, who is in bed with another nurse. "This isn't a hospital," yells Kellerman, "it's an insane asylum!" She then threatens to resign her commission. Colonel Blake simply nods, implying that if she wants to resign, that's fine with him.

The M*A*S*H loudspeaker becomes the Greek Chorus, announcing World War II movies and playing traditional American songs sung in Japanese.

When the camp dentist decides he is gay and opts to commit suicide, the other doctors oblige by giving him a dinner that parodies "the Last Supper."

When the film was later developed into one of the most popular television series, it became a long-term antiwar voice about Vietnam and the politicians who continued to manage the war.

Twentieth Century Fox producer Frank McCarthy often told about his twenty-year struggle to get the biography of General George S. Patton Jr. on film. The screenplay for *Patton* (1970) was based on source material from Ladislas Farago's *Patton: Ordeal and Triumph* and *A Soldier's Story* by General of the Army Omar N. Bradley, who also served as senior military adviser on the production. This was more than just a World War II combat film. It was a penetrating character study of a man who loved the role of a warrior, a man who was complex, contradictory, and self-destructive. Many actors, including John Wayne, expressed interest in the role. At different times Spencer Tracy and Lee Marvin turned down the script.

That it was finally produced at this time may have been coincidental, a fact not overlooked when the film won Oscars for George C. Scott in the title role; Best Picture, McCarthy; Best Director, Franklin Schaffner; Best Art Direction, Editing, and Sound.

As the first screenwriter, Francis Ford Coppola had the opening scene, in England, with Patton in khaki uniform giving his address to the 6th Armored Division in May 1944. The auditorium was filled with the entire unit. Patton sat on a card table chair and gave his noted speech. Second screenwriter Edmund H. North then put the emphasis on the man alone. The audience heard the soldiers sit down but never saw them. Patton was taken out of his khaki uniform and resplendently dressed in a class A uniform, complete with medals, a monogrammed ivory handle revolver, riding boots, and crop. The chair was taken away. Patton then paced the stage in front of a painted oversized American flag, giving his philosophy on the army, life, and war.

From the speech, the audience hears how Americans love to fight, "that all real Americans love the sting of battle." Patton then states what was to become a contradiction, that because of the way Americans are raised, they will never lose a war. "The very thought of losing is hateful to Americans."

"The army is a team. . . . This individuality stuff is a bunch of crap!" What the man demands from others and what he demands from himself are mixed at best. Patton is wearing a rogue uniform with a nonregulation sidearm. Even though he demands conformity from his men, he emerges as a larger-than-life *individual*, what he intensely dislikes. Like many such men, with outsized egos, he has come to hate the media, referring to the staff of the *Saturday Evening Post* as "bilious bastards."

His vigorous bluntness comes out in telling these soldiers to wade into the Nazis and "spill their blood." It's a rousing pregame locker room speech that many sports coaches often emulated over the years. "We're going to kick the hell out of him [the Hun] all the time.... And we're going through him like crap through a goose!"

Patton's final observation could be termed a combat veteran's credo, as opposed to a garrison soldier's role. Patton explains that what they're about to embark on "You may one day thank God for it." He adds that in another generation when the soldiers' grandsons ask, "What did you do in the great World War II, you won't have to say 'I shoveled shit in Louisiana.' "

Two slapping incidents came close to ending Patton's career before it came to fruition. The first was on August 3, 1943, at the 15th Evacuation Hospital outside of Nicosia. When Private Charles Kuhl, of the 26th Infantry Regiment, explained that he couldn't take the stress of combat anymore, Patton swore at him and called him a coward. In front of witnesses, the general slapped Kuhl with a glove and pushed him out of the tent by kicking him in the rear.

The second incident, involving Private Paul Bennett, of the 17th Field Artillery Brigade, occurred one week later at the 93rd Evacuation Hospital. Bennett explained to Patton, who was touring the hospital, that his nerves were shot. "I can't stand the shelling anymore."

Patton began shaking with anger. "Your nerves, hell, you are just a Goddamned coward, you yellow son of a bitch.... I won't have these brave men here who have been shot seeing a yellow bastard sitting here crying.... You ought to be lined up against a wall and shot. In fact, I ought to shoot you myself right now, Goddamn you!"

Patton pulled a pistol and waved it in front of Bennett's face. Patton then knocked the soldier's helmet liner off with a glancing swing. A battle surgeon, Colonel Donald Currier, then intervened, preventing the situation from getting more out of hand.

But the damage was done. The two incidents quickly became common knowledge among the troops. In a short period, the press got hold of both stories and began investigating. One reporter, John Charles Daly, thought Patton had gone temporarily crazy, a general driven mad by war.

On August 22, the medical staff and enlisted men who witnessed both incidents at the hospitals were summoned to Palermo, Sicily, to hear the general verbalize an apology.[19]

In his autobiography, *War as I Knew It*, Patton described his feelings toward what was termed "battle fatigue" at the time: "The greatest weapon against the so-called 'battle fatigue' is ridicule.... If soldiers would make fun of those who begin to show battle fatigue, they would prevent its spread, and also save the

man who allows himself to malinger by this means from an afterlife of humiliation and regret."[20]

Only one slapping incident was needed to add to the character traits in the
film. At one point Patton asks General Omar Bradley why he's being singled
out as a rogue all the time. Bradley simply shakes his head and quietly says,
"Because, George, sometimes you're just a big pain in the ass."

Scott, to his credit as an accomplished actor, studied and came to a conclusion
as to how to play the man, so complex and contradictory, a mystic, driven to
love one of civilization's horrific experiences. Like Lincoln, he was there when
we needed him and then taken away. He did what was needed at the time: He
closed with and fought the enemy. Like T.E. Lawrence, Patton was killed in a
freak vehicle accident after the fighting ended.

The absence of a war killed him, one could say. "God forgive me, I love it
so," said Scott reflectively.

Today, General George S. Patton Jr. rests with his troops in a military cemetery in Hamm, Luxembourg.

The film, during its release, also qualified for controversy because of the
complexity of the man and war. The West Point glee club was invited to a
special screening on the USC campus. On the other side of the auditorium sat
a large group of Vietnam War protestors who likewise came to view the film.
Many felt that there was the possibility of an ugly confrontation. However, at
film's end, both groups filed out peacefully, admiring the film—from different
viewpoints. This incident was clearly a tribute to the screenplay, and the portrayals, about a driven, complex, larger-than-life character.

By 1973, it was the navy's time in the barrel as Columbia released Robert
Towne's adaptation (of the same title) of Darryl Ponicsan's novel *The Last
Detail*. Ponicsan, who served in the navy, once heard the account of two petty
officers who had to escort a naive sailor from Norfolk, Virginia, to the brig at
Portsmouth, New Hampshire. The young sailor's court-martial sentence was
eight years and a dishonorable discharge for stealing $40 from a favorite charity
of the base commander's wife. The two escorts then decide to show the kid a
good time before starting his brig time. The novel ends with both petty officers
going AWOL, in disgust, after delivering the young sailor to the marine guards
at Portsmouth.

Towne changed the novel's ending, allowing the petty officers to do their
jobs and return to duty. As quoted in Peter Biskind's *Easy Riders, Raging Bulls*,
Towne explained, "I wanted to imply that we're all lifers in the navy, and
everybody hides behind doing a job, whether it's massacring in My Lai or taking
a kid to jail."[21]

Director Hal Ashby cast Jack Nicholson and Otis Young as "Bad Ass" Bud-
dusky and "Mule" Mulhall, respectively, as the petty officers. Randy Quaid
played the naive sailor, Meadows.

The script was laced with foul language and an antimilitary attitude. Bud-
dusky and Mulhall are both Vietnam veterans. When a hippie-type asks Mulhall,

who is black, how he felt about going to Vietnam, he replies, "The man says go; got to do what the man says. We are livin' in the man's world, ain't we?"

Oscar nominations came in for Ashby, Nicholson, and Quaid. Young died an untimely death shortly after.

With the success of *Patton* at 20th Century Fox, Universal turned to another flamboyant, ego-driven general: Douglas MacArthur. And again, it was producer Frank McCarthy who stayed with the project for the better part of seven years. *MacArthur* was eventually produced in 1977.

In a bit of cross casting, Gregory Peck portrayed MacArthur. The script, written by Hal Barwood and Matthew Robbins, was directed by Joseph Sargent. Dan O'Herlihy was President Roosevelt, while Ed Flanders did a turn as Harry Truman. Like Patton, the film bypasses the subject's formative years (West Point, the early Philippine years, World War I, and the Washington Bonus March) and opens with the dark beginning of World War II, the fall of the Philippines, the Bataan Death March, and the island hopping campaign of the Western Pacific, culminating with the return to the Philippines and the surrender of Japan aboard the USS *Missouri*. MacArthur was then named Supreme Commander Allied Powers and began the reconstruction of Japan, perhaps his most notable achievement.

As historians have pointed out, MacArthur's downfall was twofold: his Korean War strategy, during the 1950 Winter Offensive, and bypassing the chain of command (the Joint Chiefs of Staff) in the Truman administration, which ultimately led to his dismissal. One of the final scenes was his return to West Point in 1962, giving the "duty, honor, country" speech to the graduating cadets, many of whom were among the first army officers to serve in Vietnam.

*MacArthur* lacked the scope and grandeur of *Patton*, mainly because the budget was slashed drastically. Actual foreign locations were replaced with stateside venues like the Long Beach, California, Naval Station; Camp Pendleton, California; the Bremerton, Washington, Naval Shipyard; and the Pasadena, California, Arboretum.

Peck noted in a 1998 interview that the budget cutback had something to do with Richard Zanuck and David Brown's deal at Universal. "When that happened, I felt that the picture was being compromised," said Peck. "It was the story of a man whose virtues were many but who also had hubris and pride."

He added that the time of the film's release was post-Vietnam, "a period of discontent and disillusionment."

Peck related an anecdote of becoming the man. During production, his wife Veronique was looking for a bigger house. After much searching, she came upon a sprawling estate just above Sunset Boulevard near the UCLA campus. On that day Peck was filming a scene with hundreds of extras. At the lunch period he broke away and drove to the prospective house, aware that he had to return immediately to the studio for the afternoon shoot. Arriving at the grounds, in costume, he searched for Veronique and the real estate agent. After finding them, they asked Peck what he thought. He cast a look around the grounds and over at the house.

"Buy it!" he commanded. Then he turned on his heel, wearing a general's uniform, and walked back to the car.

"I wasn't myself at all," Peck added with a smile. "I was MacArthur."[22]

# 8

# The Vietnam Era:
# A Campus in O-hio

It was a bad time for everyone.
                        —Colonel Sam Troutman, *First Blood*

In the fall of 1969, President Richard Nixon began his Vietnamization policy, calling for the withdrawal of 35,000 Americans from Vietnam. He also appealed to the not-so-silent "Silent Majority" to support the new administration's war efforts. Vice President Spiro Agnew went on the attack, going after war protestors and the "eastern liberal establishment," intellectuals, and journalists. This only widened the gulf between the two American sides. The man who promised to bring the country together with his administration was accomplishing the opposite.

While this was taking place, the army announced that Lieutenant William L. Calley was being charged with premeditated murder in the massacre of Vietnamese civilians in the hamlet of My Lai on March 16, 1968. At first, the incident was denied. As more revelations emerged, the army was forced to admit that such an atrocity had indeed occurred. The country was stunned. Only the bad guys committed atrocities, like the North Vietnamese at Hue City. The country was introduced to a complex enemy: itself. America was no longer undeniably looked upon as the good guy. When the photos of the My Lai incident were released, they played right into the protestors' argument of "village burners and baby killers."

As the war dragged on, the Silent Majority began to lose patience. Nixon's 1968 presidential campaign strategy to end the war included a secret plan, as he called it. During the campaign Nixon first referred to it as a "pledge." Nixon said, "I pledge to you that new leadership will end the war and win the peace in the Pacific." The country was listening.

David Halberstam of the *New York Times* observed that Nixon used the ploy repeatedly: "Touching his breast pocket as if the plan were right there in the jacket—implying that to say what was in it might jeopardize secrecy."

But behind the scenes, as later revealed by Anthony Summers with Robyn Swann in *The Arrogance of Power: The Secret World of Richard Nixon*, Nixon ultimately came to the conclusion that the war could not be won. "But we can't say that, of course. In fact, we have to seem to say the opposite, just to keep some degree of bargaining leverage." What the public heard and what was really going on were two different things. Nixon's razor-thin victory over Hubert Humphrey gave the Thieu administration new hope for victory, so it was thought.[2]

In the spring of 1970, Nixon okayed the invasion of Cambodia. But the administration held off from admitting it an outright invasion, instead referring to the offensive as an "incursion" (a sudden attack or a raid). To the administration, it was felt that the American withdrawal in Vietnam was contingent upon destroying the North Vietnamese supply sanctuaries.

Nixon's secret plan was never fully defined, causing many to speculate that the secret was kept even from him.

Both ends of the American political spectrum grew angrier and increasingly frustrated. The Right wanted to go all out to win the war, whereas the Left felt that the country was drifting aimlessly in the continuing immorality of the war, veering off course by false casualty reports and deceptions.

A casual remark by an army officer in the Delta Corps after the liberation of the village of Ben Tre was constantly mocked on campuses. "We had to destroy the village in order to save it," the officer was quoted.

"Consider the mentality of that remark," said Anthony Russo (involved in the Pentagon Papers controversy) to a protest crowd at California State University, Fullerton, in 1972.[3]

The campus antiwar protests continued to make their marks: Wisconsin, UC Berkeley, Columbia, Harvard, and UC Santa Barbara.

When the Nixon administration announced, on April 30, 1970, that it had widened the war beyond Vietnam into Cambodia, many college students were enraged at what they perceived as political deception. Many had believed Nixon's campaign promises, and his pledge, to end the war. They now saw the fighting not only continuing but intensifying. Pressure from both coasts converged in the Midwest. The protests were no longer coming from the elite schools; they had spread to the rock-ribbed heartland. And they collided violently on the Kent State campus in Ohio.

Student protests were not new to Kent State. In the prior year, rallies, marches, and demonstrations were held on a peaceful note. That weekend saw many boisterous gatherings at bars. Several local stores were damaged. Mayor Leroy M. Satrom saw fit to impose a curfew on the campus and the city.

Anger and hostility escalated over Saturday and Sunday. Saturday evening a mob marched on the ROTC building. As demonstrators attempted to start a fire with a flare, a photographer positioned his camera and was immediately beaten. The flare rolled harmlessly to the ground.

But a Molotov cocktail that was thrown inside the building did ignite a fire. A fireman then moved toward the flames. He was immediately attacked and beaten. Demonstrators cut the hose with machetes, knives, and icepicks. The building continued to burn.

On Sunday, Governor James Rhodes visited the campus and declared a state of emergency. Fliers were distributed calling for the restriction of all rallies and demonstrations.

That evening guardsmen broke up another rally. Tear gas was fired at demonstrators as guardsmen advanced on line with rifles and bayonets at the ready. Several demonstrators retrieved tear gas canisters and threw them back at the advancing soldiers.

Monday morning a noon rally was announced. This time the crowd numbered approximately 2,500.

At the rally the crowd was again ordered to disperse. And, as before, many demonstrators responded by throwing rocks. Tear gas was again the option. As the gas drifted across the lawn, the troops advanced on the crowd. This forced many protestors over a hill and back toward a parking lot. The guardsmen then headed back up the hill. Suddenly, several guardsmen turned around, lowered their rifles, and fired. The vibrations from those shots were felt around the world. The killing caused by the war had now invaded the halls of learning in America. It was 12:25 in the afternoon.

Within thirteen seconds, approximately sixty-five rounds were fired. A bullet hit student Sandra Scheuer, walking to class, almost 400 feet from the firing line. Scheuer died instantly. Allison Krause, who stuck a flower down a soldier's rifle barrel the day before, went down fatally wounded, near Scheuer. Jeffrey Miller, age nineteen and ninety yards from the firing line, took a fatal hit in the face and went down on his stomach. William Schroeder, age twenty, was hit fatally in the left lung. Nine other students were wounded; another student, Dean Kahler, was paralyzed.

Mary Vecchio, a fourteen-year-old runaway, knelt down over Miller's body, screaming. Her anguished face and outstretched arms were photographed by John P. Filo, a photography major standing nearby. The photo was sent worldwide, by Associated Press, destined to become an icon of American antiwar campus protests. Filo would later be awarded a Pulitzer Prize for spot news photography.

The reaction, nationwide, was intensely polarized. Many parents of the Vietnam generation, who supported the war, were outraged at the campus tragedy. In Laguna Beach, California, a motel manager told this writer, working as a local journalist at the time, that "those hippie bums deserved it." The manager was then informed that one of the dead students, Miller, was a cadet in the ROTC. The manager attempted to respond, shrugged, and then walked away in frustration. Black and white had mixed to a murky gray. The incident was too complex and contradictory for him to define.

Indeed, this was a different war.

The National Guard claimed that their soldiers had fired in reaction to a sniper. When it was proven that there was no sniper, officials quickly shifted their rationale, contending that the soldiers fired "in self-defense." Many Americans agreed with the self-defense position. However, the psychological damage was permanent and further split an already divided nation whose president had promised to bring the country together and end the war.

Soon thereafter, Neil Young's song "Four Dead in O-hio" was released. Bumper stickers, playing off the title of the Jane Fonda film, asked, "They Shoot Students, Don't They?"

Writing in the *Chronicle of Higher Education*, on the thirtieth anniversary of the tragedy, Philip Semas, who was on the campus that day, stated, "Months later, a presidential commission found that the shootings were unjustified. And then a local grand jury, incredibly, indicted twenty-five demonstrators and no guardsmen. The guardsmen were brought to court on federal civil rights charges, but the trial ended when the judge ordered their acquittal. The wounded students and the parents of the slain sued but lost."[4]

Ten days later, two young black people were shot and killed following a barrage of police gunfire at Jackson State University in Mississippi. The victims were Phillip L. Gibbs, a twenty-one-year-old student, and James E. Green, a seventeen-year-old bystander. The Jackson State tragedy dealt more with the simmering civil rights issues; however, it came on the heels of Kent State and added to student unrest nationwide.

In June 1972, a group of burglars entered the headquarters of the Democratic National Committee in the Watergate building that bordered the Potomac River. Their objective was to plant bugs in the telephones as a Republican intelligence conduit. The following day it was discovered that the bugs were defective. The burglars were then ordered back to replace them.

Early on the morning of June 17, the burglars were apprehended by the Washington, D.C. police. The White House quickly characterized the burglary attempt as "third rate" and disavowed any connection. It was the first in a long line of administration lies and mistakes that would lead to a constitutional crisis.

The Vietnam War protests and outrage escalated into the 1972 presidential campaign. George Stanley McGovern, a former high school teacher, B-24 bomber pilot in World War II, congressman, and senator from South Dakota, won the Democratic Party's nomination for president. Already established with the left wing of the party, he quickly reinforced himself with the intellectuals, college students, and the younger war protestors.

Within a short period, things began to unravel for the Democrats. Missouri senator Thomas Eagleton withdrew as McGovern's running mate, after unfavorable public reaction that he had undergone psychiatric therapy and electric shock. Eagleton was replaced by R. Sargent Shriver, Kennedy in-law and head of the U.S. Peace Corps.

In August, the last units of U.S. ground forces in Vietnam were withdrawn. Ten days later, Richard Nixon and Spiro Agnew were renominated on the Republican ticket, despite war protestors picketing outside the Miami convention hall.

On election night, Nixon sat in the Lincoln sitting room listening to the soundtrack tape of the Emmy Award–winning World War II television documentary *Victory at Sea*.

The next morning, the nation learned that Nixon won the election in a huge landslide, taking almost 61 percent of the popular vote. McGovern carried only one state, Massachusetts. Nixon immediately initiated major cabinet and White House staff changes.

On January 26, 1973, Henry Kissinger signed a four-party pact in Paris, ending the U.S. military involvement in Southeast Asia. Nixon's approval rating then spiked to 68 percent.

A breakthrough came in the Watergate investigation on March 23. James W. McCord, one of the convicted burglars, wrote a letter to Judge John Sirica. In the letter, McCord admitted that he and the other four defendants were under pressure to remain silent. Attorney General John Mitchell was then fingered as the cabinet officer who supervised the Watergate operation.

Nixon announced, on April 30, the resignations of Presidential Chief of Staff H.R. Haldeman and Domestic Affairs Aide John Erlichman, along with Presidential Counsel John Dean. Unrelated to Watergate, the resignation of the then–Attorney General Richard Kleindienst was also announced. Nixon denied any knowledge of the Watergate break-in or the subsequent cover-up. Kleindienst felt betrayed. He was not involved in the actual White House dealings, having replaced John Mitchell. He felt that the timing of Nixon's announcement, coming on the heels of those caught in the cover-up, made it appear that he was in a conspiracy with Haldeman and Erlichman. He never spoke to Nixon again.[5]

## A SUCKER'S TOUR

In 1977, United Artists felt that the timing was right to tell an epic war failure from a recognized author. The author was Cornelius Ryan of *The Longest Day* fame. This time the book was *A Bridge Too Far*, the story of Operation Market Garden, an attempt to slash across Holland and cross the Rhine into Germany, September 17–26, 1944. Next to the debacle at Dunkirk, it ranked as the worst-planned Allied move in the European Theater of Operations. Operation Market Garden was based on poor intelligence and resulted in grave errors on the Allied side.

The Americans, British, and Polish paratroopers, 35,000 in number, went in behind Nazi lines. They were to link up with a massive British armored convoy coming forward over a series of bridges and then wheel across the Rhine into

Germany. The only trouble was that the Allies couldn't take the last bridge. And the entire plan, the brainchild of British Field Marshal Bernard Montgomery, fell apart. It caused one of the most noted Allied defeats of the war.

Richard Attenborough directed *A Bridge Too Far* (1977) from an adaptation by William Goldman.

Working the epic war script, first established by *The Longest Day*, cameo performances came from Laurence Olivier, Liv Ullman, Maximilian Schell, and Anthony Hopkins. Ryan O'Neal portrayed a young General James Gavin. Also beefing up the cast were Dirk Bogarde, Michael Caine, Robert Redford, Gene Hackman, and James Caan.

Hollywood continued to tell troubling World War II stories but distanced itself from Vietnam combat films. Slowly, the first low-budget Vietnam combat films were put into production. Like films depicting previous wars, the first group of Vietnam combat films was produced by people who did not see the war; rather, these films were their "artistic" interpretation. The first of these were *The Boys in Company C* and *Go Tell the Spartans*, both in 1978.

*The Boys in Company C* came off as a quickly made, low-budget film that was spawned from the old World War II propaganda films. The difference came in the third act. The young marines finally see the corruption of the side that they are to assist.

Director Sidney Furie wrote the script with Rick Natkin. The story was simple, following five marines through boot camp to their company in Vietnam. It mirrors *Sands of Iwo Jima, Battle Cry*, and many World War II films, with a "Greek Chorus" narration from one of the survivors about the life-and-death experience that they went through. The technical difference was that during the Vietnam War marines did not remain in the same unit, from boot camp to combat.

The training sequence was routine, taking the young men from all backgrounds and making marines out of them. After arriving in Vietnam, they soon witness atrocities on both sides. They realize that the war isn't what they envisioned, echoing themes from *The Red Badge of Courage* and *All Quiet on the Western Front*. The cast included Stan Shaw, Andrew Stevens, James Canning, Craig Wasson, and James Whitmore Jr.

*Go Tell the Spartans* was adapted from the story *Incident at Muc Wa*. Wendell Mayes wrote the script for director Ted Post. Burt Lancaster played Major Asa Barker, a burned-out, passed-over field-grade officer from another era. Lancaster's character recalls his portrayal of First Sergeant Milt Warden in *From Here to Eternity*. But now the wars and politics have taken a new turn. It's as if the regular army had no need for combat-experienced men like Barker. The McNamara "whiz kids" have taken over, making computer war presentations with charts and graphs, techniques of systems analyses. Barker is saddened when he sees a bespectacled, callow staff officer making this type of presentation.

Barker has now realized that his time has expired. And he no longer qualifies for promotion because of a sexual misdeed with his commander's wife during a Washington party attended by the president. Marc Singer, playing Lancaster's executive officer, asks what he did upon being discovered by his commander in chief. With a wry smile, Lancaster replies, "I stood up and saluted."

Because of his experiences, coming up through the ranks during World War II, Barker senses the tragic end of Vietnam. He pauses, reflectively, "World War II. Now there was a war. . . . This one's a sucker's tour going nowhere."

Just before the final firefight, Barker has a chance to go out on a helicopter. However, he chooses to remain behind where he dies the warrior's death. His dying words are, "Aw, shit." In their own ways these two low-budget films let Hollywood know that audiences were more than curious about the Vietnam combat experience.

Production elements in bigger films were already taking place. The planned major releases of *The Deer Hunter* (1978) and *Apocalypse Now* (1979) pried ajar the tightly sealed Hollywood production doors on Vietnam combat films. Like the Military Advisory Command before it, mainline Hollywood was finally venturing into the jungle.

While American audiences were taken up with counterculture films, John Milius began adapting Joseph Conrad's haunting 1902 novel *Heart of Darkness*, which was set in Africa, to make a contemporary statement about Vietnam. *Apocalypse Now* would be a wartime journey upriver into madness and horror, a surreal metaphor of the war itself. Milius, who never served in the military reportedly because of asthma, started his "first draft" in 1967. It wouldn't be completed until December 5, 1969, coming in at 131 pages.[6]

The first draft opened with a special forces ambush, introducing Colonel D. Kurtz with the rock group "Cream" singing "Sunshine of Your Love." The detachment compound is set at Nu Mung Dung, inscribed with their motto, "Apocalypse Now." Nu Mung Dung would become Nu Mung Ba in the subsequent drafts.

When Francis Ford Coppola became fascinated with making a Vietnam combat film based on Conrad's novel, the project took on another life. As Coppola was quoted in his wife Eleanor's documentary *Hearts of Darkness*, "Like the Vietnam war, it [the script] was incomplete and with a different ending."

Coppola wasn't the first filmmaker to be attracted to the Conrad novel. Orson Welles had abandoned his planned adaptation in 1940. Welles went to another project titled *The American*, which ultimately became *Citizen Kane*.

Upon its release, in 1979, Coppola explained his motivation for doing the film.

The most important thing I wanted to do in the making of *Apocalypse Now* was to create a film experience that would give its audience a sense of the horror, the madness, the sensuousness and the moral dilemma of the Vietnam war. . . . Over the period of shooting, this film became very much like the story of the film. . . . It was my thought that if the American audience[s] could look at the heart of what Vietnam was really like—what

it looked like and felt like—then they would be only one small step from putting it behind them.[7]

    The initial budget for *Apocalypse Now* came in at $12 million. Coppola, fresh
from his Oscar triumph for *The Godfather II*, chose the Philippines for his
distant location. Like the war, the production was plagued with problems: in-
numerable script changes; the firing of lead actor Harvey Keitel after one week
of shooting; Keitel's replacement, Martin Sheen, would suffer a heart attack; a
typhoon would cause a production shutdown; and the constant changes in the
third act would cause Coppola to go into his own darkness, coupled with the
possibility of personal bankruptcy. An entire sequence, involving the French
actor Christian Marquand, at a rubber plantation along the river, would end up
being shelved in postproduction. Marquand portrayed Gaston de Marais, the
head of the family that had been running the plantation for 121 years, an icon
of French colonization, a dynasty frozen in time.
    There are several versions as to the amount of the final budget. The figure
most agreed on is $31.5 million, an outrageous sum in that time. The film
eventually grossed approximately $100 million worldwide.
    The main story line seemed clear at first, being updated from the Conrad
novel. An army captain, B.L. Willard, recently divorced and beginning his second Vietnam combat tour, is given a mission by a colonel (in later drafts a
general, G.D. Spradling). Willard was selected because of his record of working
with the CIA in the back story. He completed two such assignments, including
the execution of a Vietnamese tax collector in Kontum.
    His new mission is to travel upriver in a navy patrol boat to the remote
compound of Colonel Walter Kurtz. He is to infiltrate the colonel's headquarters
"by whatever means necessary" and terminate the command. Kurtz, played by
Marlon Brando, is a Green Beret and third-generation West Pointer originally
on the army's fast track for flag rank; but he has abandoned the military advisory
chain of command (MACV headquarters in Saigon) and set up an "unlawful"
operation in Cambodia using his loyal staff and primitive Vietnamese montagnards (the mountain people) to wage his own war. The montagnards now regard
him as a god and will blindly obey any command, no matter how ridiculous.
Kurtz's rogue command has now been charged with numerous murders, and his
radio transmissions are monitored daily. Months before, a similar mission was
given to a Captain Richard Colby (Scott Glenn). The army now has reason to
believe that Captain Colby abandoned the mission and joined Kurtz's "outlaw
group."
    Captain Willard accepts the mission, taking a Marlboro from a supposed CIA
agent (Jerry Ziesmer), dressed in civilian clothes, who elaborates on the termi-
nation. "Terminate . . . with extreme prejudice." Like the vagueness of the war's
mission, extreme prejudice is never defined in the film.
    The general tells Captain Willard that everyone has a breaking point. "Walt
Kurtz has reached his." Kurtz's methods have been termed "unsound" by the

army. Willard accepts this, his third assassination mission. But this mission is different, going into the darkness to kill one of his own with the sanction of the army. Willard explains, in narration, that he knew the risks—or thought that he did. "Charging a guy with murder, in this place, is like handing out speeding tickets at the Indy 500."

As Willard meets the crew of the navy patrol boat, the audience gets a cross section of the proverbial "squad," reminiscent of the World War II films.

Willard's narration was taken both from the novel and from *Dispatches*, Michael Herr's personal narrative of his visits to various firebases in Vietnam. "They [the crew] were mostly kids, rock and rollers with one foot in their graves." Clean (Larry Fishburne) was from some south farm shit hole. Willard figured that the light from Vietnam "put the zap on his head." Chef (Frederic Forrest) was from New Orleans, raised to be a saucier. Willard thought he was "wrapped too tight for Vietnam, even wrapped too tight for New Orleans."

Lance Johnson (Sam Bottoms), the gunner on the forward .50s, was a famous surfer from the beaches south of LA (the South Bay, where Milius used to surf). To look at him you'd never guess that he even fired a .50 caliber gun, much less killed someone.

The Chief of the boat (Albert Hall) instinctively suspects something clandestine. "One look at you and I know it's hot."

"It might have been my mission but it sure as shit was his boat," narrates Willard. Willard confides to the Chief that they're going seventy-five clicks upriver above the Do Long bridge. (A "click" is a military field term for a thousand meters.)

"That's Cambodia, captain," says the Chief.

Willard responds, "That's classified."

Along the way Willard gets to know his quarry, reading Colonel Walter Kurtz's "201 file." What emerges from the file is an officer originally being groomed to go higher up in the corporation. The file is stocked with Kurtz's impressive assignments and fast-track promotions, even completing the rigorous Ranger training at age thirty-eight. Willard then comes across a letter Kurtz had written to his son, a testimony to the eternal struggle of a man in conflict with morals and ethics in a war with no clear definition. The letter conjures a feeling similar to that evoked by the letter John Wayne's Sergeant Stryker wrote to his son, unfinished, in *Sands of Iwo Jima*.

After reading the file, Willard comes to the observation that "[t]he [Vietnam] war is being run by a bunch of four star clowns who are going to give the whole circus away."

It is at this coincidental moment in the film where art follows life. As Willard narrates, "In 1964, he [Kurtz] returned from a tour with Advisory Command, Vietnam [MACV] and things started to slip. His report, to the Joint Chiefs of Staff and Lyndon Johnson [entitled *Status of United States Involvement in the Republic of South Vietnam*] was restricted. It seems they didn't dig what he had to tell 'em."

According to William Conrad Gibbons, writing a five-volume history, *The U.S. Government and the Vietnam War*, a similar study was begun in July 1965.[8] The study, titled the PROVN Report, was headed by General Harold Johnson, U.S. Army Chief of Staff. According to Gibbons, Johnson had criticized Westmoreland's staff for developing a conventional plan (Order of Battle) for using U.S. forces that did not adequately take into account the unconventional nature of the war in Vietnam. General Johnson was a strong proponent for counterinsurgency and the use of small units. However, his views were not widely supported. Johnson then commissioned a Special Study Group, made up of combat-experienced field-grade officers. General Johnson wanted a long-term study for the pacification of Vietnam "even if it took 50 years for it to be effective."

The report was completed on March 14, 1966, a 900-page, two-volume document entitled *A Program for the Pacification and Long-Term Development of South Vietnam*, or the PROVN Report. The final draft was highly critical of the way in which the war was being fought and that time was already running out.

After the PROVN Report was concluded, according to Gibbons, those who had reason to resist its conclusions took steps to conceal its distribution. The security classification was upgraded from secret to top secret.

Distribution of the PROVN Report outside of the Department of Defense was not authorized. The Joint Chiefs of Staff distributed copies inside the Defense Department only on a limited "need to know" basis. Army officials were forbidden to discuss even the existence of the report outside the Pentagon.

It is not known if President Johnson ever saw the report. It was never submitted to the National Security Council. It does appear, however, that Secretary of Defense Robert McNamara and the Secretary of the Army were briefed on the report. Gibbons adds that neither took any action. By 1967, of the 140 recommendations of the PROVN Report, 53 had been implemented and 45 partially implemented. Overall opposition to the report's conclusions continued in the army in Washington and with Westmoreland and his associates. The fictional Colonel Kurtz was paralleling the real-life General Johnson.

The mission of the Air Cavalry contributed to the most visual and memorable sequence in *Apocalypse Now*, the attack on the village. The ridiculous motivation for the attack was to go surfing. It had no military objective. The Air Cav commander, Lieutenant Colonel Bill Kilgore (Robert Duvall), is obsessed with surfing. And since Lance is a ranked surfer, Kilgore wants to have Lance ride a six-foot break at the village beach. Kilgore proudly says that his helicopter assault unit is the "first of the ninth, Air Mobile!"

As Willard notes in his narration, "The first of the ninth was an old cavalry outfit that cashiered in its horses for helicopters and went tear assing around 'Nam looking for the shit." The combination of the name is obvious, kill and gore.

The name *Kilgore* also reflects a throwback to Kilroy in World War II. Kilroy was supposedly an army supply sergeant who, after checking equipment, would write on it, "Kilroy was here." General Patton would have been proud of Lieutenant Colonel Kilgore.

As Willard noted about Kilgore, "He wasn't a bad officer. He loved his boys. They felt safe with him." Willard added that Kilgore had "that weird light around him. You knew he wasn't going to get so much as a scratch."

At the night barbecue Kilgore learns of the six-foot peak. He's fascinated. In his opinion there aren't any good surfing beaches "in this whole shitty country." But this beach is tube city. The bad news is that the village is hairy, it's Charlie's (Viet Cong) point. Kilgore then issues the verbal attack order, because "Charlie don't surf!"

Kilgore then dons his U.S. Cavalry hat and orders his bugler to blow the charge as the helicopters warm up. The images are all in line, a steak and beer barbecue, surfing, and a helicopter attack on an enemy village, as if in homage to the troops leaving the fort in a John Ford cavalry film.

The choppers look like a swarm of locusts as they head out across the water. In an echo to the Pearl Harbor attack Kilgore's helicopter assault squadron emerges from the rising sun. At this point he plays Wagner's *Ride of the Valkyries* because "it scares the hell out of the slopes [Vietnamese]." On the radio net Kilgore's call sign is "Big Duke 6" as he confers with "Eagle Thrust."

The attack on the village begins the second act of the sequence. At first the village appears peaceful, as grammar school children assemble and then are warned by a female NVA-type soldier. As the Air Cav ships come in over the breaking waves Viet Cong and NVA soldiers, carrying AK-47s and wearing pith helmets, scramble to defensive positions. The choppers quickly break off and commence the attack, catching many of the NVA soldiers in open areas, even blowing a truck off of a bridge. Then an antiaircraft emplacement is knocked out.

Kilgore congratulates the Huey commander for the direct hit as he sips from a coffee mug. "Outstanding, I'll get you a case of beer for that one, hoss!"

When Kilgore lands his command ship the attack goes to the ground. A young soldier, obviously in his first action, declares, "I'm not going, I'm not going!" He is then grabbed and pulled into the fight, symbolizing the dilemma of young draftees.

A black soldier takes a gaping leg wound, the result of a booby trap. As he is being evacuated, a village girl throws a cone hat into the Huey. Concealed in the cone hat is a grenade, which takes out the whole ship. Kilgore now refers to his enemy as "fucking savages." Retaliation then begins.

As the third act of the sequence begins, the villagers flee and are cut down from above. After landing, Kilgore strips off his fatigue blouse and calls in a napalm strike, ignoring incoming mortar rounds while soldiers around him duck for cover. As the napalm hits and flashes skyward, Kilgore parades around, bare chested, in his cavalry hat, proclaiming that "nothing in the world smells like that. . . . I love the smell of napalm in the morning!"

Kilgore then sadly realizes that "some day this war is gonna end." Like Patton,

Kilgore has to realize that his time on stage, like the war, has an exit date. The man is almost in tears, knowing that his time, in what he loves, is running out.

In an earlier draft Willard is the one who says, "Some day this war's gonna end." Kilgore then adds, "Yes, I know."

As Willard observes, after the attack, "Some day this war's gonna end. That would be just fine with the boys on the boat. All they wanted was to go home. I'd been back there. And it didn't exist anymore. . . . It wasn't just insanity and murder. There was enough of that to go around."

As the rewrite process was accelerating in the Philippines, Marlon Brando, cast as Kurtz, arrived. The good news was that he was on location; the bad news was that Brando was extremely overweight and looked nothing like a West Pointer and a seasoned Green Beret officer. Brando's contract terms called for him to be available for three weeks of shooting. After arriving, he spent an excessive amount of time with Coppola getting into character, trying to determine exactly who Kurtz is. Coppola contended that Kurtz was in a twilight zone, the way America (at the time) was in a twilight zone.

As the patrol boat approaches the USO Theatre, along the shore, the most noticeable icons are the phallic missiles, pointed skyward. The boat stops for fuel. But first they see the black market operation being run by a young supply sergeant who is able to supply Chef with the drug Panama Red. Willard then assaults the sergeant, who suddenly realizes the seriousness of the captain. Apologizing, the sergeant gives the men press box seats for the USO show, along with a bottle of brandy for Willard.

The bunnie showgirls—Playmates of the month—arrive via Huey helicopter, along with the master of ceremonies (MC) (Bill Graham). The MC congratulates the troops for working so hard on Operation Brute Force. As he introduces the women, they each dance and gesticulate around the stage, even to the point where one playmate (Cindi Wood), garbed as an Indian brave, taunts the troops. Another bunnie (Linda Carpenter), in a Union cavalry tunic, mocks with the flash suppressor of the rifle. A third (Colleen Camp), costumed in western attire, with two revolvers, is brought to center stage standing on two M-16s. She also makes several cocainesque motions with her index finger to the nose.

As the troops become more taunted, they rush the stage, causing a near riot. The MC then gets the women back onto the Huey, but not before giving a Nixonesque "V" salute, recalling former President Nixon's last White House gesture on his resignation day.

The tumultuous presidential triangle was complete here, a sayonara to them all, a trilogy that began with Kennedy ideals, conflicting Johnson, and ending Nixon. The metaphor even goes further with Lance's full name, Lance B. Johnson: LBJ.

"It's our time . . . in our moment of history," Kurtz tells Willard.

The sampan incident, where a Vietnamese boat family is needlessly slaughtered, reinforced the feeling to audiences that Americans were just as guilty as any military force. It is here where we see Willard execute a wounded Vietnamese girl rather than take her to an aid station, less he be delayed in accomplishing his mission. One assassination foreshadows the next.

Numerous elements were changed or dropped from Milius's third draft. In an account of the troubled shooting and script changes, Eleanor Coppola, in her book *Notes*, wrote:

He [Francis] couldn't go on making the original John Milius script because it really didn't express his ideas, and he couldn't stop because so much money had been spent. People were saying how anxious they were to see the film because it is such an extraordinary story. He didn't know how to turn the film into his personal vision, or if anybody would even be interested in it. He was really scared and miserable, and at just that moment the typhoon came along and gave him the excuse to stop and resolve his conflict.[9]

Coppola's draft, dated December 3, 1975, at 153 pages, kept Milius's basic structure of a "bookend flashback." There is a sequence on a luxury party boat in Marina del Rey, where Willard, dressed as a civilian, relives the entire nightmarish experience.

As the final air strike is brought to bear on Kurtz's compound, Willard is leaving on the patrol boat with Captain Colby at the helm. A mortally wounded Kurtz had been carried aboard by Willard. After Kurtz dies, Willard, reacting maniacally, raises his M-16 and fires at one of the helicopters.

The scene then flashes forward to the Marina del Rey party boat as the guests are leaving. Willard kept the more important documents from Kurtz's 201 file, including the letters to his wife. Willard adds, in voiceover, that he watched the fall of Saigon in a bar in Alameda.

Willard then goes to see Kurtz's widow, who lives with their son in a nondescript California neighborhood. Mrs. Kurtz still keeps framed photos of her husband at various stages of his career. Willard gives the packet to her and explains that he was with Kurtz when he died.

"He said his last words to me," explains Willard.

"What were they . . . tell me," pleads Mrs. Kurtz.

Willard lies to her. "He spoke of you ma'am."

In voiceover, we hear the true last words of Colonel Kurtz, "The horror . . . the horror."

This dissolves to the patrol boat, back in Vietnam, floating downriver as Jim Morrison sings "The End."

In a later essay on the film, critic Jean Baudrillard wrote, "His film is really the extension of the war through other means, the pinnacle of this failed war, and its apotheosis. The war became film, the film becomes war, the two are joined by their common hemorrhage into technology."[10]

Coppola took a "rough cut" of the film to the 1979 Cannes International Film Festival, where it shared the Palme d'Or with Volker Schlöndorff's *The Tin Drum*, based on Gunter Grass's novel. *Apocalypse Now* was later nominated for

Academy Awards for Best Picture, Best Screenplay, and Best Direction. Robert Duvall was nominated for Best Supporting Actor for his portrayal of Lieutenant Colonel Kilgore. The only Oscar it received was for Best Cinematography, Vittorio Storaro.

While *Apocalypse Now* was in production, two other significant Vietnam films were being produced, *The Deer Hunter* (1978) and *Coming Home* (1978). Like *Apocalypse Now*, both would have lasting effects on the myth and image of Vietnam veterans in American film.

Directed by Michael Cimino, in his first major release, the final script of *The Deer Hunter* was written by Deric Washburn with rewrites from Cimino, Louis Garfinkle, Quinn K. Redeker, and Washburn.

*The Deer Hunter* is an epic study of soldiers from the working class, who made up the bulk of the MACV fighting force in the Vietnam War. Raised on the tempo of World War II films, they believed in the twentieth-century American ethic. And they willingly went to serve in a cause they deemed as their duty.

Mike (Robert De Niro), Nick (Christopher Walken), and Steven (John Savage) are products of Russian immigrants in a Pennsylvania mill town, captured in early morning with Vilmos Zsigmond's cold and stark cinematography, complete with a rambling eighteen-wheel tractor trailer rig making a turn in front of smokestacks sending steel vapors skyward. The story has a definite triangular structure, of what happens to these young men before, during, and after Vietnam. They figuratively exchange the inferno of steel mill heat for the fury of a deadly wartime jungle.

In addition to the three soldiers, the supporting characters—the women and townspeople—are likewise affected by the war's tragic long arms. The film begins with the three on their last morning at the mill, leaving the graveyard shift where Mike spots an old Indian sign in the sky, giving an omen to their last hunting trip before going to war. They are also preparing for Steve's wedding to Angela (Rutanya Alda), who is carrying Nick's child. But Nick has already moved on to Linda (Meryl Streep), who Mike eyes from afar. Linda has her own problems, an overweight, physically abusive drunken lout of a father.

The reception is at the town's American Legion Hall, complete with patriotism and posters. George Dzundza's guilt comes out where he expresses that he really wanted to go in the army with them but failed the physical because of a knee injury.

In the midst of the celebration comes a multitoured Green Beret sergeant, an angel of death, like the soothsayer in *Julius Caesar* giving a warning of doom that goes unheeded, is even laughed at. The sergeant won't even look at Mike, who offers a handshake and wonders, "Well, what's it like over there?" The sergeant offers no opinion of the hell that awaits the three. He merely responds with the proverbial thousand-yard stare and a raised shot glass to the war's effort: "Fuck it." It's as if he is looking at a parade of dead comrades passing in review in his mind's eye. There's actually no reason for the sergeant to be at the reception other than to give his tragic foreshadowing.

The actual in-country combat sequence is only twenty-seven minutes of screen time. Yet it is the most harrowing, involving POWs, NVA waterlogged prison pens, rats, and a Russian roulette game.

The POW Russian roulette scene has been one of the most criticized by combat journalists and veterans groups because no such incidents were ever recorded among Vietnam POWs. However, it can also be noted that the Russian roulette was a metaphor for America placing a loaded Vietnam gun to the head of its youth, most of whom came from working-class backgrounds. The visual image of the Russian roulette scenes being perpetrated by an Asian gave rise to the racial criticism.

After the POW sequence, the three are separated and thereby sent to their individual psychological prisons. Steve is a triple amputee and ends up as a recluse, heavily medicated in a VA hospital ward; Nick remains in Vietnam, drawn into the Saigon underworld where he is addicted to heroin and becomes a pawn in a larger, corrupt maze of gambling and more Russian roulette. Mike keeps his conflict inside, unable to communicate his true feelings. Upon return to Pennsylvania, he purposefully ignores a coming-home reception, preferring to squat (like a Vietnamese villager) alone in a motel room gazing at a laminated photo of Linda that he carried all the way through.

After visiting Steve in the hospital, Mike reverts to his loyalty and returns to Vietnam to bring Nick home. By this time Nick is a hopeless victim, both to the war and corrupt Asian politics. Even though Mike finds Nick, he is unable to prevent the last deadly round from being fired in Russian roulette.

The final Vietnam effort in *The Deer Hunter* is the videotape sequence of a Huey helicopter being pushed off the deck of the aircraft carrier USS *Hancock* in the South China Sea. The diplomatic corps, including Ambassador Graham Martin, have been airlifted from the roof of the embassy.

Balancing Steve's wedding at the beginning, the film comes full circle with Nick's funeral at the end. Coming out of the church, Mike takes a final reflective look at Nick's coffin through the glass of the hearse, as if aware that part of the spirit of their generation is being buried with Nick.

Even though this working-class generation was ripped and scarred by the experience, they still are holding on to hope that there had to have been some meaning in all of this. Gathered around a table in the local bar, Linda begins singing "God Bless America." Reverently, the rest join in, giving homage that despite the tragedy, they still owe something to America, the land where their parents fled to escape persecution. Mike's final gesture is another raised glass, not to the war but to Nick's sacrifice.

Academy Award nominations came in for Deric Washburn (Best Screenplay), Vilmos Zsigmond (Best Cinematography), Robert De Niro (Best Actor), and Meryl Streep (Best Actress). Oscars went to Christopher Walken (Best Supporting Actor) and Michael Cimino (Best Director). The film was also named as Best Picture for 1978.

On Oscar night, April 9, 1979, John Wayne, terminally ill with cancer, made a farewell appearance. The man who Douglas MacArthur once said personified the American serviceman "better than the American serviceman" confided grave disappointment with the film, its message, and its award as Best Picture. It could be said that on that night the American war film had come 180 degrees from the blatant early World War II propaganda films.

According to writer Peter Biskind, in *Easy Riders, Raging Bulls*, Jane Fonda lit into Cimino, backstage, for making a "racist, Pentagon version of the war."[11] Outside the Dorothy Chandler Pavillion that night, "Vietnam Veterans against the War" picketed. Clearly, *The Deer Hunter* crossed many ideologies, being objected to by both John Wayne and Jane Fonda.

As the awards were held, it had been almost four years since the fall of Saigon. Even as the North Vietnamese closed in on the Saigon perimeter, in those final days, an element of denial existed among the American politicians, including Ambassador Graham Martin.

According to retired Marine Colonel Herbert Fix,[12] who commanded the American helicopter forces during that time, the CIA had predicted what the outfall would be even as the heavily armed North Vietnamese convoy got closer to Saigon. "At about 4:30 on the morning of April 30 [1975] President Ford wanted to know if Ambassador Martin was out of the embassy. The response was no. Ambassador Martin was refusing to leave."

Colonel Fix explained, "He [Ford] sent a seething message that the next helicopter was to land on the embassy rooftop and to wait for the ambassador. If he did not get aboard the helo the crew and Marine Security guards were authorized to physically put him aboard."

Captain Gerry Berry was flying the next helicopter in line for an embassy pickup. According to Fix, Captain Berry landed his ship on the rooftop and waited until Ambassador Martin was safely aboard. At 4:58 that morning Captain Berry's CH-46 helicopter lifted off. Over his guarded radio frequency Berry relayed the coded message "Tiger, Tiger, Tiger." This meant that he had Ambassador Martin aboard. Colonel Fix added that the American embassy was officially closed. Unofficially, a handful of marines remained behind, waiting for their ride to freedom.

The commander of the marine security detachment, Major Jim Kean, withdrew his men into the embassy and barricaded the doors. He moved through the building until he occupied only the top floor, from which he had access to the roof. After dodging rifle fire, Major Kean employed riot control agents against people attempting to storm the roof. At 7:53 that morning, Major Kean, with the last eleven embassy marines, got aboard the last helicopter flown by Captain Tom Holden.

Less than ten minutes after Holden's helicopter lifted off the embassy rooftop, the NVA tank and truck convoy crashed through the Presidential Palace gates.

Out in the gulf, helicopters from the South Vietnamese Army were looking for a safe haven. Several landed on the flight deck of the aircraft carrier the USS *Hancock*. After a while they were pushed overboard.

The Vietnam War, in terms of combat, was over.

Major General Norman W. Gourley, commanding general of the First Marine Aircraft Wing, who served in three wars, later wrote, "Never in the annals of flying, and I am including all U.S. combat air operations of any war, have a group of pilots performed so magnificently as the helicopter pilots who extracted those folks out of Saigon in late April 1975."[13]

## A KITCHEN FLASHBACK

There was still major reluctance to tell the Vietnam experience through American war films. As late as 1980 a producer at a major studio told this writer that after the release of *Apocalypse Now*, there won't be any more Vietnam war films produced. "We lost the war and the American public doesn't want to be reminded of it," explained the producer.[14]

Despite the frustrating uphill struggle that awaited the acceptance of Vietnam combat films, something notable occurred—but not without a serious and acrimonious struggle.

In March 1979, Jan Scruggs, a former infantryman with the army's 199th Light Infantry Brigade, went to see *The Deer Hunter*. At the time, many people felt that *The Deer Hunter* was the most violent war film ever produced, because of the Russian roulette scenes.

But the violence wasn't what affected the twenty-nine-year-old Scruggs. It was the subplot of three young working-class men from a Pennsylvania steel mill town who believed in doing the right thing for their country. The three became victimized by the war, tragically but contrasting. With Scruggs, this depiction struck a raw, submerged nerve. The film brought that nerve to the anguished surface. And once again, an American war film reminded the country of what had happened to a generation.

Scruggs couldn't sleep that night. At three in the morning, he was in his kitchen, a bottle of whiskey his only companion. In his mind, he was reliving combat horrors, seeing his buddies die, body parts strewn upon a clearing near a hamlet with a strange name. The faces came together in front of him.

It could have been a scene out of *All Quiet on the Western Front, The Best Years of Our Lives, Twelve O'Clock High*, or *Captain Newman, M.D.* It was the combat vet reliving the nightmare alone.

Scruggs kept thinking about the names. Nobody remembers the names, he thought to himself. It wasn't what they did; it was who they were. And Americans should remember.

Later that morning, Scruggs told his wife Rebecca, "I'm going to build a memorial to all the guys who served in Vietnam. It'll have the names of everyone killed."

Rebecca smiled. Then she began to worry that he was having delusions. She figured the best thing to do was to let the situation play itself out.

Scruggs's vow, stemming from his "kitchen flashback," began the long and difficult road to the construction of the Vietnam War Memorial. The twisting, roller-coaster, bureaucratic nightmare began with the formation of the Vietnam Veterans Memorial Fund (VVMF). And then there was the decision on the design. It came down to finalists. In his book on the 1966 West Point class, *The Long Gray Line*, Rick Atkinson told how eight jurors sat for four days in hanger number three at Andrews Air Force Base to study 1,421 entries in the competition.

When it came down to the final decision, it was entry number 1026, a simple pastel drawing that showed two black slashes joined at an obtuse angle. The black granite would list the names of every serviceman and servicewoman killed in Vietnam. They were gradual sloping walls set into a hillside, equidistant from the Lincoln Memorial and the Washington Monument. The artist was a Chinese American woman, twenty-two-year-old Maya Ying Lin who had hip-length black hair, an architecture student. According to Atkinson, her winning memorial design "was awarded a B+ by her instructor at Yale."[15]

Even though there was applause and mild celebration at the announcement, staunch opposition was festering below the surface. The nucleus of the opposition came from seasoned cold warriors such as conservative commentator and presidential candidate Patrick J. Buchanan, William F. Buckley Jr., U.S. Representative Henry Hyde (R–Illinois), President Reagan's Secretary of Interior James Watt, and Dallas entrepreneur H. Ross Perot. Some of the criticisms held that the slabs were ugly and an insult to Vietnam veterans. Also, the memorial should not be below ground, slammed into a hillside like it was hiding from the world.

Despite the arguments and furor, even among some Vietnam veterans, Lin's design held fast, and the wall was eventually constructed.

Today it is the most visited tourist site in Washington, D.C.

In 1988 a TV movie was produced, based on Jan Scruggs and Joel Swerdlow's book *To Heal a Nation*, with Eric Roberts playing Scruggs. The film, directed by Michael Pressman, captured what one man can accomplish with an idea, overcoming internecine strife and political opposition. It also brought out the element that antiwar activists were simply against the war, not the men who fought it. The airport spitting and the "baby killer syndrome" had become things of the past.

So it came to be that *The Deer Hunter*, the American war film that was criticized as being too graphic, racist, and violent, resulted in a lasting memorial to the 58,191 Americans (including 8 women) who paid the ultimate price in Vietnam.

## A TURN ON YIN AND YANG

In 1974 Nancy Ellen Dowd, a graduate screenwriting student at UCLA, wrote a thesis script titled *Buffalo Ghost*, what ultimately was to be *Coming Home*

(1978). *Buffalo Ghost* took place on the Fort Sheridan army post near Buffalo Ghost, South Dakota. The character triangle centered around Johnny and Marilyn Beaumont and a paraplegic veteran simply described as "Vet" in the script. Johnny is a thirty-year-old sergeant and goes to Vietnam to advance his career, leaving Marilyn behind in their trailer park home. Marilyn brings in extra money working at Rydell's jewelry store, which owes its existence mainly to the trade of the lowly paid soldiers. While Johnny is gone, Marilyn begins a relationship with Vet, who now has a sarcastic view toward life from the seat of his wheelchair. She also talks an unhinged, doped-up, combat veteran out of robbing the store.

Johnny returns as a distant person with an alcohol problem, preferring the company of soldiers to Marilyn. At a chamber of commerce function, Johnny is awarded the Distinguished Service Cross, second to the Medal of Honor. Later, Johnny calls Marilyn from a bar, drunk. She pleads with him to stay there, that she will come and get him. Johnny has borrowed a buddy's Porsche and will drive home, he insists. Marilyn then drives to the bar. On the way she sees the aftermath of a tragic accident, involving a Porsche. When she arrives at the car, Johnny is already dead.

The final sequence has Marilyn leaving Buffalo Ghost with Johnny's personal effects, widowed, and wounded by the experience. She picks up two hitchhikers in the rain, an AWOL soldier and his young girlfriend. They're heading to the Canadian border to avoid his going to Vietnam. Marilyn wishes them luck as they pass highway billboards advertising Esso, Shell, General Motors, the U.S. Marine Corps, and finally Nixon in '68 (who promises to bring us together).

Dowd would later reflect on studying previous war film classics, *The Big Parade, Le Grande Illusion, The Best Years of Our Lives*, and *The Men*: "I had seen the previous reels, but in those years the effect of war on women was obviously important to me because that is what I was thinking and writing about. These were not assignments, not adaptations. I wrote *Buffalo Ghost* while the war was raging. It was not a backward look. It was produced well after the American defeat, but it was written during."[16]

Dowd sold the screenplay outright to Jane Fonda. After several arbitrated drafts by Waldo Salt and Robert C. Jones, the script took a much tougher look at the military in general and Vietnam in particular. The setting was moved from the army in South Dakota to the marines in southern California. Marilyn Beaumont was now Sally Hyde (Fonda). Sally no longer lived in a trailer park but, as a captain's wife, was part of the officers' social circle.

Salt's take on the story went to different issues. The film opens in the recreation room of a spinal ward, as a group discussion of paraplegic veterans takes place. We meet Luke Martin (Jon Voight), an alienated marine sergeant who attacks his anger with alcohol. On the officer's side is Captain Bob Hyde (Bruce Dern), who is gearing up for his Vietnam tour, jogging to the Rolling Stones' "Out of Time." Bob is such a gung-ho marine that he makes love to Sally wearing his dog tags.

Bob and Luke seem to be the Yin and Yang of the Vietnam experience. One uses the war to inform others and better himself, whereas the other careens down a one-way psychological road. The music track is evocative of the 1960s and 1970s: the Rolling Stones, Buffalo Springfield, the Beatles, Jefferson Airplane, Simon & Garfunkle, Dylan, Jimi Hendrix, Richie Havens, and Steppenwolf.

After Bob leaves, Sally volunteers to work on the spinal ward, where she meets Luke (in leather restraints), who recognizes her as Sally Bender, the cheerleader for the high school football team of which Luke was cocaptain. Things are different now; Luke has an anger problem, while Sally begins questioning values and priorities. Among these are getting the support of the officers' wives club to do something for the paraplegic vets. However, the wives don't think this is the proper thing. Turning down Sally's request, they go to the next item on the agenda, supporting the upcoming little league season; thereby ignoring the problems of the spinal ward veterans.

After getting a wheelchair, Luke chains himself to the front gate of the base upon hearing of a Vietnam troop buildup. This individual act of civil disobedience begins the FBI's surveillance as Sally and Luke's relationship develops into an affair. An R&R in Hong Kong foreshadows Bob's trauma and his confusion with the mission in Vietnam, where his troops placed the heads of dead enemy soldiers on poles.

After returning to southern California, Bob becomes distant and is found asleep with a loaded .45 automatic. He is then called into the base provost marshall's office and told of the FBI surveillance on Luke and his unfaithful wife. Bob confronts Luke and tells him that the FBI has tapes and photos, beginning with the gate incident.

Bob then loads a Chinese rifle and confronts Sally as a confused warrior, distant, damaged, and hurt. He is angered by Sally's affair with Luke and feels that he doesn't deserve the medal he is about to receive. Luke, sensing trouble, enters the house and tries to calm Bob, realizing the tragic potential. Bob, losing control, calls Luke a "Jody fuck" and Sally a "slope cunt." Bob, a tangled psychological mess, then gives up the loaded rifle.

Luke contends that he is not the enemy. "The enemy is the fucking war. . . . You have enough ghosts to carry around."

Editing is the salvation in the final sequence. As Sally and friend Vi (Penelope Milford) go shopping, Luke addresses a high school assembly, while Bob discards his marine dress blues with the newly awarded Bronze Star medal at a life guard station and takes a suicidal run into the crashing California surf.

At the assembly, the high school students first hear from a marine recruiter that the Marine Corps builds body, mind, and spirit. Giving an alternative view, Luke tells the students that one grows up real quick in Vietnam. "All you're seeing is a lot of death." He recalls seeing all the films with the glory of the other wars. Even as he wanted to go out and kill for his country, it still isn't like it is in the movies, he contends.

"I have killed for my country and I don't feel good about it. . . . There's a lot of shit I did over there that I have to live with." He adds that he's a lot smarter now. All the marine sergeant can do is glare at Luke; he has no counterargument.

The last shot in the film has Sally and Vi entering a supermarket to get steaks for a barbecue. As they enter, a door swings out with a sign on it: Exit.

The FBI surveillance was obviously a statement by both Fonda and screenwriter Salt. Fonda, herself, was placed under FBI surveillance for her antiwar activism, which included numerous demonstrations and her controversial 1972 trip to North Vietnam. She was also placed on the Nixon White House "Enemies List," which was revealed during the 1973 Watergate testimony. As noted, Salt was a victim of the Hollywood blacklist and an unfriendly witness. This subplot definitely got in its licks.

The film was nominated for Best Picture, Best Director (Hal Ashby), Best Supporting Actor (Dern), Best Supporting Actress (Milford), and Best Editing (Don Zimmerman). Oscars were awarded to Fonda and Voight for Best Actor and Best Actress, respectively.

Nancy Dowd, who was given story credit for her *Buffalo Ghost* thesis script, Salt, and Robert C. Jones received Oscars for the screenplay. It was the first time Dowd met the other two.

In a 1988 ABC *20/20* interview, Jane Fonda used a Barbara Walters segment to apologize for bad judgment in going to North Vietnam in 1972 and allowing herself to be used as a propaganda vehicle. She amended that apology in June 2000, commenting on having her photo taken with North Vietnamese soldiers after visiting the infamous "Hanoi Hilton," where American POWs were being held. Fonda said, "It was the most horrible thing I could possibly have done. It was just thoughtless."[17]

At the end of World War II the realistic war films began to emerge. The veterans came home and wrote about the experience, what Ernest Hemingway once described as "seeing the elephant." A similar chain of events occurred in the 1980s where Vietnam veterans, as writers and filmmakers, got their stories made into films.

A 1980 CBS TV movie *Rumor of War* chronicled its author's Vietnam experience. Philip Caputo, born and reared in the Midwest with a patriotic fervor, had seen the old World War II movies. In addition to his patriotism, he embodied the Kennedy-era idealism of doing something for his country.

After graduating from Loyola University in Chicago, Caputo went through the rigorous Marine Corps officer training and found himself going into Danang in 1965 with the first elements of the 3rd Marine Division. In a 1996 CNN interview on the Cold War, Caputo reflected, "We were going to stay there a month to ninety days, help the South Vietnamese recover, and then get out."

One of Caputo's squad leaders echoed the gung-ho attitude at the time. "Hot damn. Vietnam," said the sergeant.

Caputo's platoon got the rugged Vietnam initiation: the enemy, the heat, the jungle, and the monsoons. As a result of a firefight, Caputo was charged with the murder of innocent civilians and court-martialed. Caputo returned embittered and disillusioned, his Kennedy-era idealism shattered as the war intensified under Lyndon Johnson and Richard Nixon.

Returning to the United States and leaving the Marine Corps, Caputo became a journalist and eventually covered the fall of Saigon for the *Chicago Tribune*. As he observed, "I was with the first American combat unit sent into the war . . . then I was among the last Americans to be evacuated from the place."

At the Rendezvous with War conference in April 2000, at the College of William & Mary, Caputo commented on his *Rumor of War* memoir and the CBS TV movie. The manuscript sat on an editor's credenza for an extended period "because the editor didn't want to read it." Caputo added that at the time to even mention Vietnam as a book was an anathema.

Brad Davis was cast to play Caputo, with Brian Dennehy as his platoon sergeant. Richard Heffron directed from John Sacret Young's script, which was rewritten considerably. This led to irritation on Caputo's part, the difference between a book and a film. In reflecting on the experience, Caputo explained that he "kicked back" the script six times. The most notable incident was when the producer wanted certain World War II sex elements inserted into the script, complete with a beach scene imitating *From Here to Eternity*. People in the conference audience laughed uproariously. Caputo reaffirmed that this actually happened.

"That was his experience, what he remembered seeing in World War II films," explained Caputo. He further railed at the changes and finally asked to have his name taken off the project. The network executives, to their credit, eventually backed him up and his corrections were followed. The script came through, reflecting the book, added Caputo. Davis and Dennehy supported Caputo in his arguments for authenticity.

In 1982, Carolco Pictures developed David Morrell's novel *First Blood* into a starring vehicle for Sylvester Stallone. It would be the first installment of what would become "The Rambo Trilogy." And it would also enhance the Vietnam psychotic stereotype to the point of comic book heroics.

Director Ted Kotcheff emphasized the action adventure angle of Morrell's novel with a heavily rewritten script from Michael Kozoll and William Sackheim, with a revision by Stallone.

John Rambo, former Green Beret, shows up in the Pacific Northwest town of Hope, looking for an old buddy who he learns has died of Agent Orange. The local sheriff, Will Teasle (Brian Dennehy), considers Rambo a vagrant and literally drives him out of town. However, Rambo is not someone with whom to mess. He returns, walking across a bridge (his own Rubicon) to actually start the film. Rambo is then arrested for coming back into town as a vagrant, resisting arrest, and carrying an oversized hunting knife.

Rambo is then abused and taunted by the deputies, one of whom is David Caruso in his first major film role. This causes Rambo to experience combat flashbacks. Rambo then goes into his "animal mode," flattening the deputies with a battery of chops and kicks, even throwing one through a window. He then turns the police headquarters upside down and escapes into the woods, thinly dressed and rearmed with his hunting knife. The caveman is now ready to face modern law enforcement.

This sets off the first phase of the chase. The deputies, in this case, are ill suited for venturing into the woods, a metaphor made in the script. Rambo takes them on, one by one, where they come to realize exactly what they're dealing with. A radio call comes through with the make on Rambo: a former Green Beret, three years in Vietnam, Medal of Honor winner. Rambo then grabs Sheriff Teasle from behind, puts the knife to his throat, and warns him, "Let it go, or I'll give you a war you won't believe."

Realizing the challenge and refusing to quit (in a Lyndon Johnson mode), Teasle then becomes the obsessed cop, referring to Rambo as a "psycho" and "maniac." He calls in the state police and the National Guard. But the guardsmen are likewise ill trained for the terrain.

Richard Crenna, as Colonel Sam Trautman, Rambo's former commanding officer, then appears and advises the ignorant authorities as to whom they are chasing. Rambo is a product of refined American combat training now relegated to the ash heap since the war is over. But he hasn't forgotten what he was taught. Troutman warns the locals that if they keep up the chase, in their present manner, they will need one more item: body bags. Trautman then becomes the "Greek Chorus," staying away from the action but subtly predicting what will happen. And then it does.

Rambo continues the fight because "they drew first blood." Rambo then commandeers a "six-by" national guard truck, which leads to obligatory chases topped off with super explosions. Rambo returns to town, this time armed with an M-60 machine gun to shoot out the town's lights. Sheriff Teasle eventually ends up on his back with a bloodied face.

It's obvious that the only one who can rein in Rambo is his former commander. After ninety minutes of steely looks, grunts, chases, and fiery explosions, the film gets to its message, the country's treatment of veterans after the war.

Trautman explains to Rambo that the mission is over, that he cannot continue doing these things to friendly civilians. "There are no friendly civilians," counters Rambo, reflecting a Vietnam syndrome.

Trautman becomes emphatic. "It's over, John."

"It's not over! Nothing's over!" yells Rambo. "It wasn't my war. You asked me, I didn't ask you." Rambo then goes into his coming home experience, "Maggots at the airport calling me a baby killer." Trautman says that it was a bad time for everybody.

Rambo's frustration goes further. "Over there I was responsible for millions of dollars of equipment. Back here, I can't even hold a job."

Trautman then completes his mission, walking out with Rambo. They pass a gurney with Teasle on it, being loaded into an ambulance. With Rambo going quietly, the avenue is now set for sequels, departing from the ending of the novel. In the novel Rambo was holed up in the woods, refusing to come out. He is eventually shot and killed.

Richard Crenna jumped in and took over the role of Trautman after Kirk Douglas dropped out. The film did well and caused much comment, including the question of what will come next.

By 1983, the military was further questioned in the surprise hit *Uncommon Valor*. Despite the worn story line of a gang of heroes with a noble goal, the film found wide acceptance. Also directed by Ted Kotcheff, from a script by Joe Gayton, it was a cross between *The Dirty Dozen* and *The Magnificent Seven*.

Gene Hackman portrayed a retired marine officer whose son is missing in Vietnam. After years of futile tracking, Hackman recruits a band of military rogues to go in for the rescue. They go through updated training, overcome obstacles, and accomplish this mission. Robert Stack plays a wealthy business-man who finances the venture because his son is also missing.

During the recruiting sequence, Hackman explains that Vietnam veterans are considered criminals in their own country, that the sons of the powerfully con-nected ducked the war. He adds that the only hope for those missing are the veterans themselves. The group is a clichéd mix, recalling the World War II films. Reb Brown is a surfer and expert in demolitions; Fred Ward is a former tunnel rat with many kills; Tim Thomerson is a crop-dusting pilot close to burnout; Harold Sylvester is a successful administrator but reluctant to sign on again; and Randall "Tex" Cobb is the stereotypical Vietnam vet who came back psychotic.

The training sequences are realistic, thanks to technical adviser Chuck Taylor, a Vietnam veteran and weapons expert. Hackman was believable as the team leader, partly because of his service as a Korean War–era marine.

The brutal and savage realism of the genocide of the North Vietnamese–backed Khmer Rouge in 1975 Cambodia was brought to the screen in *The Killing Fields* (1984), based on *New York Times* reporter Sidney Schanberg's and Dith Pran's experiences. The film is often graphic and difficult to watch simply because it shows exactly what happened.

When dictator Pol Pot came into power, he proceeded to exterminate ap-proximately 2 million people whom he considered enemies. The exact figure will never be known. Cities were emptied; villages ceased to exist. Mass exe-cutions were routinely carried out. Schanberg, reporting the horror, and his Cam-bodian assistant, Dith Pran, were separated. Schanberg got out of the country, while Pran was captured and sent to a reeducation camp.

While Schanberg continued with his journalism career in New York City, including a Pulitzer Prize for international reporting in 1976, Pran endured brutal hardships, bordering on death, and awaited the moment to escape across the fields littered with rotting corpses and the bones of those exterminated. The two ultimately reunited. And then Schanberg wrote the account, *The Death and Life of Dith Pran*.

The 1984 film was produced by David Puttnam. Roland Joffé directed from

Bruce Robinson's adaptation. Sam Waterson played Schanberg, while Haing S. Ngor, a survivor of the Cambodian holocaust, gave a stunning performance as Dith Pran. In supporting roles were John Malkovich, Julian Sands, and Craig T. Nelson. The film was nominated for Best Picture. Also receiving nominations were Waterston, Bruce Robinson, and Joffé.

Ngor, in accepting his Oscar for Best Supporting Actor, gave an emotional speech on the verge of tears. (Sadly, years later, Ngor was the victim of a Los Angeles homicide.) Chris Menges and Jim Clark won Oscars for cinematography and editing, respectively.

In 1986 Clint Eastwood directed himself from a script by James Carabatsos, *Heartbreak Ridge*. The film was produced by Eastwood's Malpaso Productions and released by Warner Bros.

It was standard war film fare—an experienced, multidecorated marine gunnery sergeant puts the recruits through rigorous training and takes them into combat. This time the combat is the invasion of Grenada.

Like *Sands of Iwo Jima*, the film received initial cooperation from the Marine Corps. One of the areas at Camp Pendleton, Camp Talega, was used in the training sequence. A bar sequence at the Swallows Inn in nearby San Juan Capistrano was also employed.

In the script Tom Highway (Eastwood) is a survivor of Heartbreak Ridge in Korea. On the downswing of his career, Highway is transferred to Camp Pendleton to qualify a new unit for combat. Everett McGill plays the regulation-orientated commander who informs Highway that the day of his type of marine is gone. No more bar room brawls and swearing in front of recruits. McGill is then met with the "Eastwood look."

Coming out of the back story is Marsha Mason, who plays Highway's ex-wife Aggie who is now working at the local bar. The love story subplot has Highway courting his ex.

The Grenada invasion sequence caused the Marine Corps to pull its support because of a scene where an unarmed Cuban soldier is killed by a marine.

After winning an Oscar for the adaptation of *Midnight Express*, Oliver Stone continued working on his combat memoir of Vietnam, what ultimately became *Platoon*. Stone, a decorated army veteran, wrote and directed the 1986 film that brought out many emotional and divided feelings about the Vietnam War. Many Vietnam veterans acknowledged Stone's position as a combat survivor but took issue with his interpretation of the experience. Major General John Cleland, upon seeing the film, wrote that it left him with feelings of "disgust and dismay . . . this ghastly film gives a totally false picture of the American infantryman in combat." Brigadier General Barry McCaffrey contended that Stone's film portrayed a terrible and distorted image of American combat troops in Vietnam.[18]

Brock Garland, in his book *War Movies*, wrote, "*Platoon* is surely one of the most profound and disturbing war films ever made about the American experience in Vietnam."[19] Michael Lee Lanning, in *Vietnam at the Movies*, stated, "In reality [*Platoon*] is an excellent picture, but poor extremely biased history."[20]

To date, no film about the American Vietnam experience brought out such reactions from across the combat spectrum. In theaters across the country, audiences sat in stunned silence as closing credits rolled. When the credits ended, they were still sitting, staring at the white screen, numbed by the cinematic experience they had just endured.

For realism Stone contracted retired Marine Corps captain, and Vietnam veteran, Dale Dye to put the actors through a two-week "boot camp," repeating what William Wellman did to the major actors in *Battleground* in 1949.

Charlie Sheen played Chris Taylor, an idealistic nineteen-year-old who drops out of college, joins the army, and heads into the experience of his life. He wanted to do something he could be proud of. His grandfather served in World War I, his father in World War II. Rich kids, Chris says, could get away with it. A biblical quote opens the film, from Ecclesiastes, "Rejoice, O young man, in thy youth."

Chris lands in Vietnam as body bags are being loaded for the flight home. As a living soldier, he passes by the parade of the dead in the first hours of his combat tour. One gaunt soldier, leaving, passes Chris, giving the look of impending death. Chris then meets two sergeants, again representing the Yin and Yang of the Vietnam War. These are Elias (Willem Dafoe) and Barnes (the scarred Tom Berenger), respectively, good and evil. The officers are likewise portrayed. Chris's youthful platoon commander is sadly ineffective, while the company commander, Captain Harris (Dale Dye) commands authority and respect.

Elias and Barnes are used for different sides of the truth. Elias tells Chris, "We're gonna lose this war. We been kicking ass for so long it's time we got our ass kicked." Barnes, who runs his squad on fear, reiterates the old basic training saw that "I am reality. . . . When the machine breaks down, we break down."

Chris is able to dictate his feelings and experiences in narrated letters to his grandmother because he no longer communicates with his father, due to an understandable generational conflict. This paralleled Stone's own paternal conflict.

The unit then proceeds on a series of jungle patrols and ambushes near the Cambodian border in 1967. Chris is the FNG, the fucking new guy. He quickly makes friends with private Gardner, who shows Chris a picture of his girl back home. As soon as the picture is brought out, it becomes a question of time before Gardner takes a mortal wound.

Along the way, the confusing war intensifies with villages being burned, civilians murdered, and bodies mutilated. Dope is used freely by the soldiers. Dopers are referred to as "heads" (potheads), while drinkers are "juicers." Chris is even offered a toke of marijuana smoke through the barrel of an M-16 while the rest of the unit gets high listening to Smokey Robinson and the Miracles singing "Tracks of My Tears." These scenes are what offended many veterans, although most will admit that those instances did exist. Marijuana had become a serious problem in Vietnam in 1967. By 1969, the "problem" was not only marijuana but heroin.

With each patrol, the conflict intensifies. And so do the arguments among the soldiers. Barnes then attempts to solve an ongoing conflict with Elias by waiting for the opportune moment and shooting him with no witnesses, reporting it as a combat death. When Chris discovers that Elias survived, he knows that Barnes was responsible. However, Elias survives only to be killed by the NVA.

After Elias is killed, with arms outstretched (Christlike) in an obvious religious metaphor, Chris takes it upon himself to have a final showdown with Barnes, who represents all the evil that the Vietnam War has brought. In killing Barnes, Chris, in his own way, balances what Vietnam did to brave and well-meaning soldiers like Elias who became unwitting victims.

As Chris is finally airlifted out of the combat zone, he intones the one thing the nation learned from the entire experience: "I think now, looking back, we did not fight the enemy, we fought ourselves—and the enemy was in us. . . . The war is over for me now, but it will always be there—the rest of my days."

Despite the negative feelings this film elicited, it emerged as a blockbuster and attracted television audiences to two Vietnam series: *China Beach* and *Tour of Duty*.

Naturally *Platoon* left American moviegoers with the impression that this was really what it was like to experience combat in Vietnam. Other veterans looked upon it as a microcosm. There were approximately 385,000 American troops in Vietnam at that time. This was just one of their stories.

Oscars were in store as Best Picture, Stone as Best Director, and Claire Simpson for Best Editing.

Berenger and Dafoe were nominated as Best Supporting Actors, with Stone for Best Original Screenplay and Robert Richardson for Best Cinematography.

*Rambo: First Blood Part Two* was released in 1985. The second of the Rambo trilogy found the mythical hero transformed into a comic book hero. Sylvester Stallone, as Rambo, leaves the beleaguered Pacific Northwest town of Hope to do what the military won't, rescue the POWs left behind in Vietnam.

A brave intention indeed. But the evil-plotting CIA gets away with betrayal. Rambo is then captured by the Vietnamese and tortured by a Russian Special Forces officer (Steven Berkoff), who apparently came in from the cold.

Befriended by a pretty Vietnamese woman, Rambo finds the emaciated Americans and brings the boys home.

Directed by George P. Cosmatos, from a script by James Cameron with a Stallone rewrite, the story is a roller coaster with megaexplosions that bring in a body count pushing three figures.

The film, despite likewise ridiculing reviews, did tremendous summer box office. Stallone even added his own touch to jungle guerrilla fashion—the marketing of his headband. This was followed by posters and dolls, which made producers realize the deep pockets of the outrageous wartime cartoon.

One of the riddles of this film was the acceptance by American audiences of a hero with obvious questionable mental stability. Russ Thurman, a technical adviser on *Platoon* and *84 Charlie Mopic* (1989) and a retired decorated Marine Corps captain, wryly observed, "Rambo would have lasted about a half hour in my outfit."[21]

President Reagan even quipped about assigning Rambo to rescue skyjacked hostages, while the Russians took umbrage with their portrayals.

It did the Russians no good to complain. By 1988, Rambo was back, in *Rambo III* resting in a Thai Buddhist monastery, perhaps a recommendation from his psychiatrist after the previous mission.

This time Rambo is called into action when Colonel Trautman (Richard Crenna) is captured by the Russkies in Afghanistan. Rambo literally rides to the rescue, on horseback wearing his signature headband.

Director Peter MacDonald took over when Russell Mulcahy left after several days of production. Stallone received first credit on the script followed by Sheldon Lettich. The stunts and explosions sent the budget into the stratosphere. Closing credits listed forty-four stuntmen.

Early in the 1980s, Stanley Kubrick was alerted to a Vietnam novella titled *The Short-Timers*, written by Gustav Hasford, who served as a Vietnam combat correspondent. It was standard wartime fare, somewhat derivative of *A Walk in the Sun, The Story of G.I. Joe, Battleground,* or *Sands of Iwo Jima.* It was the story of an infantry squad in Vietnam.

True to form, Kubrick took a comparatively unusual or forgotten novel and turned it into an intriguing film. His previous efforts were well documented: *Paths of Glory, Lolita, Dr. Strangelove, A Clockwork Orange, Barry Lyndon,* and *The Shining.* Working with Hasford and Michael Herr (*Dispatches*) on the script, Kubrick shot the film in and around London, which doubled for Hue City during the Tet Offensive. This caused criticism among some veterans who contended that the sets did not match the country.

Numerous delays came about, not uncommon in a Kubrick film. Still, he went ahead to make his Vietnam statement. *Full Metal Jacket* was finally released in 1987.

As in his previous films with war backgrounds, Kubrick met the military mentality head-on. His sledgehammer began to swing right from the get go. The first act dealt with the marine boot camp experience at Parris Island, South Carolina. Gunnery Sergeant Hartman (R. Lee Ermey, a retired marine drill instructor) terrorizes and emasculates the cross section of recruits using every Marine Corps expression and bandied cliché, right down to the "jody calls" (the limerick-type chants sung while the platoon is jogging).

Hartman explains to his new charges, "If you ladies leave my island, if you survive recruit training, you will be weapons. You will be ministers of death, praying for war." Hartman then adds, "God was here before the Marine Corps.

Now you can give your heart to Jesus . . . but your ass belongs to the corps!" He also explains that they have completed a life passage; high school is in the past. "Your days of finger-banging old Mary Jane Rottencrotch through her pretty pink panties are over. . . . I'm going to rip your balls off so you cannot contaminate the rest of the world!"

Everybody gets a nickname: Matthew Modine is "Joker," Arliss Howard is "Cowboy," Adam Baldwin is "Animal Mother," Kevyn Major Howard is "Rafterman," Dorian Harewood is "Eightball."

During the rifle qualification sequence, Hartman refers to the accuracy of Marine Corps marksmanship. His examples are two Texas killers, Charles Whitman (the 1966 Texas tower shootings) and Lee Harvey Oswald, both of whom learned how to set their deadly rifle sights from Marine Corps instruction.

Hartman proceeds to brutalize a bumbling recruit, Pyle (Vincent D'Onofrio), whom he nicknames "Gomer," after the TV sit-com character on *Gomer Pyle, U.S.M.C.* But Kubrick goes a step further. Gomer takes the insults, even a "blanket party" from the rest of the recruit platoon, but he is then transformed into a Parris Island psycho, looking much like John Hinkley. He finally shoots his main tormentor, Hartman with an M-14 rifle, firing a (7.62 millimeter round) full metal jacket. Gomer then turns the rifle on himself, barrel into the mouth.

When the Vietnam sequence begins, Joker finds himself as a journalist with Rafterman on the Danang staff of *Pacific Stars & Stripes*. Both are sent north to Hue City to cover the 1968 Tet Offensive. On the way up, Rafterman is forced to watch a door gunner on the helicopter shoot innocent villagers, a legal way in which to commit murder. Rafterman becomes physically sick but is incapable of stopping the psychotic door gunner.

At Hue City, the marines are reunited as Joker meets Cowboy, Animal Mother, and Eightball. The Hue City massacre is depicted as a mass grave is uncovered, civilians bound and gagged, thrown into a trench and covered with lye. Here, Kubrick goes along with accepted facts, that the North Vietnamese and Viet Cong did carry out a mass execution at Hue City. Also, it is here where Joker is confronted by a colonel for wearing a peace symbol.

They move into Hue and come into the sights of a sniper. As they attempt to flush out the sniper the marines pay heavily in casualties. They finally realize the true consequences of war when they discover that their enemy is a young North Vietnamese woman who turned out to be a better marksman than all of them combined.

Kubrick's established signature was repeated with the ending. In the novella, nobody is left standing at the end. In the film, Kubrick has the survivors walking off into the sunset singing the theme from *The Mickey Mouse Club*, what these young men grew up on. After all, war is fought at the ground level by kids.

Kubrick basically held forth with his defined classical pattern of looking at war, the corruption, the destruction, and the tragic loss of lives. The war itself provides the milieu with a looming tragic confrontation intertwined with the actors showing their character traits from all over the war spectrum. With *Dr.*

*Strangelove*, he ended with Vera Lynn singing the World War II 8th Army Air Force standard, "We'll Meet Again."

Kubrick, Herr, and Hasford received Academy Award nominations for Best Adapted Screenplay.

The year 1987 also brought out the second of four important Vietnam War films, *Hamburger Hill*. Based on the actual battle for Ap Bia Mountain from May 11 to May 20 in 1969, the objective was to break the enemy's grip in the A Shau Valley, west of Hue. The thinking was that whoever occupied the highest peak controlled the valley. It was classic in nature: the assault of a significant hill. It had elements of Marye's Heights at Fredericksburg, Cemetery Ridge at Gettysburg, San Juan Heights in Cuba, Verdun in World War I, Iwo Jima in World War II, and Heartbreak Ridge in Korea. For ten gruelling days, the soldiers of the 101st Airborne and marines of the 9th Regiment made repeated charges against an array of sniper nests, booby traps, and bunkers. Finally, the Americans got to the top, only to later abandon the hill. This prompted the press and the American public to ask, "What was that all about?" Because of the controversy, it was only a question of time before the battle became a film.

The script, directed by John Irvin, was written by Jim Carabatsos, a Vietnam veteran. The cast included Dylan McDermott, Don Cheadle, Steven Weber, Timothy Quill, Courtney Vance, Anthony Barrile, and Tegan West. These were the young, untried soldiers of the 101st Airborne who were about to go into combat for the first time. The "angle" on this film was the intense fire that these men were repeatedly placed under. And it became more intense with each foray up the mountain. Air strikes and artillery fire missions had little effect at first. Again, American forces realized how determined—and entrenched—their enemy was. The film portrayed closeups of the brutal fighting. Each time the order came down for another charge, the doom was evident on the men's faces. But as soldiers, they obeyed their orders.

The charges went forward, and the battle persisted for those days in May. The accounts were summarized at the daily press briefings in Saigon, notoriously dubbed "the Five O'Clock Follies." Because of the summaries given at these briefings, the battle wasn't initially given much space. And then, in the tradition of Ernie Pyle, Associated Press correspondent Jay Sharbutt managed to get to the scene and write a firsthand report.

According to Samuel Zaffiri's book *Hamburger Hill*, Sharbutt wrote the suggested headline "U.S. Assault on Mountain Continues, Despite Heavy Toll."

The paratroopers came down from the mountain, their green shirts darkened with sweat, their weapons gone, their bandages stained brown and red—with mud and blood.

Many cursed Lt. Col. Weldon Honeycutt, who sent three companies Sunday to take this 3,000-foot mountain just a mile east of Laos and overlooking the shell pocked A Shau Valley.

They failed and they suffered. "That damned Blackjack won't stop until he kills every one of us," said one of the 40 to 50 101st Airborne troopers who was wounded.[22]

Newspapers across the country picked up the story. In the early afternoon of May 20, in the well of the U.S. Senate, Edward Kennedy (D–Massachusetts), recognized as a presidential candidate, denounced the attack on Ap Bia as "senseless." Kennedy added that the attack was "symptomatic of a mentality and a policy that requires immediate attention. American boys are too valuable to be sacrificed for a false sense of military pride."[23] His remarks that day ignited a firestorm.

The Nixon White House was enraged. Quickly, Senator Hugh Scott (R–Pennsylvania ) rebutted Kennedy and supported General Creighton Abrams and the army. In Saigon, Abrams held a press conference and stated, "We are not fighting for terrain as such. We are going after the enemy."

In Phu Bai, the following day Major General Melvin Zais, commander of the 101st Airborne, added, "The hill was in my area of operations. That's where the enemy was, and that's where I attacked him. If I find the enemy on any other hills, in the A Shau, I assure you I'll attack him there also."

Senators Margaret Chase Smith and John Tower (Republicans, respectively, from Maine and Texas) supported the White House and denounced Kennedy.

In Vietnam, reinforcements helped secure Ap Bia Mountain. Bulldozers were brought in, and a road was opened. A defensive perimeter was established. But the expected NVA attack never came. The hill was abandoned on June 5, opening another chapter.

The NVA reoccupied the hill with 1,000 troops. However, the army and the new commander of the 101st Airborne, Major General John Wright, explained that there were no present plans for another assault on Ap Bia. Senator Stephen Young (D–Ohio) then went after the army in a blistering attack, criticizing both Zais and Wright.

The controversy continued. On June 27, *Life* magazine printed the photos of the 241 men killed in Vietnam that week, including 5 who died in the battle for Hamburger Hill. The cover headline was: "The Faces of the Dead in Vietnam—One Week's Toll." The piece was prefaced with a one-page introduction, a quote from a 101st Airborne soldier who was writing his parents during a lull. "You may not be able to read this. I am writing in a hurry. I see death coming up the hill."

Total casualties at Hamburger Hill came to 476, including 56 killed. The political realities quickly set in. General Abrams was ordered to avoid any further large-scale assaults. A new strategy came from Washington: "protective reaction," to fight only when threatened by the enemy. President Nixon then began his gradual withdrawal of combat troops from Vietnam. And still the question lingered, "What was that all about?"

The third important Vietnam War film in 1987 was *The Hanoi Hilton*, directed by Lionel Chetwynd, starring Michael Moriarty, Jeffrey Jones, Paul Le Mat, Lawrence Pressman, and David Soul. This was the nickname given to the Hao Lo prison where American POWs, mostly airmen, were incarcerated. This prison was one of the stops on Jane Fonda's controversial 1972 propaganda tour.

Many died while in captivity. But still others survived the brutal torture by the North Vietnamese. Seventeen former POWs served as technical advisers on the film.

The Vietnamese prison commandant explains, "The real war is in Berkeley, California, the Washington D.C. mall; in the cities of America; and what we do not win on the battlefield, your journalists will win for us on your very own doorstep."

In classic historic irony, on February 26, 1999, the 270-room Hilton Hanoi Opera hotel opened its doors, designed in classic French colonial style. An executive stated that there was no plan to associate the hotel with the wartime past.

The section of the Hoa Lo prison where the Americans were kept has since been torn down.

To further illustrate how all important things come around, President Clinton's appointed ambassador to Vietnam, Pete Peterson, a former air force pilot, was a prisoner in the Hanoi Hilton.

Comedian Robin Williams's frenetic talents were the 1987 centerpiece of *Good Morning, Vietnam*, loosely based on the 1965 tour of air force disk jockey Adrian Cronauer. Cronauer took over the early morning AFVN (Armed Forces Vietnam) show with the high-volume greeting to all servicemen, "Good morning, Vietnam!"

This was an ad-libbed showcase for the outrageous Williams who showed no mercy for the military establishment, politics, gays, and the war.

"How hot is it?"

"It's so hot, I can cook things in my shorts!"

"Flash! Former Vice President Nixon is now in country." A pause. "That's right, the big Dick is here!"

Cronauer also had a gay jungle fashion consultant, Mr. Leo, to remind all troops to wear pearls, with black pajamas, on their night patrols, and not the day patrols.

J.T. Walsh gave an angry, frustrated performance as Cronauer's immediate superior, a career master sergeant who takes exception to the new brand of outrageous GI humor. The sergeant then upbraids Cronauer, who ad-libs, sotto voce, "He reminds me a little of Donna Reed, around the eyes."

Bruno Kirby portrayed a sappy, not too bright, lieutenant who thinks that the troops would be better off listening to Montevani's 100 strings rather than the "Rolling Stones."

Forest Whitaker came in as Cronauer's sidekick, laughing all the way.

The only sympathetic officer is Noble Willingham, who sees potential in Cronauer for morale purposes.

In true character at times, Williams departed from Mitch Markowitz's script, being directed by Barry Levinson. In turn Williams got a Best Actor nomination.

Lincoln Kirstein's book *Lay This Laurel* and the letters of Robert Gould Shaw were the basis for the Kevin Jarre screenplay of *Glory* (1989), the story of the

54th Massachusetts Regiment, the first black unit recruited to fight in the Civil War. Directed by Edward Zwick, the film recounts the attitude in the Union army that black men shouldn't, and couldn't, participate in combat. Matthew Broderick portrayed Shaw, an inexperienced officer who commands the regiment. The unit is finally called upon in 1864 to assault the heavily fortified Fort Wagner, South Carolina. The black soldiers of the 54th Regiment displayed extraordinary bravery in a futile attempt to capture the fort.

Supporting Broderick were Denzel Washington, as a fiercely independent black soldier who is disciplined by being flogged, and Morgan Freeman as the sergeant who guides the men through training. Washington won a Best Supporting Actor Oscar along with Freddie Francis for Best Cinematography. Steven Rosenblum was nominated for Best Editing.

The year 1989 brought three more important Vietnam combat films to American audiences: *84 Charlie Mopic, Born on the Fourth of July*, and *Casualties of War*. The first dealt with the daily reality of the war while the latter two centered around the effects of the war, both in the field and at home.

*84 Charlie Mopic* was written and directed by Patrick Duncan, who served with the 173rd Airborne Brigade. It was totally designed to show a motion picture unit's portrayal of one patrol as seen through the eyes of the camera's lens.

The radio call signs, jargon, and air and artillery support are completely accurate. Duncan, along with technical adviser Russ Thurman, gave the audience a realistic experience of what a jungle patrol was like.

The patrol was actually the protagonist, with each of the unknown actors doing their bit. The cast included Jonathan Emerson, Nicholas Cascone, Jason Tomlins, Christopher Burgard, and Glenn Morshower.

Ron Kovic's Vietnam memoir *Born on the Fourth of July* was published in 1976. It had several false starts as a film and wouldn't be produced and released until 1989. Kovic, who came from a working-class Long Island family, joined the Marine Corps for patriotic and idealistic reasons. His favorite Marine Corps film, at the time, was *Sands of Iwo Jima*.

Being schooled on the flag-waving element of war, Kovic hoped to return as a decorated war hero. He achieved half of that. Kovic did return decorated, a Bronze Star and a Purple Heart for the wound that made him a paraplegic. He did not return as a war hero but as a war protestor. And he personified a difficult problem for the older generation—a decorated combat veteran who had turned to the antiwar faction, not as a member but as one of its leaders.

Kovic returned from the war much like Ken Wilocek, the Marlon Brando paraplegic character in *The Men*. In that 1950 film the conflict was about readjustment to life in a wheelchair. Kovic's readjustment, after his combat experience, went to another level, using his antiwar stance to the point of leading a demonstration at the Republican National Convention in 1972 where he was mocked and vilified for protesting Richard Nixon's policy.

In 1976, he addressed the Democratic National Convention, with the theme, "I am your Yankee Doodle Dandy come home."

The time Kovic spent in the Bronx VA hospital soured him on the treatment of veterans in the spinal wards. He then descended into alcohol and went to the antiwar movement. In several demonstrations he was thrown from his wheelchair and repeatedly kicked.

Director Oliver Stone wrote the Oscar-nominated screenplay adaptation with Kovic. Tom Cruise, also in an Oscar-nominated performance, portrayed Kovic. Cruise was supported by Willem Dafoe, Raymond J. Barry, and Caroline Kava. Stone won an Oscar for Best Director, while David Brenner won for Best Editing.

After the film was released Stone and Kovic admitted that they had taken "poetic license" with some of the actual incidents.

*Casualties of War* was a book by Daniel Lang about a true incident in Vietnam, the kidnap and rape of a Vietnamese village girl. David Rabe adapted the screenplay for director Brian De Palma.

Sean Penn played the squad leader who allows the kidnap of the village girl, portrayed by Thuy Thu Le. Michael J. Fox is the lone objector to what these soldiers are doing. He makes a moral stand that ultimately leads to a court-martial.

*Casualties of War* became just that, a metaphor for everything wrong that came out of the war, the kidnap and rape of another culture.

Rounding out the cast were Don Harvey, John C. Reilly, John Leguizamo, and Erik King.

## JUNGLE AFTERTHOUGHTS

In her book *Long Time Passing*, Myra MacPherson observed, "Vietnam was a war that asked everything of a few and nothing of most in America."[24]

"Coming Home" veterans saw the backside of America for at least a decade after the fall of Saigon. Upon their return friends and family members didn't want to hear about what they did or look at the combat medals they were awarded. Veterans routinely brought a civilian change of clothes upon flying to their hometowns. At the airport they would do a quick change, less they be spat upon and called baby killers by certain protestors who had no idea what the veterans had endured. These men and women paid the price that their leaders asked of them. It was a price that no other generation was asked to pay in terms of leadership.

Award-winning historian Barbara Tuchman wrote in *The March of Folly: From Troy to Vietnam*:

American refusal to take the enemy's grim will and capacity into account has been explained by those responsible on the ground of ignorance of Vietnam's history, traditions and national character: there were "no experts available," in the words of one high ranking official. But the longevity of Vietnamese resistance to foreign rule could have been learned from any history book on Indochina. . . . Not ignorance, but refusal to credit the evidence, and more fundamentally, refusal to grant stature and fixed purpose to a "fourth rate" Asiatic country were the determining factors, much as in the case of the British attitude toward the American colonies. The irony of history is inexorable.[25]

Slowly over the years, the Vietnam veterans saw themselves getting recognition that for so long had been denied. Sadly, the price is still being paid in upset lives, divorces, and tragic suicides. Many never adjusted, and many never will.

An ironic twist occurred long after the fall of Saigon. Veterans and the war protestors came together. It was a time when many Vietnam veterans who went back to college either hung out in their own groups or were "closet vets," simply assuming the role of student and not talking about it.

As pointed out in a *Los Angeles Times* op-ed piece in 1981:

Ironically, some members of the 1960's "peace movement" have shown more sympathy, understanding, and support for Vietnam veterans than the gung-ho politicians and generals who signed and supported the Gulf of Tonkin Resolution. How many of the politicians' sons and nephews received special draft board consideration during the years when we were in 'Nam and the "peace people" were being clubbed by police in Chicago? Oh, the bloody hypocrisy of self proclaimed patriots.[26]

For some, it became chic to be a Vietnam veteran. Many went on to hold public office and become successful business executives, journalists, authors, and law enforcement officers.

When the Desert Storm soldiers and marines marched in a victory parade through Hollywood, with retired General William Westmoreland as an honored guest, the largest applause was for the Vietnam veterans. Many of them, with thickened waists and graying hair wearing combat medals, bush hats, and faded fatigues, happily waved to the crowd that lined the streets. The same type of parade was held in other large cities. These men had finally "come home."

Despite statistics that suggest otherwise, Vietnam was always seen as a working-class war, cutting a tragic swath through the factories and mill towns such as the one depicted in *The Deer Hunter*. But Vietnam was also a war that was easy to avoid if one did it from the correct position, deferments, and loopholes. In the power circles, there was always the late-night phone call from a connected father to a politician. In a short period a deferment would be granted for one of many reasons. And often the father was a supporter of Lyndon Johnson, Richard Nixon—or both.

In her 1972 Pulitzer Prize–winning book *Fire in the Lake: The Vietnamese and the Americans in Vietnam*, Frances FitzGerald observed, "It was a white man's war being fought by blacks, a rich man's war being fought by the poor, an old man's war being fought by the young."[27]

As in any war, there was unfairness. It was observed long ago that those who never saw war close up have no problem sending others into it.

The Civil War gave new meaning to the word "substitute." World Wars I and II spawned the epithet "draft dodger." Vietnam took that to another level with "draft evader."

One of the aftereffects of the Vietnam War came into stark contrast with past wars, particularly World War II. In that war many war veterans achieved high office, even the White House, from Dwight Eisenhower through Gerald Ford.

But now many political leaders of the Vietnam generation who came to power in the early 1990s neither served in combat nor wore a uniform. And the syndrome clearly cut across the political spectrum.

But history, being the teacher that it is, can tell us that somewhere down the line, we will need brave men and women again. And, like the Minutemen, they will be there, younger, smarter, stronger, and better educated. And they will go, willing to die on some field with a strange-sounding name.

# 9

# The Gulf War and Beyond

It's quite a view.
—Captain John Miller at Normandy, *Saving Private Ryan*

With the fall of Saigon a new syndrome emerged in the war film genre: the individual caught up in the situation rather than the situation dictating. Vietnam was now in the past. A new generation was set to fight a new war. And the commanders in the new war would be the junior and field-grade officers who had learned their hard lessons in the previous war.

The Vietnam war protestors, like the two flag officers on the USS *Missouri* at the Japanese surrender, could ask, "What do we do now?"

Different issues caused a shift on the social and political forefront from Southeast Asia to the Middle East. On November 4, 1979, approximately 500 Iranian students stormed the U.S. embassy in Teheran and captured sixty-six Americans. After numerous setbacks in negotiations, while in the midst of campaigning for reelection, President Jimmy Carter ordered a rescue attempt. The mission was aborted when eight Americans were killed as a helicopter collided with a transport plane in the desert. Then Secretary of State Cyrus Vance resigned. The captors refused to release the hostages. In November 1980, Ronald Reagan was elected president in a landslide victory. On the day of Reagan's inauguration, the hostages were released after being in captivity for 444 days. Their subsequent treatment as heroes, complete with a ticker-tape parade, outraged many Vietnam War veterans, some of whom did two and three combat tours with no similar treatment.

The Middle East continued to be hot. In the 1980s, Saddam Hussein engaged in a bloody war with Iran over efforts to cut oil production to raise the price of oil. This war was futile and frustrating for Iraq. In the end, it resulted in Iraq plunging into massive debt. Saddam Hussein felt that the Arab community was conspiring against him. Two factors resulted from this war: Saddam had a standing army of 1 million men; and they were equipped with modern weapons.

The time was right, Saddam felt. On August 2, 1990, Iraq sent an invasion force of seven divisions (120,000 troops) supported by 2,000 tanks, into oil-rich Kuwait. He then declared that Kuwait was Iraq's new province. Saddam was banking on defending his move successfully against his neighbors. If the move worked, Saddam would be controlling 40 percent of the world's oil reserves. The next day, Iraqi troops massed along the Iraqi-Saudi Arabian border. The United Nations condemned the invasion.

The United States reacted instantly, sending a reaction force to the area. President George H.W. Bush began to build diplomatic support as allied forces joined in as the face-off continued.

Eventually, thirty nations joined the military coalition against Iraq, with an additional eighteen countries giving other forms of assistance. This preparation phase—referred to as Operation Desert Shield—continued with a U.S.-led blockade and UN sanctions against Iraq. Operation Desert Shield became the largest U.S. military deployment since Vietnam. Aircraft carriers in the Gulf of Oman and the Red Sea were called on. U.S. Air Force interceptors came in from American bases. Air transports brought in army airborne troops. A marine expeditionary brigade was rushed from Diego Garcia in the Indian Ocean to the gulf.

After a two-day debate, the U.S. Senate and House of Representatives authorized President Bush to use military force to expel Iraq from Kuwait.

The Iraqi forces refused their deadline of January 15, 1991, to pull out of Kuwait. On January 17, 1991, Desert Shield became Desert Storm. And once again, the world watched a war unfold on television. But this time it was both network and cable television. And the media did not have the freedom it enjoyed during Vietnam. Because of the vastness of the desert terrain combat correspondents were more restricted, often getting much of their information from briefings.

First came the air campaign, an intensive thirty-eight-day precise operation that destroyed or damaged every Iraqi military target, including Saddam's supply lines. On February 23, the ground war phase (Desert Saber) commenced. It was as close to a textbook operation as a war could get. Iraqi troops began to surrender in droves. Within 100 hours, the occupying Iraqi army was brought to its knees. On February 27 President Bush suspended military operations in the gulf. As wars go, the cost was cheap on the American side: 148 killed (including 11 women) with an additional 458 wounded. In addition, countless other veterans were to later learn of a new malady: Gulf War Syndrome.

Whether the Gulf War could have been averted by more adroit diplomacy is still being debated, along with the issue that in the end, Saddam Hussein was still standing. Even though Saddam's forces were defeated in the field, it was not a complete victory. Ending the ground war after a hundred hours permitted portions of Saddam's Republican Guard to escape with their weapons. Even though President Bush and Secretary of Defense Dick Cheney repeatedly emphasized the lessons learned in Vietnam, the military community was less than pleased that the enemy was allowed to escape with some forces intact. By December 1991, 80 percent of Americans believed that the United States had failed to finish the job. It is one of history's current ironies that one year later the Bush administration was voted out of office. And today Saddam continues to rule his country.[1]

The Gulf War did carry with it a redemption from the Vietnam experience. The two military commanders, Army Chief of Staff General Colin L. Powell and field commander General H. Norman Schwarzkopf, were both decorated Vietnam veterans.

## BEFORE IT IS GONE

War films from past wars continued to make contemporary statements. Kevin Costner and producer Jim Wilson knew if their project *Dances with Wolves* (1990) was to become a major film, it would need a strong base, in this case a novel. Costner, set up as director and lead actor, felt that if writer Michael Blake went to screenplay, it would end in the usual studio "slush pile." Thus, Blake's novel came first. Costner then secured financing, partly through Orion Pictures, and the project came together for preproduction.

Costner played Union army Lieutenant John Dunbar who barely escapes death at St. David's Field in Tennessee in the middle of the Civil War. His exposure, on horseback, straddling the Union and Confederate lines is thought to be a suicide by a federal general officer. Eventually, it is looked upon as bravery, headlining a Union victory.

Dunbar is then rewarded by choosing a post, a remote abandoned soldier's fort in the middle of the Sioux and Pawnee nations. Dunbar explains to a suicidal Union major (Maury Chaykin) that he wants to see the frontier before it is gone.

The Sioux are naturally suspect at the intentions of the interloper. But eventually they come to see him more as a friend than an enemy after he rescues a white woman, Stands with a Fist (Mary McDonnell), who was raised as a Sioux squaw. Suicide is again the theme as Stands with a Fist is mourning the death of her warrior husband and slashes herself with a knife.

Dunbar then finds himself torn between two cultures. Chief Ten Bears (Floyd Red Crow Westerman) is sadly aware that their civilization will soon be gone with the white man's western advance. The younger braves Kicking Bear (Graham Greene) and Wind in His Hair (Rodney A. Grant) do not accept this and vow to fight. Ten Bears explains to Dunbar, "Our country is all that we have. And we will fight to keep it."

Dunbar assimilates into the Sioux culture, marrying Stand with a Fist. He becomes the de facto "Special Forces Adviser" to the tribe.

The most spectacular sequence in the film is the buffalo hunt, a now-extinct plains ritual. The braves, demonstrating excellent horsemanship and bow shooting, bring in many trophies. Included in this ritual is the eating of a buffalo's heart. Dunbar, the only horseman in the hunt who uses a rifle, saves a young brave's life.

But the Union cavalry advances, commanded by a major who resembles John Chivington, the leader of the infamous 1864 Sand Creek massacre where U.S. soldiers slaughtered and mutilated approximately 500 Cheyenne Indians, near Fort Lyon, Colorado. Chivington, who harbored political ambitions, was investigated and later court-martialed.

Dunbar is captured by the cavalry and held prisoner. The federals are shocked that Dunbar went native. While being transported in a Union column, the soldiers are ambushed by a war party, allowing Dunbar to escape.

However, the western advance continues, as predicted. Dunbar realizes that he can no longer remain with the people he has adopted as his own. He and Stands with a Fist strike out on their own. An epilogue states that the Lakota Sioux, after thirteen years, finally surrendered to reservation life at Fort Robinson, Nebraska.

The film received seven Oscars for 1990: Best Picture, Best Director, Best Cinematography, Best Adapted Screenplay, Best Original Score, Best Sound, and Best Film Editing. As actors, Costner, McDonnell, and Greene were all nominated.

Despite the awards and nominations, *Dances with Wolves* came in for some tough reviews, citing stereotypical characters and Hollywood-type Indians. Writing in *The New Yorker* on December 17, 1990, critic Pauline Kael stated, "Costner has feathers in his hair and feathers in his head."

In 1991 CBS broadcast *Mission of the Shark*, the story of the tragic USS *Indianapolis* saga. This story would be a black mark that would follow the navy into the next century.

It began on July 16, 1945, the same day as the successful atom bomb test at Los Alamos, New Mexico. The *Indianapolis*, a cruiser with a crew of 1,196 men, departed San Francisco. On board was a classified top secret cargo in the form of a wooden box. Inside the box was uranium 235, needed for the two atom bombs. The box was off-loaded at Tinian. From Tinian the *Indianapolis* was to proceed through the Philippine Sea to Leyte in the Philippine Islands. The skipper of the *Indianapolis*, Captain Charles Butler McVay III, requested a destroyer escort for detection of Japanese submarines. The *Indianapolis* was not fitted with sonar, to detect submarines. His request was rejected. McVay's superiors contended that the submarine threat was almost nonexistent. He was told to zigzag at his own discretion, depending on visibility and the weather.

Late on the night of July 29 the ship entered an area of cloud cover. Before leaving the bridge to retire, Captain McVay left orders to resume zigzagging if the conditions changed. Around midnight the cloud cover lifted, revealing some moonlight.

The Japanese submarine *I-58* surfaced and quickly spotted the cruiser in the moonlight. In a matter of minutes, six torpedoes were fired at the *Indianapolis*. At least two hit the target. One blew off the bow, while another struck at the magazine and fuel tanks. The ship sank in twelve minutes.

It is estimated that 300 crewmen went down with the ship. Approximately 900 more, many of them jostled out of their bunks in underwear, quickly grabbed kapok life jackets and went into the oil-covered water. Several rubber rafts were also in the water.

McVay and his crew naturally assumed that they would be rescued shortly since three SOS messages were sent out before the ship went under. But no rescue came.

The first day passed, as did the second. And then a third. The kapok life jackets were designed for forty-eight hours afloat. The sailors now had to keep their chins high to continue breathing. With the sun beating down and being surrounded by oil and water the men suffered ulcers on their faces.

And then came the worst. Shark fins were sighted. The sharks then circled and attacked.

By the fourth day rescue seemed hopeless. What the crewmen didn't know was that local navy headquarters did not even know of their situation. It was the fortunate stroke of a navy patrol plane pilot, on a routine pass, who saw an oil slick and heads bobbing in the water.

Ed Brown, a native of Sioux Falls, South Dakota, and a survivor of the sinking, recalled his experience in an interview. Brown reported aboard in March 1944 as a seaman first class. He was assigned as a deckhand in the 4th Division.

"I went on watch at midnight that night. Twelve minutes into my watch we got hit. I didn't even get a chance to put my shoes on," said Brown.

Brown's watch station was a gun mount on the port side. He recalled that when the first torpedo hit the starboard bow, the *Indianapolis* was cruising at seventeen knots. Within a minute he was in the water.

"The ship rolled starboard, tilted up in the air, and went straight down," explained Brown.

To survive, the crew of the *Indianapolis* formed circles in the oil-soaked water. Brown said that initially there were 366 men in his circle.

And then the sharks appeared.

"There were fins around us all the time," said Brown. "One shark, about eight to ten feet long, swam beneath my legs."

"It was like the covered wagons and the Indians," he added. "They were around us all the time."

The crew was in the water from midnight Sunday to Thursday afternoon. Exposure, shark attack, and starvation all took their toll. Some men just gave up and drifted off. Those who drank the salt water got violently ill.

According to Brown, when they were rescued there were sixty-six left in his group. A total of 321 of the crew were picked up. Many died of pneumonia thereafter.

Brown added that while they were in the hospital, through radio news reports, they realized what the mission of the *Indianapolis* was after the dropping of the two atomic bombs.

After the rescue and initial reports Captain McVay was informed that he was being charged with "hazarding" his vessel during a time of war. The navy announced the sinking of the *Indianapolis* on the same day Japan surrendered. So it was eclipsed in the news. A court-martial was convened. After testimony was heard, including that of the Japanese submarine commander, McVay was found guilty.

It would be decades before it was uncovered that the navy knew all along how dangerous the Philippine Sea was at that time. McVay was never warned.[2]

In 1958 Richard F. Newcomb, a World War II navy man, published *Abandon Ship!* Newcomb's book set off a controversy that continues to this day. There was evidence of a massive cover-up and a complete miscarriage of military justice.

Two years later the crew of the *Indianapolis* held a reunion on the fifteenth anniversary of the sinking. McVay, reluctantly, attended with his wife. During the interim years McVay received some vicious hate mail from family members of those who died.

At the 1960 reunion McVay received salutes from those who came through that ordeal with him. Sadly, in 1968, after reading another piece of hate mail, he took his own life with a pistol.

In the TV movie Stacy Keach portrayed McVay, an Annapolis graduate and son of a four-star admiral. Richard Thomas was the ship's physician, while David Caruso played a captain in the marine detachment. Others in the cast were Bob Gunton, Steve Landesberg, and Cary-Hiroyuki Tagawa as the Japanese commander. Carrie Snodgress played Louise McVay.

Robert Iscove directed from a script by Alan Sharp.

## A RIDGE CALLED CEMETERY

Michael Shaara's 1975 Pulitzer Prize–winning historical novel *The Killer Angels* was originally intended as a Turner Network miniseries. But once producer Ted Turner realized that the Civil War epic, the story of Gettysburg from the Confederate point of view, had theatrical potential, it was scheduled for release in the fall of 1993.

Retitled *Gettysburg* (1993), the film was adapted and directed by Ronald Maxwell and filmed at the actual location with modern-day Civil War reenactors as extras. Like *The Longest Day*, the story went back and forth with the main historical characters: Robert E. Lee (Martin Sheen), James "Pete" Longstreet (Tom Berenger), Lewis "Lo" Armistead (Richard Jordan), George Pickett (Stephen Lang), General John Buford (Sam Elliott), and Joshua Lawrence Chamberlain (Jeff Daniels).

*Gettysburg* showed the setup, coincidences, accidents, and tragedies of the July 1–4, 1863, tide-turning battle. Many of the senior commanders on both sides were classmates at West Point, subsequently serving together in the Mexican War and later in California. Their wives became best friends. And now, during this decisive encounter, they found themselves on the opposite sides of Cemetery Ridge.

The battle itself began by accident. After invading the North, Lee was intending for a showdown at Harrisburg. With a quick and decisive strike, he hoped to end the war and negotiate a peace settlement. Only days before President Lincoln had appointed General George Gordon Meade as the new Union commander. Meade, an able field commander with a fierce temper, was aware of the advance by the Army of Northern Virginia and intended to make a stand near Pipe Creek.

Many Confederate infantrymen in the North Carolina brigade marched barefoot into Pennsylvania that summer. By coincidence, a June 30 newspaper advertisement in the *Gettysburg Compiler* proclaimed a sale on men's shoes and boots. The brigade was ordered to advance on Gettysburg and seize the shoes. When it was determined that Confederate forces were in the area, Union forces reacted quickly. One of the first Union elements to come upon the scene was General John Buford's cavalry. Also included in this advance was the occupation of the high ground on Cemetery Ridge under the II Corps command of General Winfield Scott Hancock. Many historians have observed that this is where the Confederate forces lost—before the battle was joined—that the Union artillery was the first to seize the high ground. This was the first of three elements that contributed to the Federal victory.

The reputation of General John Fulton Reynolds was well known in the Union ranks. Many felt that it was just a question of time before Reynolds became the Union commander. But it was not to be. After arriving in the field early on July 1, at the head of the 2nd Wisconsin, he was fatally shot off his horse by a Confederate sharpshooter.

Second in his class at West Point, Robert E. Lee had a reputation for rapidly analyzing a situation and making decisive, bold moves that often took away an enemy's advantage. Observing the entrenched Union force on the far ridge, he ordered attacks on the flanks. Lieutenant Colonel Joshua Lawrence Chamberlain's Union regiment, the 20th Maine, was quickly tied into the left side, occupying a rocky knoll known as Little Round Top. The 20th Maine numbered approximately 386 Union infantrymen.

Chamberlain, a rhetoric professor at Maine's Bowdoin College, had no formal military training. Initially, he was commissioned when the 20th Maine was formed and quickly studied military campaigns and biographies. At Gettysburg he was informed that his unit was the end of the line and had to stand fast at all costs. His understrength regiment set in and formed its skirmish lines. That afternoon, the 20th Maine steadfastly repulsed several bloody uphill frontal assaults by the 15th Alabama.

Chamberlain later explained that some soldiers in his regiment were driven back to the summit of the hill. They then reformed and charged, forcing the Confederates back down the hill. "The edge of the fight rolled backward and forward like a wave. . . . The edge of the conflict swayed to and fro with wild whirlpools and eddies," recalled Chamberlain in Mark Nesbitt's book *Through Blood & Fire: Selected Civil War Papers of Major General Joshua Chamberlain.*[3]

On the final Confederate assault, with the Union soldiers almost out of ammunition, Chamberlain ordered a bayonet charge downhill, thereby preventing his position from being overrun. This bayonet charge was a major factor in the battle that was to become the largest military engagement in the Western Hemisphere.

Little Round Top was the second element that led to the Union victory, a courageous and decisive charge that greatly contributed to the tide-turning battle. The other flank of Cemetery Ridge likewise held its ground, but not under the same series of repeated assaults. The 20th Maine not only held its line but took approximately 400 Confederate prisoners.

Nesbitt added, quoting Chamberlain, "When that mad carnival lulled from some strange instinct in human nature and without any reason in the situation that can be seen—when the battle edges drew asunder, there stood our little line, groups and gaps, notched like saw-teeth, but sharp as steel, tempered in infernal heats."

It would be thirty years before Chamberlain would be awarded the Congressional Medal of Honor for his action and leadership that afternoon on Little Round Top.

That night, July 2, Lee planned a different strategy, what was to become the biggest mistake of his career, a decision that would not only cause a clear Confederate loss but send the Southern cause down a path to ultimate defeat. First, he needed a fresh unit. General George Pickett's Virginia division had arrived late. Lee called on Pickett's division to anchor the assault on the center of the Union line, "where they are the weakest." Reinforcing Pickett's division would be the divisions of Generals Pender and Heth.

Longstreet demurred, feeling that continued attacks on the flanks would cause a rippling effect, and the Union line on Cemetery Ridge would eventually crack and be forced to retreat. To attack the center, Longstreet contended, would be "Fredericksburg in reverse." (At Fredericksburg, December 1862, Lee's forces held the high ground, resulting in a decisive victory over Union General Ambrose Burnside.) But here, Longstreet was overruled. Napoleonic tactics were still being employed with success during this era. Lee truly felt that a wide, coordinated frontal infantry assault at the center would crack the Union line, leading to Confederate victory, ending the war, and establishing the South as a separate nation.

At 1 P.M. the following afternoon, Pickett's division formed the center of the charge in the cover of a tree line facing Cemetery Ridge. The other divisions tied in with them. It was a day of stifling heat, almost ninety degrees.

Lee ordered an intense artillery barrage on the Union lines that could be heard miles away. It continued for more than two hours. Pickett, recognized for certain theatrics in the field, gave his men an inspirational and romantic "second-half locker room speech," emphasizing their role in the Southern cause and the glory of being in the Virginia division. He added that they were chosen to be the center of a great historical event. On this, George Edward Pickett was correct.

Riding up and back in front of the tree line, Pickett raised his saber and rallied his men. "Up men, up! And let no man forget today that you are from old Virginia!"

Accounts vary as to exactly how many Confederate soldiers participated in the charge. The numbers range from 10,500 to 15,000.

The Confederate artillery barrage lifted, and the divisions, with Pickett's in the center, began its on-line advance across a one-mile open wheat field that led to the slope going up to Cemetery Ridge. On the far ridge, Hancock's II Corps had eighty Napoleon cannons and 9,000 troops facing the Confederate divisions. As the Confederate line advanced, Hancock ordered an artillery barrage of solid ball. At a closer point, the Union artillery rounds would be switched to cannister (grapeshot), making them virtual shotguns at point-blank range.

Confederate General Lewis Armistead took his hat off and held it high, perched on his officer's saber as he advanced at the front of his brigade, heading right into the mouth of cannon fire. This would later be called "The Valley of Death." The Confederate advance continued through the Union barrage.

In the film, ironically, actor Richard Jordan, portraying Armisted, was diagnosed with terminal cancer. Jordan would not see the final cut of the film.

In the field, at a certain point, the advance went from walk to quick step, ninety steps per minute. The cannister rounds were then employed. Sections of the wide Confederate line were leveled with withering shot. Bodies piled up on bodies, often three deep. Yet the Confederate soldiers closed ranks and continued to march toward the slope. The artillery and rifle fire became more deadly as the Confederate assault was relentlessly ripped apart. And still the Southerners trudged forward.

Back at the tree line, Pickett watched through a heavy lens. Longstreet, fearing the worst, stared at the infantry advance across the wheat field. The senior commanders waited with their staffs as they noticed their wounded soldiers coming back under heavy smoke. There were portions in the wheat field where one could walk over a section without touching the ground, the Confederate bodies were so grouped together.

Only several hundred of the total number in Pickett's charge made the full distance up the slope. And they were either killed or captured for their heroic efforts.

The view from the Union line down the slope and across the wheat field showed a sea of torn and ripped forms of Confederate infantrymen, the flower of an entire Southern generation. By now almost half of the original number lay dead in the shimmering afternoon heat.

As the winded, wounded, and exhausted survivors drifted back to the tree line, Lee, riding his horse Traveler, approached Pickett. "General Pickett, reform your division for counter attack," ordered Lee.

Shocked and devastated by the slaughter, Pickett stared at Lee for a moment, tears welling in his eyes. Then Pickett said, "General, sir, I have no division!"

Lee took total responsibility, telling his men, "This is all my fault!" Several staff officers suggested to Lee that they make one more charge. Lee could only stare out at the wheat field and the carnage. Then he shook his head. More than the day was lost.

The next day was a stalemate. Lee then began his retreat back to Virginia that night, recognizing 28,000 Confederate killed and wounded. Total Union casualties were slightly less, bringing the total dead and wounded to approximately 50,000 for the three-day battle.

Meade declined to take advantage of the situation and pursued the retreating Army of Northern Virginia with caution. This caused great disappointment and criticism from the War Department and the White House.

To the end of his days George Pickett held Robert E. Lee with total responsibility for the loss of his division that day. The South never recovered.

*Gettysburg* was also shown on television as a three-part miniseries. The extended video version runs just under six hours.

## THE LIST

A true story once again overcame anything that fiction could imagine with Universal Pictures/Amblin Entertainment's 1993 release of *Schindler's List*, directed by Steven Spielberg, based on the novel by Australian Thomas Keneally. The path of the film actually began seven years earlier.

Keneally, on a trip to California, visited a Beverly Hills luggage store. The propietor, Leopold Page, happened to mention that he was a "Schindlerjuden," a Jew saved by Oskar Schindler. In the Holocaust years, Page was known as Poldek Pfefferberg. For more than three decades Pfefferberg had tried to interest any writer who would listen to the story of Oskar Schindler. Pfefferberg often said, "A single person, a human being, can change the world." Each attempt was futile until Keneally heard the story. It took two years to get the manuscript completed. Keneally's research included interviewing fifty Schindlerjuden in seven countries.

Schindler, an Austrian businessman who was also known as a heavy drinker and notorious womanizer, was thirty when the Anschluss (the Third Reich's annexation of Austria) was declared in 1938. Operating a factory, he managed to keep out of military service and persuaded the Nazis to allow him to use Jewish slave labor in an elaborate scheme that ultimately saved 1,200 Jews from concentration camps. Schindler, a cunning deal maker and intimate social friend of high-ranking Nazis, had many setbacks in his scheme but always managed a way out at the last moment. He even joined the Nazi Party to increase his position.

In 1962, Schindler was named a "Righteous Gentile" by Yad Vashem, a Holocaust Memorial, established by Israel, to honor those Jews who perished and the Gentiles who risked their lives to save them. Schindler, who was denied U.S. immigration because of his membership in the Nazi Party, died in 1974. Keneally's book was published in 1982.

Steven Zaillian adapted the novel for Amblin. Liam Neeson portrayed Schindler, while Ralph Fiennes turned in a chilling performance as SS Commandant Amon Goeth, a deranged reprobate who was responsible for the executions of thousands of Jews and who randomly shot concentration camp prisoners from a sniper's perch. Goeth was hanged on September 13, 1946. During his war crimes trial, he displayed indifference and uttered a final "Heil Hitler" before dying. Ben Kingsley played Schindler's loyal assistant who kept the list of names.

Both Neeson and Fiennes received Academy Award nominations. Oscars came in for Best Picture, Best Director (Spielberg), Best Screenplay Adaptation, Best Cinematography (Janusz Kaminski), Best Musical Score (John Williams), and Best Editing (Michael Kahn). Writing in *The New Yorker* in 1993, Terrence Rafferty commented, "This is by far the finest, fullest dramatic (i.e., non-documentary) film ever made about the Holocaust."

Novelist Winston Groom's loopy fantasy and chronicle of the 1960s and 1970s, *Forrest Gump* was published in 1986. It wasn't produced as a film until 1994. After producer Wendy Finerman acquired the film rights, eight studios turned down the project until it found a home at Paramount with Tom Hanks playing the lead as the slow-witted Forrest. The novel was an outrageous, overly coincidental and tragic walk-through of the Vietnam generation: the Alabama-Nebraska Orange Bowl Game, combat sequences, playing in a rock band, antiwar protests, a space flight, a four-year stint with New Guinea cannibals (whose leader is a Yale graduate), a short career as a professional wrestler, a chess tournament, filming a remake of *The Creature from the Black Lagoon*, running through Beverly Hills and Rodeo Drive with a half-naked Raquel Welch, a quick rise to millionaire status, a run for the U.S. Senate, ending up in a near-penniless state in New Orleans where he reflects on his experiences.

Eric Roth's adaptation showed a remarkable twist from Groom's episodic novel. Roth shrewdly emphasized certain sequences. And then he cut others: the space flight, the New Guinea cannibals, professional wrestling, Raquel Welch, and the U.S. Senate race. He wisely took advantage of the assignment and concentrated on the tempo of the times, the Vietnam War, the antiwar protests, the Chinese Ping-Pong tournament, and the Watergate scandal. There were also computer-generated meetings with John F. Kennedy and Richard Nixon. The massive antiwar protest on the Washington, D.C. mall was also digitally edited.

Roth also used the rooming house that Forrest's mother managed to have notables such as an unknown Elvis Presley pass through. Forrest gives the young

Presley suggestions in using hip movements to improve his singing act. He unknowingly gave John Lennon the inspiration for the song "Imagine."

The opening montage explained Forrest Gump's family and southern namesake. Nathan Bedford Forrest, a self-educated cotton farmer and slave trader, raised a Confederate regiment at the onset of the Civil War. He was then appointed its commander with the motto "Get there first with the most."

A brilliant and daring cavalry officer, Nathan Bedford Forrest's impressive combat reputation was marred at Fort Pillow, Tennessee, in 1864. He was blamed for the deaths of hundreds of black Union soldiers who were attempting to surrender. In his later years Nathan Bedford Forrest became a plantation owner and the only Grand Wizard of the original Ku Klux Klan.

The Vietnam combat scenes of *Forrest Gump* evoke the sacrifice of a generation, where Forrest's platoon commander, Lieutenant Dan Taylor (Gary Sinise), loses his legs. In Groom's novel, Forrest doesn't meet Lieutenant Dan until both are hospitalized. They later meet again in a homeless situation.

In the film, Lieutenant Dan rages at Forrest for saving his life, thereby denying him a battlefield death with honor. Someone in Lieutenant Dan's family died in every American war. Forrest also saves the life of his buddy Bubba (Mykelti Williamson). In Groom's novel, Bubba is killed in Vietnam.

Forrest's Vietnam tour is capped with the award of the Medal of Honor presented by Richard Nixon. (In the novel, Lyndon Johnson makes the presentation and allows Forrest to have lunch in the White House, watching a television episode of *The Beverly Hillbillies*.) He then reunites with his childhood girlfriend Jenny Curran (Robin Wright) at the Washington, D.C. protest. In the film's resolution, Forrest is left with a son after Jenny dies of complications from AIDS. Echoing the philosophy of his mother (Sally Field), Forrest explains, "Life is like a box of chocolates. You never know what you're gonna get."

Oscars were awarded to Hanks (his second as Best Actor), Robert Zemeckis (Best Director), Eric Roth (Best Screenplay Adaptation), and Arthur Schmidt (Best Editing). Ken Ralston, George Murphy, Stephen Rosenblum, and Allen Hall won for Best Visual Effects. Gary Sinise was nominated for Best Supporting Actor.

The book that many studios rejected ended up taking in $325 million in the United States. Worldwide, it grossed $635 million, with more than 15 million video copies sold in America.

While the Vietnam War was given to American homes every evening, the Gulf War played on CNN day and night. The company and field grade officers, typified by generals Colin Powell and H. Norman Schwartzkopf, who survived the combat of Vietnam, were now managing the fighting in the cities and deserts of Iraq.

When Vietnam veteran and screenwriter Patrick Duncan got the idea for *Courage under Fire* (1996), a woman undergoing combat, he initially thought to place it in Vietnam. Duncan, who previously did a documentary on Medal of Honor winners, decided on setting his script in the Gulf War to debunk the accepted myth that women could not handle combat situations.

"I decided on doing a story on a woman who wins the Medal of Honor being balanced by an officer who lost some men in battle," explained Duncan.

Directed by Edward Zwick, the story has Lieutenant Colonel Nathaniel Serling (Denzel Washington) giving the order for a night tank attack. In the confusion of the desert battle, Serling ends up firing on one of his own tanks. He returns to the United States with guilt as the "friendly fire" incident is under investigation. His new assignment is working for General Hershberg (Michael Moriarty) at the army awards and decorations section in the Pentagon.

Serling is given the 201 personnel file of Captain Karen Walden (Meg Ryan) who is being recommended for a posthumous Medal of Honor. Captain Walden was a Huey medevac pilot who demonstrated bravery and intrepid gallantry at the cost of her own life during a rescue mission. Walden's Huey came under fire from Iraqi forces and went in. Her copilot was seriously wounded. Walden and her downed crew had to spend the night in enemy territory and are forced to undergo more Iraqi fire. During this time Walden takes a mortal wound but still stays in command.

As Serling is still haunted by his own mistakes in the gulf he tracks down the surviving crew members: Monfriez (Lou Diamond Phillips), Llario (Matt Damon), and Altameyer (Seth Gilliam). It is here where Serling comes across conflicting accounts as to what really happened out there. Serling is initially told that the downed crew had run out of ammo during the night. But a nearby unit contends that they heard M-16 rounds from that area. When his inquiries are met with blank looks and vague answers, Serling naturally senses that the truth lies under the surface.

While Serling is conducting his investigation he learns that Tony Gartner (Scott Glenn) of the *Washington Post* is on to the "friendly fire" incident. Serling has his own demons to deal with, a lack of communication with his wife Meredith (Regina Taylor), and a growing alcohol problem.

The surviving crew members are scattered over army posts, undergoing contrasting situations. Altameyer is in a hospital dying (a reaction to Gulf War Syndrome). He's heavily medicated.

The supermacho Monfriez is a basic training drill instructor. It is here where Serling explains the problem with conflicting statements. Monfriez initially states that nothing happened out there, "It was a war." When Monfriez sees that Serling is getting to the truth, he takes himself out, driving headlong into a locomotive.

In each of the interviews, the audience views flashbacks recalling the "Roshomon Syndrome" (named after the Japanese legend where four people witness the same incident, resulting in four different versions of the truth). Despite the turmoil that Captain Walden had to endure, while mortally wounded, Serling determines that she does deserve the medal after all. He even visits her grave and places his own Silver Star on her headstone.

Duncan added that his model for the screenplay was the 1959 Gary Cooper film *They Came to Cordura*, an epic adventure, which revealed the true character traits of American military heroes in 1916 Mexico during General Pershing's pursuit of Pancho Villa.

Duncan explained that when he arrived in Hollywood, in the mid-1970s, he was told by several producers at different studios that there were three genres that were box office poison and to avoid them: boxing films, science fiction, and war films. With a chuckle, Duncan added, "This of course was later contradicted with *Rocky, Star Wars*, and *Platoon*."

While writing the screenplay for *Courage under Fire*, Duncan said that he had no particular actor in mind. "He [Serling] was just an army officer who lost people in combat. I thought Denzel was perfect in the role, one of our better actors."[4]

Michael Ondaatje's novel *The English Patient* was adapted for a 1996 Miramax film by Anthony Minghella, who also directed the love story, set against World War II. The story is told in "bookend flashback," where a dying Austrian count recalls his tragic affair with the wife of a friend.

The film was mounted as a sweeping epic, mixing the horrors of war with the attraction of doomed lovers. The film received rave reviews and was named as Best Picture. Anthony Minghella received an Oscar as Best Director. Juliette Binoche was named as Best Supporting Actress as the devoted nurse. Other Oscars were awarded to John Seale (Best Cinematography), Gabriel Yared (Best Musical Score), Walter Murch (Best Editing), and Stuart Craig for Best Production Design. Ralph Fiennes and Kristin Scott-Thomas were nominated for their depictions of the star-crossed lovers.

## THE BEACH OF DEATH

Memorable American battles have been well documented through the ages, days, or an afternoon that turned the tide. Among these are Saratoga, Gettysburg, Belleau Wood, and Midway. Before World War II ended, another place was added: Normandy. And on the beach at Normandy was a section with a code name: Omaha.

The film adaptation of Cornelius Ryan's book *The Longest Day*, as noted, was documentary in style from the Allied side to the Nazi high command. It impressed the 1962 audiences with its international cast and massive black-and-white scope. What that film didn't show was the graphic realism that was to grip audiences in July 1998 when Paramount/Amblin released *Saving Private Ryan*.

The story was evocative of assigned special operations stories: Get behind enemy lines, find Private Ryan (Matt Damon) who parachuted in with the 101st Airborne, and get him out. He is the only survivor of four sons fighting in the same war.

As Army Chief of Staff George Marshall, Harve Presnell quotes from the

November 21, 1864, letter from Abraham Lincoln to Mrs. Lydia Bixby of Boston who lost five sons in Civil War battles. Lincoln ended his letter to the grieving mother: "I pray that our Heavenly Father may assuage the anguish of your bereavement and leave you only the cherished memory of the loved and lost, and the solemn pride that must be yours to have laid so costly a sacrifice upon the altar of freedom."[5]

The film, directed by Steven Spielberg, was derivative of Paramount's *The Fighting Sullivans* (1944), where five brothers went down with the USS *Juneau* in the battle of Guadalcanal in 1942.

In a script credited to Robert Rodat, *Saving Private Ryan* is told in "bookend flashback." It is present time as a World War II veteran journeys with his wife and grandchildren to the Normandy cemetery. At a specific grave, the veteran flashes back to the June 6, 1944, line of departure, a Higgins boat going into the Dog Victor sector of the 1st Infantry Division's landing area.

Tom Hanks played army ranger Captain John Miller, who survives the Omaha Beach slaughter only to be given the special mission to find Private Ryan and bring him out. At the actual landing, Miller's unit, the 2nd Rangers, assaulted the cliffs at Pointe du Hoc at the far right of Omaha Beach. After Captain Miller is given the special assignment, he has to hold his unit together. His leadership is repeatedly tested with different combat situations and a morale problem within his own ranks. In supporting roles were Tom Sizemore, Edward Burns, Matt Damon, Jeremy Davies, Giovanni Ribisi, Adam Goldberg, and Barry Pepper.

As accounted by Stephen E. Ambrose in his book *D-Day*, the initial army assault waves at Omaha Beach waded into a withering, interlocking, buzz saw of machine gun and artillery fire. Naturally it wasn't planned that way.

Ambrose quoted General Eisenhower: "Plans are everything before the battle, useless once it is joined. . . . Nothing worked according to the plan, which was indeed useless the moment the Germans opened fire on the assault forces and even before."[6]

Allied intelligence had come to the erroneous conclusion that the German infantry defending Normandy was less than mediocre with poor morale. In his book *The Second World War*, John Keegan pointed out that the 352nd Wehrmacht Infantry Division, above Omaha Beach, was the best German unit on the coast that day. "Had all of the German defenders of Normandy been as well trained and resolute as those of the 352nd Division and had accident overtaken more of the swimming Shermans [tanks], the debacle at Omaha might have been repeated up and down all five beaches, with catastrophic results."[7]

The air support was negligible because cloud cover delayed the B-17 bombers. When they did drop their bombs they fell as much as five kilometers inland. Ambrose pointed out that not a single bomb fell on the beach or bluff. "In addition, the naval bombardment was both brief and inaccurate. Most of the rockets fell short landing in the surf, killing thousands of fish but no Germans."

As with many tide-turning battles, ordinary men performed extraordinary heroics, often paying for it with their lives. Utter chaos reigned as the first waves landed. The Germans of the 352nd controlled every field of fire going down to the beach. Ambrose cited the 16th Regiment of the 1st Infantry Division, which landed in confusion, off target, and disorganized. "There were only two types of people on that beach, the dead and those about to die."[8]

Combat correspondent Ernie Pyle later wrote, "We did it with every advantage on the enemy's side and every disadvantage on ours. . . . We sit and talk and call it a miracle that our men got on [the beach] at all or were able to stay on."[9]

The price the Allies paid to gain a foothold on the European continent that day came to 4,649 killed and wounded. The majority of that number occurred at Omaha Beach. Today, many of those killed rest in the military cemetery above the cliffs.

In preparing for production, director Spielberg used the William Wellman example from *Battleground* and put the actors through boot camp. For that he went to Dale Dye, the retired Marine Corps captain who conducted similar training with the actors in *Platoon*. Dye and his technical adviser staff wanted to come as close as possible to train actors as soldiers to endure combat conditions. They knew that they were dealing with actors and not combat soldiers. Complaints fell on empty ears with no sympathy. The two-week actors boot camp consisted of living in the field, eating rations, suffering rainstorms, handling weapons, individual movement, army language, and tactics. They even had to hike five miles a day carrying forty-pound packs.

The Omaha Beach scenes graphically brought forward the slaughter in the water and on the sand. Audiences, in a twenty-minute sequence, cringed as they watched American infantrymen vomiting in the Higgins boats, drowning, getting blown in half by artillery bursts, having exposed intestines oozing out of the stomach, in addition to suffering head wounds from the raking fire. One soldier, in obvious shock, is seen walking around the beach holding his right arm, which has just been blown off.

The film came in for criticism for being overly violent. However, the filmmakers candidly came back with the time-honored, "That was how it was." Still, many filmgoers, after several minutes, turned their heads, looking away from the realistic carnage on the screen.[10]

*Saving Private Ryan* fostered many media reflections. World War II veterans recalled not just Normandy but the entire European campaign up to and through the Battle of the Bulge. In Glendale, California, an elderly white-haired veteran had to be helped out of the theater by his wife, tears streaming down both cheeks as the film's end came back to present time with a tearful salute at the grave.[11]

Tom Hanks received an Oscar nomination. Awards came in for Best Director, Best Editing, and Best Original Screenplay. The film was also named Best Picture of 1998 by the New York Film Critics Circle.

Following *Saving Private Ryan* was the World War II remake of *The Thin Red Line* (1998), directed by Terrence Malick, who left Hollywood after an impressionable career with *Badlands* and *Days of Heaven*. As previously noted,

*The Thin Red Line* was James Jones's sequel to *From Here to Eternity*, following the infantry survivors of the Pearl Harbor attack to their first invasion, Guadalcanal in the Solomon Islands.

The idea for the remake started in 1988 when producers Robert Michael Geisler and John Roberdeau approached Gloria Jones, James Jones's widow. Malick was initially brought in only to write the adaptation for Phoenix Pictures. By September 1996 Malick was aboard to also direct for Fox 2000 Pictures.

The director quickly lined up old friends and collaborators, including cinematographer John Toll and composer Hans Zimmer. Locations took place in Australia.

The 1964 version was a black-and-white film and was criticized for being a routine war film. Malick's script emphasized the contrast of the destruction of war in a natural, pristine environment. The soldiers land unopposed, heading into an unseen enemy. As objectives present themselves to the officers the enlisted men begin questioning whether this is all worth it. Bravery abounds, but still men die. As in *From Here to Eternity*, the enlisted men acquit themselves much better than the officers.

The film opens with the infantry regiment about to land in Guadalcanal to relieve the beleaguered 1st Marine Division, which was the first unit on the island, August 1942. When the marines pulled back, after being relieved, one of them wrote a quatrain about the experience: "When I get to Heaven/To Saint Peter I will tell/One more marine reporting/ I served my time in Hell."

And now the army's time in hell was beginning. Jones's novel came right from his combat experience, that there was a thin red line between bravery and cowardice.

Sean Penn played First Sergeant Welsh, an extension of Burt Lancaster's Sergeant Milt Warden. Jim Caviezel was Private Witt, the extension of Montgomery Cliff's Private Robert E. Lee Prewitt.

Also cast were Nick Nolte, Ben Chaplin, Woody Harrelson, George Clooney, John Savage, John Cusack, and Elias Koteas.

Malick received an Academy Award nomination for Best Director, along with Toll.

Neil Sheehan's military biography of Lieutenant Colonel John Paul Vann, *A Bright Shining Lie*, was published by Random House in 1988. It was awarded the 1989 Pulitzer Prize for general nonfiction and was also given the National Book Award. The book was first optioned by Warner Bros. But it would be nine years (1998) before the film was finally produced by HBO Productions. After *Platoon* was released, many studio executives felt that the country was not ready for another controversial story centered around the Vietnam War, true or otherwise.

Like many driven men, John Paul Vann was a walking contradiction, obsessed with making his mark in what he called "the noblest profession," that of a soldier. He was more committed to military victory than he was to his marriage vows.

He was born in Norfolk, Virginia, where he grew up in a troubled home. He received an Army Air Force commission at the end of World War II. He married Mary Jane Allen in October 1945. Vann was posted in Osaka, Japan, just before the Korean War. He served with distinction during Korea. After Korea, Vann did a tour of duty in Germany with occupation forces.

In 1962, Vann was a lieutenant colonel, one of the first army advisers sent to Vietnam. It was at this time where he began to run afoul of the politics surrounding the American military advisory command (MACV) and the Army of the Republic of Vietnam. After the Battle of Ap Bac was erroneously termed a victory for the South, Vann criticized the advisory program as a complete scam. He further criticized the military on both sides for using phony statistics to prop up an ineffective army. Vann showed disgust that promotion in the South Vietnamese Army was not based on merit but politics. He felt that the ARVN could fight the North Vietnamese if it had sufficient leadership. On the personal side, Vann began an affair with a Vietnamese woman.

After returning to the United States Vann began a speaking tour, an audio-visual presentation, based on his experiences and opinions as to how the war should be conducted. Officers at army posts took note. It was impressive. Vann was then asked to brief the Joint Chiefs in Washington. However, the old guard closed ranks, and the briefing schedule was suddenly canceled. Vann was notified as he waited in an anteroom. The military establishment did not care for his message. The advisory program would continue as is, business as usual.

This echoes the Colonel Walter Kurtz character in *Apocalypse Now*. In the back story Kurtz sent a memo to Lyndon Johnson and the Joint Chiefs regarding the conduct of the war. Kurtz received a similar reaction: complete denial.

Vann then resigned from the army. However, he was itching to get back. After the Gulf of Tonkin incident, in August 1964, he applied to the U.S. AID (Agency for International Development) program as a regional adviser. He returned to Vietnam in March 1965 as the U.S. buildup was beginning. He also resumed his affair with the Vietnamese woman.

Again, John Paul Vann confronted the lack of leadership in the South Vietnamese Army, still rank with corruption and politics. It came to a head when he slapped a corrupt ARVN colonel in front of the commander's staff.

Vann's obsession with turning the war around consumed him. He worked out of Saigon with General Fred Weyand, working inordinate hours, sleeping only three and four hours a night. In the meantime, he married a second Vietnamese woman who was carrying his child.

As the Tet holiday of 1968 approached, Vann could see the signs of a completely coordinated North Vietnamese offensive. Here, he differed with General Westmoreland who felt that the real thrust would be at the northern outpost of Khe Sanh. Newsreel tape was mixed with location shooting, showing the Tet fighting on the American embassy grounds. Saigon Chief of Police General Loan was again shown executing the handcuffed Viet Cong prisoner.

Because of his actions at Tet, Vann was appointed as U.S. senior adviser to the South Vietnamese Army, carrying the rank of a major general. Westmoreland was then replaced by General Creighton Abrams.

Vann continued to achieve victories in the field but was later forced to rely more on the South Vietnamese troops after the U.S. withdrawal began. At Kontum, he called in an air strike on his own position to repel a North Vietnamese assault. Vann was killed in a helicopter crash shortly after attending a ceremony congratulating his actions at Kontum.

In Sheehan's book, John Paul Vann came off as a contradictory, idealistic officer, as flawed as the advisory mission he was attempting to correct. On June 16, 1972, he was buried at Arlington National Cemetery. His burial symbolized the end of effective American advisers in Vietnam.

Ironically, as history would have it, the Watergate burglary occurred the next day not far from Vann's grave. As one chapter ended, another began.

*A Bright Shining Lie* was written and directed by Terry George. Bill Paxton portrayed Vann, while Amy Madigan was cast as Mary Jane. In supporting roles were Donal Logue and Eric Bogosian as journalists. Vivian Wu played Lee, Vann's mistress.

Logue's character, Steven Burnett, narrated the film. Ed Lauter played General Weyand, while Kurtwood Smith was General Westmoreland. The location shooting took place in Thailand in the fall of 1997.

Many editing decisions had to be made with George's screenplay adaptation. One of them concerned Jesse Vann, the son who adamantly opposed the Vietnam War. After the Arlington burial, President Nixon invited the Vann family and relatives to the Oval Office for a reception. Jesse indicated that he was going to tear up his draft card at the reception and give half of it to the president as his protest to the war. The family pleaded with him, contending that the day was a memorial to his father and not to use the opportunity to express individual political feelings. The reception was in doubt at this point. Nixon aide Brent Scowcroft then talked the young man out of the gesture, and the reception came off as planned. In epilogue it is noted that Vann, who was not classified as active duty military, was not included in the combat deaths of Vietnam. His name does not appear on the Vietnam War Memorial.

John Ridley, a Milwaukee native, moved to New York in the 1980s with aspirations of being a stand-up comedian. He majored in East Asian studies at New York University. He then lived for a period in Japan. Returning to the United States he went to Los Angeles and found work as a comedy writer.

In the mid-1990s he wrote a speculation script (one written with no advance money) entitled *Spoils of War*, where three American Desert Storm soldiers find a map that leads them to a cache of gold in Iraq. In an interview, Ridley recalled that the script was sold to Warner Bros. It made the studio rounds with the usual script coverage and notes. Eventually it landed with director David O. Russell, who saw a movie in it and made some marked structural and character changes.

By the time the film was in postproduction, *Spoils of War* was retitled *Three*

*Kings* (1999). Ridley, who is black, had the three soldiers in his initial script as black. However, when casting came for the film, special forces Major Archie Gates was cast with George Clooney.

When the film was released in September 1999, Ridley told an interviewer: "It [the script] was sold to Warner Bros. as a spec script. It got kicked around a little bit—the usual Hollywood course—and then wound up with David O. Russell." Although the outlines of the story are the same, Ridley says Russell made significant changes. "He [has] made it more of a political story, more about America's role in the war."[12] Ridley received a "story by" and coproducer credit on the film.

The film's locations were desert areas in Arizona, California, and Mexico. The story began when Americans are classifying and searching Iraqi prisoners. Sergeant Troy Barlow (Mark Wahlberg), Sergeant Chief Elgin (Ice Cube), and Private Conrad Vig (Spike Jonze) discover a map in the buttocks of a prisoner. It is assumed that the map pinpoints the location of a cache of gold ingots— stolen from Kuwait during Saddam's invasion. Special Forces Major Archie Gates (Clooney) realizes the potential and forms a special operation to retrieve the gold, ostensibly to return it to Kuwait, although it could be to snatch a few bars for themselves.

CNN-type reporter Adriana Cruz (Nora Dunn), looking much like the international correspondent Christine Amanpour, is hungry for a story with a good combat angle. Gates then sets a false lead for her, with the hope of keeping her camera away from the treasure. It is here where the story line becomes reminiscent of both *The Treasure of the Sierra Madre* (1948) and the 1970 World War II film *Kelly's Heroes*. In the latter, Clint Eastwood, Telly Savalas, and Don Rickles happen upon a fortune of gold. The former had three prospectors taking gold out of a remote Mexican mountain, only to have it destroy their intentions, leading to tragedy, where, in the end, the gold dust is carried back to the mountain by a windstorm.

Initially, the Iraqi soldiers attempt to deceive the Americans but eventually turn and help load the ingots from an underground bunker to a truck. Here, the Americans become aware of the Iraqis who oppose Saddam. Poison gas is released during the escape attempt, forcing the Americans into another bunker. Barlow is separated from the others and gets an opportunity to phone his wife on a cell phone: technology meeting modern warfare.

Barlow is subsequently captured and tortured by Captain Sa'id (Sa'id Taghmaoui). Captain Sa'id lost his only son in the Baghdad bombing. He asks Barlow why the United States attacked Iraq. Barlow says because it (Iraq) invaded Kuwait. Captain Sa'id gives Barlow the real reason, pouring oil down his throat.

The other soldiers return to rescue Barlow. The Iraqi rebels allow them the use of pilfered limousines on the condition that they will allow safe conduct of approximately 100 Iraqi refugees to the Iranian border. The convoy then proceeds to the border. During the battle Vig is killed. At the border Gates makes the decision to give the gold ingots to the refugees, thereby giving the group redemption.

Adriana ultimately arrives and gets the story, casting the soldiers as heroes in a special operation.

The first week of April 2000, *Rules of Engagement* was released, starring Tommy Lee Jones, Samuel L. Jackson, Guy Pearce, John Speredakos, Ben Kingsley, Anne Archer, Blair Underwood, Philip Baker Hall, and Dale Dye. The final draft screenplay was written by Stephen Gaghan from an original screenplay by James Webb, who received story credit.

Directed by William Friedkin, the story of *Rules of Engagement* spans two conflicts: the Vietnam War and an uprising in Yemen where the ambassador's family has to be evacuated. Marine Colonel Terry Childers (Jackson) is the commander of a MEU (Marine Expeditionary Unit) tasked with protecting the embassy and the Americans inside.

The situation quickly turns violent, resulting in a firefight. Three marines are dead along with more than eighty Yemeni men, women, and children killed by U.S. fire. Despite securing the safety for the American ambassador (Kingsley), his wife (Archer), and family, Childers returns stateside and is notified that he will be faced with a court-martial for violating the rules of engagement that caused the deaths of unarmed civilians. Childers feels that he did his duty. And because of the ugly diplomatic crisis, he is destined to take the fall. The ambassador lies in his account of the situation, and the president's national security adviser destroys evidence that would have cleared Childers. It is here where combat loyalty and brotherhood become the theme. Childers requests Colonel Hays Hodges (Tommy Lee Jones) to represent him. He came to Hodges's aid during a Vietnam firefight, at the film's opening, when both were company-grade officers. After Vietnam, Hodges got a law degree and rose to the rank of full colonel. Guy Pearce portrayed the pit bull prosecutor who steadfastly believes in Childers's guilt. Because of this strong bonding between Hodges and Childers, they overcome the odds, and the court acquits Childers.

Like *Forrest Gump* and *A Bright Shining Lie*, *Rules of Engagement* had a lengthy metamorphosis. In an interview in the *U.S. Naval Institute Proceedings*, author James Webb (*Fields of Fire, A Country Such as This*), an Annapolis graduate and decorated marine combat veteran, explained that he conceived the idea in 1989 with producer Scott Rudin (*Angela's Ashes, Sleepy Hollow*).[13] Rudin had just read excerpts, in *Esquire* magazine, from Bob Timberg's book *The Nightingale's Song*. Timburg, also an Annapolis graduate and Vietnam veteran, profiled five men in his book: John McCain, John Poindexter, Oliver North, Webb, and Bud McFarlane. All are Annapolis alums, although from different classes. And all had served in Vietnam at different times and in different capacities.

Timburg's title came from a tale that a nightingale, raised in isolation from other nightingales, can never sing. But once exposed to the song of another nightingale it begins singing like it's been doing it all its life. In the aftermath of Vietnam, their individual voices, once lusty and full throated, had been stunned into silence by the homecoming. Putting the five stories under one cover would bring their song out for all to hear.

After the Timburg excerpts were published, Webb and Rudin discussed military loyalty as opposed to the civilian world. Webb's view was, "In the Marine Corps, loyalty means you will die for somebody even if you don't like them."

Rudin answered, "You know, there's a movie in that."

The issue had weighed heavily on Webb. As an attorney, he represented a "war criminal," ultimately gaining an acquittal. He was also upset with what he termed the "ridiculous" rules of engagement that marines in Beirut were forced to endure. Webb was appointed as Secretary of the Navy by President Reagan and served during the 1987 and 1988 Persian Gulf incidents.

Webb was gratified that his original story survived the filmmaking process. Childers tells Hodges that no matter what the outcome of the court-martial, he will never be able to command again. That is the price he pays. He has lost the one thing most precious to him in the military, the right to command troops. Webb, himself, found that to be the most satisfying element that was conveyed to the audiences.

"World War II is easy in Hollywood," said Webb. "There has never before been a film that expressly addresses the modern American military and the issues it faces." He added, "[Hollywood] had no comprehension that we had restrictions on us, even in a place like Vietnam. Where does the average American get his information? From the movies."[14]

## NEW ANGLES TO HISTORY

The year 2000 brought criticism concerning factual content in two films with American war backgrounds. The first was a World War II submarine film, *U-571*, directed by Jonathan Mostow and starring Matthew McConaughey, centering around the capture of the Nazi Enigma code machine.

American submarine films herald back to the early days: *Destination Tokyo, Crash Dive, Operation Pacific, Submarine Command, Run Silent, Run Deep, Torpedo Run,* and *The Enemy Below*. The appeal to audiences is double-edged: navy men fighting not only the enemy but the forces of the sea, above and below. The submarines had to dodge their way through the nautical maze caused by the destroyers' depth charges. The submarine crews had to endure sparse living conditions plus inordinate temperatures that spanned the mercurial spectrum. These elements greatly contributed to monumental stress hundreds of feet below the surface. Such was the background for *U-571* in a terrifying depth-charge attack.

Codes and ciphers are even referred to in the Bible. It was a method of sending important military messages in secrecy. By 1921, the term *cryptanalysis* was coined by American code breaker William F. Friedman.

This code machine was invented by Dutchman Hugo Koch in 1919. By 1923,

Arthur Scherbius, a German engineer, adapted the machine to help businesses conduct secure overseas communication through wireless transmissions. He then approached the German military as a potential buyer. But they were not interested at the time. When Hitler became chancellor in 1934, the Third Reich became a big customer for the device, now called "the Enigma machine." No one, outside of Germany, was aware of its existence.[15]

The Enigma machine was perfect for the Nazis. It was portable and simple to use. The unusual aspect was the coupling of letters. They were constantly changed so the encrypted messages were never the same. The code had billions of combinations, making it impossible to break, or so the Nazis thought.

In the early days of the Third Reich, a World War I veteran, Hans-Thilo Schmidt, was working in the War Ministry Cipher Center in Berlin. Even though Schmidt was a member of the Nazi Party, he was bitter and felt underpaid and unappreciated. He then contacted French intelligence, offering to sell classified coded documents. By 1938 Schmidt had met with French contacts, mostly in Switzerland, approximately twenty-four times, giving over classified documents on the code and taking payments.

But the French were stymied by the code variables and could only resolve three of the basic six equations to reconstruct the wiring of the machine's code wheels. This was all done on paper. The French then gave the information to the Poles, who were able to decode some messages. The Poles, in turn, gave their documentation to the British, who improved on the methods and code equations. But the actual machine was still in the hands of the Third Reich. Until May 9, 1941.

On that day, a British convoy en route from England to Nova Scotia was passing south of Iceland. Lurking underwater was the German *U-110* commanded by Fritz-Julius Lemp. (The term *U-boat* came from the German *Unterseeboot*: undersea boat.) One of the warships providing convoy security was the British corvette HMS *Aubretia*, commanded by A.J. Baker-Creswell.

A British lookout on the *Aubretia* spotted a periscope in the water. The corvette broke from the convoy line and circled around. A depth-charge attack soon resulted in severe damage, forcing the *U-110* to the surface. The crew poured out of the hatches and into the sea. Many of them, including Captain Kemp, were lost. At this point Captain Creswell made a momentous decision. Instead of ramming the crippled *U-110*, Creswell decided to send over a boarding party.

While the surviving German sailors were taken aboard a rescue vessel, Sublieutenant David Balme, twenty, led a British boarding party to the adrift submarine. Balme would later write, "I am still haunted by my climb down that last vertical ladder, fifteen feet into the bowels of the U-110 . . . I felt there must be someone below trying to open the seacocks, or setting the detonating charges. But no one was there. There must have been complete panic in U-110, and she was left to us as the greatest prize of the war. But I still wake up at night fifty-six years later to find myself going down that ladder."[16]

Balme's boarding party returned with various code books, signal logs, and pay records. They also came back with a small machine that looked like a typewriter.

The typewriter machine was turned over to British intelligence. In a short period the British knew what had fallen into their hands—one of the biggest prizes of the war. In the meantime, the Germans surmised that the *U-110* was lost with all hands.

With the deciphering formulas already in hand, the British could now crack the codes. The captured machine gave British intelligence the capability to intercept all Enigma messages for the rest of the war. These intercepts were termed "Ultra."

The seizure of the Enigma machine was later described by King George VI as the single most important event in the war at sea.

As an American naval officer in *U-571*, Matthew McConaughey expects to assume his first submarine command. But that position is given to Bill Paxton. This causes the same resentment that Burt Lancaster had for Clark Gable in 1958's *Run Silent, Run Deep*. But the mission comes first. When the American submariners encounter the *U-571*, they decide to board her. At this point the American submarine is hit and Paxton killed. McConaughey, in the meantime, is leading a boarding party toward the *U-571*. The Americans board the U-boat and, after a brief firefight, take over the vessel. They now have to survive as Germans, using the enemy's vessel. Luckily, they have an interpreter.

In the end, they realize what they have: the Enigma machine. And they connect with one of their own, bringing the machine into Allied hands. An epilogue then states the true account of David Balme (who rose to the rank of lieutenant commander and has a walk-on bit) and the HMS *Aubretia*. Supporting McConaughey and Paxton are Harvey Keitel, Jake Webber, Erik Palladino, Matthew Settle, and David Keith.

Despite the epilogue and the financial success, the film enraged British audiences, who accused Hollywood of shamelessly rewriting history, implying to the public that it was Americans who captured the machine. Addressing the House of Commons, Prime Minister Tony Blair called the film an "affront" to the British sailors who were killed in the war. "I hope that people realize there are people that, in many cases, sacrificed their lives in order that this country remained free," said Blair.[17]

Tom Carr, a British veteran, appeared on Sky Television soon after the release of *U-571* and branded it: "A pack of twisted lies."

Two months later, Sony–Tri Star released *The Patriot* (2000), starring Mel Gibson. Directed by Roland Emmerich (*Independence Day*), from a script by Robert Rodat (*Saving Private Ryan*), the film told the story of Benjamin Martin, a widower who is dragged into the American Revolution as the war reaches his South Carolina homestead. As a veteran of the earlier French and Indian War, Martin was scarred by that experience and vowed to live in peace with his family. But fate has another turn for Martin. At the beginning he quietly says, "I have long feared that my sins would return to visit me."

In supporting roles were Chris Cooper, Joely Richardson, Tchéky Karyo, Heath Ledger, and Tom Wilkinson.

The first act has Martin at odds with his sons over getting involved in another war. However, when the British dragoons arrive and kill Martin's younger son, he again takes up arms, this time leading an effective hit-and-run guerrilla campaign against the British army, ultimately leading to the defeat of Lord Cornwallis (Wilkinson). Personifying the heartless and evil antagonist is the brutal Colonel William Tavington (Jason Issacs) who murders the Martin son, shooting him point blank.

Tavington also issues the order to burn a parish church that American colonists use as a refuge. The colonists are first locked into the church, and then the order is given, by Tavington, to torch it.

The summer of 2000 was rife with British criticism about *U-571* and *The Patriot*. However, the latter film had more of a basis in history. Colonel Tavington was based on the real-life Banastre Tarleton, a master of the saber, who commanded a squadron of dragoons in Sir Henry Clinton's Carolina campaign. He quickly established a reputation and won victories. In the spring of 1780, he garnered the nicknames "Bloody Ban" and "Tarleton's quarter" when his men bayoneted Americans attempting to surrender. He was taken prisoner at Yorktown, paroled, and returned to England where he died in 1833. Although he was daring and vigorous, he was also ruthless and cold-blooded in his treatment of Americans.

Martin's character was obviously a composite of several Revolutionary War figures: Thomas Sumter, Andrew Pickens, Daniel Morgan, Elijah Clark, and Francis Marion (The Swamp Fox).

In the film, Lord Cornwallis was portrayed as an aristocrat in the King's service to corral the unruly colonists. Educated at Eton, a veteran of the Seven Years' War, and an aide-de-camp to King George III, he had his moments in the early days of the Revolutionary War. However, he later found himself trapped at Yorktown (1781) and surrendered, ending the war. Banastre was his protégé.

The climax in *The Patriot* is a battle loosely based on several of the era. In the film, Colonel Tavington is killed by Martin after the Continentals gain the upper hand with a bold flanking movement.[18]

The film set off a firestorm of controversy from British quarters and from Americans. Gibson's film history was called into question, starting with the Australian-made *Gallipoli* (1981), which brought out the slaughter of New Zealanders and Aussies in the infamous 1915 battle. In 1995, Gibson played William Wallace, the Scot who led a revolt against English King Edward I in *Braveheart*.[19]

Filmmaker Spike Lee sent off an angry letter to the *Hollywood Reporter*, denouncing the film as blatant Hollywood propaganda. Lee was particularly annoyed that the film ignored slavery. "Where are the slaves? Who's picking the cotton? Did [Robert] Rodat, a 1981 graduate of Colgate University, get his dates mixed up? Where were the native Americans? Did the two Johns—Ford and Wayne—wipe them out already?" Sony Studios had no comment to Lee's letter.

Several days later on July 7, 2000, writing to the *Los Angeles Times*, actor Charleton Heston acknowledged that the film had historical flaws. Heston added, "I found it a very fine film. There are three wars in American history that we had to win: the American Revolution, the Civil War and World War II. Mel Gibson's film on our war for independence made that point tellingly."

The Gulf War era, beginning in 1990, in American war films, brought about more story angles to past wars, going back to our first. It also opened the gates for more war films, particularly about World War II.

## TRIANGULAR HISTORY[20]

Perhaps no other contemporary American war film was more hampered by historical incidents, money, and then critics than the 2001 Disney/Bruckheimer *Pearl Harbor*. The historical incidents first conflicted with the bottom line, a reported budget that landed somewhere between $135 and $140 million.

The difficult production began in 1999 when director Michael Bay (*Days of Thunder, Armageddon*) met with Disney executives about possible future projects. After two "pitch" meetings Bay rejected every Disney proposal. As Bay was preparing to leave, an executive mentioned the possibility of doing a film about Pearl Harbor. The follow-up question was, why Pearl Harbor? What could be added to an attack that spawned more than a dozen films, including the 1970 docudrama *Tora! Tora! Tora!*?

The challenge and historical angle appealed to Bay. This project, a film with historical impact, particularly a combat film, could be considered a higher level.

Screenwriter Randall Wallace (*Braveheart*) was brought in to structure a story that would become the first draft of *Pearl Harbor*. This was before endless notes and story conferences. How does a writer come up with a new angle to tell an old story?

Wallace began with a triangular structure, both in story and character. The structure was similar to *Wings* (1927), two fliers and a nurse. The Pearl Harbor attack would be the center point of the film, anchored between the Battle of Britain in the first act and Lieutenant Colonel Jimmy Doolittle's psychologically uplifting bombing raid on Tokyo in April 1942. With the characters, Wallace resorted to an oft-told device, two brothers who fall in love with the same woman, a navy nurse, no less. This ventured close to a Hemingway cliché, a soldier in wartime falling for a nurse.

The brother angle was dropped in favor of two childhood friends who grow up loving airplanes and who join the U.S. Army Air Corps. They become separated when one volunteers for the Eagle Squadron for the Battle of Britain but reunite on the eve of Pearl Harbor and then volunteer for Doolittle's raid. As they reunite, the love story subplot threatens their relationship.

The casting was rightfully geared to the new generation of actors. Ben Affleck portrayed Rafe, the midwestern farm boy and best friend of Danny, played by newcomer Josh Hartnett. The part of Evelyn, the navy nurse, was given to Kate Beckinsale, a British actress with a background in small, arthouse films. Supporting roles went to Jon Voight as President Roosevelt and Alec Baldwin as Doolittle. Cuba Gooding, Jr. was cast as steward's mate Dorie Miller, who was the first black to be awarded a Navy Cross.

Historical research played an important part with period music, costumes, and uniforms. Underneath it all, the budget was climbing. The battle sequences called for blowing up seventeen ships with vintage Japanese planes strafing airfields and peeling off toward Ford Island and battleship row. Historical accuracy was primary; two uncredited screenwriters came in to incorporate documentation and to "polish" Wallace's dialogue.

Accounts differ as to executive reactions each time a draft was turned in. The initial number crunching went over $200 million, then was pared down from $186 million to $176 million. But it still wasn't enough. Before long, it became a distinct possibility that the project would be shelved.

Bay and the principal actors agreed to salary cuts. But the conflict between commerce and art continued. Bay was advised to drop the Doolittle raid, eliminate President Roosevelt, and to forget about the USS *Oklahoma* keeling over on its side. Frustration mounted with the suggested script cuts. They all directly related to the attack that morning. For a time it seemed that a film about major historical events was going to be produced without several of the key events.

Politics also entered the mix. Executives became increasingly concerned about offending the Japanese-American community. A scene depicting a Nisei Honolulu dentist receiving a phone call from Japanese officers concerning U.S. ship movements was requested to be cut by the Japanese-American Citizens League. However, Disney and Bay held fast, contending that the incident actually occurred and would remain in the film.[21]

Filming began in Hawaii in April 2000. Computer digital imaging played an important part, from piecing in many of the attacking Japanese planes to sailors falling from burning ships and dropping into oil-streaked water or fireballs. The major computer-generated sequence allowed the audience to follow the fatal bomb drop down on the USS *Arizona*, crashing through the deck and coming to rest in the ship's magazine, where it detonated.

The film was scheduled for a May 25, 2001, domestic release. A lavish shipboard premiere, at Pearl Harbor, was scheduled aboard the aircraft carrier USS *John C. Stennis*, with a screening of the film on the flight deck in front of 800 military brass along with survivors of the attack.

The film received scathing reviews, particularly about the love story subplot. *Daily Variety* tallied the reactions of forty-eight critics across the country.

Twenty-five reviews were negative, seventeen were mixed, with six critics giving the film a thumbs up.[22]

Writing in *The New Yorker*, Anthony Lane concluded,

Why did they (Michael Bay and Jerry Bruckheimer) go with this plan? . . . I just learned that this Hawaiian thing—with the planes and ships, right—well, it wasn't so great for us. Apparently, the Japs won. We *lost*. So they tacked on another story and went out on a high. Pearl Harbor may be stirring proof that right will prevail, but I hate to think what will happen when these guys get their hands on *King Lear*.[23]

Despite the rough reviews, *Pearl Harbor* not only opened up old controversies, it gave the *younger* generation a cinematic history lesson. The film's subplots unleashed a series of related sidebar stories. Many in the new generation had no idea of the devastation of the attack or that the death toll went to approximately 2,400 that Sunday morning. Survivors of the attack, in their seventies and eighties, were quoted in various reflections on the weekend that changed the twentieth century.

The two commanders, Admiral Husband Kimmel and Lieutenant General Walter Short, were back in the news. Were they really derelict in their duties? Supporters of Kimmel and Short had lobbied for congressional legislation to clear the commanders of the blame for the attack that ended their careers.[24] Then there was the resurrection of the much-debated issue of what President Franklin Roosevelt knew and when did he know it. One theory holds that Roosevelt was aware of the impending attack but did nothing because he knew it would pull the United States into the war, which was his objective. Another theory was that the United States and the allies knew an attack was coming based on cable traffic and purported ship movements. The probable attack targets were thought to be Manila, Singapore, Taipei, Hong Kong, or even Wake Island. Many military advisers therefore concluded that an attack on the Hawaiian Islands was extremely improbable. Naturally, this thinking contributed to the surprise factor.

When *Pearl Harbor* opened in Japan, it was marketed as an epic love story rather than a war film. It premiered before a crowd of 25,000 at the Tokyo Dome. The screening set off more controversy and questions about the attack in Japanese history books, which give the incident scant mention. It was also brought out that most Japanese history courses begin with the ancient regimes and run out of time, glossing over the twentieth century and World War II. There are a few lines about Pearl Harbor along with referrals to secondary reading.

The Japanese pilots were seen as noble warriors in the film, capped off with the frequently used quote from Admiral Yamamoto, "All we have done is awaken a sleeping giant."

The concern from the Japanese-American community did not seem as great after the film's release. By the first week of August, *Pearl Harbor* was approaching $200 million in reported domestic box office receipts.

## THE VALLEY OF DEATH

The 1992 Random House bestseller *We Were Soldiers Once . . . And Young* detailed the story of the Ia Drang Valley and came to be known as the battle that changed Vietnam. It has often been called the Gettysburg of Vietnam. Coauthored by Lieutenant General Harold G. Moore and journalist Joseph L. Galloway, the book is a powerful and factual account of the devastating three-day battle in November 1965.

Moore was a forty-two-year-old lieutenant colonel when he assumed a battalion command at Fort Benning, Georgia, on June 29, 1965. Commissioned with the West Point class of 1945, he was a combat veteran of Korea and had served in several staff capacities along with graduating from Command and General Staff College and Naval War College. He had also come to believe in air mobility as a tactic in jungle warfare.

The air cavalry was a military innovation that grew out of the vertical envelopment concept used in Korea. After Korea, the concept of a modern air cavalry was researched and developed under the leadership of Lieutenant General James M. Gavin, who won fame with the 82nd Airborne Division in World War II.

With this concept, the cavalry would still be part of the attack but horses would be replaced by helicopter mobility, transporting a battalion airmobile-size force quickly into enemy strongholds while supporting the unit with artillery and air support. When President Johnson ordered an entire airmobile division to Vietnam, Moore was troubled. Even though Johnson ordered the deployment, a state of emergency was never mentioned. And without a state of emergency, Moore would lose his most experienced men, including officers, due to transfers and enlistment expirations.

What happened at the Ia Drang Valley tested not only the airmobile concept but the will and resolution of the United States to fight a committed enemy on his own ground in the face of overwhelming odds. Up to this point in time, U.S. ground forces had engaged small units of Viet Cong. But they had yet to be tested by the People's Army of Vietnam (PAVN), the rugged and tough North Vietnamese regulars.

After assuming command Moore also learned, from his division commander, Major General Harry Kinnard, that his unit was now the 1st battalion, 7th Cavalry, 1st Air Cavalry Division. Soon they had their deployment orders, leaving the training environment of Fort Benning, Georgia.

The 7th Cavalry's history dates back to Lieutenant Colonel George Armstrong Custer and the infamous Battle of Little Big Horn at the Rosebud Creek in southern Montana on a Sunday in 1876. At that time the unit had adopted a rowdy Irish ballad, "Garry Owen." The name of the ballad was etched onto the regimental crest and the tradition held. The ballad was further popularized in the highly fictional 1941 Warner Bros. biography of Custer, *They Died with Their Boots On*, starring Errol Flynn and Olivia de Havilland.

As time went on, there would be more parallels to the 7th Cavalry's history.

Moore, like the soldiers under his command, said goodbye to his wife Julie and their children.

On the same day that the 1st Air Cavalry Division left Charleston Harbor, the 66th North Vietnamese Regiment began its move through the Cambodian sanctuary to the Central Highlands of South Vietnam. The North Vietnamese commander, Colonel Nguyen Huu An, had taken part in the defeat of a major French unit in 1954 in the same area. His strategy was simple, with comparisons to Custer and the Sioux—lure the enemy out and then surround and surprise him with overwhelming odds.

Colonel An also believed what North Vietnamese General Vo Nguyen Giap once stated, "Whoever controls the central highlands controls South Vietnam."

To set the bait, Colonel An ordered an attack on a Special Forces camp at Plei Mei. After that, assault division intelligence at 1st Air Cav made the decision to hit the enemy with an airmobile assault in the Ia Drang valley in the heart of the Central Highlands. The 1st battalion drew the assignment. The night before they went out, Moore and his sergeant major, Basil Plumley, were with the 1st battalion camped in the remains of an old French fort.

The next day was Sunday, November 14, 1965, as the battle of the Ia Drang valley was about to be joined.

What division intelligence didn't know was that approximately 2,000 North Vietnamese regulars had moved from the north, along the Ho Chi Minh trail in Cambodia, into the area and were waiting for the 450 air cavalry soldiers.

At 10:48 A.M., eight assault helicopters settled into landing zone X-Ray. The first troops reached a treeline unopposed. An eerie quiet settled in. Moore immediately sent out platoon-size patrols. A North Vietnamese soldier was captured and interrogated. When Moore heard about the size of the North Vietnamese force from the prisoner, he gave the order to call the patrols back in.

But it was too late. The patrols were ambushed with raking cross fires. Moore's command group at the landing zone also came under attack.

Under Moore's leadership, the 1st battalion then began a three-day fight where they repeatedly repulsed enemy charges, engaged in hand-to-hand combat, and held their positions against a numerically superior North Vietnamese division.

On the second day, UPI reporter Joe Galloway hitched a ride on a Huey and went into landing zone X-Ray. He would be the only journalist to not only be present and photograph the battle but to participate in it.

On the third day Colonel An massed a charge at what he thought was the weakest point of the 1st battalion, Charlie Company. The American soldiers answered with a deadly sheet of rifle and machine-gun fire, supported by artillery and helicopter gunships led by pilot Major Bruce Crandall. A final charge, led by Moore, ended it. The eerie stillness suddenly returned, this time across a field littered with enemy dead, bodies in bunches, AK-47 assault rifles lying everywhere. Approximately 230 American soldiers were killed during the three-day fight. Another 240 were wounded. The North Vietnamese left behind 1,300 dead.

Recovered among the NVA dead was a battered bugle taken from the French when they were defeated in the same area in 1954.

On November 18, 1965, the first telegrams began arriving back in the states with the dreaded salutation, "The Secretary of the Army regrets to inform you. . . ." The army's and the soldiers' families and loved ones were not prepared for this.

Because the Vietnam war was relatively new, the army had not set up casualty-notification teams to comfort relatives. The telegrams were simply handed over to Yellow cab drivers to deliver. The first telegrams caused several of the new young widows to faint dead away. The cold, indifferent manner continued as more telegrams arrived.

Julie Moore knew something had to be done, and quickly. According to the Moore-Galloway book, she followed the cabs in the Fort Benning area "to the trailer courts and thin walled apartment complexes doing her best to comfort those whose lives had been destroyed.

Mrs. Harry Kinnard, wife of the commander of the 1st Cavalry Division, and many others went public with their criticism of the heartless taxicab telegrams, and the army swiftly organized proper casualty-notification teams."[25]

It was an example of the army being totally unprepared by the aftermath of the battle.

What happened in the Ia Drang valley would plague American forces in Vietnam for years to come. Afterward, according to the Moore-Galloway book, orders came down from General Westmoreland's MACV headquarters to division brigade and battalion commanders never to speculate or suggest to any reporter "that the North Vietnamese were using Cambodia as a sanctuary or that they were passing through Cambodia on their way to South Vietnam. This refusal to admit what we all knew was true, and what even the newest reporter knew was true, struck all of us as dishonest and hypocritical."

After being the last soldier of the 1st battalion to leave landing zone X-Ray, Moore promised fellow officers Bruce Crandall and Jon Mills to have a drink with them back at Camp Holloway. Still wearing the fatigues that they wore during the length of the battle and carrying their weapons, they entered the club at the First Cav. The bartender then informed Moore that he couldn't serve them "because Moore was too dirty."

Moore then explained that they just came out of the field and would appreciate a drink. The bartender replied, "You're in the First Cav. This club doesn't belong to you; you'll have to leave."

Moore replied, "Go get your club officer and we'll settle this. But right now, I'm here and I'm going to have a drink. And I would like to have it in the next couple of minutes."

The bartender left to get the club officer.

Moore then unslung his M-16 and laid it on the bar. Mills and Crandall followed suit with their .38 pistols. When the bartender returned Moore said, "You've got exactly thirty seconds to get some drinks on this bar or I'm going to clean house."

The bartender now realized the gravity of the situation. Within seconds there were drinks on the bar. By this time the club officer had arrived. He had heard about the Ia Drang and knew who Moore was. So did the others in the club bar. From then on the three couldn't buy a drink.

For Moore it was finally over. Or was it?

On November 23, 1965, a change of command ceremony was held at An Khe. Major General Harry W.O. Kinnard, a veteran of the Battle of the Bulge where he served on Colonel Tony McAuliffe's staff, pinned colonel's eagles on Harold Moore. The division band played "Colonel Bogey," "The Washington Post March," and lastly "Garry Owen."

Six days later Colonel Harold Moore was called upon to give a briefing of his battalion's role in the Ia Drang battle. Present at the briefing were Secretary of Defense Robert McNamara; Chairman of the Joint Chiefs, General Earle K. Wheeler; Army Chief of Staff, General Harold K. Johnson; General Westmoreland; and Admiral U.S. Grant Sharp, commander in chief, Pacific.

Moore had already heard about McNamara's reputation as "a human computer, insensitive to people." As he stood in front of the group he inwardly prepared himself for a barrage of questions following his presentation. Moore wrote, "I talked without notes, using a map and pointer, for perhaps fifteen minutes. When I wrapped up, saying, 'Sir, that completes my presentation,' there was dead silence. McNamara stood, stepped forward, and without a word extended his hand looking into my eyes. He asked no questions, made no comments."

Years later, at the "Rendezvous with War" conference held at the College of William & Mary, Moore recalled the briefing over lunch: "I always felt that McNamara's opinion of the war changed because of that briefing."[26]

McNamara's memoirs also recall the effect of the battle, as he wrote about the November 29 briefing and how it changed him.

The valor and courage of U.S. troops impressed me immensely, but I saw and heard many problems. The U.S. presence rested on a bowl of jelly—political instability had increased; pacification had stalled; South Vietnamese Army desertions had skyrocketed. Westy's (General Westmoreland) talk of 400,000 U.S. troops by the end of 1966, with the possibility of at least 200,000 more in 1967, combined with the evidence that North Vietnam could move 200 tons of supplies a day down the Ho Chi Minh Trail despite heavy interdiction bombing—more than enough to support the likely level of Communist operations, taking account of supplies the Vietcong obtained in the South—shook me and altered my attitude perceptibly.[27]

The long road to a film began with Joe Galloway's reports on the Ia Drang. In the January 28, 1967, issue of the *Saturday Evening Post*, specialist Jack P.

Smith, son of network journalist Howard K. Smith, wrote about his terrifying ordeal as a soldier in the Ia Drang. It was one of many graphic accounts of the battle. Many more such accounts were to follow over the years.

By 1990 Joe Galloway was a military writer for *U.S. News & World Report.* His editors then decided to do a cover piece on the twenty-fifth anniversary of the battle. Galloway teamed up with Harold G. Moore. The two went back to Vietnam and met with an old enemy, Nguyen Huu An, who was now a lieutenant general. They had a four-hour candid discussion of the battle. The cover story ran October 29, 1990.

At that point Random House stepped into the picture, realizing that there was a book here, the detailed story of the Ia Drang battle, the men who fought and died there, and the impact it had on the families. It played right into the haunting element of the Vietnam war; the war that simply wouldn't fade into the past.

*We Were Soldiers Once . . . and Young* received critical acclaim and became a bestseller in 1992. By spring 2000, screenwriter Randall Wallace, coming off of the script for *Pearl Harbor*, finished his first draft adaptation from the Moore-Galloway book. Approximately one year and many drafts later, filming began at the locations of Fort Benning in Georgia, and Fort Hunter-Liggett in California. The film was now titled *We Were Soldiers.*

Mel Gibson was cast as Moore, with Madeline Stowe as Julie. Sam Elliott would portray Sergeant Major Basil Plumley. Barry Pepper, the Bible-quoting sniper from *Saving Private Ryan*, garnered the role of Joe Galloway.

An important historical incident was first written about in magazine pieces, then became a book, and finally a film, once more showing audiences worldwide what happens when a generation is committed to a war. A war that will, forever, stay within the American dark psyche like no other.

As these pages close, it is interesting to note that as many as eight World War II projects are in various stages of development at major studios and independent production companies.

It has been an accepted fact that as long as two men stand on this planet, the possibility of a war exists. And then afterward, someone will record it, either on the wall of a cave, in a book, or in a movie theater.

# 10

# Ending at the Beginning

I am the enemy you killed, my friend.
—Wilfred Owen

It was a peacefully clear March afternoon in 1998 when a Vietnam veteran and his wife went to Honolulu to celebrate the anniversary of their R&R reunion, when he met her in a respite from the fighting.

On this tranquil afternoon, they went to the memorial at Pearl Harbor. Across the harbor was the USS *Arizona* memorial, where "Battleship Row" once stood. The white memorial stood over the *Arizona*, still underwater at Ford Island, the sailors forever entombed from that fateful morning that brought the United States into its ultimate experience of the twentieth century.

As the veteran and his wife were looking at the view of the *Arizona*, they suddenly heard a tour guide speaking in Japanese. The guide was explaining to a group of young Japanese women how the American ships came under attack that morning. The Japanese women, many of whom were obviously born during the Vietnam War era, appeared serious and interested in what the guide was saying.

It was a curious mix—a Vietnam veteran and his wife plus a group of Japanese women who didn't speak English, all looking out at the sight that brought their two nations into a horrific conflict while their generation was being born.

The veteran moved his gaze from one of the plaques and gave a long look at the Japanese women. They were so engrossed in the tour guide's description that they didn't even notice him. As the guide pointed in the direction of where the first attack wave came from, the Japanese women quickly turned and looked skyward.

It was as if they were trying to envision what the Japanese planes must have looked like as they moved in to attack the American fleet.

The veteran and his wife stood several feet from the tour group, bookends from nations apart. The only sound came from the loudspeaker on a U.S. Navy launch taking another group across the harbor to the *Arizona* memorial.

The group of Japanese women slowly moved in line toward the launch dock. The veteran and his wife watched as they went aboard.

Minutes later, the launch was heading across the harbor to Ford Island, where the Japanese women would read the names of the Americans etched onto the memorial wall.

The Vietnam veteran took his wife's hand and walked away in silence.

It was definitely a long time in passing from that Sunday morning that changed the twentieth century.

## War Film Chronology

| Year | Title | Studio | Writer(s) | Director(s) |
|------|-------|--------|-----------|-------------|
| 1898 | *Tearing Down the Spanish Flag* | Independent | J. Stuart Blackton | J. Stuart Blackton |
| 1915 | *The Birth of a Nation* | Epoch | D.W. Griffith<br>Frank E. Woods | D.W. Griffith |
| 1918 | *Hearts of the World* | Artcraft | D.W. Griffith | D.W. Griffith |
| 1919 | *The Girl Who Stayed Home* | Paramount Artcraft | D.W. Griffith | D.W. Griffith |
| 1921 | *The Four Horsemen of the Apocalypse* | Metro | June Mathis | Rex Ingram |
| 1924 | *What Price Glory* | Metro-Goldwyn-Mayer | Maxwell Anderson<br>Laurence Stallings | Raoul Walsh |
| 1925 | *The Big Parade* | Metro-Goldwyn-Mayer | Laurence Stallings<br>Harry Behn | King Vidor |
| 1927 | *Seventh Heaven* | Fox | Benjamin Glazer | Frank Borzage |
| 1927 | *Wings* | Paramount | Hope Loring<br>Harry D. Lighton | William A. Wellman |
| 1929 | *Flight* | Columbia | Frank Capra<br>Ralph Graves | Frank Capra |
| 1930 | *All Quiet on the Western Front* | Universal | Maxwell Anderson<br>Lewis Milestone<br>George Abbott | Lewis Milestone |
| 1930 | *The Dawn Patrol* | Warner Bros. | John Monk Saunders<br>Seton I. Miller | Howard Hawks |
| 1930 | *Hell's Angels* | Howard Hughes | Howard Estabrook<br>Harry Bahn | Howard Hughes |

| Year | Title | Studio | Writer(s) | Director(s) |
|---|---|---|---|---|
| 1933 | *Today We Live* | Metro-Goldwyn-Mayer | Edith Fitzgerald<br>Dwight Taylor<br>William Faulkner | Howard Hawks |
| 1935 | *So Red the Rose* | Paramount | Laurence Stallings<br>Maxwell Anderson<br>Edwin Justus Mayer | King Vidor |
| 1936 | *The Charge of the Light Brigade* | Warner Bros. | Michael Jacoby<br>Rowland Leigh | Michael Curtiz |
| 1937 | *The Last Train from Madrid* | Paramount | Louis Stevens<br>Robert Wyler | James P. Hogan |
| 1937 | *The Road Back* | Universal | R.C. Sherriff<br>Charles Kenyon | James Whale |
| 1938 | *The Dawn Patrol* | Warner Bros. | Seton I. Miller<br>Dan Totheroh | Edmund Goulding |
| 1939 | *Confessions of a Nazi Spy* | Warner Bros. | Milton Krims<br>John Wexley | Anatole Litvak |
| 1939 | *Drums along the Mohawk* | 20th Century Fox | Lamar Trotti<br>Sonya Levien | John Ford |
| 1939 | *Gone with the Wind* | Metro-Goldwyn-Mayer | Sidney Howard<br>(and others) | Victor Fleming<br>(and others) |
| 1939 | *Goodbye, Mr. Chips* | Metro-Goldwyn-Mayer/<br>APJAC | R.C. Sherriff<br>Claudine West<br>Eric Mashweitz | Sam Wood |

| Year | Title | Studio | Writers | Director |
|---|---|---|---|---|
| 1939 | *Gunga Din* | RKO | Joel Sayre<br>Fred Guiol<br>Charles MacArthur<br>Ben Hecht | George Stevens |
| 1940 | *The Fighting 69th* | Warner Bros. | Norman Reilly Raine<br>Fred Niblo Jr.<br>Dean Franklin | William Keighley |
| 1940 | *The Mortal Storm* | Metro-Goldwyn-Mayer | Claudine West<br>George Froeschel<br>Anderson Ellis | Alan Rudolph |
| 1941 | *Dive Bomber* | Warner Bros. | Frank "Spig" Wead<br>Robert Buckner | Michael Curtiz |
| 1941 | *I Wanted Wings* | Paramount | Richard Maibaum<br>Beirne Lay Jr.<br>Sig Herzig | Mitchell Leisen |
| 1941 | *Man Hunt* | 20th Century Fox | Dudley Nichols | Fritz Lang |
| 1941 | *Sergeant York* | Warner Bros. | Abem Finkel<br>Harry Chandler<br>Howard Koch<br>John Huston | Howard Hawks |
| 1941 | *A Yank in the RAF* | 20th Century Fox | Karl Tunberg<br>Darrell Ware | Henry King |
| 1941 | *A Yank on the Burma Road* | Metro-Goldwyn-Mayer | George Kahn<br>Hugo Butler<br>David Lang | George B. Seitz |
| 1942 | *Across the Pacific* | Warner Bros. | Richard Macaulay | John Huston |

| Year | Title | Studio | Writer(s) | Director(s) |
|---|---|---|---|---|
| 1942 | *Captains of the Clouds* | Warner Bros. | Arthur T. Horman<br>Richard Macaulay<br>Norman Reilly Raine | Michael Curtiz |
| 1942 | *Casablanca* | Warner Bros. | Julius J. Epstein<br>Philip G. Epstein<br>Howard Koch | Michael Curtiz |
| 1942 | *Desperate Journey* | Warner Bros. | Arthur Horman | Raoul Walsh |
| 1942 | *Flying Tigers* | Republic | Kenneth Gamet<br>Barry Trivers | David Miller |
| 1942 | *Joe Smith, American* | Metro-Goldwyn-Mayer | Allen Rivkin | Richard Thorpe |
| 1942 | *Mrs. Miniver* | Metro-Goldwyn-Mayer | Arthur Wimperis<br>George Froeschel<br>James Hilton<br>Claudine West | William Wyler |
| 1942 | *Saboteur* | Universal | Peter Viertel<br>Joan Harrison<br>Dorothy Parker | Alfred Hitchcock |
| 1942 | *Somewhere I'll Find You* | Metro-Goldwyn-Mayer | Marguerite Roberts | Wesley Ruggles |
| 1942 | *To Be or Not to Be* | Alexander Korda/Ernst Lubitsch | Edwin Justus Mayer | Ernst Lubitsch |
| 1942 | *To the Shores of Tripoli* | 20th Century Fox | Lamar Trotti | H. Bruce Humberstone |
| 1942 | *Wake Island* | Paramount | W.R. Burnett<br>Frank Butler | John Farrow |
| 1942 | *Yankee Doodle Dandy* | Warner Bros. | Robert Buckner<br>Edmund Joseph | Michael Curtiz |

| Year | Title | Studio | Writers | Director |
|---|---|---|---|---|
| 1943 | *Action in the North Atlantic* | Warner Bros. | A.I. Bezzerides<br>W.R. Burnett<br>Guy Gilpatric | Lloyd Bacon |
| 1943 | *Air Force* | Warner Bros. | Dudley Nichols | Howard Hanks |
| 1943 | *Bataan* | Metro-Goldwyn-Mayer | Robert H. Andrews | Tay Garnett |
| 1943 | *Crash Dive* | 20th Century Fox | Jo Swerling | Archie Mayo |
| 1943 | *Cry Havoc* | Metro-Goldwyn-Mayer | Paul Osborn | Richard Thorpe |
| 1943 | *Destination Tokyo* | Warner Bros. | Delmer Daves<br>Albert Maltz | Delmer Daves |
| 1943 | *Five Graves to Cairo* | Paramount | Charles Brackett<br>Billy Wilder | Billy Wilder |
| 1943 | *Flight for Freedom* | RKO | Oliver H.P. Garrett<br>S.K. Lauren | Lothar Mendes |
| 1943 | *For Whom the Bell Tolls* | Paramount | Dudley Nichols | Sam Wood |
| 1943 | *Guadalcanal Diary* | 20th Century Fox | Lamar Trotti | Lewis Seiler |
| 1943 | *Gung Ho!* | Universal | Lucien Hubbard | Ray Enright |
| 1943 | *Hangmen Also Die!* | Arnold Pressburger/<br>Fritz Lang | John Wexley | Fritz Lang |
| 1943 | *Hitler's Children* | RKO | Emmet Lavery | Edward Dmytryk |
| 1943 | *Hitler's Madman (Hitler's Hangman)* | Metro-Goldwyn-Mayer | Peretz Hirschbein<br>Melvin Levy<br>Doris Malloy | Douglas Sirk |
| 1943 | *The Immortal Sergeant* | 20th Century Fox | Lamar Trotti | John M. Stahl |
| 1943 | *Mission to Moscow* | Warner Bros. | Howard Koch | Michael Curtiz |

| Year | Title | Studio | Writer(s) | Director(s) |
|---|---|---|---|---|
| 1943 | Sahara | Columbia | John Howard Lawson<br>Zoltan Korda | Zoltan Korda |
| 1943 | So Proudly We Hail | Paramount | Allan Scott | Mark Sandrich |
| 1943 | Watch on the Rhine | Warner Bros. | Dashiell Hammett | Herman Shumlin |
| 1944 | The Fighting Seabees | Republic | Borden Chase<br>Aeneas MacKenzie | Edward Ludwig |
| 1944 | A Guy Named Joe | Metro-Goldwyn-Mayer | Dalton Trumbo | Victor Fleming |
| 1944 | Lifeboat | 20th Century Fox | Jo Swerling | Alfred Hitchcock |
| 1944 | The Purple Heart | 20th Century Fox | Jerome Cady<br>Darryl F. Zanuck | Lewis Milestone |
| 1944 | Since You Went Away | Selznick International Pictures | David O. Selznick | John Cromwell |
| 1944 | Song of Russia | Metro-Goldwyn-Mayer | Paul Jarrico<br>Richard Collins | Gregory Ratoff |
| 1944 | The Story of Dr. Wassell | Paramount | Alan Le May<br>Charles Bennett | Cecil B. DeMille |
| 1944 | The Sullivans (The Fighting Sullivans) | 20th Century Fox | Mary C. McCall Jr. | Lloyd Bacon |
| 1944 | Thirty Seconds over Tokyo | Metro-Goldwyn-Mayer | Dalton Trumbo | Mervyn LeRoy |
| 1944 | Tomorrow the World | United Artists | Ring Lardner Jr.<br>Leopold Atlas | Leslie Fenton |
| 1944 | The White Cliffs of Dover | Metro-Goldwyn-Mayer | Claudine West<br>Jan Lustig<br>George Froeschel | Clarence Brown |

| Year | Title | Writers | Studio | Director |
|---|---|---|---|---|
| 1945 | *A Bell for Adano* | Lamar Trotti<br>Norman Reilly Raine | 20th Century Fox | Henry King |
| 1945 | *Blood on the Sun* | Lester Cole | Cagney Productions | Frank Lloyd |
| 1945 | *Captain Eddie* | John Tucker Battle | 20th Century Fox | Lloyd Bacon |
| 1945 | *God Is My Co-Pilot* | Peter Milne<br>Abem Finkel | Warner Brothers | Robert Florey |
| 1945 | *The House on 92nd Street* | Barré Lyndon<br>Charles G. Booth<br>John Monks Jr. | 20th Century Fox | Henry Hathaway |
| 1945 | *Objective Burma!* | Ranald MacDougall<br>Lester Cole<br>Alvah Bessie | Warner Bros. | Raoul Walsh |
| 1945 | *Pride of the Marines* | Albert Maltz | Warner Bros. | Delmer Daves |
| 1945 | *The Story of G.I. Joe* | Leopold Atlas<br>Guy Endore<br>Philip Stevenson | United Artists | William A. Wellman |
| 1945 | *They Were Expendable* | Frank Wead | Metro-Goldwyn-Mayer | John Ford |
| 1946 | *The Best Years of Our Lives* | Robert E. Sherwood | Samuel Goldwyn | William Wyler |
| 1946 | *O.S.S.* | Richard Maibaum | Paramount | Irving Pichel |
| 1946 | *13 Rue Madeleine* | John Monks Jr.<br>Sy Bartlett | 20th Century Fox | Henry Hathaway |
| 1946 | *Till the End of Time* | Allen Rivkin | RKO | Edward Dmytryk |
| 1946 | *A Walk In the Sun* | Robert Rossen | Lewis Milestone Productions | Lewis Milestone |
| 1947 | *Beginning of the End* | Robert Considine | MGM | Norman Taurog |

| Year | Title | Studio | Writer(s) | Director(s) |
|---|---|---|---|---|
| 1947 | *Calcutta* | Paramount | Seton I. Miller | John Farrow |
| 1947 | *Crossfire* | RKO | John Paxton | Edward Dmytryk |
| 1948 | *Beyond Glory* | Paramount | Jonathan Latimer<br>Charles Marquis Warren<br>William Wister Haines | John Farrow |
| 1948 | *Command Decision* | Metro-Goldwyn-Mayer | William R. Laidlaw<br>George Froeschel | Sam Wood |
| 1948 | *Fighter Squadron* | Warner Bros. | Seton I. Miller | Raoul Walsh |
| 1948 | *A Foreign Affair* | Paramount | Charles Brackett<br>Billy Wilder<br>Richard L. Breen | Billy Wilder |
| 1948 | *Homecoming* | Metro-Goldwyn-Mayer | Paul Osborn | Mervyn LeRoy |
| 1948 | *The Search* | Metro-Goldwyn-Mayer | Richard Schweizer<br>David Wechsler<br>Paul Jarrico | Fred Zinnemann |
| 1949 | *Battleground* | Metro-Goldwyn-Mayer | Robert Pirosh | William A. Wellman |
| 1949 | *Home of the Brave* | Stanley Kramer | Carl Foreman | Mark Robson |
| 1949 | *Sands of Iwo Jima* | Republic | Harry Brown<br>James Edward Grant | Allan Dwan |
| 1949 | *Task Force* | Warner Bros. | Delmer Daves | Delmer Daves |
| 1949 | *Twelve O'Clock High* | 20th Century Fox | Sy Bartlett<br>Beirne Lay Jr. | Henry King |
| 1950 | *Halls of Montezuma* | 20th Century Fox | Michael Blankfort | Lewis Milestone |
| 1950 | *Kansas Raiders* | Universal International | Robert L. Richards | Ray Enright |

| | | | |
|---|---|---|---|
| 1950 | *The Kid from Texas* | Universal-International | Kurt Neumann |
| | | Robert Hardy Andrews | |
| | | Karl Kamb | |
| 1950 | *The Men* | Stanley Kramer | Fred Zinnemann |
| | | Carl Foreman | |
| 1951 | *The African Queen* | IFD Horizon | John Huston |
| | | James Agee | |
| 1951 | *Bright Victory* | Universal-International | Mark Robson |
| | | Robert Buckner | |
| 1951 | *Decision before Dawn* | 20th Century Fox | Anatole Litvak |
| | | Peter Viertel | |
| 1951 | *The Desert Fox* | 20th Century Fox | Henry Hathaway |
| | | Nunnally Johnson | |
| 1951 | *Fixed Bayonets* | 20th Century Fox | Samuel Fuller |
| | | Samuel Fuller | |
| 1951 | *Flying Leathernecks* | RKO | Nicholas Ray |
| | | James Edward Grant | |
| 1951 | *Force of Arms* | Warner Bros. | Michael Curtiz |
| | | Orin Jannings | |
| 1951 | *Go for Broke!* | Metro-Goldwyn-Mayer | Robert Pirosh |
| | | Robert Pirosh | |
| 1951 | *Operation Pacific* | Warner Bros. | George Waggner |
| | | George Waggner | |
| 1951 | *The Red Badge of Courage* | Metro-Goldwyn-Mayer | John Huston |
| | | John Huston | |
| 1951 | *The Steel Helmet* | Lippert Pictures | Samuel Fuller |
| | | Samuel Fuller | |
| 1952 | *Above and Beyond* | Metro-Goldwyn-Mayer | Melvin Frank |
| | | Melvin Frank | Norman Panama |
| | | Norman Panama | |
| 1952 | *Five Fingers* | 20th Century Fox | Joseph L. |
| | | Michael Wilson | Mankiewicz |
| 1952 | *One Minute to Zero* | RKO | Tay Garnett |
| | | Milton Krims | |
| | | William Wister Haines | |
| 1952 | *Retreat, Hell!* | Warner Bros./United | Joseph H. Lewis |
| | | States Pictures | |
| | | Milton Sperling | |
| | | Ted Sherdeman | |
| 1952 | *What Price Glory?* | 20th Century Fox | John Ford |
| | | Phoebe and Henry Ephron | |

| Year | Title | Studio | Writer(s) | Director(s) |
|------|-------|--------|-----------|-------------|
| 1953 | *From Here to Eternity* | Columbia | Daniel Taradash | Fred Zinnemann |
| 1953 | *Stalag 17* | Paramount | Billy Wilder Edwin Blum | Billy Wilder |
| 1954 | *The Bridges at Toko Ri* | Paramount | Valentine Davies | Mark Robson |
| 1954 | *The Caine Mutiny* | Columbia | Stanley Roberts | Edward Dmytryk |
| 1954 | *On the Waterfront* | Columbia | Budd Schulberg | Elia Kazan |
| 1955 | *Battle Cry* | Warner Bros. | Leon Uris | Raoul Walsh |
| 1955 | *The Colditz Story* | British Lion | Guy Hamilton Ivan Foxwell | Guy Hamilton |
| 1955 | *The Court-Martial of Billy Mitchell* | United States Pictures Warner Bros. | Milton Sperling Emmet Lavery | Otto Preminger |
| 1955 | *Marty* | United Artists | Paddy Chayefsky | Delbert Mann |
| 1955 | *To Hell and Back* | Universal-International | Gil Doud | Jesse Hibbs |
| 1956 | *Attack* | United Artists | James Poe | Robert Aldrich |
| 1957 | *The Bridge on the River Kwai* | Columbia | Carl Foreman Michael Wilson | David Lean |
| 1957 | *Darby's Rangers* | Warner Bros. | Guy Trosper | William A. Wellman |
| 1957 | *A Farewell to Arms* | 20th Century Fox | Ben Hecht | Andrew Marton, then Charles Vidor (formerly John Huston) |

| Year | Title | Studio | Writer(s) | Director |
|---|---|---|---|---|
| 1957 | *Heaven Knows Mr. Allison* | 20th Century Fox | John Lee Mahin, John Huston | John Huston |
| 1957 | *Paths of Glory* | United Artists, Bryna | Stanley Kubrick, Calder Willingham, Jim Thompson | Stanley Kubrick |
| 1957 | *Sayonara* | Goetz Pictures-Pennebaker | Paul Osborn | Joshua Logan |
| 1958 | *Kings Go Forth* | United Artists | Merle Miller | Delmer Daves |
| 1958 | *The Naked and the Dead* | RKO | Denis and Terry Sanders | Raoul Walsh |
| 1958 | *Run Silent, Run Deep* | United Artists | John Gay | Robert Wise |
| 1958 | *The Young Lions* | 20th Century Fox | Edward Anhalt | Edward Dmytryk |
| 1959 | *The Diary of Anne Frank* | 20th Century Fox | Frances Goodrich, Albert Hackett | George Stevens |
| 1959 | *Never So Few* | Metro-Goldwyn-Mayer | Millard Kaufman | John Sturges |
| 1959 | *Pork Chop Hill* | United Artists/Milville Prods. | James R. Webb | Lewis Milestone |
| 1959 | *They Came to Cordura* | Columbia/Goetz-Baroda | Ivan Moffat, Robert Rossen | Robert Rossen |
| 1960 | *The Alamo* | United Artists/Batjac | James Edward Grant | John Wayne |
| 1960 | *All the Young Men* | Columbia | Hall Bartlett | Hall Bartlett |
| 1960 | *The Gallant Hours* | United Artists/Cagney-Montgomery | Bierre Lay Jr., Frank Gilroy | Robert Montgomery |
| 1960 | *The Magnificent Seven* | United Artists/Batjac | William Roberts | John Sturges |
| 1961 | *The Four Horsemen of the Apocalypse* | Metro-Goldwyn-Mayer | Robert Ardrey, John Gay | Vicente Minnelli |

| Year | Title | Studio | Writer(s) | Director(s) |
|---|---|---|---|---|
| 1961 | *The Guns of Navarone* | Columbia | Carl Foreman | J. Lee Thompson |
| 1961 | *Judgment at Nuremburg* | United Artists | Abby Mann | Stanley Kramer |
| 1961 | *The Outsider* | Universal-International | Stewart Stern | Delbert Mann |
| 1962 | *Lawrence of Arabia* | Columbia/Horizon | Robert Bolt | David Lean |
| 1962 | *The Longest Day* | 20th Century Fox | Cornelius Ryan<br>Romain Gary<br>James Jones<br>David Pursall<br>Jack Seddon | Andrew Marton<br>Ken Annakin<br>Bernhard Wicki |
| 1962 | *The Manchurian Candidate* | United Artists/MC | George Axelrod | John Frankenheimer |
| 1962 | *To Kill a Mockingbird* | Universal-International | Horton Foote | Robert Mulligan |
| 1962 | *War Hunt* | T-D Enterprises | Stanford Whitmore | Denis Sanders |
| 1962 | *The War Lover* | Columbia | Howard Koch | Philip Leacock |
| 1963 | *Dr. Strangelove; Or: How I Learned to Stop Worrying and Love the Bomb* | Columbia | Stanley Kubrick<br>Terry Southern | Stanley Kubrick |
| 1963 | *The Great Escape* | United Artists | James Clavell<br>W.R. Burnett | John Sturges |
| 1963 | *PT 109* | Warner Bros. | Richard Breen | Lewis Milestone<br>Leslie Martinson |
| 1963 | *The Victors* | Columbia | Carl Foreman | Carl Foreman |
| 1964 | *The Americanization of Emily* | Metro-Goldwyn-Mayer | Paddy Chayefsky | Arthur Hiller |

| Year | Title | Studio | Screenwriter(s) | Director(s) |
|---|---|---|---|---|
| 1964 | *The Thin Red Line* | Allied Artists | Bernard Gordon | Andrew Marton then Charles Vidor (formerly John Huston) |
| 1965 | *In Harm's Way* | Paramount | Wendell Mayes | Otto Preminger |
| 1966 | *Is Paris Burning?* | Paramount | Francis Ford Coppola, Gore Vidal | René Clément |
| 1966 | *The Sand Pebbles* | 20th Century Fox | Robert Anderson | Robert Wise |
| 1967 | *The Dirty Dozen* | Metro-Goldwyn-Mayer | Nunnally Johnson, Lukas Heller | Robert Aldrich |
| 1967 | *The Night of the Generals* | Columbia | Joseph Kessel, Paul Dehn, Hans Helmut Kirst | Anatole Litvak |
| 1968 | *The Green Berets* | Warner/Batjac | James Lee Barrett | John Wayne, Ray Kellogg |
| 1969 | *Alice's Restaurant* | United Artists | Venable Herndon, Arthur Penn | Arthur Penn |
| 1969 | *Easy Rider* | Columbia | Peter Fonda, Dennis Hopper, Terry Southern | Dennis Hopper |
| 1969 | *Midnight Cowboy* | United Artists, Jerome Hellman | Waldo Salt | John Schlesinger |
| 1969 | *They Shoot Horses, Don't They?* | Palomar, Chartoff-Winkler-Pollack | James Poe, Robert E. Thompson | Sydney Pollack |

| Year | Title | Studio | Writer(s) | Director(s) |
|------|-------|--------|-----------|-------------|
| 1969 | *The Wild Bunch* | Warner Seven Arts | Walon Green<br>Sam Peckinpah | Sam Peckinpah |
| 1970 | *Getting Straight* | Columbia | Robert Kaufman | Richard Rush |
|      |  | The Organization |  |  |
| 1970 | *Little Big Man* | Stockbridge-Hiller<br>Cinema Center | Thomas Berger<br>Calder Willingham | Arthur Penn |
| 1970 | *M\*A\*S\*H* | 20th Century Fox | Ring Lardner Jr. | Robert Altman |
| 1970 | *Patton* | 20th Century Fox | Francis Ford Coppola<br>Edmund H. North | Franklin Schnaffer |
| 1970 | *Soldier Blue* | Arco | John Gay | John Gay |
| 1970 | *The Strawberry Statement* | MGM<br>Robert Chartoff<br>Irwin Winkler | Israel Horovitz | Stuart Hagmann |
| 1970 | *Tora! Tora! Tora!* | 20th Century Fox | Larry Forrester<br>Hideo Oguni<br>Rynzo Kikishima | Richard Fleischer<br>Ray Kellog<br>Toshio Masuda<br>Kinji Fukusaku |
| 1971 | *Johnny Got His Gun* | World Entertainment | Dalton Trumbo | Dalton Trumbo |
| 1971 | *A Time for Dying* | Corinth Films (no<br>U.S. release) | Budd Boetticher | Budd Boetticher |
| 1973 | *The Last Detail* | Columbia/Acrobat | Robert Towne | Hal Ashby |
| 1974 | *The Execution of Private Slovik* | TV Movie | Richard Levinson<br>William Link | Richard T. Heffron |

| Year | Title | | Studio | Director |
|---|---|---|---|---|
| 1977 | *The Boys in Company C* | Rick Nankin<br>Sidney J. Furie | Golden Harvest | Sidney J. Furie |
| 1977 | *A Bridge Too Far* | William Goldman | United Artists/Levine | Richard Attenborough |
| 1977 | *MacArthur* | Hal Batwood<br>Matthew Robbins | Universal/Zanuch-Brown | Joseph Sargent |
| 1977 | *Young Joe, The Forgotten Kennedy* | | TV Movie | Lamont Johnson |
| 1978 | *Coming Home* | Waldo Salt<br>Robert C. James<br>Nancy Ellen Dowd | United Artists | Hal Ashby |
| 1978 | *The Deer Hunter* | Deric Washburn<br>Michael Cimino<br>Louis Garfinkle<br>Quinn K. Redeker | Universal/EMI | Michael Cimino |
| 1978 | *Go Tell the Spartans* | Wendell Mayes | Spartan Company | Ted Post |
| 1979 | *Apocalypse Now* | John Milius<br>Francis Ford Coppola | OMNI/Zoltcope | Francis Ford Coppola |
| 1980 | *The Big Red One* | Samuel Fuller | United Artists/Lorimar | Samuel Fuller |
| 1980 | *Lili Marlene* | William Anthony McGuire | 20th Century Fox | Irvin Cummings |
| 1980 | *Rumor of War* | | TV Movie | Richard T. Heffrom |
| 1983 | *Uncommon Valor* | Joe Gayton<br>John Milius<br>Buzz Feitshans | Paramount | Ted Kotcheff |
| 1984 | *The Killing Fields* | Bruce Robinson | Goldcrest/Enigma | Roland Joffe |

| Year | Title | Studio | Writer(s) | Director(s) |
|------|-------|--------|-----------|-------------|
| 1985 | *Rambo: First Blood Part Two* | Anabasis/Tri-Star | Sylvester Stallone<br>James Cameron | George P. Cosmatos |
| 1986 | *Platoon* | Hemdale/Kopelson | Oliver Stone | Oliver Stone |
| 1987 | *Full Metal Jacket* | Warner Bros.<br>Stanley Kubrick | Stanley Kubrick<br>Michael Herr | Stanley Kubrick |
| 1987 | *Hamburger Hill* | Paramount/RKO | Jim Carabatsos | John Irvin |
| 1987 | *The Hanoi Hilton* | | Lionel Chetwynd | Lionel Chetwynd |
| 1988 | *Rambo III* | Columbia/Tri-Star/<br>Carolco | Sylvester Stallone<br>Sheldon Lettich | Peter McDonald |
| 1989 | *Born on the Fourth of July* | UIP/IXTLAN | Oliver Stone<br>Ron Kovic | Oliver Stone |
| 1989 | *Casualties of War* | Columbia/Tri-Star | David Rabe | Brian de Palma |
| 1989 | *84 Charlie Mopic* | Charlie Mopic Co. | Patrick S. Duncan | Patrick S. Duncan |
| 1989 | *Glory* | Columbia/Tri-Star | Kevin Jarre | Edward Zwick |
| 1990 | *Dances with Wolves* | TIG Productions | Michael Blake | Kevin Costner |
| 1991 | *Mission of the Shark* | | | |
| 1993 | *Gettysburg* | New Line Cinema | Ronald F. Maxwell | Ronald F. Maxwell |
| 1994 | *Forrest Gump* | Paramount | Eric Roth<br>Winston Groom | Robert Zemeickes |
| 1996 | *Courage Under Fire* | | Patrick S. Duncan | |
| 1996 | *The English Patient* | Buena Vista/Saul<br>Zaentz | Anthony Minghella<br>Michael Ondaatze | Anthony Minghella |
| 1998 | *A Bright, Shining Lie* | HBO | | Terry George |

302

| Year | Title | Production Company | Writer | Director |
|---|---|---|---|---|
| 1998 | *Saving Private Ryan* | Amblin Entertainment<br>DreamWorks SKG<br>Mutual Film Company<br>Paramount Pictures | Robert Rodat<br>Frank Darabont (uncredited) | Steven Spielberg |
| 1998 | *The Thin Red Line* | | | Terrence Malick |
| 1999 | *Three Kings* | Warner Bros. | John Ridley (I) (story)<br>David O. Russell | David O. Russell |
| 2000 | *The Patriot* | Columbia Pictures<br>Columbia Tri-Star<br>Sony Pictures<br>Entertainment<br>Mutual Film Company | Robert Rodat | Roland Emmerich |
| 2000 | *Rules of Engagement* | Seven Arts Pictures<br>Paramount Pictures | James Webb (III) (story)<br>Stephen Gaghan | William Friedkin |
| 2000 | *U-571* | Universal Pictures | Jonathan Mostow | Jonathan Mostow |

# Noted Documentaries of World War II

| Year | Title | Director | Production Company |
|---|---|---|---|
| 1942–45 | *Why We Fight* (series) | Frank Capra | U.S. War Office |
| | *The Battle of Britain* | | |
| | *The Battle of China* | | |
| | *The Battle of Russia* | | |
| | *Divide and Conquer* | | |
| | *The Nazis Strike* | | |
| | *Prelude to War* | | |
| | *War Comes to America* | | |
| 1944 | *Thunder Bolt* | William Wyler | U.S. War Office |
| 1944 | *With the Marines at Tarawa* | Louis Hayward | Department of the Navy |
| 1945 | *The Battle of San Pietro* | John Huston | U.S. Army Signal Corps |
| 1945 | *The Fighting Lady* | Louis De Rochemont | Department of the Navy |
| 1945 | *The Memphis Belle* | William Wyler | U.S. War Office |
| 1946 | *Let There Be Light* | John Huston | Warner Bros. |

# Notes

## CHAPTER 1

1. Elaine Dutka, "Dawn Steel, 1st Female Studio Chief" (Obituary), *Los Angeles Times*, December 22, 1997.

2. Frances Marion, in Anthony Holden, *Behind the Oscar: A History of the Academy Awards* (New York: Simon & Schuster, 1993), p. 84.

3. Jack Kroll and Tessa Namuth, "The Movies: The Art Form of Our Era," *Newsweek*, Special Issue, December 1997.

4. Billy Wilder and Charles Brackett, *Sunset Boulevard* (Screenplay), Paramount Pictures, 1950.

5. Theodore K. Rabb, "Artists on War: Mathew Brady and Antietam," *Quarterly Journal of Military History* 10, no. 2 (Winter 1998): 40.

6. Timothy M. Gray, "Celebrities as the Gods of Mount Olympus," *Daily Variety*, Reel Life, September 12, 1997, p. 71.

7. Steve Proffitt, "David Brown: On the Nature of Celebrity," *Los Angeles Times*, March 23, 1997, p. M3.

8. Gore Vidal, "Americans Wanting to Be Movie Stars," *United States: Essays 1952–1992* (New York: Random House, 1993), p. 296.

9. David Culbert, ed., *Film and Propaganda in America: A Documentary History*, vol. 2 (Westport, CT: Greenwood Press, 1990), pp. ix, x.

10. Frank R. Wilson, Director of Publicity, War Loan Organization, U.S. Treasury Department, letter to Wallace Reid, Lasky Studies, Hollywood, CA, October 15, 1918, In Special Collections, Academy of Motion Picture Arts and Sciences.

11. Michael Satchell, "Star-Struck Charities," *U.S. News & World Report*, September 22, 1997, p. 33.

12. Jeanne Holm, "Women: A History of Service," *Army Times*, October 20, 1997, p. 14.

13. Battle deaths and other deaths from Department of Defense data. "Casualties in

Principal Wars of the U.S.," In *The World Almanac* (Mahwah, NJ: Funk & Wagnalls, 1994).

14. D.W. Griffith, *The Historical Review*, Hollywood Roosevelt Movie Museum, Transition to Talkies, 1927, Hollywood, CA.

15. Michael Thomas, "The Wonderful Life of Frank Capra," *Los Angeles Times*, May 17, 1997.

16. Lewis Milestone, undated note, c. 1964, Aspen Meadows, CO, in Special Collections, Academy of Motion Picture Arts and Sciences.

17. Lew Ayres, letter to Dr. Harley U. Taylor Jr., West Virginia University, College of Arts & Sciences, Morgantown, WV, December 17, 1975, in Special Collections, Academy of Motion Picture Arts and Sciences.

18. Thomas, "The Wonderful Life of Frank Capra."

19. Katharine Hepburn, *Me: Stories of My Life* (New York: Knopf, 1991), p. 180.

20. Margaret Mitchell Marsh, letter to Kay Brown, Selznick International, New York City, October 6, 1936, in Special Collections, Academy of Motion Picture Arts and Sciences.

21. Rudy Behlmer, ed., *Memo from David O. Selznick* (New York: Viking, 1972), p. 192.

22. Gwen Robyns, *Light of a Star* (London: Leslie Frewin Publishers, 1968), pp. 68–69.

23. Jane Ellen Wayne, *Gable's Women* (New York: Prentice Hall, 1987), p. 169.

24. Location schedules for central California regarding *Gunga Din*, research notes compiled by Hilda Grenier, RKO, customs of India, personnel and rank structure, British army; RKO Inter-Department memo, August 5, 1938, to George Stevens from Pandro Berman regarding use of the Rudyard Kipling poem for the film's finale, both from Special Collections, Academy of Motion Picture Arts and Sciences.

25. Robert Stack, letters to Calendar, *Los Angeles Times*, April 13, 1997.

## CHAPTER 2

1. The Pearl Harbor attack, "Battleship Row," and the sinking of the USS *Arizona*; losses on December 7, 1941, USS *Arizona* Memorial, National Park Service, Pearl Harbor Naval Base, U.S. Department of Interior.

2. D. Clayton James, "The Other Pearl Harbor," *Quarterly Journal of Military History* 7, no. 2 (1994): 22.

3. Thaddeus Hall, "King of Bataan," *Quarterly Journal of Military History 7*, no. 2 (1994): 32.

4. David Wallechinsky and Irving Wallace, *The People's Almanac* (New York: Doubleday, 1975), p. 232.

5. Edwin P. Hoyt, *Yamamoto: The Man Who Planned Pearl Harbor* (New York: McGraw-Hill, 1990), p. 139.

6. Michael Renov, "Hollywood's Wartime Women: Representation and Ideology," in *Studies in Cinema*, no. 42 (Ann Arbor: University of Michigan Press, 1988). Courtesy, USC Cinema Library.

7. Susan King, "Silver Screen's Role in WW II," *Los Angeles Times*, May 18, 1997.

8. "Hollywood Stars Hit Road for Army-Navy Relief," *Life*, June 1, 1942, Special Collections, Academy of Motion Picture Arts and Sciences.

9. Roy Hoopes, *When the Stars Went to War: Hollywood and World War II* (New York: Random House, 1994), pp. 168–70.

10. Stephen Ambrose, "World War II Remembered," in *The World Almanac* (Mahwah, NJ: Funk & Wagnalls, 1995), p. 37.

11. Callum MacDonald, *The Killing of Obergruppenfuehrer Reinhard Heydrich* (New York: The Free Press, 1989), p. 186.

12. Robert Brent Toplin, *History by Hollywood: The Use and Abuse of the American Past* (Urbana: University of Illinois Press, 1996), pp. 86–87.

13. John Bowers, "The Mythical Morning of Sergeant York," *Quarterly Journal of Military History* 8, no. 2 (1996): 38.

14. Jane Ellen Wayne, *Gable's Women* (New York: Prentice Hall, 1987), p. 183.

15. Aljean Harmetz, *Round Up the Usual Suspects: The Making of Casablanca, Bogart, Bergman, and World War II* (New York: Hyperion, 1992), p. 36.

16. Ibid., p. 30.

17. Ingrid Bergman and Alan Burgess, *Ingrid Bergman: My Story* (New York: Delacorte Press, 1980), p. 109.

18. Ibid., p. 110.

19. Julius Epstein, guest lecturer for instructor Frank McAdams, "Preparing the Screenplay," Summer Quarter, UCLA Extension, 1986.

20. Robert Gessner, "Suggestions for a War Film Pattern in 1943," *New York Times*, January 17, 1943; in Special Collections, Academy of Motion Picture Arts and Sciences.

21. President Franklin D. Roosevelt, letter to the Motion Picture Academy, March 3, 1943; in Special Collections, Academy of Motion Picture Arts and Sciences.

22. Edward Dmytryk, interview with the author, Encino, CA, February 3, 1998.

23. "Selected Comments on American Opinion, the Negro and the War," *Office of War Information*, April 1942; in Special Collections, Academy of Motion Picture Arts and Sciences.

24. Lt. Colonel Darryl Zanuck, Army Signal Corps, testimony before the Army Inspector General Division Panel, Los Angeles, CA, January 4–5, 1943, in Culbert, ed., *Film and Propaganda in America*, vol. 2, Document 42.

25. William Bendix's dialogue in *Guadalcanal Diary*, screenplay by Lamar Trotti; book by Richard Tregaskis; produced by 20th Century Fox, 1943.

26. Michael Renov, "Hollywood's Wartime Women: Representation and Ideology," in *Studies in Cinema*, no. 42 (Ann Arbor: University of Michigan Press, 1988). Courtesy, USC Cinema Library.

27. "Amelia Earhart Vertical File," Special Collections, Academy of Motion Picture Arts and Sciences.

28. Bergman and Burgess, *Ingrid Bergman*, p. 116.

29. Ibid., p. 116.

30. Zanuck memo to Hitchcock and MacGowan, August 19, 1943, Special Collections, Academy of Motion Picture Arts and Sciences.

31. Captain Ronald Morse, U.S. Navy, Office of Information, phone interview with author, October 15, 1997, Los Angeles, CA.

32. David Selznick, note to Milestone, Culver City, CA, April 10, 1944, Special Collections, Academy of Motion Picture Arts and Sciences.

33. Bernard Asbell, *When F.D.R. Died* (New York: Holt, Rinehart, and Winston, 1961), pp. 14–100.

34. Bill King, letter to E.M. Nathanson, January 17, 1999, Pomona, CA.

35. Samuel Fuller, letter to Lewis Milestone, June 6, 1946, Special Collections, Academy of Motion Picture Arts and Sciences.

36. Merle Miller, *Plain Speaking: An Oral Biography of Harry S. Truman* (New York: Berkley, 1974), p. 205.

37. Peter Maslowski, "Truman, the Bomb, and the Numbers," *Quarterly Journal of Military History* 7, no. 3 (Spring 1995): 103–7.

38. Miller, *Plain Speaking*, p. 227.

39. Ibid., p. 243.

40. Faubion Bowers, "The Bomb and Hiroshima," in *The People's Almanac* (Garden City, NY: Doubleday, 1975), pp. 507–10.

41. Douglas MacArthur, *Reminiscences* (New York: McGraw-Hill, 1964), pp. 270–71.

42. Ibid., pp. 275–76.

## CHAPTER 3

1. Robert Plunkett, "Classic War Films, Contemporary Echoes," *New York Times*, March 21, 1993, Sunday film section.

2. Neal Gabler, "Sinatra: Cocktail Brinkmanship," *Los Angeles Times*, May 17, 1998, p. M–1.

3. Fred Stanley, "War Films Resume in Hollywood," *New York Times*, July 15, 1945, Art section, p. 1.

4. Peter Neushul and Second Lieutenant James D. Neushul, USMC, "With the Marines at Tarawa, Captain Louis Hayward's Documentary," *U.S. Naval Institute Proceedings*, April 1999.

5. The John Huston Collection, Special Collections, Academy of Motion Picture Arts and Sciences.

6. Ibid.

7. Peter Maslowski, "Reel War vs. Real War," *Quarterly Journal of Military History* 10, no. 4 (Summer 1998): 68–75.

8. The John Huston Collection, Special Collections, Academy of Motion Picture Arts and Sciences.

9. Jay Carmody, film review of *The Battle of San Pietro, Washington Evening Star*, May 1, 1945, pp. 3–16, in Special Collections, Academy of Motion Picture Arts and Sciences.

10. Frances McFadden, *Harper's Bazaar*, May 1946, in Special Collections, Academy of Motion Picture Arts and Sciences.

11. Dorothy Wheelock, letter to John Huston, March 20, 1946, from the John Huston Collection, Special Collections, Academy of Motion Picture Arts and Sciences.

12. Surgeon General's Memo to John Huston, March 28, 1946, from the John Huston Collection, Special Collections, Academy of Motion Picture Arts and Sciences.

13. Ibid.

14. Archer Winsten, "Movie Talk," *New York Post*, July 2, 1946, in Special Collections, Academy of Motion Picture Arts and Sciences.

15. Ibid., September 21, 1946.

16. John Huston, *An Open Book*, p. 126.

17. Jan Herman, *A Talent for Trouble: The Life of Hollywood's Most Acclaimed Director, William Wyler* (New York: Putnam, 1996), p. 261.

18. Ibid., p. 266.

19. Merle Miller, *Plain Speaking: An Oral Biography of Harry S. Truman* (New York: Berkley, 1974), p. 391.

20. Edward Dmytryk, interview with the author, February 3, 1998, Encino, CA.

21. Steven Jay Rubin, *Combat Films 1945–1970* (Jefferson, NC: McFarland, 1981), p. 129.

22. Darryl F. Zanuck, memo to Henry King, November 3, 1949, in the Henry King Collection, Academy of Motion Picture Arts and Sciences.

23. Gregory Peck, interview with the author, June 8, 1998, Los Angeles, CA.

24. Leonard Fribourg, son of the late Brigadier General Leonard Fribourg, USMC, interview with the author, July 2, 2000.

25. *Daily Variety*, December 14, 1949, n.p.

26. Ron Kovic, *Born on the Fourth of July* (New York: Pocket Books, 1976), p. 43.

27. James Bradley, with Ron Powers, *Flags of Our Fathers* (New York: Bantam Books, 2000), pp. 321–22.

28. Joseph L Galloway and Douglas Pasternak, "The Warrior Class," *U.S. News & World Report*, July 5, 1999, pp. 29–30.

29. Patrick Goldstein, "Hollywood's Blackest Hour," *Los Angeles Times*, October 19, 1997, p. 79.

30. Donna Perlmutter, "The Birth of the Hollywood Blacklist," *Los Angeles Times*, October 28, 1993, p. F–5.

31. Robert Vaughn, *Only Victims: A Study of Show Business Blacklisting* (New York: G.P. Putnam's Sons, 1972), pp. 113–14.

32. Carl Foreman, interview with the author, June 1979, Universal Studios, Los Angeles, CA.

33. Alfred Friendly, "Exiles" (part 3), *Washington Post*, 1971.

34. Howard Suber, quoted by Peter A. Brown, "Blacklist: A Black Tale in Filmland," *Los Angeles Times*, February 1, 1981, calendar.

35. Tom O'Neil, "And the Winners Were," *Written By*, March 2001.

36. Carl Foreman, letter to the editor, *London Daily Express*, July 25, 1957.

37. Mrs. George Willner, PBS documentary *The Hollywood Blacklist*, produced by Judy Chaikin.

## CHAPTER 4

1. Marlon Brando, with Robert Lindsey, *Songs My Mother Taught Me* (New York: Random House, 1994), p. 147.

2. Myrna Oliver, "Gene Evans: Actor Known for 'Tough Guy' Roles" obituary, *Los Angeles Times*, April 3, 1998.

3. Dick Williams, film review of *The Steel Helmet, Los Angeles Daily Mirror*, January 5, 1951, in Special Collections, Academy of Motion Picture Arts and Sciences.

4. Darryl F. Zanuck, memo to Henry King, October 12, 1950, in the Henry King Collection, Academy of Motion Picture Arts and Sciences.

5. Letters and audition requests to John Huston, John Huston Collection, Academy of Motion Picture Arts and Sciences.

6. Associated Press, "John Huston Proves He Has Much Talent," September 6, 1951.

7. Lillian Ross, *"The Red Badge of Courage*—Saga of a Monster and a Movie," *The New Yorker* series, May 24, May 31, June 4, and June 14, 1952.

8. Vic Heutschy, "Huston Films Novel of Civil War" (film review), *Los Angeles Collegian*, Fall 1951.

9. Katherine Lloyd Collins, Archivist, 442nd Archives, Honolulu, Hawaii, interview with the author, March 16, 1998.

10. Sadayo S. Munemori received the Congressional Medal of Honor posthumously, for action on April 5, 1945.

11. Letter from Anthony Coldeway to Earl Finch, May 23, 1950, in the 442nd Regimental Combat Team/100th Battalion, Archives and Learning Center, Honolulu, Hawaii.

12. Letter from Akira Fukinaga to L.K. Sidney, Metro-Goldwyn-Mayer, August 24, 1950, in the 442nd Regimental Combat Team/100th Battalion, Archives and Learning Center, Honolulu, Hawaii.

13. Letter from Akira Fukinaga to Daniel "Balloon" Aoki, October 17, 1950, in the 442nd Regimental Combat Team/100th Battalion, Archives and Learning Center, Honolulu, Hawaii.

14. Jacqueline Newmyer, "Asian Heroes of WWII Get Tardy Honors," *Los Angeles Times*, June 22, 2000.

15. The Korean Winter Offensive of 1950–51 is detailed in David McCullough, *Truman* (New York: Simon & Schuster, 1992), pp. 853–55.

16. Merle Miller, *Plain Speaking: An Oral Biography of Harry S. Truman* (New York: Berkley, 1974), p. 302.

17. Ibid., pp. 298–99.

18. McCullough, *Truman*.

19. Carl Foreman, interview with the author, June 1979, Universal Studios, Los Angeles, CA.

## CHAPTER 5

1. Gore Vidal, "John Horne Burns," *New York Times Book Review*, May 30, 1965, pp. 343–46.

2. The James Jones Society, compiled by J. Michael Lennon, Ph.D., Wilkes University, Wilkes-Barre, PA, September 7, 1999.

3. Daniel Taradash, Oral History, series of interviews conducted by Barbara Hall, 1996, Academy of Motion Picture Arts and Sciences.

4. Ibid.

5. Mario Puzo, *The Godfather Papers and Other Confessions* (New York: Putnam, 1972), p. 46.

6. Daniel Taradash, telephone interview with the author, May 6, 1998.

7. Jay Hyams, *War Movies* (New York: W.H. Smith, 1984), p. 124.

8. Edward Dmytryk, interview with the author, February 3, 1998, Encino, CA.

9. Herman Wouk, letter to the author, June 7, 1999.

10. Elihu Rose, "The Court-Martial of Billy Mitchell," *Quarterly Journal of Military History* 8, no. 3 (Spring 1996): 16–25.

11. Don Graham, *No Name on the Bullet: A Biography of Audie Murphy* (New York: Viking, 1989), p. 69.

12. Rudy Behlmer, ed., *Memo from David O. Selznick* (New York: Viking, 1972), p. 431.

## CHAPTER 6

1. Steven Jay Rubin, *Combat Films 1945–1970* (Jefferson, NC: McFarland, 1981), p. 152.

2. Edward Dymytrk, interview with the author, February 3, 1998, Encino, CA.

3. Gregory Peck, interview with the author, June 8, 1998, Los Angeles, CA.

4. *Inaugural Addresses of the Presidents of the United States* (Washington, D.C.: GPO, 1989), p. 308.

5. Elian P. Demetraopoulos, "Muzzling Admiral Burke," *U.S. Naval Institute Proceedings* (January 2000), pp. 67–68.

6. Peck, interview, June 8, 1998.

7. *Creative Quotations of Lowell Thomas.*

8. Arthur Durand, *Stalag Luft III: The Secret Story* (Baton Rouge: Louisiana State University Press, 1988), p. 287.

9. Walter Cronkite, *A Reporter's Life* (New York: Knopf, 1996), p. 254.

10. Alexander Baron, *The Human Kind* (New York: Dell, 1963), p. 189.

## CHAPTER 7

1. Frank J. Wetta and Stephen J. Curley, *Celluloid Wars: A Guide to Film and the American Experience of War* (Westport, CT: Greenwood, 1992), p. 2.

2. E.M. "Mick" Nathanson, series of interviews with the author, January and July 2000, Dana Point, CA.

3. Ibid.

4. Randy Roberts and James S. Olson, *John Wayne: American* (New York: Free Press, 1995), p. 536.

5. Michael Herr, *Dispatches* (New York: Alfred Knopf, 1977), p. 82.

6. Leo Cawley, "The War about the War: Vietnam Films and American Myth," *The Village Voice*, September 1987, pp. 69–80.

7. Richard Pyle, Associated Press memos, June 6 and June 12, 2000.

8. "Rendezvous with War: A Reflection on the Vietnam War Twenty-five Years After," symposium, College of William & Mary, sponsored by Vietnam Veterans of America, April 6–9, 2000. Reflections include those made by Phillip Caputo, William Conrad Gibbons, Ron Spector, and Peter Arnett.

9. Walter Cronkite, *A Reporter's Life* (New York: Knopf, 1996), pp. 257–58.

10. Ibid.

11. Michael Jackson, KABC radio talk show, circa 1972–73.

12. Abigail Van Buren, "Dear Abby," *Los Angeles Times*, March 5, 1986.

13. *World Almanac* (1995), pp. 155–292; *New York Times Almanac* (1998); U.S. Department of Defense, pp. 145–53; *Parade*, August 18, 1996, p. 10; R.G. Burkett and Glenna Whitley, *Stolen Valor: How the Vietnam Generation Was Robbed of Its Heroes and Its History* (Dallas, TX: Verity, 1998).

14. Thomas Doherty, "He's a Candidate, but Not Manchurian," *Los Angeles Times*, February 11, 2000, op/ed page.

15. Elaine Woo, obituary for Joseph Heller, *Los Angeles Times*, December 14, 1999.

16. Ibid.

17. Frederic L. Borch III, "Guilty as Charged?" *Quarterly Journal of Military History* (Winter 2001): 55–63. The U.S. Senate decided in May 1999 to recommend the post-humous promotions of Admiral Husband E. Kimmel and General Walter C. Short for their performances at Pearl Harbor. The controversy continues.

18. John Lyday, *Los Angeles Times*, December 25, 1999, obituary section.

19. Carlo d'Este, "Two Slaps Heard Round the World," *Quarterly Journal of Military History* (Winter 1996): 64–71.

20. George S. Patton, Jr., *War as I Knew It* (New York: Houghton, 1947), 232.

21. Peter Biskind, *Easy Riders, Raging Bulls: How the Sex, Drugs, and Rock 'n Roll Generation Saved Hollywood* (New York: Simon & Schuster, 1998), p. 174.

22. Gregory Peck, interview with the author, June 8, 1998, Los Angeles, CA.

## CHAPTER 8

1. David Halberstam, In Anthony Summers with Robyn Swann, *The Arrogance of Power: The Secret World of Richard Nixon* (New York: Viking, 2000), p. 294.

2. Summers with Swann, *The Arrogance of Power*, p. 295.

3. Author's assignment as journalist for *Anaheim Bulletin*.

4. Philip Semas, "30th Anniversary of Kent State," *Chronicle of Higher Education* (May 1, 2000): 8–11.

5. Robert L. Jackson, obituary for Richard Kleindienst, *Los Angeles Times*, February 4, 2000.

6. John Milius, *Apocalypse Now*, first draft, December 5, 1969, courtesy of Special Collections, UCLA Research Library.

7. Karl French, *Apocalypse Now* (London: Bloomsbury Publishers, 1999), p. 191.

8. William Conrad Gibbons, *The U.S. Government and the Vietnam War: Executive and Legislative Roles and Relationships*, Part IV (Princeton, NJ: Princeton University Press, 1995), pp. 207–12.

9. Eleanor Coppola, *Notes* (New York: Simon & Schuster, 1979), p. 101.

10. Jean Baudrillard, "Apocalypse Now," *Movies*, ed. Gilbert Adair (London: Penguin Books, 1999), pp. 265–76.

11. Peter Biskind, *Easy Riders, Raging Bulls: How the Sex, Drugs, and Rock 'n Roll Generation Saved Hollywood* (New York: Simon & Schuster, 1998), p. 372.

12. Colonel Herbert Fix, USMC, Ret., memo to the author, May 17, 2000.

13. Ibid.

14. Interview with the author, September 1980, MGM Studios, Los Angeles, CA.

15. Rick Atkinson, *The Long Gray Line* (New York: Pocket Books, 1989), pp. 585–90.

16. Nancy Ellen Dowd, memo to the author, October 9, 2000.

17. *U.S. News & World Report*, July 3, 2000, p. 10.

18. *Army Reserve Magazine* (Fall 1987): 34.

19. Brock Garland, *War Movies* (New York: Facts on File, 1987), p. 160.

20. Michael Lee Lanning, *Vietnam at the Movies* (New York: Fawcett Columbine, 1994), p. 293.

21. Capt. Russ Thurman, USMC, "Rendezvous with War: A Reflection on the Viet-

nam War Twenty-five Years After," symposium, College of William & Mary, sponsored by Vietnam Veterans of America, April 6–9, 2000.

22. Samuel Zaffiri, *Hamburger Hill: May 11–20, 1969* (Novato, CA: Presidio Press, 1988), pp. 248–52.

23. Ibid.

24. Myra MacPherson, *Long Time Passing* (New York: Doubleday, 1984), p. 701.

25. Barbara Tuchman, *The March of Folly: From Troy to Vietnam* (New York: Ballantine Books, 1984), p. 376.

26. Frank McAdams, "Cry Babies No More—Except in Mourning," *Los Angeles Times*, June 7, 1981, op/ed. page.

27. Frances FitzGerald, *Fire in the Lake: The Vietnamese and the Americans in Vietnam* (New York: Random House, 1972), p. 563.


## CHAPTER 9

1. Melissa Healy, "100 Hours in March 1991 Shaped Cheney's Place in History," Campaign 2000: A Historical Perspective, *Los Angeles Times*, August 27, 2000.

2. Peter Maas, "The Untold Story of an American Tragedy," *Parade* (August 20, 2000): 4–6.

3. Mark Nesbitt, *Through Blood & Fire: Selected Civil War Papers of Major General Joshua Chamberlain* (Harrisburg, PA: Stackpole Books, 1996), p. 72.

4. Patrick S. Duncan, telephone interview with the author, July 28, 2000.

5. Abraham Lincoln, letter to Lydia Bixby, November 21, 1864, Boston; quoted in *Saving Private Ryan*, Historical Documents Co., 1996.

6. Stephen E. Ambrose, *D-Day* (New York: Simon & Schuster, 1994), p. 324.

7. John Keegan, *The Second World War* (New York: Viking-Penguin, 1989), p. 387.

8. Ambrose, *D-Day*, p. 323.

9. Ernie Pyle, *Ernie's War: The Best of Ernie Pyle's World War II Dispatches* (New York: Simon & Schuster, 1986), p. 278.

10. Susan King, "Ranking Hollywood's Depictions of the Horrors of War," *Los Angeles Times*, July 24, 1998.

11. Amy Wallace, " 'Ryan' Ends Vets' Years of Silence," *Los Angeles Times*, August 6, 1998; James P. Pinkerton, "Coming Home to Appreciation of Americanism," *Los Angeles Times*, July 23, 1998.

12. *Los Angeles Times*, September 28, 1999, p. F-6.

13. Fred L. Schultz, "Interview with Author James Webb," *U.S. Naval Institute Proceedings* (April 2000): 78–81.

14. Ibid.

15. David Kahn, "Greatest Spy," *Quarterly Journal of Military History* 12, no. 2 (Winter 2000): 12.

16. David Balme, in Kahn, "Greatest Spy," p. 12.

17. *Guardian/Observer*, June 8, 2000.

18. Bill Desowitz, "The Battle Plan behind 'The Patriot,' " *Los Angeles Times*, June 27, 2000, calendar section.

19. David Gritten, "Need a Villain? Any Brit Will Do," *Los Angeles Times*, July 12, 2000, calendar section.

20. Information following on script and budget problems, casting, survivor recollec-

tions, and computer-generated imaging taken from John Horn, Donna Foote, Andrew Muir, and Ryan Rippel, "Pearl Harbor: Hollywood vs. History," *Newsweek* (cover story), May 14, 2001.

21. Dave McNary, "Anti-discrimination Orgs 'Harbor' Fears," *Daily Variety*, May 22, 2001.

22. Phil Gallo, "Nation's Film Critics Bomb 'Pearl Harbor,' " *Daily Variety*, May 29, 2001.

23. Anthony Lane, "Bombs Away, Love and Rivalry in 'Pearl Harbor,' " *The New Yorker*, June 4, 2001.

24. Andrew Curry, "Blamed for Pearl Harbor," *U.S. News & World Report*, June 4, 2001.

25. Moore and Galloway, *We Were Soldiers Once . . . and Young*, p. 382.

26. Harold G. Moore, "Rendezvous with War: A Reflection on the Vietnam War Twenty-five Years After," symposium, College of William & Mary, sponsored by Vietnam Veterans of America, April 6–9, 2000.

27. Robert S. McNamara, with Brian VanDeMark, *In Retrospect: The Tragedy and Lessons of Vietnam* (New York: Times Books, 1995), p. 222.

# Selected Bibliography

Alexander, Joseph, with Don Horan and Norman C. Stahl. *A Fellowship of Valor: The Battle History of the U.S. Marines*. New York: HarperCollins, 1997.

Ambrose, Stephen E. *Citizen Soldiers: The U.S. Army from the Normandy Beaches to the Bulge to the Surrender of Germany*. New York: Simon & Schuster, 1997.

Ambrose, Stephen E. *D-Day*. New York: Simon & Schuster, 1994.

Ambrose, Stephen E. *The Victors: Eisenhower and His Boys: The Men of World War II*. New York: Simon & Schuster, 1998.

Arnold, James R. *Tet Offensive 1968: Turning Point in Vietnam*. London: Osprey, 1990.

Asbell, Bernard. *When F.D.R. Died*. New York: Holt, Rinehart and Winston, 1961.

Atkinson, Rick. *The Long Gray Line*. New York: Pocket Books, 1989.

Barker, Christine R., and R.W. Last. *Erich Maria Remarque*. New York: Harper & Row, 1979.

Baron, Alexander. *The Human Kind*. New York: Dell, 1963.

Basinger, Jeanine. *The World War II Combat Film: Anatomy of a Genre*. New York: Columbia University Press, 1986.

Behlmer, Rudy, ed. *Memo from David O. Selznick*. New York: Viking, 1972.

Berg, A. Scott. *Goldwyn, a Biography*. New York: Knopf, 1989.

Bergman, Ingrid, and Alan Burgess. *Ingrid Bergman: My Story*. New York: Delacorte Press, 1980.

Biskind, Peter. *Easy Riders, Raging Bulls: How the Sex, Drugs, and Rock 'n Roll Generation Saved Hollywood*. New York: Simon & Schuster, 1998.

Blair, Clay. *The Forgotten War*. New York: Times Books/Random House, 1987.

Bogdanovich, Peter. *Who the Devil Made It*. New York: Knopf, 1997.

Boulle, Pierre. *The Bridge over the River Kwai*. Trans. Xan Fielding. New York: Vanguard Press, 1954.

Bradley, James, with Ron Powers. *Flags of Our Fathers*. New York: Bantam Books, 2000.

Brando, Marlon, with Robert Lindsey. *Songs My Mother Taught Me*. New York: Random House, 1994.

Brickhill, Paul. *The Great Escape*. New York: W.W. Norton, 1950.

Brodie, Fawn. *Richard Nixon: The Shaping of His Character*. New York: W.W. Norton, 1981.

Brown, Harry. *A Walk in the Sun*. New York: Alfred A. Knopf, 1945.

Burgett, Donald R. *The Road to Arnhem: A Screaming Eagle in Holland*. Novato, CA: Presidio Press, 1999.

Burkett, R.G., and Glenna Whitley. *Stolen Valor: How the Vietnam Generation Was Robbed of Its Heroes and Its History*. Dallas, TX: Verity, 1998.

Campbell, Craig W. *Reel America and World War I*. Jefferson, NC: McFarland, 1985.

Capra, Frank. *The Name above the Title, an Autobiography*. New York: Macmillan 1971.

Caputo, Phillip. *A Rumor of War*. New York: Ballantine Books, 1977.

Ceplair, Larry, and Steven Englund. *The Inquisition in Hollywood: Politics in the Film Community, 1930–1960*. New York: Anchor Press, 1980.

Connell, Evan S. *Son of the Morning Star*. San Francisco: North Point Press, 1984.

Conrad, Joseph. *Heart of Darkness*. 1929. Cambridge, MA: Bentley, 1981.

Coppola, Eleanor. *Notes*. New York: Simon & Schuster, 1979.

Cronkite, Walter. *A Reporter's Life*. New York: Knopf, 1996.

Culbert, David, ed. *Film and Propaganda in America: A Documentary History*. Vol. 2. Westport, CA: Greenwood Press, 1990.

Dick, Bernard F. *The Star Spangled Screen: The American World War II Film*. Lexington: University Press of Kentucky, 1985.

Dmytryk, Edward. *Odd Man Out: A Memoir of the Hollywood Ten*. Carbondale: Southern Illinois University Press, 1996.

Doherty, Thomas. *Projections of War: Hollywood, American Culture and World War II*. New York: Columbia University Press, 1993.

Dupuy, Trevor N., Curt Johnson, and David L. Bongard. *The Harper Encyclopedia of Military Biography*. New York: HarperCollins, 1992.

Durand, Arthur. *Stalag Luft III: The Secret Story*. Baton Rouge: Louisiana State University Press, 1988.

Egri, Lajos. *The Art of Dramatic Writing*. New York: Touchstone, 1960.

Ellis, John. *World War II: The Encyclopedia of Facts and Figures*. Military Book Club, 1993.

Emerson, Gloria. *Winners & Losers*. New York: Random House, 1976.

Eyman, Scott. *The Speed of Sound: Hollywood and the Talkie Revolution, 1926–1930*. New York: Simon & Schuster, 1997.

FitzGerald, Frances. *Fire in the Lake: The Vietnamese and the Americans in Vietnam*. New York: Random House, 1972.

French, Karl. *Apocalypse Now*. London: Bloomsbury Publishers, 1999.

Frost, David. *I Gave Them a Sword: Behind the Scenes of the Nixon Interviews*. New York: William Morrow, 1978.

Garland, Brock. *War Movies*. New York: Facts on File, 1987.

Gibbons, William Conrad. *The U.S. Government and the Vietnam War: Executive and Legislative Roles and Relationships*. Part IV. Princeton, NJ: Princeton University Press, 1995.

Goldman, William. *Adventures in the Screen Trade*. New York: Warner Books, 1983.

Gordon, William A. *Four Dead in Ohio*. Laguna Hills, CA: North Ridge Books, 1995.

Graham, Don. *No Name on the Bullet: A Biography of Audie Murphy*. New York: Viking, 1989.

Groom, Winston. *Forrest Gump*. New York: Doubleday, 1986.

Halliwell, Leslie. *Halliwell's Film Guide*. Ed. John Walker. New York: Harper-Perennial, 1999.

Hamilton, Nigel. *JFK: Reckless Youth*. New York: Random House, 1992.

Harmetz, Aljean. *Round Up the Usual Suspects: The Making of Casablanca, Bogart, Bergman and World War II*. New York: Hyperion, 1992.

Haver, Ronald. *David O. Selznick's* Gone With the Wind. New York: Wings Books/ Random House, 1986.

Hendrick, George, ed. *To Reach Eternity: The Letters of James Jones*. New York: Random House, 1989.

Hepburn, Katharine. *The Making of* The African Queen: *Or How I Went to Africa with Bogart, Bacall, and Huston and Almost Lost My Mind*. New York: Knopf, 1987.

Hepburn, Katharine. *Me: Stories of My Life*. New York: Knopf, 1991.

Herman, Jan. *A Talent for Trouble: The Life of Hollywood's Most Acclaimed Director, William Wyler*. New York: Putnam, 1996.

Herr, Michael. *Dispatches*. New York: Alfred Knopf, 1977.

Herring, George. *America's Longest War: The United States and Vietnam 1950–1975*. New York: McGraw-Hill, 1986.

Holden, Anthony. *Behind the Oscar: A History of the Academy Awards*. New York: Simon & Schuster, 1993.

Hoopes, Roy. *When the Stars Went to War: Hollywood and World War II*. New York: Random House, 1994.

Hoyt, Edwin P. *The Alamo: An Illustrated History*. Dallas, TX: Taylor, 1999.

Hoyt, Edwin P. *Yamamoto: The Man Who Planned Pearl Harbor*. New York: McGraw-Hill, 1990.

Hughes, H. Stuart. *Contemporary Europe: A History*. Englewood Cliffs, NJ: Prentice Hall, 1965.

Huston, John. *An Open Book*. New York: Alfred Knopf, 1980.

Hyams, Jay. *War Movies*. New York: W.H. Smith Publishers, 1984.

*Inaugural Addresses of the Presidents of the United States*. Washington D.C.: GPO, 1989.

Jones, James. *From Here to Eternity*. New York: Charles Scribner's Sons, 1951.

Jones, James. *The Thin Red Line*. New York: Charles Scribner's Sons, 1962.

Kagan, Norman. "The War Film." In *Pyramid Illustrated History of the Movies*, ed. Ted Sennett. Seattle, WA: Pyramid Communications, 1974.

Keegan, John. *The Second World War*. New York: Viking-Penguin, 1989.

Keneally, Thomas. *Schindler's List*. New York: Simon & Schuster, 1982.

Kirchberger, Joe H. *The First World War: An Eyewitness History*. New York: Facts on File, 1992.

Knock, Thomas J. *To End All Wars: Woodrow Wilson and the Quest for a New World Order*. New York: Oxford University Press, 1992.

Kovic, Ron. *Born on the Fourth of July*. New York: Pocket Books, 1976.

Langman, Larry, and Ed Borg. *Encyclopedia of American War Films*. New York: Garland Publishing, 1989.

Lanning, Michael Lee. *Vietnam at the Movies*. New York: Fawcett Columbine, 1994.

Lay, Beirne, Jr., and Sy Bartlett. *Twelve O'Clock High*. South Yarmouth, MA: John Curley & Associates, 1981. Originally published by Harper & Row, 1948.

Leaming, Barbara. *Marilyn Monroe*. New York: Crown Publishers, 1998.

Lossing, Benson J. *Mathew Brady's Illustrated History of the Civil War.* New York: Portland House, 1996. Originally published as *A History of the Civil War.*

MacArthur, Douglas. *Reminiscences.* New York: McGraw-Hill, 1964.

MacDonald, Callum. *The Killing of Obergruppenfuehrer Reinhard Heydrich.* New York: The Free Press, 1989.

MacPherson, Myra. *Long Time Passing.* New York: Doubleday, 1984.

Manchester, William. *American Caesar.* Boston: Little, Brown, 1978.

Marshall, S.L.A. *Pork Chop Hill.* Nashville, TN: Battery Press, 1986.

McCombs, Don, and Fred L. Worth. *World War II Super Facts.* New York: Warner Books, 1983.

McCullough, David. *Mornings on Horseback, a Biography of Theodore Roosevelt.* New York: Simon & Schuster, 1981.

McCullough, David. *Truman.* New York: Simon & Schuster, 1992.

McNamara, Robert S., with Brian VanDeMark. *In Retrospect: The Tragedy and Lessons of Vietnam.* New York: Times Books, 1995.

Meade, Marion. *Buster Keaton: Cut to the Chase.* New York: HarperCollins, 1995.

Michener, James A. *Tales of the South Pacific.* New York: Macmillan, 1947.

Miller, Merle. *Plain Speaking: An Oral Biography of Harry S. Truman.* New York: Berkley, 1974.

Moore, Lt. Gen. Harold G. (Ret.), and Joseph L. Galloway. *We Were Soldiers Once . . . and Young.* New York: Random House, 1992.

Moore, Robin. *The Green Berets.* New York: Crown Publishers, 1965.

Morrell, David. *First Blood.* New York: Evans, 1972.

Nathanson, E.M. *The Dirty Dozen.* New York: Random House, 1965.

Navasky, Victor S. *Naming Names.* New York: Viking Press, 1980.

Nesbitt, Mark. *Through Blood & Fire: Selected Civil War Papers of Major General Joshua Chamberlain.* Harrisburg, PA: Stackpole Books, 1996.

Newcomb, Richard F. *Abandon Ship!* New York: Henry Holt & Co., Inc., 1958.

Newcomb, Richard F. *Iwo Jima.* New York: Holt, Rinehart and Winston. 1965.

Nolan, Keith William. *The Battle for Saigon: Tet 1968.* New York: Pocket Books, 1996.

Ondaatje, Michael. *The English Patient.* New York: Knopf, 1992.

Patton, George S., Jr. *War as I Knew It.* New York: Houghton, 1947.

Pitt, Barrie, ed. *The Military History of World War II.* New York: Military Press and Crown Publishers, 1988.

Puzo, Mario. *The Godfather Papers and Other Confessions.* New York: Putnam, 1972.

Pyle, Ernie. *Ernie's War: The Best of Ernie Pyle's World War II Dispatches.* New York: Simon & Schuster, 1986.

Regan, Geoffrey. *SNAFU: Great American Military Disasters.* New York: Avon Books, 1993.

Roberts, Randy, and James S. Olson. *John Wayne: American.* New York: Free Press, 1995.

Robyns, Gwen. *Light of a Star.* London: Leslie Frewin Publishers, 1968.

Rubin, Richard. *American History of the 20th Century.* New York: Guild America Books, 1998.

Rubin, Steven Jay. *Combat Films 1945–1970.* Jefferson, NC: McFarland, 1981.

Ryan, Cornelius. *A Bridge Too Far.* New York: Simon & Schuster, 1974.

Ryan, Cornelius. *The Longest Day.* New York: Simon & Schuster, 1959.

Schessler, Ken. *This Is Hollywood*. Redlands, CA: Schessler Publishing, Universal Books, 1991.

Schindler, Colin. *Hollywood Goes to War: 1939–1952*. London: Routledge & Kegan Paul, 1979.

Schlesinger, Arthur M., ed. *The Almanac of American History*. Greenwich, CT: Brompton Books, 1993.

Searls, Hank. *The Lost Prince: Young Joe, the Forgotten Kennedy*. New York: World Publishing, 1969.

Sheehan, Neil. *A Bright Shining Lie: John Paul Vann and America in Vietnam*. New York: Random House, 1988.

Smith, Gene. *When the Cheering Stopped: The Last Years of Woodrow Wilson*. New York: William Morrow, 1964.

Snyder, Louis L. *Hitler's Elite: Biographical Sketches of Nazis Who Shaped the Third Reich*. New York: Hippocrene Books, 1989.

Summers, Anthony, with Robyn Swann. *The Arrogance of Power: The Secret World of Richard Nixon*. New York: Viking, 2000.

Thomas, Gordon, and Max Morgan Witts. *Enola Gay*. New York: Stein & Day, 1977.

Toland, John. *Adolf Hitler: A Biography*. New York: Ballantine Books, 1981.

Toplin, Robert Brent. *History by Hollywood: The Use and Abuse of the American Past*. Urbana: University of Illinois Press, 1996.

Tuchman, Barbara. *The March of Folly: From Troy to Vietnam*. New York: Ballantine Books, 1984.

Vaughn, Robert. *Only Victims: A Study of Show Business Blacklisting*. New York: G.P. Putnam's Sons, 1972.

Vidal, Gore. *United States: Essays 1952–1992*. New York: Random House, 1993.

Vinacke, Harold M. *A History of the Far East in Modern Times*, 6th ed. New York: Appleton-Century-Crofts, 1961.

Wallenchinsky, David, and Irving Wallace. *The People's Almanac*. New York: Doubleday, 1975.

Warr, Nicholas. *Phase Line Green: The Battle for Hue, 1968*. New York: Ballantine, 1997.

Wayne, Jane Ellen. *Gable's Women*. New York: Prentice Hall, 1987.

Wetta, Frank J., and Stephen J. Curley. *Celluloid Wars: A Guide to Film and the American Experience of War*. Westport, CT: Greenwood, 1992.

Whitney, Courtney. *MacArthur: His Rendezvous with History*. New York: Knopf, 1956.

Wiley, Mason, and Damien Bona. *Inside Oscar: The Unofficial History of the Academy Awards*. New York: Ballantine Books, 1987.

Wills, Garry. *John Wayne's America: The Politics of Celebrity*. New York: Simon & Schuster, 1997.

Wise, James E., Jr., and Paul W. Wilderson III. *Stars in Khaki: Movie Actors in the Army and Air Services*. Annapolis, MD: Naval Institute Press, 2000.

Zaffiri, Samuel. *Hamburger Hill: May 11–20, 1969*. Novato, CA: Presidio Press, 1988.

# Index

LeMay, General Curtis (USAAF), 105–6, 134

Lemmon, Jack, 36, 150

Lemp, Fritz-Julis, 273

Lennon, J. Michael, Ph.D., xii

Leone, Sergio, 154

LeRoy, Mervyn, 67, 149

Leslie, Joan, 44

*Let There Be Light*, 98–99, 175

Lettich, Sheldon, 242

Levene, Sam, 104

Levent, Pierre, 180

Levin, Barry, xii

Levinson, Barry, 246

Levy, Melvin, 60

Levy, Raoul J., 178

Lewin, David, 156

Lewis, Robert, 88

Lewton, Val, 21

*Lexington,* USS, 41

Leyte (Philippine Islands) 254

Leyte Gulf (Philippine Islands), 71

Liberty Loan Drives, 7, 10

Lidice village (Czechlosovakia), 42, 60

*Lifeboat*, 64–65

*Life* magazine, 40, 63, 128, 152

Lighton, Louis, 106–8

Lin, Maya Ying, 232

Lincoln, President Abraham, 6, 265–66

Lincoln Brigade, 117

Lincoln Memorial, 232

Lindberg, Corporal Charles W. (USMC), 174

Lindbergh, Charles, 13, 19

Liri Valley (Italy), 97

Litel, John, 63

Little Big Horn (Montana), 207, 279

*Little Big Man*, 195, 207

Little Round Top (Gettysburg), 257–58

Litvak, Anatole, 26, 197

Lloyd, Frank, 94

Lloyd, Harold, 6, 10, 15

Lloyd, Norman, 50, 83

Loan, General Nguyen Ngoc (Saigon Police), 203, 268

Lockhart, Gene, 57, 60

Logan, Josh, 35, 140, 149

Logue, Donal, 269

*Lolita*, 242

Lollobrigida, Gina, 163

Lombard, Carole, 23, 45–46

*London Daily Express*, 123, 156, 177

"London Gun, The," 187

Long, Dewey, 76

Long, Huey, 110

*Longest Day, The*, 69, 131, 177–80

Longstreet, General James "Pete" (CSA), 256–58

*Long Time Passing*, 248

Loo, Richard, 68, 80, 127

Lopez, Perry, 148

Lopez, Trini, 196

Lorre, Peter, 19, 52

Los Alamos (New Mexico), 254

*Los Angeles Collegian*, 129

*Los Angeles Daily Mirror*, 127

*Los Angeles Times*, 205, 249

Lost Battalion, The, 131

Lovat, Lord (U.K.), 180

Lovejoy, Frank, 104, 132, 138

Loy, Myrna, 100

Luftwaffe (German Air Force), 27, 69, 103, 106, 173, 183

Lund, John, 103

Lupton, John, 148

Lyndon, Barre, 94

Lynn, Vera, 190, 244

Lyon, Ben. 16

Lyon, William, 144

MacArthur, General Douglas, xv, 33–34, 40, 61, 71, 80–81, 85–91, 100, 103, 125–26, 213–14, 230

MacDonald, Peter, 242

MacDougall, Ranald, 94

MacGowan, Kenneth, 65

*MacKenna's Gold*, 122

MacKenzie, AEneas, 66

Maclean, Alistar, 172

MacMurray, Fred, 95, 110, 147

MacPherson, Myra, 248

Macready, George, 155

Macrorie, Alma, 146

MACV (Military Advisory Command Vietnam), 171, 202, 221–23, 228, 268, 281

96, 129, 140–44, 147, 150, 189, 194, 208, 267, 276–78, 283
Peck, Gregory, xii, xviii, 109–11, 162–63, 173, 176, 182
Peck, Stephen, xii
Pender, General (CSA), 258
Pendleton, Camp (California), 72, 96, 239
Penn, Arthur, 206
Penn, Sean, 189, 248, 267
Peppard, George, 163, 188
Pepper, Barry, 265, 283
Percival, General Sir Arthur (U.K.), 90
Perkins, Anthony, 194
Perkins, Millie, 161
Perry, Commander Matthew (USN), 90
Pershing, General John J. (AEF), 7, 264
Persin, Henri, 180
Petacci, Clara, 84
Peters, Jean, 153
Peterson, Pete, 246
Pettet, Joanna, 197
Pfeffeberg, Poldek, 260
Philbrook, James, 189
Philip, Sister Jean (O.P.), xvii
Philip Neri, St., xv
Phillips, Lou Diamond, 263
Phoenix Pictures, 267
*Photoplay* magazine, 2
Picerni, Paul, 132
Pichel, Irving, 102, 119
Pickett, General George E. (CSA), 256
Pickens, Andrew, 275
Pickens, Slim, 190
Pickford, Mary, 10, 15
*Picture*, 129
Pillow, Fort (Tennessee), 262
Pipe Creek (Pennsylvania), 257
Pirosh, Robert, 114–15, 129–31
*Plain Speaking*, 85, 102
*Platoon*, 115, 239, 264, 266–67
Pleiku (Vietnam), 201
Plei Mei (Vietnam), 280
Pless, C.A., 74
Plumley, Sergeant Major Basil, 280, 283
Plunkett, Robert, 93
Poe, James, 155, 206
Poindexter, John, 271
Pointe du Hoc (Normandy), 179, 265

Poitier, Sidney, 36, 135
Pollack, Sydney, 177
*Pork Chop Hill*, 162–63
Porter, Edwin S., 3
Post, Ted, 220
Poston, Tom, 36
Potsdam Conference (Germany), 85, 88
Po Valley (Italy), 157
Powell, General Colin L., 252, 262
Powell, William, 150
Power, Tyrone, Jr., 36–37, 44, 62, 108
Power, Tyrone, Sr., 11
Powers, Ron, 113
Prague (Czechlosovakia), 42
Pran, Dith, 238–39
Preiss, Wolfgang, 180
Preminger, Otto, 122, 194
Prentiss, Paula, 208
Presnell, Harve, 264
Pressman, Lawrence, 245
Preston, Robert, 49
Price, Carolyn, 151
*Pride of the Marines*, 95
*Prince of Foxes*, 108
*Projections of War*, 205
*Proof through the Night*, 61
PROVN Report (A Program for the Pacification and Long-Term Development of South Vietnam), 224
*PT 59*, 186
*PT 109*, xix, 184–86
*Pueblo*, USS, 199
Pulitzer Prize, 203, 217, 238, 249, 267
Puller, Colonel Lewis "Chesty" (USMC), 135
Pursall, David, 180
Pusan Perimeter (Korea), 125
Puttnam, David, 238
Puzo, Mario, 143
Pyle, Ernie, 81–82, 244, 266
Pyle, Richard, xii, 202

Quaid, Randy, 212
Quantrill, William Clarke, 153
*Quarterly Journal of Military History, The*, 43, 97
Quayle, Anthony, 173
Quill, Timothy, 244

**About the Author**

FRANK McADAMS is Adjunct Professor, Department of Cinema/TV at the University of Southern California and an instructor in the screenwriting programs of the University of California, Los Angeles and the University of California, Irvine. He also is the recipient of two Sam Goldwyn screenwriting awards.